MYTHOLOGY AND THE RENAISSANCE TRADITION IN ENGLISH POETRY

New Revised Edition

Mythology and the Romantic Tradition by Douglas Bush

a sequel to the present volume

is available in the paperbound Norton Library

MYTHOLOGY AND THE RENAISSANCE TRADITION IN ENGLISH POETRY

BY

DOUGLAS BUSH

New Revised Edition

W · W · NORTON & COMPANY · INC ·

NEW YORK

Library of Congress Catalog Card No. 63-15868

PRINTED IN THE UNITED STATES OF AMERICA
FOR THE PUBLISHERS BY THE VAIL-BALLOU PRESS
123456789

CONTENTS

Preface to the Second Edition

This book was first published by the University of Minnesota Press in 1932 and reprinted by the Pageant Book Company in 1957. When W. W. Norton & Company Inc. decided to reissue it, I was graciously given the opportunity for revision. Even if other commitments allowed, complete rewriting would be a dubious enterprise, since the author has not, like Aeson, been rejuvenated by being boiled in Medea's magical stew. But I have rewritten parts of the text, especially in the chapters on Spenser and Milton. I have not enlarged—and blurred—the focus by taking account of the broad modern conception of "myth" or "archetypal myth," since this book deals strictly with classical myths and stories and with the theory and poetical practice of Renaissance writers—who, for that matter, had their own equivalent and no less valid conceptions. Small changes have been made all along the way, because of altered opinions or advances in scholarly knowledge. Wherever it was feasible, footnotes have been reduced in bulk and number, and these and the revised bibliography include a fair amount of the material published since 1932; general criticism of the major poets and many notes on their use of mythology have had to be left out. I may hope to be forgiven for inconsistency in quoting poetry sometimes in original and oftener in modernized and more easily readable form. No doubt everyone has a special tenderness for his first book, and I am glad that this is to have a new lease of life.

D. B.

Preface

This study set out, with Elizabethan confidence, to describe the uses of mythology in English non-dramatic poetry from the Middle Ages to the present. The result of such an ambition can perhaps be suggested in the apt words of a university poet concerning Actaeon:

> His hands were changed to feet, and he in short
> Became a stag.

In plain prose, this volume ends at 1680; I hope in another volume to complete the tale.

The purpose of the book is to follow some threads through the rich web of the classical tradition in English poetry of the sixteenth and seventeenth centuries. Not of course that mythological poetry and the classical tradition are equivalent terms, or have indeed any essential connection. The truism may be emphasized at the beginning that *In Time of "the Breaking of Nations"* or *The Death of the Hired Man* is far more truly classical than a multitude of poems inspired by a vision of Olympus. That, however, was not the general attitude in the period covered by this book, and historically, though not absolutely, mythology is a part of the classical tradition in European poetry.

The material had to be limited, and, unless incidentally or for a special reason, nothing has been said of classical influences in general, of formal translations from the classics, of dramatic treatments of classical themes; such huge subjects would need volumes to themselves. Some space is necessarily given to minor figures who bulk larger in relation to the mythological genre than they do in the history of English poetry. But while a number of corpses have been disinterred, almost all of these are on view in the Appendix, and the curious may satisfy their "gowlish gusto" (in Mr. Polly's phrase) by wandering through the morgue. At any rate it can be honestly affirmed, if one may profane Browne's solemn music, that the author, who hath an art to make dust of all things, hath yet spared some minor monuments.

Abbreviations used for references are listed at the beginning of the Bibliography.

It is pleasant to acknowledge the kindness of officers and attendants of the British Museum, the Bodleian, the Harvard University Library, and the University of Minnesota Library; and to express my gratitude to the authorities of Harvard University for a fellowship which enabled me some years ago to work in England. I am under special obligations to the governing board and editorial staff of the University of Minnesota Press. For criticisms of some chapters I am indebted to Professor Charles G. Osgood of Princeton University and Professor Warner G. Rice of the University of Michigan.

I would emphasize the responsibility of Professor Lowes as the only begetter of this book if it were not for some fear that even so wise a father might not know such a child. What his encouragement means his pupils best know, even if their feet move more easily down to Avernus than along the road to Xanadu.

Finally, my wife did not compile the index; her manifold help in other ways I am not allowed to acknowledge.

DOUGLAS BUSH

University of Minnesota

Introduction

There are always readers and writers who know, like Peacock, that there are no dryads in Hyde Park, nor naiads in the Regent's Canal; who rejoice with Mr. Weller when they find in a poem "no Wenuses, nor nothin' o' that kind"; who echo Whitman's familiar prayer,

> Come Muse migrate from Greece and Ionia,
> Cross out please those immensely overpaid accounts,
> That matter of Troy and Achilles' wrath, and Æneas', Odysseus'
> wanderings,
> Placard "Removed" and "To Let" on the rocks of your snowy
> Parnassus . . .
> For know a better, fresher, busier sphere, a wide, untried domain
> awaits, demands you.

But Peacock was the author of *Rhododaphne*, a good deal of Whitman is a close parallel to the Homeric catalogue of the ships, and, in general, a particular subject matter should not be blamed for the faults of its compromising votaries. Myths and tales can hardly be banished to the museum when they have attracted almost all the major English poets, not to mention minor ones, from Chaucer to the present.

Poetry is largely a matter of symbol, and the complete rebel, like Blake, who flouts tradition and insists on making his own symbols, may achieve originality of a kind, but at a high price, as the most ardent devotee of the prophetic books must admit. The greatest artists, I think Clive Bell has remarked, always look forward. It is equally true that they always look backward. Of course feeble poets who try to write in a great tradition remain feeble poets, and the bright world of classic myth has allured a number of persons who, in the words of Coleridge, mistake an intense desire to possess the reputation of poetic genius for the actual powers. But what is called realism has its own compromising army of camp followers, who, in our day, forget that the din of riveters in poetry may become as smooth a cliché as Phoebus or Diana. An authentic poet may be moved to authentic utterance by the excitement of reading—witness such diverse examples as Chapman and Milton—and the more original he is the more he gains from drawing upon the accumulated artistic heritage, which is surely as essential a part of "life" as any aspect of human behavior.

Hundreds of poets have written about Helen of Troy; she is the rich source of a many-colored stream of associations. One thinks at once of Marlowe's rapturous lines, or of that astonishing lyric from the most boisterous of Elizabethan pens:

> Brightness falls from the air;
> Queens have died young and fair;
> Dust hath closed Helen's eye:
> I am sick, I must die.
> *Lord, have mercy on us!*

Here the one name evokes glamor and romance, the brevity of life and love and beauty, with such concentrated suggestion that the imagination is filled with undertones and overtones which no "original" image or cumbrous circumlocution could give. We have even a Celtic Helen, in the inspired talk of the "playboy": "If the mitred bishops seen you that time, they'd be the like of the holy prophets, I'm thinking, do be straining the bars of Paradise to lay eyes on the Lady Helen of Troy, and she abroad, pacing back and forward, with a nosegay in her golden shawl." Hundreds of poets have written of Leda, but the theme is far from threadbare when touched by Yeats. And Mr. Eliot sets up similarly complex reverberations in those lines about the nightingales singing near the Convent of the Sacred Heart, which

> sang within the bloody wood
> When Agamemnon cried aloud,
> And let their liquid siftings fall
> To stain the stiff dishonoured shroud.

Helen, Leda, Agamemnon are only a few symbols from the inexhaustible treasury of classical myth. Beautiful or horrible simply as tales, the myths have constituted for modern poets a kind of poetic shorthand of infinite imaginative and emotional value. Mythological allusions have not lost their spell merely because at times bad poets turn them into glass beads. We are in this book concerned partly with allusions, but mainly with more elaborate manifestations of the same impulse, narrative poems on classical themes. One has only to run over the list of English poets to see that myths have appealed to the most diverse minds, have been put to the most diverse uses. They have been the vehicle for sermons on morality, for revolts against morality, for mystical theology, for obscene burlesque, for decorative tapestry, for human comedy and tragedy, for poems of escape from life, for humanitarian amelioration of life.

We moderns have a pleasant way of using, and using interchangeably, such phrases as "the Greek spirit," "the classic spirit," "the pagan spirit," and doubtless often with a meaning. Our instinct for synthesis welcomes an expression that sums up in a couple of words the essential kinship of Pindar and Sappho, Aeschylus and Lucian, Plato and Aristotle, Herodotus and Thucydides, Sophocles and Euripides—not to mention the Romans. While we are possibly nearer than our ancestors ever were to a definition of the Greek mind—to take it for the moment, as more elusive and un-English than the Roman—we continue, as they did, to make the Greeks in our own image, to see in the ancient as well as in the modern classics the reflection of our changing philosophies and prejudices. The strictly neoclassic intelligence, admiring if not fully understanding Virgil, regarded Homer as a genius, though a somewhat rude and uncouth one; for the sentimental primitivists of the eighteenth century Homer's faults of incorrectness became the virtues which proclaimed him an inspired child of nature, a true primitive bard, finally a whole committee of bards. Demosthenes, said Dr. Johnson, spoke to brutes. The German Hellenists saw the Greek as a being of superhuman beauty of body and mind, of godlike serenity and calm. In our own time we have had an anthropological and corybantic Hellenism that makes Dionysus more potent than Zeus or Apollo. And so the search for truth proceeds.

Of the writers to be discussed here the earlier ones at least, less philosophic than we, were content with a rather vague apprehension of the classical genius, but, like us, they did find in ancient literature the reflection of themselves. When we think of "unclassical" variations of theme and treatment in English mythological poems, we may well qualify our judgments in the recollection that ancient mythology was not a rigidly fixed body of "authentic" material which only in the Middle Ages began to be wondrously transmogrified. The Greek dramatists, when they cut slices from the banquet of Homer (the whole body of cyclic poems, that is), trimmed and seasoned them, within limits, to suit their own purposes. To summarize a good many centuries, the names of Pindar, Aeschylus, Sophocles, Euripides, Theocritus, Virgil, Ovid, Lucian, testify to the widest variety of conception and handling. However poetic mood and poetic genius may vary, such material has enduring vitality. In spite of the vast bulk of Arthurian stuff, old and new, we can imagine a world without Arthur; we can hardly conceive of a world without Apollo.

This volume attempts to outline both the changing moral and intellectual conceptions of myth and the changing fashions in artistic treatment, for the two are of course inseparable. The cycle of taste is roughly parallel to that represented by the ancient writers already named; it begins with religious seriousness and ends with irreverent burlesque. We shall follow the poetic handling of myth from the period of infant simplicity through that of adolescent exuberance to the mature and chastened splendor of the last poet of the English Renaissance, and, finally, sink by a logical anticlimax to the immature and unchaste travesties of the Restoration.

We shall not arrive at any startling conclusions; on the contrary everyone knows the direction to be taken and at least the chief landmarks along the way. But by surveying a single aspect of the Renaissance tradition that is not unrelated to the central principles of neoclassicism we may be able to see a little more clearly and consecutively the struggle between the virtues and vices of possession of the soul of poetry. One moral that will emerge, a moral which might be called a truism if it were not so often ignored, is that in the history of English poetry there is no absolute classicism, there are only conceptions—perhaps misconceptions—of classicism. Critics who write of the changeless laws of taste must have in mind a set of tables laid up in some Platonic heaven, for the literature of earth, which, in the absence of an aesthetic revelation, must be our criterion, does not warrant such comfortable doctrine.

But there is a stream of continuity, and for that reason, as well as from the academic instinct to commence *ab ovo*, the first chapter is devoted to a sketch of mythology in the Middle Ages. For another moral, to be perhaps relentlessly emphasized, is that the essential quality of Renaissance poetry, at the best as well as at the worst, is its medievalism. We shall find ourselves dealing continually with the heritage of medieval religion, with the spirit and technique of medieval art. The bulk of the poetry surveyed may be described, with due reservations, as a "Gothic" and edifying tapestry into which are woven more and more silver threads from Ovid and threads of gilt from

Italy. Such poetry, heavily encrusted with Renaissance brocade, is obviously seldom "classical." But how many of the Latin poets are classical, when tried by the standards that we catalogue so glibly? However, the genial Ovid would probably have been less disturbed than scholars if he had known not merely that he would not wholly die, but that through the centuries he would be, like Caesar's wife, all things to all men. For a history of mythology and the Renaissance tradition must be largely an account of the metamorphoses of Ovid.

CHAPTER I

Classical Themes
in the Middle Ages

I. THE STORY OF TROY

Without going into evidence which suggests that a few men were acquainted with Homer, one may safely assert that the *Iliad* and *Odyssey* were virtually unknown in western Europe during the Middle Ages. Of course men praised him, as we still do, without having read him. Dante, master of the learning of his time, saluted Homer as lord of the loftiest song who soars above the others like an eagle, but knew him only vaguely as a great name. The mass of readers were as ignorant of Greek as they are today.

Trojan saga, therefore, reached the medieval man by devious paths. Passing over the brief epitome of the *Iliad* by "Pindarus Thebanus" (Baebius Italicus?), which was read in the sixteenth century as well as in the sixth, we come to the great twin brethren, Dictys Cretensis and Dares Phrygius, who were the sources of nearly all medieval and many Renaissance versions of the Trojan story. Our Latin text of Dictys (fourth century A. D.), which is orderly and adequate in style, describes events from the rape of Helen to the death of Ulysses. Dares (sixth century), though much briefer, takes in everything from the Argonautic expedition to the destruction of Troy; his prose style has been sufficiently damned.

These books had an enduring popularity far beyond that of our modern outlines of the universe; they were exactly what the public wanted. The reasons are worth noting, for their potency did not end with the Middle Ages. One has been mentioned, the general ignorance of Greek. There were also abundant positive reasons. Both writers had taken part in the Trojan war and derived information from experience or from eyewitnesses; they said so themselves. Benoit de Sainte-Maure expressed the common opinion when he commended the absolute veracity of Dares and observed that Homer, though a marvelous clerk, did not live until a hundred years after the war.

These truthful historians had the gifts requisite for popularizing material. The supernatural events of the story were freely rationalized. Dictys omitted debates in heaven, divine assistance given to the heroes, fights among the gods. Even the wooden horse ceased to be hollow. Homer in his simplicity had described characters with a few broad strokes. Dares and Dictys sprinkled their work with convincing touches of realism, the kind of corroborative detail of which Pooh-Bah was such a master. Thus in Dares Aeneas has sparkling black eyes, and Polyxena is cursed with large hands. Dictys, with no less journalistic skill, gives the satisfying information that at the time of the elopement Paris was thirty-three and Helen twenty-six. The motivation is sometimes made more plausible and human; Menelaus is less disturbed because his wife left him than because two of his female relations helped her to leave.

Homeric heroes undergo a curious transformation, the last becoming first and the first last. Troilus, hardly mentioned by Homer, is described in Dares as equal to Hector. Achilles is far from heroic when he stabs Hector in the back, strangles Troilus, and is ready to betray the Greeks for the sake of Polyxena. Naturally Dictys, one of the Greek force, and Dares, a Trojan, viewed the facts from different standpoints, as historians of wars generally do. Dictys sneered at the Trojans as barbarians, and Dares placed responsibility for the war on the shoulders of the Greeks, since Paris had only taken revenge for the abduction of his aunt, Hesione. Such divergence of opinion did not weaken the authority of the historians. Dictys became the oracle of truth in the East, while Dares was preferred in the West—since many western nations were descended from Trojan heroes. Before leaving the pair in the mire of disrepute where they used to be thrown, we may remember that, however slight their literary merits, they do derive material from heroic tradition and have some "authority."

Another un-Homeric element in Dares and Dictys, which became much more important in works based on them, was romantic love. The story of that evolution has been told many times, and only a few landmarks need be noticed here. In the vast *Roman de Troie* Benoit de Sainte-Maure developed the romance of Achilles and Polyxena and invented or elaborated the story of Troilus, Briseida, and Diomede. Like other western authors Benoit used Dares chiefly, but had recourse to Dictys for events beyond the point where Dares stopped. The manners and setting were of the twelfth century, and

Hector appeared as the ideal knight of medieval chivalry.

Another version of Dares that Chaucer knew was a paraphrase in Latin verse by Joseph of Exeter, written toward the end of the twelfth century. The style and technique of the *Bellum Troianum* remind one frequently of both post-classical and Renaissance poetry; in other words it is typically medieval. The versification, modeled especially on that of Lucan and Claudian, has been pronounced "little, if any, inferior to the average of the Silver Age." [1] Colors of rhetoric, as prescribed in medieval textbooks, are laid on in profusion. We have a catalogue of trees, and, in connection with Helen, the orthodox medieval catalogue of female beauties, along with "a physio-psychological description of her interior." W. B. Sedgwick remarks that Joseph's style displays "the luxuriance of the young Shakespeare of *Lucrece* and *Venus and Adonis*, or of the young Pindar who 'sowed not with the hand but with the whole sack.'" The *Bellum Troianum* continued to be read for centuries; it was praised, for instance, by Samuel Daniel, William Browne, and Milton.[2]

We need not rehearse the familiar story of the paraphrase of Benoit by Guido delle Colonne and the development by Boccaccio and Chaucer of the tragic romance of Troilus and Cressida, though it is of interest to recall that Boccaccio's account of the enamorment drew not only upon the author's always useful experience but upon Benoit's episode of Achilles and Polyxena. Of those formidable saurians, the Middle English redactions of the whole story of Troy, the best is that of the much-enduring if not over-cunning hero, John Lydgate. His *Troy Book* (1412–20) is a solid performance of more than thirty thousand lines. While most of us, like Mr. Wegg in the matter of Gibbon, have not been "right slap through him very lately," one can by searching find bits of something like poetry.

II. VIRGIL IN THE MIDDLE AGES

The reasons for Virgil's unique authority in the Middle Ages were manifold and sometimes strange. Very early he became a textbook, and the stateliest measure ever moulded by the lips of man was

1. W. B. Sedgwick, "The *Bellum Troianum* of Joseph of Exeter," *Speculum*, V, 49–76. Cf. R. K. Root, "Chaucer's Dares," *MP*, XV, 1; N. Griffin, *JEGP*, XX, 45, note. My sketch of Dares and Dictys is indebted to the studies of Griffin cited in the Bibliography.

2. Gregory Smith, *Elizabethan Critical Essays*, II, 370; *Works of John Milton* (Columbia ed.), X, 12; and below, VIII, note 66.

chanted by rows of grubby children in hot schoolrooms. The beauty and subtlety of Virgil's language delivered him into the remorseless hands of grammarians. Rhetoric, too, claimed Virgil for her own. The speeches of his characters were studied and spouted in the schools of declamation; the question could be debated, "Was Virgil a poet or an orator?" There is testimony to his literary pre-eminence in the practice of making centos of Virgilian lines and phrases, such as the partly roguish composition of Ausonius.

But Virgil's universal sway did not rest merely on literary and artistic greatness. The purity of his writing, his ethical and philosophic tone, commended him to Christians who recoiled from Catullus or Lucretius. The lines that sounded forever of imperial Rome could not cease to inspire members of a church whose rulers were the successors of Augustus as well as of St. Peter. Then, like Homer among the Greeks, and Shakespeare among nineteenth-century critics, Virgil came to be regarded as an encyclopedia of knowledge, a complete guide to life. The *sortes Vergilianae*, which we may associate with Panurge's anxious project of matrimony, could be invoked by a Roman emperor. Hints of allegory in the early commentators were developed into a complete allegorization of the *Aeneid*; of this something will be said later. Finally, as everyone knows, on the strength of the fourth eclogue Virgil was revered as a prophet of the Messiah and hence came to occupy a place apart from other pagan poets; the traditional belief appears among scholars of the Renaissance. We need not concern ourselves with the popular metamorphosis of the poet into a wizard and hero of ignoble amorous adventures.

It was inevitable that the chief work of the universal poet should be adapted to medieval taste, and the latter half of the twelfth century produced the *Roman d'Eneas*. The very elaborate episode of Lavinia and Aeneas, which is the redactor's invention, is familiar, yet it is such a significant example of the medievalizing process that it must be summarized. For the technique of situation, dialogue, soliloquy, analysis of love and its effects, all this and more shows that for the medieval writer the successful reworking of Virgil consists to a large degree in borrowing from and imitating Ovid.

The queen visits Lavinia in order to speak to her about Turnus and tell her what love is. Aeneas happens to come out of his tent and Lavinia, seeing him, suddenly understands more than her mother could impart. She pours forth long amorous lamentations. When Aeneas pays no attention to her, she faints; recovering, she goes on again. She passes a restless night. The queen, calling the next day, sees that her daughter is in love, and is furious on learning that the object is Aeneas instead of Turnus. She rails at Aeneas, accusing him of unnatural vice. Lavinia faints, and revives to consider what she shall do. She has a letter sent to her unsuspecting idol. He reads it, turns toward Lavinia, who is on the watch, and salutes her. Going back to his tent, he feels so stricken that he has to take to the medieval lover's usual refuge, his bed. The next day Lavinia waits in the tower to see Aeneas come under the walls. Not knowing of his prostration she fears coldness, and begins to believe her mother's charges. But when Aeneas, weak and pale, rides out and shows himself to Lavinia, she repents of her lack of faith. The two gaze lovingly at each other. Aeneas' fellow warriors observe his passion and mock him. The lovers turn away, trembling. Here the author takes up Virgil, in order to describe the battle in which Turnus is killed. But for an adequate conclusion, the removal of the last doubts and obstacles and the happy marriage, he has to abandon Virgil again. Thus is a slow-moving classic speeded up to please sophisticated taste.

The whole setting of the romance is of course medievalized. Supernatural machinery, in Virgil decorative or symbolic or both, is reduced to a minimum, though romancers were fond enough of some kinds of wonders. For instance, whereas in Virgil Venus substitutes Cupid for Ascanius, in the romance Venus gives to Ascanius the power of exciting Dido's love. In general, of the *Aeneid* that we know the poet sees, or chooses to see, nothing. A religious epic, celebrating the divine mission of the Roman Empire, the venerable traditions and the ancient loveliness of Italy, touched everywhere with Virgil's sense of the burthen of the mystery and with the intricate beauty of Virgilian style—all this goes over the head of the redactor. For him and his readers the *Aeneid* is a thin tale of knightly deeds and romantic love. And yet, before shuddering at such medieval obtuseness, we may remember again that, if the romance is far from Virgil's conception and handling of the Trojan story, it is by no means so far from Ovid's.[3]

3. Edmond Faral, *Recherches sur les sources latines des contes et romans courtois du moyen age* (1913), pp. 125 ff. Writing on "Ovid's *Aeneid* and Vergil's," F. J. Miller finds the essential difference in motivation, and contrasts with the *Aeneid* "Ovid's presentation of a humdrum story, or what had, traditionally, become so; in a humdrum manner; with an un-heroic hero; his slurring over or entire omission of pertinent, important incidents, and his over expansion of entirely unrelated tales" (*Classical Journal*, XXIII, 33–43).

To mention one more item, in the *Roman de Jules César*, developed out of Lucan, Caesar's *Civil War*, and minor sources, the most notable episode is the love of Caesar and Cleopatra. An ample picture of Cleopatra's beauty, which

III. Ovid

"Next to Virgil in the Middle Ages came Ovid," says Charles Haskins, "indeed, one suspects that with the more carnally minded Ovid often came first. First he seems to have been in the twelfth century, that 'age of Ovid' which followed the Carolingian 'age of Virgil.' Any one who still believes that the Latin classics were a sealed book to the men of the Middle Ages, who cared only for the next world and had no appreciation of the beauties of literary art and the joys of the realm of sense, should ponder the popularity of Ovid and grow wiser." [4]

Some, though by no means all, of the elements of that popularity were alien to the real Ovid, but we can ill afford to patronize medieval students who, whatever their occasional vagaries, had a vital contact with Latin literature. Their classical past was a usable one—as ours hardly is—and the diversity of uses that the Latin authors served is the best proof of a fruitful tradition. The influence of Ovid ranged from the wandering scholars' very practical eulogies of Venus to the idealisms of the *Roman de la Rose*, from mythological romances to allegories of Christ's love for the human soul, from fairy tales to treatises on amatory etiquette.

To glance for a moment at these last works, how was a medieval translator, living in the midst of feudal society, to understand and make intelligible to readers such a poem as the *Ars Amatoria*, a detailed picture of the gilded life of Augustan Rome? With the self-confidence and independence that is sometimes called medieval naïveté he made over Ovid for his own purposes, and to suit his own world. It is significant that the *Ars Amatoria* was translated by Chrétien de Troyes, that twelfth-century master of the female heart; his version is not extant. A version entitled *Clef d'Amors* opens with a dream; instead of Roman entertainments we have dances, carols, tournaments; where Ovid suggests that a moistened hand may give the effect of tears our practical author recommends an onion. Still

---

resembles that of Iseult, prepares us for Caesar's immediate subjugation and consequent insomnia. A friend, acting as ambassador for the prostrated lover, is well received. When Caesar declares his passion Cleopatra, though already won, desires to consult her chamberlain. The conqueror of hearts and empires hastens to bribe this functionary, and victory is achieved. It seems hardly fair to regard this as more naïve than Shakespeare or Shaw, whatever its literary quality.

4. *The Renaissance of the Twelfth Century* (1928), p. 107.

another redaction, by Jacques d'Amiens, gives models of amorous conversation. With Chesterfieldian detail he tells how to approach an old woman, a woman of rank, a young girl.

Ovidian irony was not always carried over into these pieces, for the didactic form was congenial and might be taken rather seriously. Ovid, like other ancients, was considered a repository of wisdom, as in truth he was. "I am love's professor," he had said, and his works, which bear such testimony to a lifetime of research, might well serve as a guide to a society becoming conscious of love as the finest of fine arts. For Ovid and the courtly poets assumed that love is an art, subject to laws—artistic laws—and that the novice may take lessons in it. The redactors of the *Ars Amatoria* might miss Ovid's wit and mockseriousness, but their medievalizing of the poem was both inevitable and rational.

The *Metamorphoses* offered a different problem. A highly romantic version, in Old French, of the story of Pyramus and Thisbe is discussed in a later chapter, for the good but perhaps unexpected reason that an English poem derived from it appeared in an Elizabethan miscellany.[5] We have some indication of the character of *Piramus et Tisbé* in the fact that it was of service to the author of *Aucassin et Nicolette*.[6] The *Narcisse,* also of the twelfth century, is another illustration of the humanizing of a myth.

More elaborate than either of these poems is the *Philomena*.[7] Every reader of Chrétien de Troyes knows how dear to his heart, and to the courtly circle for whom he wrote, were amorous dialogue and psychological analysis. Whether or not Chrétien was the author, such elements are conspicuous in *Philomena*. The changes made in the Ovidian story are much the same as those favored in the sixteenth century. The most obvious one is that the Old French poem is six times as long as Ovid's. While Ovid has only a few words about Philomela's beauty, the medieval poet gives an exhaustive catalogue of her charms, from her nose to her knowledge of grammar. There is a long debate whether Philomela shall accompany Tereus or not, and the author discusses the metaphysics of love and madness. Tereus' growing passion is recorded through all its stages. Rhetoric is everywhere. Tereus

5. Page 48.
6. Faral, *Recherches*, p. 27.
7. Since we are concerned only with the technique of the poem, the question of authorship may be left to the experts, who disagree. See, for example, Karl Voretzsch, *Einführung in das Studium der altfranzösischen Literatur* (1925), p. 256; and De Boer's edition of *Philomena* (Paris, 1909).

first tries to win Philomela with a flood of eloquence. When he gives to his wife a circumstantial report of the supposed death of her sister, Progne delivers a harangue against death. She greets the discovery of her husband's villainy with a compendious tirade against men. Although there is an elaborate account of her funeral sacrifices, the general setting is medieval. Tereus in Ovid is *opibusque virisque potentem*, Pandion becomes *poissanz et larges et cortois*. While it is Ovid's great vice that he will always be clever, in this grim tale even he seems to be a trifle moved; there is no emotion at all in the ambling little couplets of the French poem. Thus the Ovidian story, rhetorical enough in itself, but still neat, compact, objective, is richly embellished with romantic, courtly, and even more rhetorical decorations.

Another mode of treating myth is illustrated at its best in the well-known tale *Sir Orfeo*. Instead of Hades we have the Celtic otherworld; instead of Pluto a fairy king with a band of knights and ladies clad in white and riding white horses; and "Heurodis" does not die, she is won by the king of the otherworld because she falls asleep under a fairy tree.[8] Chaucer, who is so rationally minded in his treatment of classic story, speaks of Pluto as "the king of fayërye." Henryson's poem on Orpheus and Eurydice mixes "goddes Infernall" and the "quene of fary." [9] In the not altogether dry light of the later sixteenth century this hybrid blossom, so far from withering, took on new life and color.

To follow the fortunes of individual Ovidian tales would lead us everywhere, but one example may be noticed. The myth of Io traveled as far as, in the drama, the gnat-stung damsel herself did. The *Gesta Romanorum* has a version that shuns connection with the pagan gods. A nobleman gives a favorite heifer to a hundred-eyed servant, Argus. A covetous man, Mercury, who wants this animal with golden horns, tries to charm and bribe the shepherd. The latter, whose integrity is shaken by opportunity, holds an imaginary dialogue with his master, represented by his staff set up in front of him. The rest of the tale is closer to the myth.[10] There are other versions in Latin, Italian, Span-

8. The story of Orpheus and Eurydice was known in the Middle Ages through Virgil (*Georg.* iv.454), Ovid, and Boethius (bk. iii, met. 12). See L. Hibbard, *Mediæval Romance in England* (1924), p. 197; J. Wirl, *Orpheus in der englischen Literatur*, Wiener Beiträge, XL, 18; and items in the Bibliography for this chapter.

9. *Poems of Robert Henryson*, ed. Gregory Smith, III (Edinburgh and London, 1908), 35; Wirl, p. 26.

10. *Gesta Romanorum*, ed. Oesterley, c.111, p. 451. See E. Bourne, "Mediæval Wanderings of a Greek Myth," *JEGP*, XXIV, 184; and "Classical

ish, German, Turkish, sometimes so remote from the original that it is only through knowledge of the intervening links that the relationship can be recognized. But the debatable land of folklore we may contemplate from afar.

Though medieval readers and writers liked Ovid the story-teller, they worshiped Ovid the poet of love. Chaucer's tribute illustrates the common opinion:

> And next hym on a piler was,
> Of coper, Venus clerk, Ovide,
> That hath ysowen wonder wide
> The grete god of Loves name.[11]

Not merely the troubadours and their successors, but clerics, historians, moralists, bear testimony, joyously or reluctantly, to the great teacher of the art of love, the painter of women who were faithful to at least one god. In fact the most potent of deities might be regarded as the son of Venus and Ovid.

If medieval authors generally missed the witty, ironic, cynical tone of the sophisticated poet of love, they also read the *Metamorphoses* in their own way. They were less likely than a modern reader to see Ovid plain, since they often met him in expanded paraphrases or abridgments, often, too, encrusted with astrological, allegorical, euhemeristic deposits. They were less likely to perceive Ovid's firm control of his material, his rhetorical tricks, his sustained verve, his creation of a clear daylight world of magic. Scholars such as John of Salisbury may praise Ovid's *levitatem versificandi*,[12] poets such as Chaucer may learn artistic lessons, but in comparison with later ages—for these statements are only relative—it is the substance of the *Metamorphoses* rather than its spirit or the niceties of its technique that the medieval writer lays hold of.

IV. ALLEGORY

Allegory might almost be said to constitute the bone, muscle, and nerves of serious medieval literature. The medieval mind, inhabiting a

---

Elements in the *Gesta Romanorum*," *Vassar Mediæval Studies* (1923), p. 345.

The allegorical interpretation is this: the nobleman is Christ, the heifer the soul, Argus a prelate, and Mercury, of course, the devil. The music with which Mercury captivates Argus is the wanton charms of women.

11. *Hous of Fame*, ll. 1486 ff.

12. Migne, *Patrologiæ Latinæ*, CXCIX, 484.

more intelligible world than ours, saw everywhere correspondences between sets of facts and ideas that to us seem unrelated. Knowledge was of three kinds, material, moral, spiritual, and up and down the ladder joining these three planes the allegorists moved like the angels in Jacob's dream. Yet the habit of allegorizing—for us the word means the reading of allegory into literature—was by no means purely medieval. It was common before Plato, and Plato himself counts as one of the germinal forces. And we shall escape from it only toward the end of this book, when the rationalism of the later seventeenth century bores through things mysterious with a cool hard stare. The octopus of allegory, then, lies floating many a rood, and at intervals we shall pause and survey the creature, though we must be content with a few prominent features of the great anatomy.

Since Homer was the Greek Bible in almost everything except the claim of divine authority, the time arrived when the devout or the skeptical reader had difficulty in reconciling the ideals of religion or the dictates of reason with the behavior of Zeus and Ares and Aphrodite. An avenue of escape opened up in the doctrine that things were not what they seemed, that underneath the fiction was concealed precious truth. However particular modes of interpretation might differ, the allegorical reading of myths became almost universal.

Such a magical sword and shield were naturally seized by Neo-Platonists and Christian apologists. Philo Judaeus and his school tried to show that the Pentateuch contained Greek philosophy, and Christian writers proved that the Hebrew prophets and poets contained Christianity. The Old Testament includes episodes of doubtful religious quality, and allegory came to the rescue. The most familiar example is the conversion of a sensuous love song (perhaps a survival from a liturgy of the fertility cult) into an allegory of Christ and the church. The invaluable method was carried over into the New Testament as well; the five barley loaves and two fishes, for instance, might become the law and the prophets. Despite protests from some of the fathers, such an instrument of exegesis was too effective to be laid down. Augustine tells how the allegorical expositions of Ambrose removed his difficulties, and illuminated passages "which when I understood literally, I was slain." [13]

Although, after the first battles between classical literature and Christianity, the practical necessities of education established Latin authors in the medieval curriculum, they were never so secure that

13. *Confessions* (Loeb Classical Library), bk. v, c. 14 (I, 259); bk. vi, c. 4 (I, 279).

they did not need defenders. Allegorical interpretation could be used by both friends and foes of classical writings and classical mythology. Euhemerism, for example, might be turned against pagan religion; gods who had originally been mere men were no fit objects of worship. With or without polemical motives euhemeristic interpretation continued to be popular throughout the Middle Ages and long afterward. Still other modes of thought turned the ancient gods into demons, or into astrological influences. Such topics are alluring, but have less concern for us than the religious and ethical methods of interpreting the classics. Apologists invoked the doctrine which had proved its strength, and classical literature was found to contain Christian truth hidden under the attractive coating of fable. The *Virgiliana continentia* of Fulgentius, written apparently in the early sixth century, launched an interpretation of the *Aeneid*—the pilgrimage of the soul through life—that was to be accepted for many centuries. In various forms this notion appeared in John of Salisbury, in Petrarch (who had moments of doubt), and other "modern men." And indeed, apart from the arid literalness of the allegorizers, is it in essence altogether un-Virgilian? [14]

Fulgentius also wrote a handbook of classical mythology, and his interpretations we shall meet again, for they lived more than a thousand years. In his hands the judgment of Paris, for instance, became a sermon on three modes of life, the contemplative, active, and sensual. This association with Minerva of the contemplative life (*quæ ad sapientiam & ad veritatis inquisitionem pertinet*) seems the most probable source of the medieval and modern version of the myth. In classical literature the offer of Minerva or Pallas is victory in war, in the medieval and modern tradition it is wisdom.[15]

14. "Vergil set before himself a Ulysses, perhaps even an Achilles. Nature set before him a St. Louis—a crusading knight and a '*holy*' war.' In the issue he hovers between the two conceptions—and fails. Yet there emerges from the failure something greater, at any rate in hope and suggestion, than any epical success: an ideal and mystical figure standing outside time and place, that seems to be now Aeneas, now Rome, now the soul of Man setting forth doubtfully on the pilgrimage of a dimly descried eternal glory." H. W. Garrod, "Vergil," *English Literature and the Classics*, ed. G. S. Gordon (1912), p. 152.

15. W. C. Curry, *MLN*, XXXI, 114–16. The first literary appearance of the offer of wisdom Mr. Curry finds in *Floir et Blancefloir* (ca. 1160), and it occurs in the Middle English *Destruction of Troy* (ca. 1375). The source of the various Middle English versions is probably, sometimes certainly, Guido delle Colonne. Cf. Edmond Faral, "Le récit du jugement de Paris dans l'Énéas et ses sources," *Romania*, XLI (1912), 100–02.

The sprightly Ovid might seem to offer intractable material to the most devout and ingenious interpreter, yet all things were possible when the *Ars Amatoria* could be reproduced as a sober didactic manual. The *Heroides* also contributed moral lessons; in his picture of Penelope Ovid was upholding chaste love, while guilty passion was condemned in the person of Phaedra.[16] Much more important was the immense reworking of the *Metamorphoses* called the *Ovide moralisé*, produced somewhere around the end of the thirteenth century. No tale was too sensuous and pagan to yield its quota of theological and moral lessons, not to mention other kinds.[17] Since the *Philomena*, which has been outlined already, was incorporated in the *Ovide moralisé*, we may ask what the interpreter makes of it. Pandion is God, who marries the soul, Progne, to the body, Tereus, in order that their offspring may replace the wicked angels who were cast out of heaven (these being the barbarians who were besieging Athens). The soul and body lived well together, and had a son Itys, "le bon fruit de sainte vie." But Progne longed to see her sister (the world and its pleasures), and sent Tereus over land and sea to obtain those earthly delights which God had granted to be used in moderation. The body, however, fixed all its thoughts upon these (Tereus' violation of Philomela), and hoarded them with avaricious care (the immuring of Philomela in the charge of an old woman). The soul forsakes the good for the evil life (Progne sacrifices to Pluto and doffs her golden robes to put on black ones), and gives itself up to sin (the releasing of Philomela). The fruit of good life is destroyed (the murder of Itys). The soul flies to hell, the vile body becomes a hoopoe, and Philomela is changed into a nightingale.[18]

Another allegorized version of the *Metamorphoses*, composed in

---

Fulgentius is quoted from *Mythographi Latini*, ed. T. Muncker (Amsterdam, 1681). For Paris, see ii. 1. As an instance of survival I might quote the allegory of L. Scoto prefixed to the second canto of Marino's *L'Adone* (Amsterdam, 1679, p. 45), where there are remarks on the three ways of life, "l'attiva, la contemplativa, & la voluntaria."

16. S. B. Meech, "Chaucer and an Italian Translation of the *Heroides*," *PMLA*, XLV, 110 ff.

17. The method of allegorizing, as formulated by Origen, Pope Gregory, and others, involved the elucidation of three or four meanings. A convenient exposition of fourfold interpretation, literal, allegorical, moral, anagogical, is given in Dante's *Il Convivio* (Trattato Secondo, c.1). For authorities on ancient and medieval mythographers and allegory see my Bibliography (under "General" and "Chapter One"), in particular O. Gruppe, Sir J. E. Sandys, L. Rick, J. Seznec, L. K. Born, E. C. Knowlton, and C. G. Osgood.

18. *Ovide moralisé*, ed. De Boer, vi.3719 ff.

the fourteenth century, was the Latin prose work that went under the name of Thomas Waleys but was written by Petrus Berchorius. The story of Pyramus and Thisbe, for example, seems almost made to the interpreter's hand. Pyramus, the son of God, loves Thisbe, the human soul, but the wall (sin) stands between them. Through the blessed incarnation they are to come together under the cross (the mulberry tree), at the baptismal font (the fountain). But the soul cannot approach the font because of the devil (the lion), and awaits the coming of Christ in silence. The son of God endures death for the human soul (Pyramus commits suicide). The soul should imitate his death, as Thisbe kills herself, and suffer the same anguish mentally. Or, to take an alternative exposition, Thisbe is the maiden to whom the son came in the flesh; he died on the cross, and she in compassion transfixed herself with a sword.[19]

There was an unbroken chain of such works which extends into the seventeenth century. In addition to miscellaneous compilations of allegorized myths, such as those of Boccaccio and Christine de Pisan, there were successive moralized versions of the *Metamorphoses* in Latin and the vernaculars. About 1370 Giovanni dei Buonsignori put together a volume based on an earlier translation of Ovid and the allegories of Giovanni del Virgilio. In 1484 the house of Colard Mansion issued a French rendering of Ovid, with bits from Waleys, Guido, and others woven into the text. And so we reach Caxton. But this is to anticipate, and we shall return to some of these books later.

The religious and moral and other lessons embodied in the *Ovide moralisé* and kindred works would of course have made Ovid stare and gasp. Haskins remarks that such Ovidian exegesis "must ordinarily have been the rationalizing effort to find justification for what men were reading for other reasons." [20] While an amateur may well hesitate to question any observation of Haskins concerning the Middle Ages, I cannot help thinking that, in his rehabilitation of an abused period, he inclines to make it too modern, to underestimate the sincerity of the moralizers and their public. No doubt many deceived

19. *Metamorphosis Ovidiana moraliter explanata* (Paris, 1509), fol. xxxvi. I might mention the romance of *Amoryus and Cleopes*, by John Metham, apparently written in 1448–49 (*Works of John Metham*, ed. H. Craig, E.E.T.S., 1916). The author makes use of the story of Pyramus and Thisbe, though with some remarkable changes. The lovers are revived through the prayer of a hermit, are baptized, married, and enjoy a long life.

20. *Renaissance of the Twelfth Century*, p. 108.

themselves, but surely many more read the allegories in good faith. What proportion of the Victorian middle class honestly believed it was reading poetry when it was only looking for Great Thoughts? In the first place, there is the sheer appalling bulk of allegorical commentary, far too large to spring from a perfunctory official piety. Then, if one habitually thinks in terms of allegory, if the physical world and everything else are an allegory of the spiritual, mythology becomes a natural part of one's subject matter. Finally, a mode of thought which maintained a vigorous life well into the seventeenth century—indeed far beyond—must have had deep and authentic roots. Of course this is not to say that Ovid the poet was not enjoyed. Nor can one generalize about medieval simplicity in the age of the Freudians.

V. Chaucer

If Chaucer had lived in the sixteenth century or in the twentieth his classical erudition would probably not have been infallible, for, though learned, he was not a mousing scholar, and he read with the swift and selective eye of a poet. But there were more than temperamental reasons for inaccuracy in the fourteenth century. Though much scholarly exploration has been done, it is still often difficult to ascertain how far Chaucer and other medieval men got information directly from the classical texts, and how far indirectly, through medieval redactions, books of extracts, quotations in grammars, and such things. Chaucer's sixty books constituted a large library, and his knowledge of Latin, French, and Italian was more than respectable. If he does sometimes make errors in classical matters he has also sometimes been wrongfully accused.[21] In any case such details have little to do with his art.

We can here only recall a few well-worn illustrations of Chaucer's attitude toward classical themes and classical authors. To begin with the outline of the *Aeneid* in the *Hous of Fame,* the first three books receive about a hundred and eighteen lines in Chaucer; the fourth book, the story of Dido, receives ninety-two lines, of which sixty are

21. For instance, there is classical authority, probably known to Chaucer, for the uncertain identity of Ascanius, so that he cannot be safely charged with a schoolboy blunder in making Ascanius and Iulus two persons. See E. K. Rand, "Chaucer in Error," *Speculum,* I (1926), 222. As for the telescoping of Brutus and Cassius, there was at least an established medieval tradition, which is a mitigating circumstance. See H. T. Silverstein, *MLN,* XLVII (1932), 148. I think Thomas Phaer, the Elizabethan translator of Virgil, regarded Pyrrhus and Neoptolemus as two men.

taken up with Dido's complaint; the remaining eight books are dispatched in thirty-five lines. Arithmetic alone indicates that epic has become romance. The *Legend of Dido*, though closer to the corresponding portion of Virgil, reveals a similar shift of emphasis, which of course is justified by the title. Dido's violation of her oath of loyalty to her husband is not mentioned, and much is made of Aeneas' broken vows. In neither poem does Chaucer present Aeneas as the prospective founder of Rome, traveling under divine guidance, temporarily seduced from his high destiny by a grandly passionate woman. Dido is a faithful saint of Cupid deceived and abandoned by a treacherous man, and the conception is in obvious accord with medieval romance —and Ovid.[22]

Another medieval element, likewise already encountered in romance, is the rationalization of the pagan supernatural. Chaucer relates, but with strong misgivings, that in "the book" Venus makes Aeneas invisible; he omits the divine agencies which secured a welcome for the Trojans; and he questions Cupid's personal activity in the kindling of Dido's love. In connection with Chaucer's rationalistic attitude it may be noted that his armor of common sense leaves him almost untouched by the allegorical mania.[23] Of course the setting of the poems is medievalized.

Thus Virgil is a source of material for Chaucer, but of spiritual affinity between the two there is not much. Chaucer's favorite ancient, one of his three or four favorite authors, was Ovid, whose influence ranges from decorative allusions to narrative method and conception of character. The familiar list of concrete borrowings need not be repeated here, but one question may be dwelt upon for a moment. Since we shall be much concerned with the technique and style of mythological poems in the sixteenth century, I should like to quote here an analysis of one of Chaucer's Ovidian pieces which, in almost every detail except the precise arithmetical figures, will be found true of *Venus and Adonis* and *Lucrece*. J. M. Manly thus dissects the Manciple's Tale:

It consists of 258 lines, of which 41 are devoted to describing Phebus, his wife, and the crow, and 50 to telling the incidents of the story. The re-

22. See E. K. Rand, *Ovid and His Influence* (1925), pp. 24–26; Elizabeth Nitchie, *Vergil and the English Poets* (1919).
23. J. D. Cooke, "Euhemerism," *Speculum*, II, 396 ff. Chaucer does of course make use of the "astrologised" gods. See W. C. Curry, "Astrologising the Gods," *Anglia*, XLVII, 213, and *Chaucer and the Mediaeval Sciences* (New York, 1926).

maining 167 lines—61 per cent. of the tale—are patches of rhetoric. Even this high percentage is perhaps too low, for the 25 lines of description devoted to Phebus are so conventional, so much in accordance with rhetorical formulas, that they might fairly be added to our estimate of the percentage of rhetoric. No effort was made by the author to conceive any of his characters as living beings or to visualize the action of the tale . . . Instead of attempting to realize his characters psychologically and conceive their actions and words as elements of a dramatic situation, he padded the tale with rhetoric. Thus he thrust into it and around it 32 lines of *sententiae*, 36 of *exempla*, 18 of *exclamatio*, 14 of *sermocinatio*, 3 of technical transition, 17 of *demonstratio*, and 63 of *applicatio*—all external and mechanical additions, clever enough as mere writing, but entirely devoid of life.[24]

To this general pattern Shakespeare, writing in the convention of his day, added pagan and pictorial sensuousness, but not much more. Further, Shakespeare carried to excess the balance and antithesis of the Ovidian line, but the trick is common in Chaucer; he learned it both from Ovid and from poets nourished on Ovid.[25]

Chaucer gathered his classical materials with an impartial hand. Statements regarding his sources are constantly subject to revision, but we need not go into detail. The legends of good women are compounded from a variety of authors, Ovid, Virgil, Guido delle Colonne, Boccaccio, the *Ovide moralisé*, Filippo "Ceffi," and others. The story of Ceyx and Alcyone in *The Book of the Duchesse* combines, with original variations, Ovid and a dash of Machaut. The Physician's Tale of Virginia may combine Livy and the *Roman de la Rose*. Trojan material is taken from Joseph of Exeter's version of Dares, from Guido and Benoit. Sometimes, as John L. Lowes pointed out, mythological allusions are colored by Dante. The classical purist might accuse Chaucer of sowing cockles in his clean corn, but the charge would of course only exhibit a quite uncritical conception of medieval ways. Chaucer was not writing works like Becker's *Gallus*, he was a story-teller looking for stories; he assumed, as Shakespeare did, that human nature is the same in all times and places.

But, with all his classical borrowings, Chaucer was on the whole least Chaucerian and most medieval in his treatment of ancient stories. The tales of good women are perfunctory and contain frequent admissions of haste and boredom; he never finished the book. Nor are the

24. "Chaucer and the Rhetoricians," *Proceedings of the British Academy*, XII (1926), 108.
25. M. A. Hill, "Rhetorical Balance in Chaucer's Poetry," *PMLA*, XLII (1927), 845. Cf. C. S. Baldwin, "Cicero on Parnassus," *ibid.*, p. 106.

classical stories told by the pilgrims among his successes. Yet would one expect anything else? The ironic observer of the human comedy moved more easily and happily among creatures of flesh and blood than in the less substantial world of mythological figures. Here and there, to be sure, are pleasant touches of simplicity and pathos, and the inimitable irony is not wholly wanting:

> She fledde hireself into a litel cave,
> And with hire wente this Eneas also;
> I not, with hem if there wente any mo;
> The autour maketh of hit no mencioun.

But the comment is in the vein of Ovid rather than Virgil.

We cannot linger over the more elaborate "mythological" poems, the Knight's Tale and *Troilus,* since they are of medieval origin. In the latter Chaucer had the room and the material he needed; his characters live as they never could in brief Ovidian tales. Here and in the best of the *Canterbury Tales* Chaucer revealed himself as, in the main, a classical artist, and Dryden with his usual insight said so, finding the medieval poet more simple and natural, in a word, more classical, than Ovid. Yet to say that Chaucer is nearest to classical art when he is furthest from classical material, that his Dido is less classical than his Wife of Bath, is only to say that the deepest influence of the ancients upon him cannot be measured. For would the Wife be what she is if Chaucer had not learned much from Ovid and the poets whom the classics taught, such as Jean de Meun and the rest?

If Chaucer represents the incalculable accident of genius, his friend the moral Gower represents something better than the average mind of the fourteenth century. His knowledge of the Latin classics was considerable, though not invulnerable; he could make two persons of "Tullius" and "Cithero," and was content to write of Virgil the wizard and his magic mirror. Gower is assuredly not a tricksy spirit, but as a story-teller he has virtues, in spite of the portentously didactic framework of the *Confessio Amantis.* While, except in a few moments of pathos, classical myths left Chaucer cold, they found in Gower an often spirited and sympathetic narrator; he was really moved by the fate of Medea, Canace, Lucrece. Besides, he had command of pure and simple English. Altogether his tales are much better than many later mythological poems. The remarkable evenness of Gower's thousands of lines has been unkindly described as the fluency of running lead, and doubtless he is not for continuous reading; but neither is William Morris.

VI. THE MEDIEVAL ATTITUDE

Although the fallacious implications of such a heading as "the medieval attitude" arouse the just ire of scholars, the phrase may serve to introduce a few words on certain important aspects of classical culture in the Middle Ages. Some familiar generalizations have a bearing on the medieval heritage of the sixteenth century. In the first place knowledge of classical, that is, Latin literature, was limited to a small minority. Then, although the range of Latin authors known was wide, it was often only partial. Horace's *Epistles* and *Satires*, for instance, had a considerable circulation, while the *Odes* were almost unread. Ovid's *Amores* was little known, though his other major works had such an immense popularity. The list might be extended indefinitely. Further, if the Latin authors were seldom read as wholes, and if spurious works had got into the canon, they could not be appreciated as distinct personalities. Nor could the classical writers be seen in a historical setting. Horace and Lucan, Virgil and Statius, were simply lumped together; they were all ancients.

But in the absence of our historical and critical view of antiquity the story-teller did not greatly suffer. Classical epics and romances based on them were read side by side, and were equally useful as sources. A story was a story, wherever found, though an ancient name, such as Lollius, might add weight and prestige. Whatever went into the capacious melting pot, the *Aeneid* or a tale from the *Metamorphoses*, came out a romance, or a sermon, or both.

Since medieval art in general is characterized by the mixture of alien elements, we have abundant illustrations in the treatment of classic and pseudo-classic themes. The mingling of the classical and medieval includes of course the mingling of the pagan and the Christian. "I am not Aeneas, I am not Paul," says Dante to his master and guide. In his untroubled use of classic myth the most religious of poets is typical of the reconciling spirit of the best medieval minds; perhaps one should say typical of a spirit unconscious of the need for reconciliation. Chaucer may exclaim

> Lo here, the fyn and guerdoun for travaille
> Of Iove, Appollo, of Mars, of swich rascaille!

But these lines occur in that remarkable epilogue to *Troilus*, where, recoiling from his own vivid presentation of physical passion, Chaucer exhorts young people to turn from earthly loves to the abiding love of God. That is not the normal mood of Chaucer or other secular writers. Chaucer is normal when he casually dubs Amphiaraus a bishop,[26] or thinks of Ovidian love stories as "the Seintes Legende of Cupyde."

The untroubled assimilation of all manner of things, so evident in the mixture of sources and of Christian and pagan ideas, has an obvious bearing upon critical appreciation of classical art. The timeless virtues of clear vision, disinterested reasonableness, precision of line, architectonic form, are not the most conspicuous qualities of medieval writing, though they are not wholly absent. Even Chaucer, in many ways truly classical, is sometimes naïve in matters of form. Despite the plentiful evidence of rich enjoyment of the classics, and despite the intensive study of rhetoric, it was not in the main aesthetic lessons that the medieval writer absorbed from his reading. John of Salisbury, the best scholar and one of the best minds of the twelfth century, read the *Aeneid* as an allegory of the life of man, found precepts of morality in the *Georgics*, and drew wisdom even from the talk of shepherds in the *Eclogues*. He esteemed Lucan highly as a moral teacher; Ovid also, with reservations. Horace is *ethicus;* likewise Juvenal and Persius. Terence contains excellent lessons in morals and manners. Altogether, for this Christian humanist, the ancients transmit *informationem virtutis quae facit bonum virum.*[27] Such an approach to the classics does not preclude aesthetic appreciation, but it certainly does not emphasize those qualities which would have helped to restrain and mold and rationalize medieval literature. On the other hand it proves that the classics, however altered and Christianized, were a living source of culture to a degree which we with all our knowledge hardly attain.

While the nineteenth century in general saw the Middle Ages and the Renaissance in terms of black and white, modern scholars have in the first place shown the importance of medieval achievement, and, in the second, have made it clear that the Renaissance was no sudden break with the medieval past. In all fields of activity men of the Renaissance were much less emancipated than they thought they were; most of them, even such heralds of modernity as Bacon and Descartes, were rooted in medieval tradition. The medieval mind ac-

26. Golding, by the way, renders *sacerdos* as "bisshop" (*Metam.* xv.778; Golding, ed. Rouse, p. 311, l. 855).

27. A. C. Krey, "John of Salisbury's Knowledge of the Classics," *Wisconsin Academy of Sciences,* XVI, Part 2 (1910), 948 ff.; Migne, *Patrologiæ Latinæ,* CXCIX, *passim.*

cepted the irrational if it came in the guise of religion, we accept the irrational if it comes in the guise of science; the difference is called progress. Though, in relation to the general march of mind, the study of myths is a bypath, a main effort in this book will be to show the persistence, for good and ill, of the medieval spirit.

CHAPTER II

The Background
of Classical Mythology
in the Sixteenth Century

I. The Character of English Humanism

Though the religious and ethical quality of early Tudor humanism is a commonplace, it is one that must be emphasized here. Without it Spenser and Milton, even Marlowe and Shakespeare, are inconceivable. For what vitalized the Renaissance in Europe generally was the spiritual energy inherited from medieval religion. That energy, however disguised or transmuted, made possible, for a time, a Christian humanism more liberal and cultivated—and perhaps less devout—than the Middle Ages had developed. But for it the revived classical culture would have been less solid, less fruitful, less enduring; the fact will find illustration even in these pages.

From the very beginning the movement revealed some dangerous symptoms. The spiritual chaos of the present day may leave it open to question whether the separation that finally took place between humanism and religion was both an inevitable and a triumphant stride forward, or, on the part of humanism, a self-destructive cutting off of its own life-giving roots. There can at any rate be no question about the fatal results of the divorce between literary humanism and life. At first the classics mirrored an ideal of civilized sweetness and light, a world in which man enjoyed dignity and freedom; in the hands of dilettanti and pedagogues they became too often an ideal of *eloquentia*. Humanism ceased to be humanistic when it made style a supreme object, when Bembo could give his well-known advice to Sadoleto. For one bold mind like Valla, who had absorbed the critical spirit (if not the urbanity) of the ancients, there were a hundred stylists and grammarians; and Latin was slain in the house of its friends. The human-

ists, at first the party of progress, became the party of academic orthodoxy and reaction, while scientists and other more legitimate heirs of
antiquity took the lead.

The paganism of the Italian Renaissance has usually been exaggerated by glowing or gushing pens, for popular writers still embellish
some misconceptions of Burckhardt and Symonds. But certain large
differences between Italian and English religion and culture cannot be
overlooked. Religious instincts in many leaders of the Italian Renaissance flowed into mystic or "heretical" channels; we recall such names
as Ficino, Pico della Mirandola, Pomponio Leto, Pomponazzi, Ago-
stino Nifo, Giordano Bruno, not to mention the ascetic fervor of
Savonarola. Among classical scholars, humanists in the special sense of
the word, a soul is not always to be discerned, though one Vittorino
had more influence than a score of Poggios and Filelfos.

But early Tudor Englishmen felt no great urge toward mystic
ecstasy, high philosophic speculation, or bold and critical rationalism.
Instead we find orthodox Catholicism followed by more or less orthodox Calvinism, and an unceasing preoccupation with practical morals.
Paganism, real or affected, did not flourish among English scholars of
the fifteenth and sixteenth centuries. The first generations of English
students, with such rare exceptions as the luckless Tiptoft, brought
back from Italy serious books and ideas, not the empty purse, queasy
stomach, and naughty conscience of the later Italianate Englishman.
The names of most early Tudor humanists are virtually a roll-call of
religious leaders, or at any rate sober and pious teachers. As a pendant
to Bembo and Sadoleto we may think of Erasmus and Colet walking
in Colet's garden and talking of Christ.

Not only was the early English Renaissance extremely religious,
it was also extremely practical. The shallow elegances of some continental culture were alien to the English temper. Besides, in bar-
barous Britain, "situated outside the world," as Battista Guarino said,
it was natural that the fruits of the movement should for some time be
devoted mainly to education, education especially directed—as it was
up through Milton's tract—toward humane knowledge, virtue, and
civic responsibility. If Tudor humanism sometimes lapsed into sterile
pedantry and pedagogy, for the most part it labored in the best spirit
of learning and patriotism to spread enlightenment.

Propagation and popularization of classical literature was a first
necessity. Over and over again the translators lament that England
lags behind other countries in making classical wisdom available for
the mass of unlearned readers; their own desires, they say, exceed

their competence, but they go manfully to work. And these translators were not merely or mainly university teachers, official custodians of the classics, but ardent unofficial scholars, young authors and Inns of Court men.[1] A chronological summary of works translated from the classics might try the reader's patience, but a very brief survey may be allowed.

To pass over the beginnings in the first quarter of the century, we find about thirty-five translations in the second quarter. There are half a dozen medical books, some history (including Thucydides, done from a French version of a Latin version), but the largest group is that of moral and philosophical works, Aristotle, Cicero, Seneca, Plutarch, "Cato," and others. In the third quarter about eighty translations appear, and we have, in addition to such perennials as Galen, more history, some science, textbooks on rhetoric; moral works are still prominent, from Cicero, with seven or eight pieces, to Philo Judaeus. So far the century is running true to form.

But now there is also a considerable bulk of translation from ancient fiction, drama, and poetry. Many of these works, to be sure, were not officially labeled as entertainment, since the early Elizabethans hardly admitted such a category. At any rate we have Adlington's *Apuleius*, Underdowne's *Heliodorus*, the classical tales in Painter's *Palace of Pleasure*, and other such books, though Italian and French fiction is taking the lead. There are numerous renderings of Ovid and Virgil, some of which will be noticed later, and most of the Senecan plays appear in English. Some treatments of Horace are significant. The versions of two odes in Tottel's *Miscellany* represent, not the urbane observer of life or the heart-whole lover, but the sober moralist who flees extremes and meditates on the brevity of life and the approach of death.[2] And in his version of the *Satires* and *Epistles* (1566–67) Thomas Drant, who complacently "wyped awaye" all of Horace's "vanitie and superfluitie of matter," turned the sophisticated ironist into a Tudor preacher.

The fourth quarter of the century shows some decline in the number of classical translations; there are only about sixty. Most of the works which attracted Elizabethan readers were already in English,

---

1. In addition to Whibley's chapter in the *Cambridge History of English Literature* and H. R. Palmer's *List of English Editions and Translations of Greek and Latin Classics* (1911), see, in the Bibliography, the books of F. R. Amos, H. B. Lathrop, *et al.*

2. The odes are ii.10 and iv.7. See *Miscellany*, ed. Rollins, II, 152, 273, and index.

and there was increasing competition in a multitude of translations from modern languages. Besides, the first phase of the English Renaissance, that of education and assimilation, had passed into the second, that of re-expression, and the immense creative energy of the time was pouring along a dozen channels. Yet the same kinds of books were being read, and in about the same proportions. One work alone would have made the fortune of the period, North's *Plutarch* (1579), and in 1600 came Livy, announcing the arrival of the translator-general, Philemon Holland. More translations of the Greek romances bear witness to an interest reflected in Elizabethan fiction, yet Greek tragedy and comedy and Plato had not yet found their way into English. Among many versions of classical poets we may remember that Homer first appeared in Arthur Hall's ten books of the *Iliad,* done from the French, and before the end of the century came the first installments of Chapman's *Homer,* one of the uncertain glories of that April day.

Most of the works mentioned indicate not only popularization of classical story but increasing knowledge and understanding of antiquity. When we come to Philemon Holland we have reached the beginnings of modern scholarship. Yet men had not laid aside the ethical spectacles of John of Salisbury. Even if Tudor writers and readers, like their medieval predecessors, fell short of the modern in aesthetic appreciation of the classics—an assumption that we may make too easily—they had a far more immediate and vivid sense of ancient literature as a part of their life, of ancient civilization as a not unattainable ideal. It is a commonplace that to North Brutus and Antony are as real as Cecil and Leicester. In 1570 Thomas Wilson issued a translation of Demosthenes' orations against Philip, "most nedefull to be redde in these daungerous dayes, of all them that loue their Countries libertie, and desire to take warning for their better auayle, by example of others." The Macedonian was not the only King Philip Englishmen thought of when they read Demosthenes.

If the ancients, who in general held a rather didactic view of literature, had returned to earth in the sixteenth century, they would not have complained, as I think Ruskin did, "I show men their plain duty, and they reply that I have a beautiful style." Ciceronians were relatively few in England, experiments with classical meters were largely a coterie affair (nor were they so irrational around 1580 as they might seem a decade later), and the general influence of the classics was solid and healthy. That their direct influence on poetic theory and practice was somewhat weak is partly, but not altogether, a matter for regret. The native and medieval tradition was too strong to be subdued; thanks to that Elizabethan drama, for instance, displayed a vitality lacking in the classicized drama of France. Poetry in general owed more directly to the older English poets and modern continental writers than to the classics, and the classics were read by a half-medieval light. But even if a characteristic of Elizabethan writing is a rich lawlessness, such an earnest and sometimes moving poem as *Musophilus,* a sixteenth-century *Culture and Anarchy* in verse, shows both the fertilizing and the disciplinary power of classical literature over sober minds. Nor was Daniel ever a more authentic classicist than when in his prose essay he spoke out against slavish imitation of the ancients and declared that English literature must develop in accordance with its own genius.

A word more must be said on the matter of imitation or plagiarism, especially since we are following in mythological poems a very imitative tradition. George Saintsbury once ranked source-hunting with the sport of worrying cats, and it is a popular attitude among the foes of pedantry. But in studying poetry of the Renaissance it is somewhat uncritical to ignore one of the main tenets of the poetical creed. Imitation, which for Aristotle meant ideal imitation of life, by the first century B. C. had come to mean, for Dionysius of Halicarnassus, imitation of authors. This early perversion of the Aristotelian doctrine was encouraged by the strong tendency of Greek and Roman critics to link poetry with rhetoric. The precept of literary imitation appeared in Cicero's *De Oratore,* and in the pseudo-Ciceronian *Ad Herennium,* which was extremely popular in the Middle Ages. It was approved by Quintilian and even by "Longinus." [3] Having flourished throughout the medieval period, the doctrine of plagiarism was powerfully reinforced by such Italian critics as Bembo, Vida, Daniello, Minturno. The modern author, it was said again and again, learns his craft from the masters; if he improves what he borrows he justifies his theft.

The critical tradition was of course carried on by English writers—Ascham was a notable early exponent—and although, as in Italy, there was a growing reaction against servility, a growing confidence in native genius, the doctrine of imitation was abundantly preached and practiced. Consistency was not always observed. Lodge could

3. *Instit.* x.i–ii; *On the Sublime,* xiii.2–4; xiv.1. See G. Fiske, *Lucilius and Horace* (University of Wisconsin Studies, 1920), c.1, "The Classical Theory of Imitation"; W. L. Bullock, "The Precept of Plagiarism in the Cinquecento," *MP,* XXV, 293; H. O. White, *Plagiarism and Imitation During the English Renaissance* (Harvard University Press, 1935).

write in an essay of the *furor poeticus;* when he wrote verse the divine and presumably original inspiration was not incompatible with wholesale thefts. On some levels, naturally, plagiarism was vicious, as a mass of sonnets makes clear, but it was imitation of great poets that made possible great Elizabethan poetry. E. K. pointed out that Spenser in his first book was devoutly following literary tradition, and in the strength of maturity Spenser invaded authors like a monarch. He went to school to some ancients and the best moderns, and, having done so, he created a style, a style essentially original. If English poetry was to be great it had to be not merely English but European, and Spenser more than anyone else made it so. Whatever sins, therefore, are to be traced to the Renaissance theory of imitation, and we find a good many, it may be remembered that the two greatest non-dramatic poets of the English Renaissance are also, to use our disparaging term, the most derivative.

II. The Sources of Classical Mythology

Sources were of course vastly more abundant in the sixteenth century than in the Middle Ages. More ancient authors were known, and they were better known. Of these Ovid was the most important, and it would need many volumes to catalogue the adventures of that most capricious poet among the Goths. But the use of Ovid and some other ancient sources will be noticed in connection with individual poets. In this section I shall try to indicate the nature of what may be called popular authorities, for, as every student of the Renaissance knows, medieval sources and medieval ideas were not abandoned in a general return to the pure fountains of classical literature.

Since a large share of mythological and historical allusion was given a didactic turn in both prose and verse, we find a large debt to such books as Plutarch's *Lives* and *Morals,* the collections of Valerius Maximus, Aelian, Aulus Gellius. The sixteenth-century reader had a keen relish for the sober shrewdness and point of ancient anecdote. Then there were countless modern compilations, such as the *Adagia* of Erasmus, a book which helped as much as any to reveal to Europe the intellectual and moral character of antiquity. To the ordinary reader such books may not always have brought emancipation, but they were inexhaustible treasuries of classical story.[4]

4. For instance, the story of Ulysses' stopping his own ears with wax appears in Ascham, Lyly, Pettie's translation of Guazzo, and Chapman. The un-Homeric detail seems to come from Erasmus (*Similia*), who was imperfectly recollecting

Medieval redactions of classical stories reached the English reader mainly through the paraphrases of Caxton and Lydgate, but in the sixteenth century the originals continued to be printed and read— Dares and Dictys, "Pindarus Thebanus," Guido, and Joseph of Exeter. Such writers, especially Dares and Dictys, were still authorities on the Trojan war, and they survived, though with diminishing prestige, beyond the age of Scaliger and Casaubon. Sidney contrasts "the fayned Aeneas" of Virgil with "the right Aeneas" of Dares.[5]

In spite of more modern rivals Boccaccio's respectable labors, the *De Genealogia Deorum, De Claris Mulieribus,* and *De Casibus,* were constantly reprinted, translated, and borrowed from. Mythological handbooks later in date, and more learned, but not much more modern in spirit, were the *De Deis Gentium* of Lilius Giraldus (1548), the *Mythologiae* of Natalis Comes (1551), and *Le Imagini, con la Spositione de i Dei degli Antichi* of Vincenzo Cartari (1556).[6] These books, especially the last two, had an enormous influence throughout literary Europe, and the number of editions perplexes the bibliographer. Natalis Comes (Natale Conti) is perhaps the most attractive of the compilers, and he has his merits. He summarized mythological tales in easy Latin, assembled abundant references, quoted and translated Greek authors, and altogether provided the means which enabled many men, such as Chapman, to appear more learned than they were. Of the value of such books to writers Marston gives a satirical hint:

> Reach me some poets' index that will show.
> *Imagines Deorum,* Book of Epithets,
> Natalis Comes, thou I know recites,
> And makest anatomy of poesy . . .[7]

But well-arranged stories and references, however inviting, would not in themselves have given such works the authority they had. The

an allusion in Plutarch. See M. P. Tilley, *Classical Philology,* XXI, 162. Even Ben Jonson accepts the variant (*Bartholomew Fair,* III.i). One finds everywhere a similar process of transmission going on; we do the same thing ourselves.

5. *Elizabethan Critical Essays,* I, 168. Geffrey Whitney compares the treatment of Hector by Dares, the eyewitness, and that of Achilles by the later Homer (*Choice of Emblemes,* 1586, dedicatory epistle). See the Appendix, under Thomas Fenne (1590) and Thomas Milles (1613).

6. For these and other mythographers, see especially Jean Seznec and D. T. Starnes and E. W. Talbert (Bibliography, "General").

7. *Works,* ed. Bullen, III, 270. *Imagines Deorum* is the title of the Latin editions of Cartari.

great mass of sixteenth-century readers were far from pagan in their tastes, and mythology was especially appetizing when the cup was coated with the honey of morality. Comes and the rest carried on the tradition of Fulgentius, Neckam, Boccaccio, and the whole tribe of authors who had made mythology safe for the world. The myths were enriched with edifying interpretations, sufficiently medieval in character, though now moral expositions replaced theological. It was this allegorical element in Comes which commended itself to Chapman, and Chapman was not unique, unless perhaps in the magnitude of his debt.

There were some small English books of similar character. Thomas Cooper's *Thesaurus* (1565 and later editions) was not small but was much used. Stephen Batman's *Golden Booke of the Leaden Goddes* (1577) was a didactic compendium of mythology which described the appearance and insignia of the gods (not without glances at "sectarian gods" and misguided Anabaptists) and appended their "signification." Abraham Fraunce's *Third part of the Countesse of Pembrokes Ivy-church* (1592) contained sixteen Ovidian tales in verse and the fullest allegorical commentary which appeared in English before that of Sandys; Fraunce's "philosophicall explications" were drawn from Cartari, Comes, and others. Richard Linche's *Fountaine of Ancient Fiction* (1599) was an abridged version of Cartari.

There was plenty of mythological lore in older English books. Chaucer, Gower, and Lydgate were widely read in the sixteenth century, but, so far as classical tales are concerned, it does not appear that Chaucer (apart from *Troilus*) and Gower had much influence. For earlier Tudor readers at least Lydgate often stood first in the trinity —he was a master of aureate diction—and his staggering paraphrases had a popularity out of proportion to anything but their length. His *Troy Book,* however, was overshadowed by Caxton's *Recuyell;* we shall return to Caxton in a moment.

The mythological compilations of Christine de Pisan, that doughty feminine invader of Grub Street, had some slight importance in the fifteenth and early sixteenth centuries, if several translations are adequate evidence. The first one was made about 1444–50 by Stephen Scrope, a stepson of Sir John Fastolf, from Christine's *L'Epistre d'Othea a Hector de Troie,* and, as one would expect, the book was included in the Pastons' library.[8] Drawing upon a popular ancient

8. Ed. G. F. Warner, Roxburghe Club, 1904. Another translation has been edited by James D. Gordon (Philadelphia, 1942). See P. G. C. Campbell, Laigle, and Pinet, in the bibliography to this chapter. For other translations from Christine, see the Appendix, under 1521 and 1536–45.

history, the *Ovide moralisé,* and other sources, Christine recounted numerous myths and appended a moralization to each. Andromeda stands for the soul, Penthesilea is the virtue of charity, Bacchus the sin of gluttony; one may wonder if the lessons took effect on the rather mundane Pastons.

Equally medieval was the pedigree of Caxton's vastly more important versions of classic stories. His *Recuyell of the Historyes of Troye* was done from the French of Raoul le Fevre, who had embellished Guido. The choice of such a book to inaugurate Caxton's publishing career is significant enough regarding popular interest in the matter of Troy. It was frequently reprinted during the next two and a half centuries; the last of the twenty or so editions appeared thirteen years after the town had welcomed the *Iliad* of Pope.[9] Far more than any other book the *Recuyell* established the Elizabethan conception of the Trojan story. We shall often encounter it in pages to come.

In 1480 Caxton finished translating *Ovyde Hys Booke of Methamorphose* but apparently he did not print it.[10] The French original sometimes incorporated the moralizations of Berchorius, which Caxton mostly omitted, and Trojan matter was considerably expanded by passages interpolated from Guido delle Colonne and others. But the stories and the pictorial quality of Ovid remain; if they have lost a good deal of their polished art and sophistication, they have gained something rich and strange. Hector and Achilles are medieval knights, of course, and romance is more romantic, magic more magical, than in Ovid. But Ovid, whose text Caxton probably never looked at, might not have been displeased by a rendering so spirited and so opulent in style.

Other medievalized tales which Caxton translated from the French were *Jason* (*ca.* 1477) and *Eneydos* (1490). The French redactor had treated Virgil with the usual freedom, omitting, abridging, changing, adding matter from Boccaccio and similar indispensable sources. Some of the most familiar Virgilian episodes—Sinon and the wooden horse, the loss of Creusa—do not appear at all, while there is a long account, taken from Boccaccio, of the life and death of Dido. Epic

---

9. A. Esdaile, *English Tales and Prose Romances Printed before 1740,* p. xii.

10. There is only one MS extant, containing books x–xv, which may have been Caxton's own copy. It had an eventful history before it reached the hands of that lover of books, women, and song, Samuel Pepys. See the handsome reprint (1924) edited by S. Gaselee and H. F. B. Brett-Smith. Caxton translated from the French version—which was published by Colard Mansion in 1484—perhaps from Mansion's own MS, since the two men had been associated at Bruges.

elements are slighted, but the work was not conceived of as an epic; such a scholar as Gavin Douglas might well exclaim in his wrath that it was no more like Virgil than the devil like St. Austin. Though the *Eneydos* was not so popular as the *Recuyell*, we shall meet it again.

The multitude of later and more direct translations from the classics cannot be considered here. The influence of particular works, such as the all-important *Metamorphoses* of Golding, will be noticed in subsequent chapters. Such formal and relatively accurate versions had an immense and obvious share in the popularization of classical culture. They did not always catch the spirit of an author, and had a tendency to reduce the ancients to a common denominator, but they had the not negligible advantage of enthusiasm and a rich, fresh, vigorous idiom. They also enabled a number of persons, in Nashe's words, to vaunt "Ouids and Plutarchs plumes as theyr owne" and "feed on nought but the crums that fall from the Translators trencher" [11]—which is a rather good instance of Satan rebuking sin.

A few words may be added concerning miscellaneous books which, increasing in number as the century advanced, helped to make mythological allusions more familiar to the reading and theater-going public than they have ever been since. No one in the period could set pen to paper without invoking classical authority—"this pitch, as ancient writers do report, doth defile"—and a multitude of anecdotes and allusions passed from hand to hand in English books. Such ornaments, either in a journalist like Nashe or a scholarly poet like Chapman, cannot, any more than in the Middle Ages, be taken as evidence of profound learning. The mass of this material in Elizabethan books is quite overwhelming, and it will be enough to mention a few titles by way of emphasizing the fact that mythology reached both readers and writers by circuitous paths.

When one is told of the seething current of ideas that swept through Elizabethan England it is well to remember some of the best-selling books, such as *A Mirror for Magistrates*, which had many offspring, or the works of the most episcopal Guevara. The chief translations from the latter, Lord Berners' *Golden Boke* (1534) and North's *Diall of Princes* (1557), with their appalling prolixity, unwearied sententiousness, and hundreds of classical anecdotes, perfectly suited Tudor taste.[12] Manuals of rhetoric, such as those of

11. Preface to *Menaphon* (*Works*, ed. McKerrow, III, 312). One might mention such a book as Underdowne's translation of Ovid's *Ibis* (1569), the notes to which constitute a small dictionary of myth.

12. It may be put down to Guevara's credit that he pleased Montaigne's excellent father (*Essays*, ii.2). And he contributed something to Burton, Jeremy

Leonard Cox (1524) and Thomas Wilson (1553), illustrated their more or less classical principles with classical examples. Mindful of the rhetorical value of illustrations, Wilson explains the allegorical meaning of Danae and Isis, Tantalus and Icarus, Midas and Hercules. From Wilson came the story of Zaleuch and his son which is versified in *The Paradise of Dainty Devices;* [13] and from Elyot's *Governour* was taken the subject of a companion poem, also by Richard Edwards, *A yong man of Ægipt and Valerian.*[14] An Italian work based on Plutarch, Baptista Gelli's *Circe,* made the story of Ulysses and Circe the vehicle for a series of debates on the comparative merits of human and bestial life.[15] Such are a random few of the innumerable works which have unexpected dealings with mythology. Elizabethan prose and verse were sometimes dropsical with classical allusions, and, while a portion of such lore was honestly begotten by the ancients, a goodly portion also was of more recent parentage. The Elizabethan reader and writer could no more escape it, whatever they read, than the modern can escape the jargon of psychology.

III. CLASSICAL TALES IN ENGLISH PROSE

Painter's *Palace of Pleasure* (1566–67), which introduced Italian and French *novelle* to English readers and especially to English dramatists, concerns us here on account of its forty-one classical stories. The sources make a significant list: Herodotus (two stories); Aelian (three); Plutarch's *Morals* (one); Aulus Gellius (twelve); Livy (eight); Quintus Curtius (three); Xenophon (one); Pedro Mexia (two); Guevara's *Letters* (three); Bandello (six).[16] The col-

---

Taylor, and Sterne (E. Bensly, *TLS*, February 13, 1920, p. 106). Of course he influenced such earlier writers as Pettie and Lyly and others, though the theory of his euphuism has long been exploded.

13. *Paradise,* ed. Rollins, pp. 58, 221; *Wilson's Arte of Rhetorique,* ed. G. H. Mair, p. 28.

14. *Paradise,* pp. 57, 220; *The Governour,* ed. Croft, II, 315.

15. The book was translated into English in 1557. See M. A. Scott, *Elizabethan Translations from the Italian* (1916), pp. 10–11, and Collier, *Bibl. Acct.* (New York, 1866), II, 155–57. T. Brown's translation of *Circe* has been edited by R. M. Adams (Cornell University Press, 1963).

16. This correct list of sources is taken from my article on Painter, *JEGP,* XXIII, 331 ff. The list in Jacobs' edition (1890), which is repeated in the *D.N.B.,* is full of errors, including such an absurdity as making Tacitus the source of the account of Queen Zenobia. These errors are repeated again in Peter Haworth's volume of selections from Painter, *An Elizabethan Story-Book* (London and New York, 1928); when he touches on sources, in E. A. Baker's

lection was indeed put together to be "delectable . . . for al sortes of men."

With one exception [17] the twenty-eight classical tales of Part One are taken from ancient sources; in Part Two only four are from ancient authors, the other nine from Bandello, Guevara, and Mexia. In Part One Painter was feeling his way, and nearly half of the classical stories belonged to the jest book category; in fact several had appeared in the *Mery Tales, Wittie Questions, and Quicke Answeres* (*ca.* 1535). But the reception of his book apparently showed the compiler what the public wanted, and in Part Two classical sobriety gave way to more modern tales of love and hot blood; even classical stories were mostly taken from modern versions adapted to modern taste. Thus Painter's solid tomes in a manner epitomize the changing literary fashions of the age, and this new appetite for amorous intrigue, courtly romance, lurid action, other translators quickly endeavored to satisfy, to the scandalizing of middle-aged puritans and patriots, such as Ascham.

Painter attempted to forestall the moralists, and his didactic motives, or professions, were expounded with fervor and fluency in the preface; stories of intrigue and rape and murder show young and old what not to do. (The useful word "frank" had not yet come into vogue.) Painter's additions to stories taken from classical sources were nearly all in the way of "morals"; a number of the longest ones, which introduce tales drawn from Belleforest, were carried over from the original. Otherwise, apart from occasional words of explanation,

---

History of the English Novel, II (London, 1929) ; and in the edition of Painter issued in 1929 by the Cresset Press.

From Livy Painter took the stories of the Horatii and Curiatii, Lucrece, Mucius Scaevola, Coriolanus, Appius and Virginia, Camillus, Tanaquil, and Theoxena; from Herodotus (Valla's translation, apparently) the stories of Candaules and Gyges, Solon and Croesus; from Xenophon the story of Panthea; from Plutarch that of Timoclea; from Bandello, Antiochus, Ariobarzanes, Aristotimus, Sophonisba, Pompey and the lady of Hidrusa, Faustina; from Guevara the correspondence of Trajan and Plutarch, the lives of the courtesans Lamia, Lais, and Flora (as examples to be avoided), and the energetic Queen Zenobia; from a French version of Mexia, the accounts of Timon and the Amazons; and so forth.

Greek authors were translated from Latin versions. In rendering Xenophon, Painter even made wholesale use of William Barkar's English translation of six books of the *Cyropaedia*. He likewise took some liberal extracts from Brende's version of Quintus Curtius.

17. Novel 27. There are two exceptions if one counts the story of Timon, but it differs from Plutarch in arrangement rather than substance.

and occasional abridgment of historical matter, Painter was an almost colorless medium.

A Petite Pallace of Pettie his Pleasure (1576) has a small niche in literary history because it is the most notable document before *Euphues* in the development of euphuism.[18] It is of interest here as a collection of prose tales, all but one classical in subject and all highly unclassical in manner. Ovid was one main quarry for plots, and from him came a good many incidental bits as well; Pettie, an Elizabethan professor of love, could not overlook the first and greatest incumbent of the chair.[19] Pettie's treatment of his plots is so very free, and most of them are familiar in so many versions, that sometimes one can only guess at his sources.[20]

As his title implies, Pettie was one of the numerous followers of Painter, but his method was quite different. So far from being a mere translator, Pettie often changed his stories out of all likeness to the originals. A few examples may be outlined, though outlines involve the loss of most of what Pettie adds. The tale of Tereus and Progne, opening with three pages on the misery of the human lot, proceeds through five pages of courtship; of all this Ovid knows nothing. The marriage is dispatched "out of hand" in one sentence. Tereus' report to Progne preserves the spirit of Ovid, but the dialogue is expanded to emphasize his hypocrisy. Philomela sends her message through a chivalrous gentleman, not through a mere woman. Progne, planning revenge, soliloquizes for two pages, with copious classical allusions.[21] Another invention, a little scene between Progne and Itys—who talks of his "Christcross"—has some tender pathos which reminds one of

18. Ed. Gollancz, London, 1908; ed. H. Hartman, Oxford University Press, 1938.

19. Speaking of Lyly Miss Jeffery remarks that "within this system of reasoning the turning to classical mythology, especially to Ovid, for arguments and illustrations, is probably derived originally from Boccaccio" (*John Lyly and the Italian Renaissance*, p. 129). But it is difficult to name any one original model.

20. The story of Sinorix and Camma was based on *The Courtier* (Tudor Translations, p. 236). The plots of the other tales came mostly from Ovid and Thomas Cooper's *Thesaurus* (Starnes and Talbert, *Classical Myth and Legend in Renaissance Dictionaries*, 1955, pp. 29–34).

21. "Without doubt, Boccaccio was the original source of inspiration for another motive used freely by Lyly,—the motive of depicting the lover shutting himself up in his chamber, and locking his door, to fling himself on his bed and indulge in a sad soliloquy" (V. M. Jeffery, pp. 63–64). But the motive is also that of Old French romance, which was revived by Belleforest and others. Pettie is full of such soliloquies.

Greene. Pettie spares his readers some of the more repulsive elements; he omits the evil omens which attended the wedding and the details regarding the Bacchic costume; he allegorizes the metamorphoses. One third of the story is occupied with dialogue and soliloquy. In general though not in particular features such a psychologized and romanticized version recalls the medieval *Philomena*.

The title *Icilius and Virginia* shows the bent of Pettie's mind; a tragedy in which Icilius is a mere lay-figure becomes a romantic love story. Icilius meets Virginia at a house party, falls in love, and seeks fame and fortune in order to win her as a bride. Although at the moment of death Pettie gives Virginia a long speech, he ends the tale with dispatch, in order to address his Gentlewomen Readers on the texts that virtue is to be preferred above wealth, and that girls should not marry old men. The story of Scilla and Minos crams almost all the action of the Ovidian tale into twelve lines. It becomes a romance in which a girl, having repulsed one lover (of the author's invention), falls in love with a stranger, and goes through acute distress in wondering if she can tell him so and win him. The myth of Cephalus and Procris is localized in "the Duke's court of Venice"; the supernatural elements are omitted or rationalized.

Thus, whatever the original plot, Pettie creates a romantic love story concerned with the difficulties of young lovers, the obduracy of parents, the problems of matrimony. Action counts for little, and Pettie hastens over it in order to develop psychology. He always has his Gentlewomen Readers in mind, and he bows and smirks and rallies them like an old master of ceremonies. He presents, in the form of entertaining fiction, a manual of the ethics and etiquette of courtship and marriage. His story-telling technique Pettie might have learned partly from the versions of Bandello done by Boaistuau and Belleforest; a number of these had been included in Painter's book, not to mention Fenton's, and Pettie often refers to them. The elements which Pettie makes so much of are the elements which Belleforest in particular added to the usually plain *novelle*, moralizing, romantic love-making, dialogue, soliloquies, letters, tirades—these last Pettie delivers with a wink. This technique takes us back to Chrétien and the classical romances and tales of the Middle Ages.

There is another strain in Pettie's little stories which becomes more obvious in Lyly. It was not a mere accident that Pettie's first tale should have been borrowed from *The Courtier*, or that his other literary work should have been a translation of Guazzo's *Civile Conversation*. Pettie's endless discussions of the problems of love owe a great deal to the social customs of Renaissance Italy, customs reflected in the many books which testify to Italian interest and success in making an art of life.[22] The *Petite Pallace* is one of the books which, stemming from *The Courtier* and lesser works, made possible the birth of Benedick and Beatrice. And this has led us a long way from classical mythology.

Equally remote from antiquity is such a tale as Greene's *Euphues his Censure to Philautus* (1587).[23] Greek and Trojan knights and ladies entertain each other at the Greek camp and in Troy, where they discuss the ideal soldier and other topics in the Italianate manner. Ovid and Caxton's *Recuyell* contribute to the setting, but not a great deal to the subject matter. In *Penelopes Web* (1587) Greene does not attempt a re-creation of Homeric Ithaca, but takes Penelope's name as a peg on which to hang tales and conversations about feminine virtues.

Thus the Elizabethan reader found mythology and pseudo-mythology even in prose fiction. Writers like Pettie and Greene were better classical scholars than their medieval progenitors, but in dressing up more or less classical material in the Franco-Italian manner they were following a medieval tradition; we have had similar novels in our own day, with flippancy and satire in place of courtly romance and moral ballast. Pettie and Greene help to prepare us for quite unclassical poems on classical subjects.

IV. NEW TROY

A sketch of the Elizabethan attitude toward classical myth would leave a gap if it passed over a myth that is not strictly classical, the story of the Trojan origin of Britain.[24] The legend flourished for at least five hundred years, and we are limited to about five paragraphs. Whether Geoffrey of Monmouth was or was not "a master of grave,

22. See T. F. Crane, *Italian Social Customs of the Sixteenth Century* (Yale University Press, 1920), and Miss Jeffery.

23. *Works,* ed. Grosart, VI, 147–284. See J. S. P. Tatlock, "The Siege of Troy in Elizabethan Literature," *PMLA,* XXX, 682.

24. This section owes several references to the charming essay by George Gordon, "The Trojans in Britain," *Essays and Studies by Members of the English Association,* IX (1924), 9 ff. The standard full account is Sir T. D. Kendrick's *British Antiquity* (London, 1950). See also Greenlaw's "The Battle of the Books" (*Studies in Spenser's Historical Allegory*), and Roberta F. Brinkley's *Arthurian Legend in the Seventeenth Century.*

imperturbable lying," [25] he started on its way the tale which was to inspire for centuries almost equal quantities of poetry and controversy.

Brutus, the descendant of Aeneas, having involuntarily killed his father, was driven out of Italy. Collecting in Greece a band of Trojans, which was augmented during the westward voyage, he landed in Albion. The first task was to rid the country of giants, and the sportive Corineus, having his choice of districts to rule, chose Cornwall, since nothing gave him greater pleasure than to wrestle with the giants, who were especially numerous there. Brutus built a city on the Thames which was called Troia Nova, later Trinovantum or Troynovant, and finally Lud's Town; the country itself was called Britain, after the Trojan leader. Brutus was followed by the long and famous line of kings, Locrine, Lear, Gorboduc, and the rest.

Geoffrey's book was a patriotic monument, and Spenser, when he came to glorify the Tudor house, was moved by a similar spirit. Everyone read Geoffrey's history, and it was paraphrased and elaborated in endless ways. Skeptics there were from the beginning; witness William of Newburgh, and the familiar tale of Giraldus Cambrensis about the man troubled by demons. But what the skeptics disliked was the Arthurian matter; throughout the Middle Ages the Trojan dynasty stood unshaken. Since Englishmen, like other western nations, found it agreeable to trace their origin to Troy, it is not surprising that the first important iconoclast was a foreigner, the historian Polydore Vergil, who worked in England under Henry VII and Henry VIII. (There was an earlier English skeptic, but he, happily for himself, failed to draw fire.) Polydore discussed the silence of the Roman historians, of Gildas and Bede, and cited William of Newburgh's animadversions upon Geoffrey's "most impudent lyeing." But he felt the strength of popular sentiment, and, for "the avoydinge of evel will," decided that he could not escape rehearsing the story, "albeit not altogether without indignation." [26] Alas for his hopes of avoiding evil will! He had said enough, and the curses of loyal antiquaries rained upon him. If he had not quite sapped a solemn creed with solemn sneer, he had questioned the entire holiness of the Pilgrim Fathers and laid a sacrilegious hand upon the cherry tree.

Grafton's *Chronicle* considered opinions pro and con, and men-

25. On the questions regarding Archdeacon Walter and the British book see Acton Griscom's edition of the *Historia Regum Britanniae* (London and New York, 1929), and J. J. Parry's review, *JEGP*, XXX (1931), 95.

26. *Polydore Vergil's English History, from an Early Translation,* ed. Sir H. Ellis (Camden Society, 1846), p. 33.

tioned among the skeptics the learned Thomas Cooper. But Grafton's heart is with the Trojans. After citing Cooper he proceeds: "And nowe I will returne to the Historie of Brute where I left. . . ." [27] Holinshed accepted the Trojan pedigree with confidence. The great Camden did not, but showed a diplomatic discretion which attests the weight of traditional belief. Edmund Howes, the continuator of John Stow's *Annales,* achieved a compromise. Attacking Polydore, not without thoughts of Camden, he exclaims that "this man with one dash of a pen, cashireth threescore Princes together," but, while he will not insist on the descent of Brutus from Aeneas, he does maintain that there was a King Brute or Brito.[28]

John Speed has an encyclopedic discussion of the subject. Like Stow he cites perhaps the earliest English skeptic, "Iohn Weathamstead Abbat of' Saint Albanes, a most judicious man that wrote in *Anno* 1440," who had pronounced the story of Brute "rather poeticall, then historicall" and "built more upon opinion then truth." [29] Speed, a thorough patriot, declares that it is no honor to be descended from the Trojans, who lasted for only six reigns and were three times vanquished. He is also a thorough moralist, and these words are of interest not only in this connection, but as one of the increasingly numerous expressions of hostility toward pagan myth:

And therefore as France hath cast off their Francio King Priamus his sonne, Scotland their Scotia King Pharaoes daughter, Denmarke their Danus, Ireland their Hiberus, and other Countries their Demi-gods; so let Britaines likewise with them disclaime their Brute, that bringeth no honour to so renowned a Nation, but rather cloudeth their glory in the murders of his parents, and imbaseth their descents, as sprung from Venus that lascivious Adulteresse: of whom saith du Plessis, I am ashamed that the heathen were not ashamed of this shamefulnesse; but much more that Christians blush not to name her in their verses.

Meanwhile the British kings and their numerous relations had appeared again and again in dramatic and non-dramatic writings, from

27. Ed. Sir H. Ellis (1809), I, 27.

28. *Annales* (ed. 1631), pp. 6–7; see J. A. Bryant, *MLR,* XLV (1950). One might give ear to loud if not authoritative skepticism, the remarks of Nashe on one of the Harveys whose sins included a Trojan bias: "Dick the true Brute or noble Troian, or Dick that hath vowd to liue and die in defence of Brute, and this our Iles first offspring from the Troians" (*Works,* ed. McKerrow, III, 85). In 1593 Richard Harvey produced *Philadelphus, or a defence of Brutes and the Brutan history.*

29. *The History of Great Britaine* (ed. 1627), pp. 164 ff. Cf. Stow, p. 7.

Gorboduc and *A Mirror for Magistrates* to less weighty productions. We meet the story in Spenser, William Warner, Drayton, Thomas Heywood. But it could not retain its hold upon intelligent opinion in the face of the critical antiquarianism of the seventeenth century. The name of Drayton reminds us that the omniscient Selden could argue for Brute "but as an advocate for the Muse." And it was mainly advocacy for the muse that inspired kind treatment of the legend in the *History of Britain,* at the hand of one who had already sung of the

> Virgin, daughter of Locrine,
> Sprung of old Anchises' line . . .

Here we may end, though this is not the end of the tradition.

V. THE GREEK SPIRIT

As a challenging text for a brief consideration of the Greek element in the Renaissance one might take the dictum of a nineteenth-century scholar: "Greece rose from the dead with a New Testament in her hand." This is still a popular notion, whether or not it may be called a classical myth.

The renaissance of the twelfth and thirteenth centuries did not accomplish a great deal for the study of Greek. Aristotle became a bulwark of Catholic theology, but the mass of Greek literature remained buried; I am speaking of course of literature only, not of science and philosophy proper. A slender Greek tradition persisted in southern Italy and Sicily, and it was through a Calabrian monk that Petrarch was introduced to Greek. Petrarch scarcely knew the alphabet, but Boccaccio gained some knowledge of Homer at least, and took honest pride in being the first Italian Grecian. Everyone has read the words of Leonardo Bruni on hearing that Chrysoloras was coming to Florence, and his enthusiasm was shared by other young men. The revival of Platonism, which Plato might not have fully understood, encouraged the new fashion. By assembling utterances like that of Bruni one might suggest that fifteenth-century Italy was a new Athens, but as a matter of fact or inference there was probably at any one time only a handful of men who could read Greek with ease. All the charges that are now made against the study of Greek were made then, and there were reasons besides. Lack of adequate grammars and dictionaries, the decline of an enthusiasm which had been something of

a high-brow fad, the multiplication of translations, the lessening prestige of Greek teachers, all these factors combined to make a knowledge
of Greek the possession of a few. Nor did the study of Greek in Italy
have the patriotic stimulus that helped to revive Latin. Most men who
knew anything of the language read a little with a teacher—if especially ambitious they produced a translation as a *specimen eruditionis*
—and thereafter relied upon Latin or vernacular renderings. The evidence of printing is clear enough. By 1500 about five thousand books
had been printed in Italy, and, before 1495, only a dozen were
Greek.[30] Here and there a man like Poliziano might seem to have
breathed Athenian air, but there were not many Polizianos.

In France—if one can survey French Hellenism in a paragraph—
Greek was better known than elsewhere, in the sixteenth century as
well as later. There were illustrious scholars from Budé onward. But
among the great writers of the century perhaps only Montaigne would
have been at ease in Athens, and Montaigne's Greek culture was decidedly indirect. In general, what Hellenic current there was in
France soon flowed into the narrower and shallower channel of neo-
classicism.

Greek studies in England, if we can believe Anthony à Wood,
were of more than respectable antiquity, for when Brute came to the
land about 1108 B. C. he had some Greek scholars in his train. This
efflorescence of Hellenism must be passed over; likewise the more
authentic if not very extensive revivals connected with various individuals from Archbishop Theodore to Grosseteste. After about 1300
the English universities declined from the high position they had occupied in the thirteenth century; the scholastic program was entering
upon its long period of decay. The catalogue of Oriel College Library
in 1375 contains, among about a hundred titles, not a single reference
to classic Latin literature, much less Greek.[31] Concerning Duke
Humphrey's gifts to Oxford it has been said: "Of 130 books which
he presented to the University in 1439, not one is Greek; of 135
given in 1443, only one—a vocabulary—is certainly Greek, four
more are possibly, but not probably so." [32] And even this library did
not remain intact. The situation at Cambridge was still worse. Some

30. Sandys, *History of Classical Scholarship*, II, 97.

31. M. W. Wallace, *The Birthe of Hercules* (Chicago, 1903), p. 8. See
Collectanea (ed. C. R. L. Fletcher, Oxford Historical Society, 1885), I, 61.
There are some translations from Aristotle and Euclid in the catalogue.

32. P. S. Allen, *The Age of Erasmus* (1914), p. 121. See also W. F.
Schirmer, *Der englische Frühhumanismus* (1931), pp. 55 ff.

catalogues of college libraries in the fifteenth century reveal no Greek books at all, and almost no classical Latin.[33]

But Duke Humphrey's interest in humanism had not been fruitless at Oxford, especially at Balliol. Such Oxonians as Grey, Free, Gunthorp, Flemming, Selling, studied in Italy. Of these only Free and Flemming seem to have been productive. Flemming is credited with a Latin-Greek dictionary, and Free made a Latin version of Synesius' treatise on baldness; one could have wished for a more inspiring introduction to the glory that was Greece. There are several candidates for the honor of having first taught Greek in England. Perhaps the first teacher was Emmanuel of Constantinople, a Greek who was working in England as a copyist, before 1470.[34] At least as early as 1475 the Italian Vitelli taught *bonae literae* at Oxford, and the phrase, which is Polydore Vergil's, may or may not include Greek. William Grocyn knew some Greek before he went to Italy, as a middle-aged man, in 1488, and he might have learned it from Emmanuel or Vitelli. The names of Grocyn, Linacre, William Latimer, bring us to a less misty period in the history of Greek studies. Yet the group of competent Grecians was small, and the instruction in Greek given by Erasmus at Cambridge in 1511 was rudimentary. As P. S. Allen says, "eminent scholars do not teach the elements at a university if boys are already learning them at school."

But from this time onward the fortunes of Greek rose. Corpus Christi College was founded in 1516, the first permanent establishment for the teaching of Greek in England, and, in spite of "Trojan" opposition, Greek made its way in the universities. Under Colet and Lily Greek was taught in St. Paul's School, but it was not until Elizabeth's time that the precedent was followed in public schools. Such men as Elyot pleaded for the study of Greek. Ascham even set Greek literature above Latin. The Greek lectures of Cheke and Smith gave Cambridge an international repute. And of course everyone knows of Lady Jane Grey and other learned women, though their names, as evidence of the state of scholarship, have been somewhat overworked.

Unhappily this flowering in the first half of the century was followed by a decline. Religious strife between Catholics and Protestants was the main cause. The dissolution of the monasteries had helped to

33. J. Bass Mullinger, *The University of Cambridge*, I (1873), 323 ff., 327; Wallace, p. 10.

34. H. L. Gray, "Greek Visitors to England in 1455–56," *Haskins Anniversary Essays* (1929), pp. 81 ff. Schirmer's book, already cited, is invaluable on the whole subject of early English humanism.

cut off the supply of students for the universities. The minds of scholars were more or less preoccupied with religious controversy. The city of the violet crown might well seem a remote fairy tale when Latimer and Ridley were burned outside college walls. Then from about the middle of the century we have the successive phases of controversy between prelacy and puritanism. The central tenet of puritanism, that the Bible was the only and sufficient guide in ecclesiastical government, ritual, and doctrine, and in personal conduct, was not favorable to the study of ancient literature. In the sixteenth and early seventeenth centuries the steady enlargement of the reading public, which included puritans, involved, as it always does, the rise of middle-class illiberality and morality, and the aristocratic humanism of the Renaissance was hardly intelligible to the new masses. Erasmus, with his ideal of Christian culture, had foreseen the dangers of purely religious fervor, of uneducated passion and prejudice.

In Elizabethan England we do not, at any rate, find Grecians like Budé, or scholar-printers like the Estiennes. The materials for Greek study were nearly all of foreign origin. The first Greek text of the *Iliad* printed in England seems to have appeared as late as 1591; the first scholarly English *Homer* was the celebrated edition of Joshua Barnes (1711), which is said to have been financed by Mrs. Barnes on the understanding that the *Iliad* was the work of Solomon. Nor, in the later sixteenth century, was the general level of Greek studies high enough to lead to much scholarly research; the domain of Hellenism was on the whole bounded by educational requirements. Even among scholars learning was less disinterested than it was on the continent, for few were untouched by religious controversy. Besides, Greek was often studied merely as a key to the New Testament. Similar reasons supported the claims of Hebrew, which became an increasingly formidable rival; on this point orthodox divine and puritan could agree. Thus a movement which had promised well had not gathered sufficient momentum to make head against a variety of obstacles.[35]

A real knowledge of Greek was obviously rare among Elizabethan

35. "The Elizabethan age is almost a blank in the history of Greek learning in England. It produced a few translations—mostly of books bearing on matters of theological controversy—but there is hardly a trace in it of that large interest in Greek antiquity which characterized the humanists of the early part of the century.

"Whatever the explanation may be, the situation changes when we come to James I's reign, and from that moment there is no dearth of distinguished names in the annals of English learning." I. Bywater (*Oxford Lectures on Classical Subjects*, 1919, p. 13).

writers. We have observed the usual procedure of translators, such as Painter, Nicolls,[36] North, and Hall. Even Chapman, who worshiped Homer, used Latin aids, and worked humanistic commentary into his text. The almost total ignorance of Greek drama, which was not translated at all—except for one play of Euripides taken from Italian —is a commonplace.[37]

In such circumstances there could be little understanding of the special virtues of Greek art, virtues moreover which have always been alien to the English genius. Not merely the qualities which Greek authors possessed in common, but their wide individual differences, had small chance of surviving when the text filtered through one or more diffuse mediums. If translators failed to perceive and reproduce Greek clarity of line, the mass of readers, who depended upon translations, were still further removed from the manner and spirit of the originals. It is perhaps ungrateful to quarrel with a theory of translation which gave us North's *Plutarch* and Chapman's *Homer*, yet the bad results are obvious. The freest sort of paraphrase or redaction might pass as a translation, and there was no established standard of scholarly judgment such as nowadays, for instance, distinguishes between Plato and Jowett's Plato, between Euripides and Gilbert Murray's Euripides. Of course even in the eighteenth century, the age of generally diffused scholarship, translators had a way of missing some essential qualities of their originals, not only Greek but Latin, and most people had no very clear conception of the real virtues of classic art.

While an author of any age may possess Greek virtues without knowing Greek, the point here is that those virtues were in general neither understood nor admired by men of the Renaissance. The note of Renaissance art was not restraint but excess. The period nourished every kind of stylistic extravagance—Ciceronianism, euphuism, Gongorism, Marinism. Writers seldom saw an object quietly or described it temperately. Form is perhaps the last quality that one looks for in the mass of Renaissance literature, even in the greatest. Taste was not Attic but Asiatic, or rather Alexandrian. While the literature of the golden age of Athens was comparatively neglected, that of the silver and brass ages—the Greek romance, for example—was highly popular. We constantly find Renaissance authors attracted by the florid and rhetorical in late Greek writing. If these facts were true of the

36. The translator of Thucydides.
37. In addition to Gascoigne's *Jocasta* one might mention Peele's translation of one of the Iphigenia plays of Euripides. See T. Larsen, *Library*, Fourth Series, XI (1931), 310.

continent, they were even more true of Elizabethan England. The virtues which the Elizabethans admired and possessed were at the opposite pole from the Greek, and they lacked the first-hand knowledge of the best Greek literature which might have supplied a corrective and an ideal. The dramatists, from the greatest down, were addicted to over-expression; in both central conceptions and details one misses a severe, rational, critical instinct. Nothing could be less Greek than *The Faerie Queene,* or almost any typical work of the period. The prodigal excellences of Elizabethan literature, which are a large if not a full compensation, do not need to be discussed.

In short, the resurrection of Greece was a slow process, not accomplished in the sixteenth century. And the mere revival of Greek was not enough to establish it on an independent footing. Greek learning was valued not only for theological reasons, but as an aid to Latin; Battista Guarino esteemed the dialogues of Plato as collateral reading for the student of Cicero. The classical revival was mainly a Latin revival, and it was not over-discriminating, as the welcome accorded the Senecan dramas indicates. In England solid critical scholarship came with the seventeenth century, and antiquity began to be understood, by the few, as we understand it today. But English culture, so far as it was derived from the ancients, continued throughout the neoclassic period to be Latin rather than Greek. In the matter of style poets in general preferred Latin rhetoric to Greek simplicity. The codifying habit of the neoclassical mind, moreover, had early begun to reduce Aristotelian principles to neat Horatian rules, with so many half-medieval and modern additions that not merely the Greeks but the Romans would have had difficulty in recognizing the aesthetic laws fathered upon them. The Renaissance, far from being Hellenic, was only imperfectly Latin, but this Latin culture so greatly predominated over Greek that only in the romantic period did the pendulum swing in the other direction. In modern times the tendency has been, especially among persons with a tincture of Greek and anthropology, to depreciate and neglect the real legacy of Rome.

CHAPTER III

Myths in Earlier Elizabethan Verse

When a period of sterility occurs in the progress of poesy it is customary for literary historians to call it a seedtime and discover abundant promise of harvests to come. We shall, however, skip the long interval between Chaucer and the early sixteenth century without examining such modest seeds as the works of Lydgate. The practice of versifying tales from Ovid had virtually expired, and the genre was born anew in the Elizabethan age. But the medieval manner had not expired, and this chapter may achieve some coherence through the fact that the pieces described are almost untouched by Italian influence. Very few of those pieces are of more than historical interest, but they demand some attention because the origins of the modern mythological poem lie in the period from 1557 to 1589. It is hard to classify representative types, for the early Elizabethans were quite indifferent to the scholarly pigeonholes of posterity, and did not distinguish between translation and the freest kind of redaction. With this proviso the poems to be discussed may be divided into five groups, mythological tales proper, miscellaneous pieces, amatory pieces, ballads, and long poems. A survey of these, if it does nothing more, should give one a new appreciation of Spenser and Marlowe.

I. MYTHOLOGICAL TALES

An interest out of proportion to literary merit attaches to *The fable of Ouid treting of Narcissus, translated out of Latin into Englysh Mytre, with a moral ther unto* (1560).[1] The narrative, which fol-

1. Reprinted in full by W. E. Buckley in his edition of Thomas Edwards (Roxburghe Club, 1882), pp. 133 ff.; the narrative portion by O. Jiriczek, *Specimens of Tudor Translations from the Classics* (1923), pp. 77 ff. The piece is discussed by T. Corser, *Collectanea*, IX, 101 ff.; Brydges, *Restituta*, III, 265–67, and *Censura Literaria*, VIII, 337–41; E. Witz, *Die englischen*

lows Ovid closely, and apparently at first hand, occupies one hundred
and ninety-two lines, while the moral receives eight hundred and
ninety-six, in seven-line stanzas. The matter of edification consists of
sermonizing on the topics traditionally connected with the story of
Narcissus—"richis and bewty be vayne"; "the transitory thinges of
this world are not to be trustyd"; "all dysdayne ful folkes are compared unto Narcyssus." The preacher is good enough to name some
of his sources. Thirty-five lines elaborate Boccaccio's interpretation of
Echo, the voice of earthly delights and vanities which lures men to
their ruin.[2] We have a Platonic discourse on the power of the soul
over the body, taken from "Ficius," that is, Ficino.[3] There is a reference to one who

> asence deuine, doth make
> No foole he semethe, that walles hath to name
> And englyshe man, whych thus doth undertake
> For sowles behoufe, to deskant on this same . . .

"Walles" is no other than the moralized *Metamorphoses* which, as we
have already noticed, passed under the name of Thomas Waleys, so
that we receive a sufficiently instructive "deskant." [4] Our author also

---

Ovidübersetzungen des 16. Jahrhunderts (1915), pp. 27–29; L. Rick, *Ovids
Metamorphosen in der englischen Renaissance* (1915), pp. 29–32.

The author is unknown. The piece ends with "Finis. Quod. T. H.," and it
was therefore assigned by Ritson and others to Thomas Howell. This ascription is repeated in the *Cambridge History of English Literature*, IV, 438; in
the *Short-Title Catalogue* (1926); in C. H. Conley, *First English Translators
of the Classics* (1927); and elsewhere. But the poem is not like Howell's
known work, and one may agree with the note added to Warton's *History of
English Poetry* (London, 1871), IV, 298: "It is supposed that T. H. may be
the initials of the printer Hacket: the work appears to have been written some
years before it was published, from the unpolished and archaic style." Even
the few quotations given in the text should confirm this judgment.

2. Buckley, p. 150; Boccaccio, *De Genealogia Deorum* (Venice, 1511), bk.
vii, c. 59, p. 60.

3. Buckley, pp. 165 ff. The reference is apparently to the passage on Narcissus in Ficino, *Comm. in Convivium* (*Omnia Divini Platonis Opera*, Lyons,
1548), vi.17, p. 277.

4. Buckley, p. 168. Buckley reprints the passage from Waleys, page 176;
see fol. xxxv in the edition of Waleys already cited (Paris, 1509). Echo represents flatterers who frequent prelates (mountains), and others in high place;
or, Echo signifies quarrelsome women and servants who must have the last
word, etc. The story of Narcissus shows that pride leads to aloofness. People
see in the fountain of worldly prosperity the shadow of their condition, which
passes away like a shadow and destroys the life of the soul.

deals with an interpretation of the story put forth by one "whome Italye dyd brede," namely, Buonsignori or Niccolò degli Agostini; it does not matter which, since Agostini's work was a version of Buonsignori's.[5] It is clear that the author has got up the literature of his subject with commendable zeal. The whole sermon is of course plastered with examples, from Helen, Cleopatra, and Phaethon to Lucifer, Dives, and David. As poetry it is naught, but it remains a not insignificant congeries of ancient, medieval, and Renaissance elements. And in the narrative the versifier does make some attempt to carry the Ovidian manner over into English. At any rate Golding, who to be sure was only loosely Ovidian in style, did not disdain, when he reached the story of Narcissus, to borrow a good many phrases from this version.

A Gorgeous Gallery of Gallant Inventions (1578), a miscellany which does not live up to the fine Elizabethan swagger of its title, contains a poem of about four hundred and fifty lines called *The History of Pyramus and Thisbie truely translated.*[6] I have not found any version from which it could be said, at least in our sense of the words, to be truly translated, but it derives ultimately from the Old French redaction of Ovid, *Piramus et Tisbé.*[7] Both the Old French

5. See above, page 15. For the passage in the English poem, see Buckley, page 169. Cf. Agostini, *Tutti gli Libri de Ouidio Metamorphoseos tradotti dal litteral in uerso uulgar con le sue Allegorie in prosa,* Venice, 1522 (no pagination).

6. *Gorgeous Gallery,* ed. Rollins (1926), p. 103.

7. Ed. De Boer (Paris, 1921). Of later foreign versions of the story there are many, and a number I have not seen. Georg Hart throws no light on our poem (*Die Pyramus-&-Thisbe-Sage,* 1891). The essential un-Ovidian details mentioned in my outline occur in the version in *Les XV. liures de la Metamorphose D'ouide . . . contenans L'olympe des Histoires poëtiques traduictz de Latin en Francoys* (Paris, 1539), pp. 54 ff.; and in *Les Histoires des Poetes: comprises au Grand Olympe* (1595). These works derive from the *Bible des Poetes*—a significant title, by the way, as regards the reputation of Ovid.

Some of the details, though not the visit to the temple, had already appeared in English, in the two translations of Christine de Pisan's *Epistre d'Othea* (chapter 38), and in Anslay's *Boke of the Cyte of Ladyes,* translated from another work of Christine's (see above, page 30). Anslay's chapter is reprinted in *Anglia,* XII (1889), 14.

Among other versions of the tale before 1578 were Chaucer's, in the *Legend;* that of Gower, *Confessio Amantis,* iii.1331–1494; Lydgate, *Reson and Sensuallyte,* ll. 3960–4001; a poem taken from Gower (printed in *Anglia,* XII, 16 ff., 631); *La conusaunce damours,* printed before 1531 (see the Appendix); a mysterious book "intituled Perymus and Thesbye" of 1562–63 (see *Gorgeous Gallery,* pp. 198, 203); *A New Sonet of Pyramus and Thisbie* in *A Handful of Pleasant Delights* (see below, page 57); and of course Golding's translation.

and the English poem have much to say about the childhood of the pair, who were touched by love at the age of seven, and were consumed by desperate passion at fourteen. In the French piece Pyramus utters a long complaint and then goes to the temple of Venus to pray, though the substance of his prayer is not given; in the English, Pyramus does not make a complaint, but he does go to the temple, and his prayer is set down. In both Thisbe finds a hole in the wall and hangs the pendant of her girdle through it; Pyramus, returning from the temple, catches sight of the pendant and begins to talk. Thus the Ovidian tale is spun out with amorous dialogue and soliloquy and romantic incidents. It may be a little surprising to find in a miscellany of 1578 a poem which, whatever its immediate original, is directly descended from a French work of the twelfth century, and, what is more, retains its medieval character.

In 1589 George Peele published together a *Farewell* to Norris and Drake and a *Tale of Troy*. The latter piece was included ostensibly to rouse his countrymen to emulate "their glorious and renowned predecessors, the Trojans," but really, it would appear, in order to swell the volume to a respectable size.[8] In nearly five hundred lines Peele narrates events from Hecuba's dream to the departure of Aeneas from Troy. The story lacks continuity and coherence, and the verse, apart from a few lines, is far from Peele's best. In its treatment of classical material, however, the poem has interest. We might not expect an Oxford man, publishing in 1589, to handle the Trojan saga in this manner:

Not even the exalted consciousness of knowing more about Pyramus and Thisbe than anyone else gives warrant for setting down here a detailed comparison of countless versions of the tale, from notes compiled in my lusty youth, but a word may be said about Gower. G. C. Macaulay (*Works of Gower*, I, 497–98) remarks, for example, that in his story the lovers make the hole in the wall; that Ninus' tomb is not named; that (to be Irish) the lioness is a lion; that Thisbe hides in a bush, not a cave; that Pyramus dies before Thisbe returns, etc. In such items Gower is closer to Christine's versions than to others. Thus in Anslay Thisbe sees a small hole and makes it larger; Ninus' tomb is not mentioned; there is a lion; Thisbe hides in a bush; Pyramus dies at once. Some, though not all, of these un-Ovidian details are, as we see, in *Piramus et Tisbé* (and in the tale in the *Gorgeous Gallery*); cf. Boccaccio, *De Claris Mulieribus* (Berne, 1539), c. xii. Since this note was written S. B. Meech has discussed some details (*PMLA*, XLVI, 201, note 105).

8. *Works of Peele*, ed. Dyce (London, 1829), I, xvi; ed. Bullen (1888), I, xxix. The text is quoted from Bullen, II, 241 ff.

Peele refers to the piece as "an old poem." D. H. Horne (*The Life and Minor Works of George Peele*, p. 149) dates the composition 1579–81.

> How many Greeks, how many Troyan knights,
> As chivalry by kind in love delights,
> Upon their helmets can their plumes advance,
> And twist their ladies' colours on their lance . . .[9]

We are in the world of the *Roman de Troie*. The presence of incongruous materials is explained when we examine Peele's sources. Ovid contributes some events and details, Virgil most of the description of the fall of Troy, but the groundwork of the whole, and many incidents, appear to be derived from Caxton's *Recuyell*.[10] The narrative method, the medieval and chivalric tone, of Caxton are clearly reflected in Peele.

Along with romance we have the pastoral note, especially in the passage describing that "jolly swain," Paris:

> How he can nymphs and shepherds' trulls beguile,
> And pipen songs, and whet his wits on books,
> And rape poor maids with sweet-alluring looks:
> So couth he sing his lays among them all,
> And tune his pipe unto the water's fall,
> And wear his coat of grey and lusty green,
> That had the fair Œnone never seen
> His ticing curlèd hair, his front of ivory,
> The careless nymph had ne'er been so unhappy . . .

Nearly all these lines, and more that follow, are paralleled in the pastoral drama, *The Arraignment of Paris* (published in 1584).[11] The close relations between the Italian pastoral and the Italian mythological poem will be noticed later.[12] Here we may observe that the pastoral element, though slight, is a trifle incongruous in an unItalianate and medieval story of Troy.[13] A casual bit of Platonism

9. Ll. 276 ff. Cf. ll. 289–90, 295–96.

10. For details see Tatlock, *PMLA*, XXX, 680–82.

11. With the passage quoted (ll. 66 ff.) compare, in the play, III.i.55–56, 116 ff., I.i.49 ff., and see Horne, p. 150.

12. See below, pages 73, 87.

13. Paris appears in a pastoral background in Ovid's epistle of Oenone, and in Colluthus' *Rape of Helen* (trans. A. W. Mair, Loeb Classical Library, ll. 102 ff.). This latter piece was popular enough in the period to attract two translators (see the Appendix, under 1586, 1587).

Miss V. M. Jeffery (*MLR*, XIX, 175 ff.) has argued that Peele based his *Arraignment* on *Il Giuditio di Paride* (1566), by Anello Paulilli. A. H. Gilbert offered reasons against this view (*MLN*, XLI, 36 ff.). Miss Jeffery is least convincing in regard to the judgment scene proper, since the material is traditional, and her parallels could be multiplied from other versions than adds further variety; the idea is elaborated by the thrifty author in the *Arraignment*.[14]

Peele's archaisms in diction form a noticeable element in the poem. In addition to the general influence of Caxton he seems to have had both Chaucer and Spenser in mind.[15] In fact a number of the archaisms are words that E. K. saw fit to explain—but the details may be left to a footnote.[16]

The poem as a whole is poor enough, and lacks the charm and lyrical sweetness of much of the *Arraignment*. But the pastoral bits are pleasant, and there are occasional other good lines. A happy addition in the revised text describes Paris' flight with Helen—"As blithe as bird of morning's light in May." The Greeks set sail from Aulis "As shoots a streaming star in winter's night." [17] But the significance of

---

Paulilli's. Mr. Gilbert also fails to take account of the number and variety of sources. For instance, he remarks that Euripides and Paulilli make Hermes the guide of the three goddesses, while Ovid (epistle of Oenone) and Peele do not. But Hermes appears in Ovid's epistle of Paris, in Colluthus, in Lucian's dialogue, in Apuleius (x. 30), in Lydgate's *Reson and Sensuallyte* (ll. 1601 ff.), in a pseudo-Chaucerian piece (see the Appendix, under 1561), and in pageants. Pageantry is especially important in connection with Peele's compliment to Elizabeth, though the critics do not deal with it, apart from Miss Jeffery's mention of Gascoigne's *The Grief of Joy* (page 176). See T. S. Graves, "*The Arraignment of Paris* and Sixteenth Century Flattery," *MLN*, XXVIII (1913), 48–49; and, in the Bibliography (III), notes by I-S. Ekeblad and J. D. Reeves. Cf. also a poem in the *Gorgeous Gallery*, page 63. Miss Jeffery's case is plausible on some points, and one may accept her argument for the general influence of Italian pastoral on English even if it is difficult to prove a connection between Peele and Paulilli.

14. *Tale*, ll. 117 ff.; *Arraignment*, II.i.68 ff. The whole passage on the judgment of Paris in the *Tale*, though relatively short, has numerous correspondences with the play.

15. The 1589 version has a reference to the story of Troilus and Cressida, while the 1604 edition has a direct allusion to Chaucer and another to the "House of Fame." (The version published in 1604 was apparently written in 1595–96; see Bullen, I, xxix; II, 241, 255.)

One line in the passage quoted above was taken from Spenser's *April* (l. 36): "And tuned it unto the Waters fall." Though variations on the phrase later became conventional, they were not in 1589 and earlier. (Spenser also liked it well enough to use it in other places.)

16. Peele uses "y-clyppèd" (l. 11), "y-blinded" (l. 120), etc. E. K. explains "y" as "a poeticall addition" (*April, May*). Other words occurring in Peele which E. K. glosses are "of yore," "couth," "dight," "swain," "won" (i.e., "dwell"), "uncouth," "hight," "surquedry," "hent," "mickle." See Horne, p. 150.

17. The simile, like the phenomenon, was not new. For example, cf. Ovid, *Metam.* ii.320–22; *Pearl*, ll. 115–16; *Canterbury Tales*, A 267–68; see also *Venus and Adonis*, l. 815.

the piece is not in its few gleams of poetry. It appears rather, as I have said, in the medieval substance and spirit. In narrative method the poem is the exact opposite of Lodge's mythological poem issued in the same year, for while Lodge, inaugurating the Italianate style, slighted action in favor of sensuous picture-making, Peele crammed the matter of half a dozen epics into a chronicle of five hundred lines. Whether or not *The Arraignment of Paris* had a particular Italian source, almost everything in *The Tale of Troy* is in accord with the native tradition.

II. Miscellaneous Pieces

The poems so far mentioned represent the more strictly narrative species. "Strictly" is a relative term, since the *Narcissus* of 1560, and some other tales noticed in the Appendix, were adorned with an impressive caudal member in the form of a sermon. The early Elizabethans were equally fond of what may be called sermons with a mere prefatory hint of narrative. Indeed a single example, from the *Gorgeous Gallery*, testifies that the Helen of Troy who haunted pedestrian imaginations was not the vision beheld by Marlowe; in *The reward of Whoredome by the fall of Helen* the repentant sinner avows all her errors in lurid language. The *Mirror for Magistrates*, like Falstaff, was not only witty in itself but the cause that wit was in other men.

George Turberville was one of the most typical and popular writers of the pre-Spenserian generation. His talents show to better advantage in his translation of the *Heroides* than in original work. He anticipated Keats in handling the war of gods and Titans, and his treatment of this high argument bears the very Elizabethan title *A Myrrour of the fall of Pride*.[18] The war is dispatched in one and a half pages, but the

A possible instance of Marlowe's influence on Peele is the expansion of ll. 25–26, which in the 1589 text read thus:

> His court presenting to our earthlie eyes
> A skye of starres or shyning paradise.

The revised version was:

> His court presenting to our human eyes
> An earthly heaven or shining paradise,
> Where ladies troop'd in rich disguised attire,
> Glistering like stars of pure immortal fire.

Cf. *Hero and Leander*, i.97 ff.; and also *Romeo and Juliet*, I.ii.25.

18. *Epitaphes, Epigrams, Songs and Sonets* (1567), ed. Collier, pp. 152 ff. There was an earlier edition apparently, published in or after 1565 (H. E. Rollins, *MP*, XV, 518).

real theme requires five and a half more.

> Let giants fall and shipmens case
> a myrrour be, therefore,
> To such as seeke to hie a place,
> for like shall be their lore.

This specimen may relieve us from the need of describing the story of Aristotimus in Turberville's *Tragical Tales*.[19]

Another representative of the mob of gentlemen who wrote with ease is Thomas Howell. He treated the story of Cressida twice, the second poem being a recasting of the first. Their character is indicated in the titles, *The britlenesse of thinges mortall, and the trustinesse of Vertue* and *Ruine the rewarde of Vice*.[20] There is the usual debt to Chaucer and Henryson, but in place of Chaucer's subtle irony and Henryson's grim tragedy we have only flat moralizing.[21] Yet Howell had a spark somewhere in him. His editor, Sir Walter Raleigh, justly praised these lines:

> At strife to whom I might
> Commit my secret tears,
> My heart the mountains' sight
> And hollow Echo fears.
>
> I doubt the Dryades
> Amidst the forest chace,
> And thinking on the Seas,
> I dread the Mermaids' grace.[22]

19. Ed. Edinburgh (1837), pp. 203 ff. Extant copies of the book were printed in 1587, but the first edition must have appeared in 1574–75 (Rollins, pp. 520 ff.). Bandello's novel of Aristotimus (iii.5) had been translated by Painter (ii.5), and a version of the story was included in Thomas Fortescue's *The Foreste*, 1571. Turberville follows Bandello quite closely. An envoy of twelve stanzas makes clear the evils of despotism.

20. *Poems of Thomas Howell*, ed. Grosart, pp. 121–22; *Howell's Devises*, ed. W. Raleigh, pp. 18–19. See below, note 29.

21. Another piece of didactic earnestness, evidently inspired by the *Mirror for Magistrates*, is *The infortunate ende of Cresus Kynge of Lydia, a worthy note for Couetousnesse sake* (ed. Grosart, "Newe Sonets," p. 124). Howell has two versions of *The lamentable ende of Iulia Pompeis Wyfe* (ibid., p. 138; *Devises*, p. 26). He probably took the story from Valerius Maximus (iv.6.4) rather than from Plutarch (*Pompey*, 53; North, Tudor Translations, IV, 263). It is also in Boccaccio, *De Claris Mulieribus*, c. 79. Cf. Lucan, *Pharsalia*, i.111 ff.

22. *Devises*, pp. xvii, 64.

The brief suggestion, the gleam of magic, in that second stanza are beyond the conscientious poet's normal reach.

Such a heading as "miscellaneous" may justify our turning for a moment to that Theocritean translation called *Sixe Idillia*, which was published anonymously at Oxford in 1588.[23] The translator chose an author who was relatively little read, and his work is attractive. Although Bullen with unwonted sournesss pronounced it worthy of Turberville or Googe, the transparent ease of the *Sixe Idillia* is far removed from the heavy flatness of the older generation. The style has some charm and grace, and occasional rustic words add vividness and flavor. Thus Polyphemus consoles himself:

> For many Maidens in the evening tide with me will play,
> And all do sweetly laugh, when I stand heark'ning
> what they say . . .

The singers of the bridal hymn to Helen

> will, every Spring, unto the leaves in meadow go
> To gather garlands sweet; and there, not with a little woe,
> Will often think of thee, O Helen! as the suckling lambs
> Desire the strouting bags and presence of their tender dams.[24]

III. Amatory Pieces

Even amatory verse shows the influence of the study of rhetoric and the long rhetorical tradition in poetry. The courtly lover's first object was to convince his mistress, real or imaginary, of the sincerity of his passion and the hardness of her heart. Ovid had been a master of the *suasoria*, and in his various poems about love he had shown himself not only a brilliant wit and psychologist but a superlatively clever rhetorician. The Elizabethan amorists were portentously serious—the

23. The six pieces are reprinted in Bullen's *Longer Elizabethan Poems* (1903), pp. 125 ff. The one on Adonis is given by O. L. Jiriczek in *Jahrbuch der Deutschen Shakespeare-Gesellschaft* (1919), p. 30; parts of others are in Ward's *English Poets*, I, 379. See R. T. Kerlin, *Theocritus in English Literature* (1910), p. 27.

24. The translator, by the way, in a note prefaced to his last idyll, that on Venus and Adonis, gives an allegorical interpretation of the story:

"The Poet's drift is to shew the power of Love, not only in men, but also in brute beasts: although in the last two verses, by the burning of the Boar's amorous teeth, he intimateth that extravagant and unorderly passions are to be restrained by reason."

Petrarchan mood was not altogether favorable to levity—and they borrowed Ovidian myths to incorporate in their own special kind of *suasoria*. Gascoigne gives this advice to the poet-lover:

Likewise, if I should disclose my pretence in loue, I would eyther make a strange discourse of some intollerable passion, or finde occasion to pleade by the example of some historie, or discouer my disquiet in shadowes *per Allegoriam* . . .[25]

For versifiers seeking "the example of some historie" no matter lay readier to hand than the familiar tales of mythological lovers.

Tottel's *Miscellany* contained a number of short poems exploiting what was to remain a popular formula, that is, the narration of a mythological tale and the application of it to the lover's own hard lot. The pattern soon became sufficiently stereotyped to find a place in a practical manual on the art of writing letters.[26] Rosalind advised lovers who were gravelled for lack of matter to kiss; the courtly lover who lacked not only matter but a mistress at hand was compelled to use mythology. Thus we meet in Tottel's *Miscellany* such self-explanatory titles as *The tale of Pigmalion with conclusion upon the beautye of his loue*; *The louer praieth his seruice to be accepted and his defaultes pardoned* (concerning Cephalus and Procris); *The louer complaineth his harty loue not required* (Phoebus and Daphne).[27] In harmony with such themes is a translation of the first twelve lines of Ovid's epistle from Penelope to Ulysses, apparently the first published version of any part of the *Heroides*.[28]

One of the most popular stories to be adapted to the amatory formula was that of Troilus and Cressida. The tale was, as the poets testify, in every man's mouth, and allusions to it are spread like a rash over Elizabethan verse.[29] Turberville and the rest wrote amorous plaints on various mythological themes, but we must put wax in our ears and pass by. In addition to poems outlining a single myth brief

---

25. Smith, *Elizabethan Critical Essays*, I, 48.
26. See the Appendix, under William Fulwood (1568).
27. Ed. Rollins, I, 125, 202, 253.
28. *Ibid.*, p. 219. But see the Appendix, under 1526.
29. For example, Tottel's *Miscellany*, I, 183. On the debasement of Cressida's character between Chaucer and Shakespeare, a process started mainly by Henryson's beautiful *Testament*, see H. E. Rollins, "The Troilus-Cressida Story," *PMLA*, XXXII, 383 ff.; F. Haynes and J. S. P. Tatlock, in my Bibliography, under "General"; W. W. Lawrence, *Shakespeare's Problem Comedies* (New York, 1931), c. 4, especially pp. 144 ff., and the Variorum Edition of *Troilus and Cressida* (1953).

allusions were fashionable too. In one passionate "sonnet" Thomas Watson mentions Leander, Hero, Pyramus, Thisbe, Haemon, Antigone, Orpheus, Eurydice, Cerberus, "the Wheele, the Stone, the Fire and Furies." [30] Any further illustration would be an anticlimax. Sidney might well complain that the "swelling phrases" of literary lovers would never persuade a mistress.[31]

One more author, George Gascoigne, must be noticed, not because he sometimes wrote poetry but because he wrote *The Complaynt of Phylomene* (1576).[32] This poem, begun when the author was riding, was broken off when he was "overtaken with a sodaine dash of Raine." The narrator listens to the nightingale, which declares that she sings for true lovers, of whom one is not far away. While she sings the poet falls asleep and dreams that a nymph appears to "paraphrase" the song. We may observe that the author uses the medieval dream-convention and also associates himself with the piece in the character of a lover. In the narrative, which occupies twenty-three pages, Gascoigne's management of an unhappily popular meter suggests that his ride to London was in the right butter-women's rank to market. He follows Ovid closely, except in a few details, but adds an abundance of sententious morality. In his long analysis of the nightingale's notes he may have been the first to isolate *Tereu,* a doleful and dubious mark of originality.[33] The poem ends with the departure of the nymph, the awakening of the poet, and the application of a sermon to him; though Gascoigne was rather a gay blade in private life he could be heavily didactic in public.[34] To appreciate the incredibly swift maturing of Elizabethan poetic art—in other words, the accident of genius—one may set this piece beside Sidney's *The Nightingale.*

30. *Poems,* ed. Arber, p. 66.

31. Smith, *Elizabethan Critical Essays,* I, 201. Even King James wrote a lyric invoking the examples of Leander and Pyramus (*New Poems by James I of England,* ed. A. F. Westcott, 1911, p. 24).

32. *Works,* ed. Cunliffe, II, 177 ff. The poem is discussed by Starnes and Talbert, *Classical Myth and Legend,* pp. 34–40. One might mention also *Davids salutacions to Berzabe* (I, 463), which quaintly links Apuleius and the Bible, Fotis and David.

33. H. W. Garrod, *The Profession of Poetry* (Oxford, 1929), p. 150.

34. In the introduction to his *Steele Glas* (*Works,* II, 144) Gascoigne allegorizes the story of Philomela in a cumbrously medieval way:

> My Systers name, was pleasant Poesys,
> And I my selfe had Satyra to name.

They are the daughters of "Playne dealyng" and "Simplycitie." Tereus turned from Progne to Philomela; that is, "Satyrical Poetry is somtimes ravished by vayne Delight." In his comments on Ovid's tale George Sandys takes the sisters as representing poetry and oratory (*Ovid's Metamorphosis,* 1632, pp. 228–29).

IV. BALLADS

In that eloquent testimonial to the breadth of Elizabethan literary interests, the Stationers' Register, among "ballets" on monstrous pigs and still more monstrous children, on maids undone and maids who would like to be, we find dozens of pieces on classical themes. A list of ballad titles, if we had room for it, would show that classical myths which, in more pretentious versions, appealed to the polite, were known in racier form to the eager customers of Autolycus. When all shops were stuffed with rhyming pamphlets, anecdotes, sermons, critics who had the good of literature at heart groaned aloud over the mangling of poetry by rude smatterers. "Scarce a cat can look out of a gutter," snorted one enemy of popular journalism, "but out starts a half-penny chronicler, and presently A propper new ballet of a strange sight is endited." [35]

When mythological ballads kept such company one would not look in them for the qualities of Spenser and Marlowe. But it would be a mistake to regard the early Elizabethan ballads as a distinct stratum of verse quite different from and inferior to the "sonnets" written by the courtly poets. It must be remembered that in the first half of Elizabeth's reign ballads were being composed by such men of letters as Turberville, Googe, Gascoigne, and Howell. Many pieces in the miscellanies, from Tottel's onward, were ballads; many were entered separately, as such, in the Stationers' Register. There was not, then, in this period an impassable gulf between the courtly ballads and their poor relations of the street. In later times, as the mention of Autolycus suggests, ballads as a class did come down in the world.

Since the character of the Elizabethan broadside is familiar, and since pieces on classical subjects possess the generic qualities, it will be enough to recall a very few specimens. Some, either real or virtual ballads of the courtly type, have been noticed already in this chapter. Mythological ballads were fairly numerous through most of the period covered in this book, but they were especially abundant between 1560 and 1575. They must have helped greatly to popularize the commoner myths among people who did not keep Ovid under their pillow.

The most representative collection of what may be called upper-class ballads was *A Handful of Pleasant Delights,* which first appeared

35. *Epistle to Martin Mar-sixtus,* 1592 (quoted by F. O. Mann, *Works of Thomas Deloney,* Oxford, 1912, p. x).

in 1566 and was enlarged in 1584.[36] One piece of particularly tragical mirth is *A New Sonet of Pyramus and Thisbie. To the, Downe right Squier.*[37] This affecting version of one of the most popular myths may have been in Shakespeare's mind when, in providing a tragic vehicle for Bottom, he burlesqued the theatrical heroics of an earlier age. Here at any rate is Ercles' vein, a part to tear a cat in:

> Oh Gods aboue, my faithfull loue
>   shal neuer faile this need:
> For this my breath by fatall death,
>   shal weaue Atropos threed.
> Then from his sheathe he drew his blade,
>   and to his hart
> He thrust the point, and life did vade,
>   with painfull smart.

Ballad narratives may pause for moralizing, or for bursts of rhetoric, but they seldom waste time in mere decoration; the story must march. In a piece on Diana and Actaeon (sung "To the Quarter Braules"), which was reprinted or imitated many times, the crisis of the tale is thus dispatched:

> As she began to shoot, Acteon ran about,
> To hide he thought no boote,
>   his sights were dim:
> And as he thought to scape,
> Changed was Acteons shape,
> Such was unluckie fate,
>   yeelded to him.[38]

Longer but hardly more moving is Thomas Howell's *The lamentable historie of Sephalus with the Unfortunat end of Procris. To the tune of Appelles (ca. 1568).*[39] It discards all of the Ovidian story ex-

36. Ed. Rollins, 1924. See Baskervill's review, *MP*, XXIII, 119 ff., and his own *Elizabethan Jig* (Chicago, 1929), pp. 30–31.

37. *Handful*, ed. Rollins, pp. 35, 99. See G. Hart, *Die Pyramus-&-Thisbe-Sage* (1891), pp. 22–23, and *Cambridge History of English Literature*, III, 191. Rollins remarks that this ballad "could have been, and probably was, in the 1566 *Pleasant Sonnets.*"

38. *Handful*, pp. 25, 91.

39. *Poems of Thomas Howell*, ed. Grosart ("Newe Sonets," pp. 146 ff.). For the story of Cephalus and Procris see *Metam.* vii.694 ff., and *Ars Amat.* iii.685 ff. A brief love poem in Tottel makes use of the death of Procris, omitting the rest of the tale (ed. Rollins, I, 202–03; II, 309).

cept the catastrophe, and, for the earlier part, transfers to Cephalus and Procris the experiences of Pyramus and Thisbe. And at the end the Ovidian motive of Procris' jealousy is abandoned in favor of pure romantic tragedy, in the style of the other pair of lovers:

> When Sephalus his Procris founde,
> Imbrude with blood on euery side,
> The arowe stickinge in the wounde,
> That bleedinge sore did gape full wyde,
>   He curst the gods that skies possesst
>   The systers three and all the rest.

Indeed Shakespeare had only too many models for his Pyramus and Thisbe.

One more specimen must be enough. *The Wandering Prince of Troy* was an extremely popular ballad, or rather ballads, for there were many issues or versions from 1564–65 onward. The text of 1624 has two parts. The first follows the Virgilian story, from the arrival of Aeneas to the death of Dido. The second part opens with Dido's funeral. Her sister wrote to Aeneas, who was sojourning on an island of Greece, and the hero's "lofty courage then did fall." Dido's ghost appeared and foretold his death.

> And like one being in a Trance,
>   A multitude of ugly fiends
> About this wofull Prince did dance,
>   No help he had of any friends:
>   His body then they tooke away,
>   And no man knew his dying day.

We may smile with Bishop Percy over the engrafting of "a Gothic conclusion" upon the story, and agree that the author of the ballad "dealt out his poetical justice with a more impartial hand" than Virgil.[40]

Sound morality was generally a strong point with ballad-makers, whether courtly or popular, as it was with almost any writer of the Tudor age. Middle-class virtue was the special concern of the puritans, who had no love for courtly and worldly ballads, and, since they could not banish them, they could at least try to moralize them. If a multitude of readers clung to the old songs and, like Sir Andrew

---

40. *Roxburghe Ballads*, VI, 547; Percy's *Reliques* (Everyman's Library), II, 307; Rollins, *Analytical Index*, 2710, 2839 ff.

Aguecheek, cared not for good life, the old songs might be made to yield a lesson. Thus we find a number of moralized ballads registered in the fifteen-sixties. These years seem to have witnessed special efforts to snatch merry tunes from the devil. Some of the titles are rather pathetic examples of popular paganism conquered by the stern daughter of the voice of God—*I myghte have leved meryly morralysed* (1564–65); *O Sweete Olyver altered to ye scriptures* (1586).[41] The moral fervor of this period, so clearly marked in the ballads, had other manifestations, some of which we have already encountered, such as the *Fable of Narcissus* (published in 1560) and the works of Peend (1565), Underdowne (1566), Golding (1565–67), Painter (1566–67).[42] While the classical translators inherited a moralistic tradition, the warm professions of such men as Golding and Painter were doubtless heightened by the consciousness that popularizers of pagan and immoral stories needed to be on the defensive.

There is no need of citing ballads of later periods. Religious and political and topical broadsides might undergo some changes of style, or at least of sentiment, but those on classical themes have a strong family likeness in all ages. Moralistic or romantic or sentimental, they lived on—as the chapbook stories of Leander or Hercules did—into the eighteenth century. Their increasingly subterranean existence was hardly touched by changing fashions in poetry in the world above.

V. Long Poems

Sackville's *Induction,* though only incidentally mythological, is an early and highly significant example of the working of classical influences, and is moreover the most important poem between Skelton —some would say Chaucer—and Spenser. It was published in 1563.[43]

41. Rollins, *Analytical Index*, 1193, 1994. See also 819, 820, 1051, 1175, 1627, 1693, 2033, 2035, 2331, 2332, 2333, 2334, 2612, 2840, 2921. Only one of these is on a classical theme, *The wanderynge prynce moralyzed* (2840).

42. For Peend and Underdowne see the Appendix. The ungodly *Couurte of Venus* (1557) provoked two attempts to counteract its pernicious influence. One was John Hall's *The Couurte of vertu contaynynge many holy or spretuall songes Sonettes psalmes ballettes shorte sentences as well of holy scriptures as others &c.* (1565; *Stat. Reg.*, I, 268; ed. R. A. Fraser, London, 1961). The other was *The Couurte of Venus moralized,* by Thomas Bryce (1567; *Stat. Reg.*, I, 343).

43. *The Mirror for Magistrates,* ed. Lily B. Campbell (Cambridge University Press, 1938). Cf. *The Complaint of Henry Duke of Buckingham Including the Induction,* ed. M. Hearsey (Yale University Press, 1936). The fullest

In this really noble work of the young lawyer we have, treated with dignity and somber emotion, that theme which above all others haunted the Renaissance mind, mutability, the theme which links together Spenser's *Cantos,* Hamlet's speeches in the graveyard, Ralegh's apostrophe to death, so much of the prose of Drummond, Donne, Burton, Browne, Taylor, and those lines from the last of the great race,

> The glories of our blood and state
> Are shadows, not substantial things . . .

Walking forth into the fields on a bleak winter evening, and thinking of "the sundry changes that in earth we find," the poet sees a woman, clad in black, who is overcome with grief. She is Sorrow, and she will guide him to the underworld where he may see those who have fallen from pomp and power, and may learn that there is no duration in earthly happiness. They enter Hades by "an hideous hole, all vast, withouten shape," and meet a series of figures, Remorse of Conscience, Dread, Revenge, Misery, Care, Sleep, Old Age, Malady, Famine, Death, War, all of whom are described with vivid physical detail. The shield of War is pictured at still greater length, for it contains scenes from ancient history, especially the fall of Troy. The poet and his guide pass on, cross over Acheron in Charon's boat, appease Cerberus, and enter Pluto's realm, where the air is filled with groans and wailing of babes and maids unwed, and princes of renown

> That whilom sat on top of fortune's wheel,
> Now laid full low . . .

Then the Duke of Buckingham appears, to commence his story.

Even this brief summary reveals the combination of medieval and classical motives. At the outset we have for example the dream-allegory convention, echoes of Chaucerian language, four stanzas about the signs of the zodiac to emphasize the fact that it is evening. The theme of the whole, the fickleness of fortune and the tragedy of fall from high estate, recalls Chaucer's droning monk and other medieval preachers.[44]

---

critique of the Induction is in Jacobus Swart, *Thomas Sackville: A Study in Sixteenth-Century Poetry* (Groningen, 1948).

44. Sackville is quoted from the text in Hebel and Hudson, *Poetry of the English Renaissance* (1929), pp. 56 ff.

Koeppel pointed out (*Archiv,* CI, 145–46) that some lines in Sackville's description of Sorrow (87, 90–91, 123) echo phrases in Chaucer's *Romaunt of*

But when he approaches the underworld the author inevitably re-calls Aeneas. The description of Avernus is obviously based on Virgil, yet Sackville's phrasing and slight additional details almost suggest the hell-mouth so popular in the Corpus Christi plays. Virgil's personified abstractions are given epithets only. Sackville's list roughly corre-sponds, so that the passage has a classical rather than a Christian tinge, but his treatment is quite different from Virgil's. This is only one of a number of stanzas describing Old Age, the *tristis Senectus* of Virgil:

> Crookbacked he was, tooth-shaken, and blear-eyed,
> Went on three feet, and sometimes crept on four,
> With old lame bones that rattled by his side,
> His scalp all pilled and he with eld forlore;
> His withered fist still knocking at Death's door,
> Fumbling and drivelling as he draws his breath;
> For brief, the shape and messenger of Death.

One is reminded at once of the much-discussed old man in the Par-doner's Tale; in fact both pictures have been traced to a common source, an elegy of Maximian.[45] Such technique is a medieval develop-ment of the post-classical, and is most familiar to us in Spenser. Sack-ville's lines have a concrete, half-Dantesque actuality, yet the very fullness of physical detail loses something of the timeless universality and vague horror of Virgil's personifications.

Some other imitations and borrowings are palpable—the shield of War, suggested by the shield of Aeneas; the account of the fall of Troy, with the capture of Cassandra and the death of Priam; the embarkation with Charon; the subduing of Cerberus; the lamenta-tions of the shades. Sackville shares the Virgilian mood more keenly than Spenser,[46] but he lacks the power of suggestion, the sustained greatness of style, which raise the commonplaces of death to the Vir-gilian level. "Here puled the babes" hardly approaches

---

the Rose (312, 336 ff.) which describe a painting of "Sorowe." Reminiscences of Sackville in *The Faerie Queene* have been noticed by commentators, but not, I think, in *The Shepheardes Calender*. Cf. the pictures of winter in Sackville (ll. 1, 5, 13, 16–17), and Spenser's *January* (ll. 19, 24, 31, 35). Courthope, *History of English Poetry* (II, 122–23), notices Sackville's debt, in this descrip-tion of winter, to the lines of Gavin Douglas prefixed to his version of *Aen.* vii.

45. Chaucer's debt was pointed out by G. L. Kittredge (*American Journal of Philology*, IX, 1888, 84–85; see Skeat, V, 287). A. M. Clark added Sack-ville (*TLS*, January 23, 1920, p. 52).

46. See below, pages 100–102.

> Continuo auditae voces vagitus et ingens
> infantumque animae flentes, in limine primo
> quos dulcis vitae exsortis et ab ubere raptos
> abstulit atra dies et funere mersit acerbo.

Nor does

> the maids unwed
> With folded hands their sorry chance bewailed,

attain the concentration of the one word *innuptae* with which Virgil suggests the untimely blighting of rose-lipt maidens; Sackville's maids might almost be disappointed wallflowers. But then, in the expression of pity, who does not fall short of Virgil? And as a whole Sackville's poem is moving.

It would be odd if the young man who collaborated in *Gorboduc* did not reveal Senecan influence in this poem also. The stanzas concerning the zodiac have many parallels in medieval writers, but the passage, more mythological than mathematical, is nearer Seneca than Chaucer.[47] The main theme of the *Induction* is no less Senecan than medieval, and the sketch of the fall of Troy, though Virgilian in substance, yields the Senecan moral of mutability.[48] While Seneca's personified abstractions are generally labeled in an epithet or a phrase,[49] his apostrophe to sleep suggested Sackville's finest stanza, the second of these two:

> By him lay heavy Sleep, the cousin of Death,
> Flat on the ground and still as any stone,
> A very corpse, save yielding forth a breath;
> Small keep took he whom fortune frownèd on
> Or whom she lifted up into the throne
> Of high renown; but as a living death,
> So, dead alive, of life he drew the breath.
>
> The body's rest, the quiet of the heart,
> The travail's ease, the still night's fere was he,
> And of our life in earth the better part;
> Reaver of sight, and yet in whom we see

47. Cf. the opening of *Hercules Furens*, or *Thyestes*, ll. 844 ff.

48. For example, see the opening of the *Troades*, or the first chorus in *Agamemnon*. The description of Avernus may be compared not only with Virgil, but with *Hercules Furens*, ll. 664 ff.

49. E.g., *Herc. Fur.*, ll. 96 ff., 690 ff. (Tudor Translations, I, 12, 31).

Things oft that tide, and oft that never be;
Without respect, esteeming equally
King Crœsus' pomp, and Irus' poverty.[50]

Chaucer, Virgil, Seneca—it is a characteristic Tudor combination. And Sackville is not a mere stumbling translator or imitator, like most of the men treated earlier in this chapter. His borrowings are wrought into an original poem, at once medieval and classical, which is the most ample poetic expression before Spenser of the moral seriousness of Tudor humanism.

To subsist in bones, says Browne, and be but pyramidally extant, is a fallacy in duration, yet that mortuary monument, the *Mirror for Magistrates,* demands a sigh from the passing reader, if only because of its size and influence. The 1587 edition contained a number of pieces on Roman emperors, from the pen of the worthy John Higgins. They vary in length from six to over fifty stanzas; variations in style are less readily discernible. The narratives in this group, like the rest, embody the medieval conception of tragedy as a dolorous fall from high estate, and Julius Caesar begins his tale of sin with a reference to the medieval models of the book, "Bocas" and Lydgate.

Among this nice derangement of epitaphs the life of Tiberius will serve for illustration. After some inevitable stanzas on the dangers of fortune we learn of the divorce of Agrippina, of wars in Illyria, of professed hesitation to accept the throne. Less familiar to classical students is a letter written by Pilate to Tiberius, reporting the birth, miracles, death, and resurrection of Christ. It is translated literally from the *Flores Historiarum,* with a comment from Higgins by way of higher criticism.[51] Then the fate of Sejanus, Drusus, and Germanicus is mentioned, and some lines are given to the depravities of the court. With a literary tact unusual in the *Mirror* Tiberius decides to tell no more of his life now, since his evil deeds do not bear repetition.

Such an imperial precedent may absolve us from the necessity of gazing any longer into a mirror which, says its compiler to the reader, shows "the slipery deceiptes of the wavering lady, and the due rewarde

50. Cf. *Herc. Fur.* (Tudor Translations, I, 43):
. . . and thou O tamer best
O sleepe of toyles, the quietnesse of mynde,
Of all the lyfe of man the better parte . . .
Although there is nothing in the first stanza which might not have arisen naturally out of Sackville's theme, it may have been partly inspired by the picture of the sleeping Hercules which motivates the Senecan chorus.
51. *Mirror*, ed. Haslewood, I, 279; *Flores Historiarum*, ed. Luard, I, 108.

of all kinde of vices." The motive of the book is medieval, the manner
is medieval, and even in these Lives of Roman emperors much of the
substance is medieval too. The bulk of it is taken from Suetonius and
Herodian, but some details and episodes are drawn from the *Flores
Historiarum,* Grafton's *Chronicle,* and Lanquet's *Chronicle.*[52] Such a
combination of ancient, medieval, and Renaissance sources, done in a
medieval spirit, is still another illustration of the more sluggish of the
innumerable cross-currents in sixteenth-century literature. And here
we may leave the *Mirror,* floundering, as Augustine Birrell somewhere says of Hannah More, like a huge conger eel in an ocean of
dingy morality.

One would not at first thought expect to find classical myths in a
versified history, but in his *Albion's England* William Warner, like
medieval chroniclers (not to mention Ralegh and others), thought it
well to get a flying start by beginning at the beginning.[53] So Warner,
with little of Ralegh's knowledge, imagination, or eloquence, but with
a sincere desire to glorify the nation's ancestry, began with the father
of Saturn. The birth of Jupiter, the overthrow of Saturn, and kindred
matters lying at the root of British history, lead on to the career of
Hercules, whose labors are amply described. One of several inset tales
narrated by the daughters of King Picus has romantic touches:

> Wheare braue aspects of louely dames
>   Tantara to the fight,
> Whose forms perhaps are weg'd in harts,
>   When fauours wag in sight . . .
>
> Wheare ladies doffe their champions' helmes,
>   And kisse their beauers hid,
> And parlie under canapies
>   How well or ill they did.[54]

The chivalric note is frequently sounded in the poem. Warner was,
according to Anthony à Wood, "a friend to poetry, history, and romance."[55] Taste as well as the habit of the times would lead him to

52. The sources of the classical Lives are discussed in detail in my article in
SP, XXII, 256 ff.
53. *Albion's England* appeared in successively enlarged editions, the first
four books and the prose history of Aeneas in 1586, the first six books in 1589,
the first nine in 1592, and so on.
54. Chalmers, *English Poets,* IV, 527. Most of the first stanza, by the way,
is woven into Baron's *An Apologie for Paris* (1649, p. 55); see the Appendix.
55. *Athen. Oxon.,* ed. Bliss (London, 1813–20), I, 766.

Caxton, and in the first two books he did little more than versify the *Recuyell*.[56] In addition to the relics of chivalry there are other non-classical details. One of the inset tales is that of Callisto, and we might expect an Ovidian interlude, but even this story is based on Caxton.[57] Caxton's version, however, is serious, pathetic, courtly; Warner develops the motive of Jupiter's feminine disguise and the progress of the seduction with sportive and rakish detail, his Jupiter is a Don Juan in the harem.[58]

Jogging along at an even trot Warner deals with the Trojan war and the death of Aeneas, and reaches at length the all-important Brute.

> And thus the Brutons bring
> Their petigree from Iupiter,
> Of pagane gods the king.

And thus two books are filled. The rest of the work, apart from some inset tales, is devoted to Brute's successors on the British throne.

In the sixth book Owen Tudor relates to Queen Katherine several classical or pseudo-classical stories, and the spirit of them is rather more Jacobean than Elizabethan. The thirtieth chapter tells of Venus and Vulcan, with a good deal of dialogue and realistic or burlesque detail. The gods proceed to consider the case, and Pan, Mercury, and Mars contribute tales and opinions which reveal the disconcerting ways of women. In the forty-sixth chapter the story of Narcissus and Echo follows Ovid, with variations,[59] but Ovidian myth fades away when the ghost of Narcissus and the voice of Echo are sent, with the Furies, to do what damage they can on earth. Mythological machinery becomes a vehicle for satire.

The chief claim of *Albion's England* to the title of epic is that it has twelve books. Francis Meres, with characteristic exuberance, declared that "the best wits of both our Universities" regarded Warner as "our English Homer." For us Warner's interest lies mainly in the medieval and English quality of his work which appears not only in

56. See Hans Huf, in the Bibliography.

57. Chalmers, pp. 531–33; *Recuyell*, pp. 48 ff.

58. Both in *Troia Britanica* and in *The Golden Age* Heywood, in his episode of Jupiter and Callisto, follows Warner, and elaborates the details of dalliance in the same spirit. There are even verbal correspondences.

59. For example, Echo cries "Let's meete," and Narcissus, thinking that his shadow in the pool has spoken, jumps in and drowns. See below, Chapter VI, note 29.

his treatment of myth but in the poem as a whole; in an age of borrowing Warner reveals only a few traces of Italian influence.[60]

A further illustration of Warner's medievalism is the prose "breuiate of the true historie of Aeneas" which was appended to the second book.[61] In the poem, in accordance with a venerable tradition, Aeneas appears as a traitor. In the first sentence of his "true historie" Warner repudiates this view. After that we might look for an abstract of the *Aeneid;* instead we get a summary of Caxton's *Eneydos,* with a few borrowings from Virgil. The narrative, following Caxton, proceeds by the chronicle, not the epic method. Epic portions are condensed, for Warner frankly avows his desire to reach the love story; speeches and dialogue are altered and expanded. In addition to chivalric touches we have rationalizing of the supernatural; even though Caxton, like Virgil, has Mercury sent with a warning message, here "a noble Troian" is substituted. Then there are realistic details which add verisimilitude; Ascanius is twelve years old. Thus in following Caxton Warner treats the classical epic exactly as Chaucer did in the *Legend of Dido.*

Looking back over the mass of material touched upon in this chapter, one remains certain at least of the great and increasing popularity of classical themes. They furnish wings (or pattens) to the translator and the literary aspirant, the story-teller and the puritan preacher, the courtly amorist and the ballad-monger, the patriotic chronicler and the philosophic moralist. Every quill-driver of the age has slept, more or less soundly, on Parnassus hill. In two types of writing especially we find the beginnings of the mythological poem proper, in paraphrases of single tales from the *Metamorphoses,* and in mythological narratives used to decorate the plea of a despairing lover. The former were natural products of an age of translation. The latter were partly responsible for the style and tone of mythological poems, which inherited the rhetorical tricks and conceits of the courtly lover.

The most pronounced and consistent quality of this body of writing is its medievalism, usually in the bad sense of the word. It is often heavily didactic, and a poem may embody a sermon or an allegory or both. Ancient, medieval, and modern sources are mingled with medieval indifference—Ovid, the *Ovide moralisé,* "Waleys," Boccaccio, Ficino, Chaucer, Virgil, Caxton's *Recuyell* and *Eneydos,* Seneca, Herodian, Suetonius, Geoffrey of Monmouth. Even in those narratives which are free from a moral the manner of treating myths is

60. See Huf, and F. Brie, *Archiv,* CXXVII, 328 ff.
61. For a fuller account see *MLN,* XLIV, 40–41.

medieval. The authors want a story, find it in Ovid or elsewhere, and retell it as best they can, with little originality and no attempt at rich decoration. Before turning to Lodge and later exponents of the Italianate Ovidian poem we must take fuller account of old and new conceptions of Ovid.

CHAPTER IV
Ovid Old and New

I. ALLEGORY

The persistence of the habit of allegorizing myths has been and will be noticed in connection with individual poems, but here we may pause to invoke a few out of the cloud of witnesses by way of reminding ourselves that most Elizabethans, in their whole theory of poetry, relied upon the medieval method of defense. There is no need of more than a reminder, since the subject has often been discussed.

Although, as Spingarn said, the first problem of Renaissance criticism was the justification of imaginative literature, the victory of aesthetic disinterestedness (a victory which has proved something of a great illusion) was long delayed. The tradition of many centuries could not be quickly overthrown. Aristotelian doctrine, considerably modified by Horatian and medieval ideas, gradually changed the status of literature from what had been a dubious province of heaven into a bravely independent kingdom of man. The process was not completed in the sixteenth century—in England it was only beginning—for the allegorical defense could not become obsolete so long as the conditions which created it still subsisted. When historical criticism of the Bible, for instance, was only faintly stirring, allegory might be needed, even by such a clear-eyed ironic humanist as Erasmus, to explain biblical stories. As for classical myths, Erasmus seems to have wavered, sometimes accepting allegory, sometimes laughing at it.[1]

The allegorizing of Virgil and Ovid flourished on the continent in

---

1. "And here they bring in some foolish insipid Fable out of *Speculum Historiale* or *Gesta Romanorum*, and Expound it Allegorically, Tropologically, and Anagogically . . ." (*Praise of Folly*, trans. J. Wilson, ed. Mrs. P. S. Allen, Oxford, 1913, p. 135). But the allegorical commentary in Sandys' *Ovid* (1632) draws upon Erasmus two or three times.

Our concern is with prevailing orthodoxy rather than with sporadic hints of skepticism, but we may recall something more than a hint in the prologue to *Gargantua*, and the amusing mockery in *Epistolæ Obscurorum Virorum*, Letter 28 (ed. F. G. Stokes, London, 1925, pp. 72 ff.).

the sixteenth century.[2] The medieval version of the *Metamorphoses* by Buonsignori was revamped by Agostini. The free translations of Dolce (1539–53) and Anguillara (1554–61) had their moral baggage. Handbooks of moralized mythology, such as those of Comes and Cartari, have been mentioned already; they were widely read not only in the sixteenth but throughout the seventeenth century. In France, to mention one item, Barthélemy Aneau translated part of the *Metamorphoses* (1556), and, though reacting to some degree against religious interpretations, he was rationalistic mainly in a Pickwickian sense. Jupiter's amorous exploits signified for him the effort of the world-soul to unite all things in itself. The general tendency of interpretation in the sixteenth century was ethical rather than theological; the fact marks both the strength and the limitations of the secularizing spirit of the Renaissance. On the other hand there was the mystical vein which, branching out from Pico and other Platonists (to go no further back), was inextricably mixed with Cabbalism; the mixture was likely to be more fantastic than fruitful.

Perhaps the best proof of the dominance of allegory is found in the notorious cases of the two chief poets of sixteenth-century Italy. Ariosto had incorporated some actual and obvious allegories in the *Orlando*, but the intuitions of pious commentators soon uncovered many more which the gay and gallant author would not have recognized.[3] And Tasso, harassed by criticism and by his own morbid conscience, declared, to save his poem, that it was allegorical throughout.[4]

In England the medieval notion of allegory held firm sway. The opinions of Thomas Wilson we have met already. The poets, says Ascham, "oftentymes under the couering of a fable, do hyde & wrappe in goodlie preceptes of philosophie." [5] The Elizabethan critics who defended poetry against puritans and ballad-mongers had commonly no better argument than the allegory underlying poetical fiction. Lodge, Webbe, and Puttenham are quite orthodox. The mystical Tom Nashe accounts poetry a hidden and divine kind of philosophy, and duly interprets the tales of Ovid.[6]

Sidney, with more important ideas to expound, only glanced at al-

---

2. For the continent, see Rick, Gruppe, pp. 26 ff., the references above in chapter II, note 6, and the chapter on allegorical interpretation of the *Aeneid* in M. Y. Hughes, *Virgil and Spenser* (1929).

3. S. J. McMurphy, *Spenser's Use of Ariosto for Allegory* (1924).

4. Angelo Solerti, *Vita di Torquato Tasso* (Turin and Rome, 1895), I, 233; Courthope, *History of English Poetry*, III, 113–15.

5. *English Works of Ascham*, ed. W. A. Wright, p. 17.

6. *Works*, ed. McKerrow, I, 25, 28, 286.

legory, and perhaps did not have much faith in it. He found parables and allegories edifying, but his parables were Christian, and his allegories the fables of Aesop. Yet his strong moralizing instinct is apparent. He appeals constantly to classical *exempla* and sees in the *Aeneid* a picture of the excellent man, in the *Cyropaedia* "an absolute heroicall Poem" designed to give us *effigiem iusti imperii;* he embodied similar ideas in the revised *Arcadia.* Further, at the very end of the *Apology* Sidney seems, in a mood both playful and serious, to share in part the current view when he cites Clauser and Cornutus and agrees that the fables of Hesiod and Homer "giue us all knowledge." [7]

A moralist no less versatile than Nashe was Sir John Harington, author of the *Metamorphosis of Ajax* and of a version of Ariosto which did not bowdlerize erotic passages. In his preface to the latter work (1591) he borrows both from Fornari, the allegorical interpreter of Ariosto, and from Leo Hebraeus.[8] Following Leo he moralizes the myth of Perseus and Andromeda. "The weaker capacities" will be content with the story, "stronger stomackes" will taste the moral sense, while "a third sort, more high conceited then they, will digest the Allegorie."

For Elizabethan orthodoxy concerning Ovid one may turn back to Golding's "Epistle" and "Preface," where the translator expounds his author's "dark Philosophie." He marches resolutely through the fifteen books, demonstrating the moral lessons of the tales, reducing them to "ryght of Christian law." Ovid is reconciled with the Bible quite satisfactorily. In the "Preface" Golding explains the meaning of the gods in such a way as not to offend Christian scruples, and further celebrates the rule of reason over the flesh. Gavin Douglas had pronounced Ovid "expert of all thing as it semit," [9] and Golding is of the same mind. He proclaims that Ovid is a repository of all knowledge, that he has profitable lessons for all classes of people, young and old, rich and poor, learned and unlearned. Such words are not a mere blurb (done in Elizabethan fashion by the author instead of the publisher), they spring from real conviction; though some allowance may be made for humanistic exuberance of expression, and also for a con-

7. *Elizabethan Critical Essays,* I, 206. An appeal, in the same passage, to supposed Aristotelian authority, may be taken from Boccaccio's *De Genealogia Deorum.*

8. McMurphy, pp. 19–20 (on Fornari). As for Leo, see his *Dialoghi d'Amore,* ed. Caramella (1929), pp. 98–99; and *Elizabethan Critical Essays,* II, 201 ff. See the Appendix, under Abraham Fraunce, 1592.

9. *The Palice of Honour (Works,* ed. Small, I, 47).

sciousness of censors in the offing.[10]

These representative opinions are enough to show that the Elizabethan conception of poetry, and of myth in particular, was on the whole the medieval substitute for an aesthetic theory. Yet, as on the continent, interpretations of myth are mainly ethical and humanistic. The Elizabethan love of morality is manifest everywhere, in the briefest allusion and in the plan of *The Faerie Queene*. In the matter of allusions it is often hard to say—as it is in the case of preachers' use of the Bible—whether an author is consciously allegorical, whether he is employing a poetic symbol or metaphor, or whether a petrified allegory has become a mere conceit. A single familiar example will do:

> O! when mine eyes did see Olivia first,
> Methought she purg'd the air of pestilence.
> That instant was I turn'd into a hart,
> And my desires, like fell and cruel hounds,
> E'er since pursue me.

So well-worn an idea could not retain much allegorical edification.[11]

10. Symptoms of puritan sobriety have been noticed already in connection with ballads, and puritan dislike of mythology becomes increasingly significant. Warton quotes *The Ungodlinesse of the Hethnicke Goddes or The Downfall of Diana of the Ephesians, by J. D. an exile for the word, late a minister in London, MDLIV,* and says: "The writer, whose arguments are as weak as his poetry, attempts to prove that the customary mode of training youths in the Roman poets encouraged idolatry and pagan superstition"; see *History of English Poetry* (1871), IV, 231. Warton also mentions one "H. G.," "a painfull minister of God's word in Kent," who condemned Linche's *Fountaine of Ancient Fiction* or some similar book as "spawne of Italian Gallimawfry" (*ibid.*, p. 351). Thomas Bryce exclaims

> We are not Ethnickes, we forsoth at least professe not so;
> Why range we then to Ethnickes' trade? Come back, where will ye go?
> Tel me, is Christe or Cupide lord? Doth God or Venus reign?

        (Quoted by Raleigh, *Milton*, London, 1909, pp. 173–74.)
See the Appendix under Thomas Salter, 1579; and the quotation from Speed, page 39 above.

11. The interpretation of Actaeon's hounds as his own emotions appears, for example, in the Epistle Dedicatory of Adlington's *Golden Asse* (1566); Whitney's *Choice of Emblemes* (1586), p. 15; the fifth sonnet of Daniel's *Delia* (1592); Fraunce, *Third part of the Countesse of Pembrokes Ivychurch* (1592), p. 43; B. Barnes, *El.* iii (Lee, *Elizabethan Sonnets*, I, 240); B. Griffin, *ibid.*, II, 269; Drayton, *Heroical Epistles*, "Rosamond to Henry" (Chalmers, IV, 58; *Works*, II, 137). Cf. *Adonais*, st. xxxi.

In this period, as earlier, euhemerism is common, but it has not much interest for us and may be neglected. One might cite examples ranging from Greene's *Planetomachia* to the travel books of Moryson and George Sandys.

There is a serious purpose in Spenser's summary of the ethical allegory of the great heroic poets:

In which I haue followed all the antique Poets historicall, first Homere, who in the Persons of Agamemnon and Ulysses hath ensampled a good gouernour and a vertuous man, the one in his Ilias, the other in his Odysseis: then Virgil, whose like intention was to doe in the person of Aeneas: after him Ariosto comprised them both in his Orlando: and lately Tasso disseuered them againe, and formed both parts in two persons, namely that part which they in Philosophy call Ethice, or vertues of a priuate man, coloured in his Rinaldo: The other named Politice in his Godfredo . . .

The didactic attitude must be accepted if we wish to understand a large share of Elizabethan literature. It may amuse or offend our aesthetic sophistication, but it would have been understood, and partly endorsed, by Plato and even Aristotle as well as Horace. If the classics received sometimes wrong-headed appreciation from Elizabethan readers, they were not a mere innocuous genteel tradition. Besides, a moral purpose did not hamper Elizabethan freedom of feeling and expression, as *The Faerie Queene* again makes amply evident, in the "Bower of Bliss" and elsewhere.[12]

II. THE NEW OVID

With full recognition of the fact that in the sixteenth century a large proportion of readers and writers regarded, or professed to regard, Ovid as a moral teacher, we may here outline the growth of a more aesthetic and "pagan" conception of mythology in general and the *Metamorphoses* in particular. It is of the first importance for the mythological poem throughout its history that from the beginning the new mythology was closely associated with the developing pastoral conventions. Further, the new and warmer treatment of myth was often not incompatible, outwardly at least, with didactic allegory.

We may recall the character of Boccaccio's elaborate pastoral, the

---

12. To take a minor example, Peele's *The praise of Chastitie* includes a passage which was apparently imitated in *Venus and Adonis* (397 ff.). Thus Peele (*Phœnix Nest*, ed. Rollins, p. 22; ed. Macdonald, p. 14):

    Who hath beheld faire Venus in hir pride,
        Of nakednes all Alablaster white,
    In Iuorie bed, strait laid by Mars his side,
        And hath not bin enchanted with the sight . . .

This, however sincere, is not the vein of *Comus* or *A Dialogue between the Resolved Soul and Created Pleasure.*

Ameto (*ca.* 1341). Ameto, a rough hunter, comes upon a group of nymphs sitting by a stream, and, overhearing the song of one of them, Lia, he falls in love. Later, at the feast of Venus, Ameto listens while each nymph, at Lia's suggestion, tells the story of her love, and his pulse is considerably stirred by their tales. Then, after what has appeared to be a celebration of very earthly love, a pillar of fire is seen —it is likened to that which led the Israelites—and the voice of Venus explains,

> Io son luce del cielo unica e trina,
> Principio e fine di ciascuna cosa,
> Del qual nè fu nè fia nulla vicina.[13]

The faces of the nymphs shine with unearthly beauty, and the dazzled Ameto becomes aware that it is the goddess of sacred, not profane, love who has spoken. Baptized with elaborate rites by the nymphs, he, the representative of untaught humanity, can now comprehend the heavenly mysteries and feel the divine fire. The work is an early illustration of what was to be a widespread and enduring quality of Renaissance writing, the mixture of sensuous paganism (not to mention erotic realism) with a more or less Christian allegory. Such a combination is no doubt more congenial to the Latin than to the English temperament, though it can appear in England.

Closer to the mythological poem was Boccaccio's *Ninfale fiesolano,* which "uses a pagan allegory to convey a favourite *novella* theme. The shepherd Affrico loves a nymph of Diana, and the tale ends by the goddess changing her faithless votary into a fountain." [14] A similar Ovidian motive appeared in the *Ambra* of Lorenzo de' Medici, for the poem is virtually a redaction of the story of Apollo and Daphne.[15] Likewise Ovidian was Sannazaro's graceful *Salices,* which described the flight of nymphs from pursuing satyrs and their metamorphosis, through Diana's power, into willows. Pastoral and mythological poems shade into each other, for pastoral writing in both prose and verse was drenched with mythology, and the mythological poem obviously owed much to the pastoral. In both is an artificial Arcadian

---

13. *Opere Volgari* (Florence, 1833), XV, 186.

14. W. W. Greg, *Pastoral Poetry and Pastoral Drama* (1906), p. 37. For Boccaccio's poem, see *Opere Volgari,* XVII, 1 ff., and the separate edition, ed. A. F. Massèra (1926). See also the works on Boccaccio by Edward Hutton (1910) and T. C. Chubb (1930); and J. A. Symonds, *Italian Literature* (1909), I, 103–04, 108, and *passim.*

15. *Opere,* ed. A. Simioni (Bari, 1913), I, 291 ff.

scene, exhaustively described, inhabited by artificial nymphs and swains and mythological figures, also—especially the nymphs—exhaustively described, and of course there is interminable sensuous or sensual love-making.

Among mythological poems must be mentioned the *Giostra* of Poliziano.[16] In it the thread of narrative hardly does more than unite mythological pictures of the richest ornamentation. In Italy, as later in England, the ornate manner rapidly became a convention, and the mythological poem was one of the most popular genres in the fifteenth and sixteenth centuries.[17] The style was encouraged by Ariosto, whose *Orlando* contained elaborately sensuous variations on Ovidian and Virgilian themes. And then, in addition to many versions of tales from the *Metamorphoses*, there were such large works as the paraphrases, often freely expanded, of Dolce, Anguillara, Maretti.[18]

The weaknesses of the Italian mythological poem, amply evident in English pieces, were almost inevitable. Emphasis on luscious descriptions of the beauties of art, nature, the human and especially the female body, resulted often in long invertebrate poems compounded of voluptuous imagery and word-spinning.[19] In their pictorial richness, artificial rhetoric, erotic themes, and general slightness of content, they were typical young man's poetry, beautiful words about beautiful things, things and bodies which can be seen and touched. Style cultivated smooth softness of diction and rhythm, diffuseness instead of concentration, bookishness instead of emotion. Love of color and detail was not favorable to purity of line and pattern. But poetry needed a rediscovery of sensuous beauty, and not all poets ran to excess.

Though the inexhaustible Ovid was far and away the chief source of themes, there were other tales, such as the late Greek *Hero and Leander*. Boscán's *Leandro y Hero* (1543), which was inspired by Bernardo Tasso's much superior Italian version, established the elaborate mythological poem in Spain.[20] In both countries Ovidian narra-

16. *Le Stanze per la Giostra: L'Orfeo*, ed. E. Rho (Milan, 1927). See Greg, p. 37, and De Sanctis, *Storia della Letteratura Italiana*, ed. B. Croce (Bari, 1912), I, 339 ff.

17. See A. Belloni, *Il Poema Epico e Mitologico* (1912), especially chapter xii.

18. For a convenient list of Italian versions of Ovid, see R. Schevill, *Ovid and the Renascence in Spain* (1913), pp. 234 ff.

19. For instance, see Symonds' account of Molza's *Ninfa Tiberina*, in his *Italian Literature* (1909), II, 199 ff.

20. Menéndez y Pelayo, *Antología de Poetas Líricos Castellanos* (*Tomo XIII*), *Juan Boscán* (Madrid, 1908), 334 ff.; F. Flamini, *Studi di Storia Let-*

tives multiplied with a rapidity quite appalling to the investigator. In France the Italianate fashion took less hold, though mythology was rampant there as elsewhere, and the works of Ronsard and others are full of mythological pieces.

Conservative humanistic tradition might prefer to follow the narrative method of the Latin epic, without frills, except those sanctioned by the *Aeneid*, and Petrarch's *Africa* was the first of many neoclassic epics which, as Porson said of Southey's, will be read when Homer and Virgil are forgotten. Conservatism also, supported by the principle of *utile et dulce*, found expression in half-mythological or pastoral didactic pieces, such as the *Scacchiae Ludus* of Vida or the extraordinary work of Fracastoro. But in general the sensuous Italian fancy applied itself to decorative embellishment of Ovid.

Although, as neoclassic principles hardened into a rigid convention, Virgil became the ideal heroic poet, and although, on the strength of critical dicta, he might be given that place even in the sixteenth century, the more concrete testimony of imitation proclaims Ovid the favorite of the Renaissance. The fact explains a good deal in the history of poetry. Renaissance dramatists, even if they sometimes knew Greek, were much better able to imitate or surpass the rhetoric, the sententiousness, and the violence of Seneca than to fathom the spiritual depths of Greek tragedy. The most Virgilian qualities of Virgil, when appreciated, were not within easy reach, but an unhappily large number of men throughout the neoclassic period thought that a combination of "correctness," funeral games, historical prophecy, and "machines" made an epic poem. Thus the very defects of Ovid, as well as his real virtues, contributed to his popularity in the sixteenth century.

While the strength of medievalism continued to manifest itself, Ovid did by degrees slough off his didactic and allegorical skin sufficiently to emerge as something more like the poet we know.[21] Increasing scholarship placed him, for some men, in a recognizable milieu, and gave to readers a tolerably authentic text of his work. Despite layers of allegorical interpretation Ovid could be better appreciated as a personality. Although his narrative and stylistic tech-

---

teraria (1895), pp. 385 ff.; F. Pintor, *Delle liriche di B. Tasso* (1900), pp. 137 ff.; M. H. Jellinek, *Die Sage von Hero und Leander in der Dichtung* (1890). For the general influence of Ovid in Spain, see Schevill.

21. For the survival in our day of popular legends of Ovid as "magician, trader, prophet, preacher, saint, paladin," see R. H. Coon, "The Vogue of Ovid since the Renaissance," *Classical Journal*, XXV, 277–90.

nique was by no means wasted on medieval scholars and writers, knowledge, understanding, and the capacity for imitation were now more generally diffused. Ovid's morality was less of a stumbling-block. In short, his combination of brilliant rhetoric and soulless subject matter was exactly suited to Renaissance taste.

The foundation of Ovid's medieval fame shifted somewhat in the later period. Advancing knowledge and aesthetic appreciation put the *Metamorphoses* definitely in the forefront of the poet's work, not merely as a great body of narrative matter, but as the revelation of a carefree world of the imagination inhabited by beings who live only for love and beauty. As Gilbert Murray said, in an admirable characterization of Ovid,

> He was a poet utterly in love with poetry: not perhaps with the soul of poetry—to be in love with souls is a feeble and somewhat morbid condition —but with the real face and voice and body and clothes and accessories of poetry. He loved the actual technique of the verse . . . He loved most the whole world of mimesis which he made . . .

What a world it is that he has created in the *Metamorphoses!* It draws its denizens from all the boundless resources of Greek mythology, a world of live forests and mountains and rivers, in which every plant and flower has a story, and nearly always a love story; where the moon is indeed not a moon but an orbèd maiden, and the Sunrise weeps because she is still young and her belovèd is old; and the stars are human souls; and the Sun sees human virgins in the depths of forests and almost swoons at their beauty and pursues them; and other virgins, who feel in the same way about him, commit great sins from jealousy and then fling themselves on the ground in grief and fix their eyes on him, weeping and weeping till they waste away and turn into flowers; and all the youths and maidens are indescribably beautiful and adventurous and passionate, though not well brought up, and, I fear, somewhat lacking in the first elements of self-control; and they all fall in love with each other, or, failing that, with fountains or stars or trees; and are always met by enormous obstacles, and are liable to commit crimes and cause tragedies, but always forgive each other, or else die. A world of wonderful children where nobody is really cross or wicked except the grown-ups; Juno, for instance, and people's parents, and of course a certain number of Furies and Witches. I think among all the poets who take rank merely as story-tellers and creators of mimic worlds, Ovid still stands supreme. His criticism of life is very slight; it is the criticism passed by a child, playing alone and peopling the summer evening with delightful shapes, upon the stupid nurse who drags it off to bed. And that too is a criticism that deserves attention.[22]

22. "Poesis and Mimesis," *Tradition and Progress* (1922), pp. 116–17. See also E. K. Rand, *Ovid and His Influence*, 54 ff., 172.

The pure story-telling faculty, when not actually despised, is nowadays generally regarded as a half-spurious thing, within the reach of those who are not true poets. Yet the gift for narration, at its best, is rare enough to be valued more highly. How many great poetic storytellers can one count up? At any rate Ovid possessed that gift in a supreme degree. He may not appeal to the immortal in man, but he has stirred to enthusiasm such various poets as Dante, Chaucer, Shakespeare, Milton, Wordsworth. And the writers of the Renaissance accepted Ovid without damaging reservations. His limitless invention and untiring verve, his delight in the sensuous, his taste for scenery at once pleasing and conventional, his easy mastery of every rhetorical artifice, such qualities were more fully enjoyed in the sixteenth than in any other century. Further, we now hear less of Ovid the respectable professor of the theory of love, and more of Ovid the guide to not quite respectable practice. The tolerant but scarcely Bohemian Roman gentleman is on his way to becoming the patron saint of neo-pagans.

Such a brief outline of a general tendency through a long period, or rather different periods in different countries, must of course be qualified at every point. As we have seen, and shall see, the moralized Ovid enjoyed a prolonged euthanasia. While the complete works in the original text were read by more people than in the Middle Ages, numerous translations had a still wider circulation, and Elizabethan translations were even less likely than modern ones to preserve the special character of an ancient classic. A diligent and moderately faithful translator, like Golding, often missed or blunted Ovidian points, while many versifiers freely expanded and altered the original.

In Elizabethan England opposed attitudes toward Ovid existed side by side, even within the same mind. He was a treasury of moral wisdom, and he was the archetype of the loose and immoral poet. In the course of a quite un-Ovidian anatomical catalogue, Sidney, reaching thighs, pronounces them for Ovid's song more fit.[23] Lodge found moral lessons in Ovid, but in his own *Glaucus and Scilla* he slighted that aspect of his master in favor of sensuous picture-making. Spenser, whose soul moved above Ovid's mundane level, constantly wrote in the Ovidian tradition. No literary compliment was more esteemed than the bestowal of Ovid's crown, and the names of poets who received it—Shakespeare, Daniel, Drayton, Chapman—suggest rather mixed notions of the real Ovid.[24] For Ovid was inextricably en-

23. *Arcadia*, ed. Feuillerat (1912), p. 220.
24. Of course it might be a particular rather than a general appellation. Drayton was Ovidian by virtue of his *Heroical Epistles*, Chapman on the strength of *Ovid's Banquet of Sense*.

tangled with the work of his Renaissance imitators, who often exaggerated or distorted Ovidian qualities.

Ovidian influence on the mythological poem was not that of the *Metamorphoses* alone. The *Amores* contributed erotic suggestions. The *Heroides* taught the arts of amatory rhetoric and complaint. From Ovid too came the trick of scattering moral aphorisms through immoral poems, for, as the Middle Ages well knew, Ovid was a keen observer of human behavior, and, intermittently, a sound moralist.

Then there was the poet's immense indirect influence, which reached the mythological poem through such various intermediaries as pastoral verse and prose, Greek romances, Italian discussions of love, courtly fiction, Petrarchan sonnets, painting, tapestry. Pastorals and Franco-Italian fiction we have glanced at already. Greek romances stimulated both the erotic and the pictorial impulses in mythological verse.[25] The sonneteering tradition contributed its familiar virtues and vices to the technique of mythological poems, for these, dealing with amatory themes, naturally absorbed the whole jargon, Ovidian, chivalric, Petrarchan, which composed the rhetorical pleading of very articulate lovers. The numerous parallels, for instance, between Ovid and Shakespeare's sonnets, between the sonnets and *Venus and Adonis*, are a commonplace. In general the style of mythological poems inclined to the artificial and bookish, and it is significant that two eminent practitioners in this genre were Marino and Góngora.[26]

As for painting, the brush and the pen stimulated each other. Poets of all kinds subscribed to the dogma *ut pictura poesis*. One cannot race too quickly through the Louvre or the Italian galleries to observe that Ovid rivaled, or excelled, the Bible as a storehouse of subjects. While even lean Madonnas acquired a figure, they might, in their ample robes, be less attractive than buxom Venuses clad in sunshine. And mythological poets vied with painters in rich ornamentation and warm

---

25. Here may be mentioned the half-medieval *Hypnerotomachia* (1499) of Colonna, which was translated into English in 1592. As Andrew Lang said, it "is a specimen of the Renaissance in its fever of paganism. He is a Christian monk, vowed to poverty and chastity, and nothing is dear to him but heathenism and luxury in all its forms. Beautiful naked bodies, beautiful faces, beautiful buildings, fountains, temples, triumphs of dead gods, a Venus of onyx and sardonyx, nursing a Cupid above the sepulchre of Adonis, these things and such as these are his sole delight" (Introduction to the reprint, 1890, of the English translation). See Symonds, *Italian Literature* (1909), I, 190.

26. Góngora, though he could use mythology abundantly and seriously, could also burlesque Boscán's poem on Hero and Leander. See Jellinek, *Die Sage von Hero und Leander*, p. 16.

flesh tints. The body had come into its own, although in mythological verse it often seems to be under glass.

The Renaissance conception of mythological characters was by no means wholly bookish. There were popular and alien influences which help considerably to explain unclassical qualities. In England especially, where paintings were less familiar than on the continent, tapestries were common, and the myths pictured in them are not always recognizable at first sight. Whatever the popularity of Ovid and the mythographers, they could not altogether counteract the effect of a tapestry on the wall which more often than not showed mythological figures in modern dress. Or, even if such figures were classical to the extent of having no dress at all, the pictorial details and conventions of tapestry were transferred to verse; one has only to recall the character of the pictures promised to the bewildered Christopher Sly.[27]

Thus tapestries might simply vivify a traditional myth with abundant pictorial detail, or might embellish or alter it in various unorthodox or romantic ways. Another powerful influence of a similar kind came from the living pictures of pageants and masques, which made the Elizabethan eye familiar with mythological figures placed in strange settings and combinations. Pageantry had a long native tradition behind it, and when, under the impulse of Renaissance classicism, mythological characters were introduced, they naturally took color from the older and stronger popular conventions.

French influence may account for the fact that the first mythological pageant was performed, not in England, but in Scotland.[28] At Edinburgh in 1503 the daughter of Henry VII was welcomed with a representation of the judgment of Paris. The pageant included, in addition to Paris, Mercury, and the goddesses, the salutation of Gabriel to Mary, and the four virtues, Justice, Fortitude, Temperance, Prudence, treading upon Nero, Holofernes, Epicurus, and Sardanapalus respectively—surely a comprehensive scheme.[29] Thirty years later, at the coronation of Anne Boleyn we have, among other things, Apollo and the Muses sitting on Parnassus, St. Anne, the three

27. There is no need of citing other familiar examples, especially as we shall meet them from time to time, but Sandys' remark concerning Ovid's palace of the sun may be quoted: "In this description our Poet imitates Homer in the sheild of Achilles; and is imitated by the moderne in their Screenes and Arasses" (*Ovid*, 1632, p. 65).

See F. Hard, "Spenser's 'Clothes of Arras and of Toure,'" *SP*, XXVII, 162 ff.; Joan Evans, "Chaucer and Decorative Art," *RES*, VI (1930), 408 ff.

28. Robert Withington, *English Pageantry*, I (1918), 81.

29. *Ibid.*, I, 169.

Marys, the three Graces, and Udall's elaborate pageant, "almost a play," on the judgment of Paris. The three goddesses of course were unworthy to receive the apple in the presence of their superior, Anne [30]—a courtly compliment which Peele repeated, to Anne's daughter.

Under Elizabeth, who loved shows if they did not "put her to charges," pageants and masques became more and more lavish. In the entertainments at Kenilworth old English and Arthurian characters rubbed shoulders with Arion and Proteus. The shows at Elvetham (1591) opened with an oration, "during which six virgins, representing the Graces and the Hours, removed blocks from her majesty's path, which Envy had placed there to impede Virtue's progress." [31] On the second day there were water sports. "From a bower, built at the further end of the pond, rose Nereus, Neptune, and Oceanus, Phorcus and Glaucus with a pinnace, in which three virgins played Scottish jigs with their cornets." Later Sylvanus appeared, to be "spilt into the lake by Nereus, then ducked by the hooting sea-gods."

Obviously mythological characters underwent a sea-change. They were similarly "romanticized," if the term be adequate, when they appeared in drama both courtly and popular. At Dublin in 1528 there was at Christmas a dramatic festival "wherein the taylors acted the part of Adam and Eve; the shoemakers represented the story of Crispin and Crispinianus; the vintners acted Bacchus and his story; the Carpenters that of Joseph and Mary; Vulcan, and what related to him, was acted by the Smiths; and the comedy of Ceres, the goddess of corn, by the Bakers." [32] We cannot, however, either here or elsewhere take time to do more than record a phenomenon which must be studied in scores of plays, and may fall back on a summary of some results of the mixture of classical and native traditions:

30. *Ibid.*, I, 180 ff. A contemporary account is printed in Arber, *English Garner*, II, 41 ff. For a list of dramatic treatments of the judgment of Paris, see C. R. Baskervill, *MP*, XIV, 483.

31. Withington, I, 216; on Kenilworth, I, 207. For further accounts of Kenilworth, etc., see E. Greenlaw, *SP*, XV, 105 ff., and C. R. Baskervill, *MP*, XVIII, 49 ff.

32. Sir E. K. Chambers, *The Mediaeval Stage*, II, 365. Concerning this list Baskervill remarks: "The treatment in these plays, in spite of their classical themes, was probably as free and romantic as that of Venus and Diana in court of love romance, of Venus in *The tryumpe of Love and Bewte*, 1514, or of classical figures in plays about the middle of the sixteenth century, particularly in Lyly" ("Some Evidence for Early Romantic Plays in England," *MP*, XIV, 479). Baskervill's article, especially pp. 245 ff., 478 ff., 483 ff., has much material on the mixture of classical and native tradition in drama.

. . . An argument for old traditions can be made in the case of practically every mythological play before 1600. Moreover, the particular combination of material in these plays suggests dramatic tradition. Like love allegory of the Middle Ages, they show divergences from classical story toward the conventions of mediaeval pageantry and festival play; but the presence of clowns, pages, fairies, and shepherds is suggestive of the melting pot of earlier romantic drama rather than of the somewhat more harmonious court of love poems. Some such mingling of elements must have appeared in the pastoral presented before Elizabeth by Italian actors in 1574, features of which were a scythe for Saturn, shepherds, a wild man, arrows for nymphs, and garlands, the last possibly for festival dances and games.[33]

Lyly of course combined mythological, pastoral, and romantic elements. In Marlowe's *Edward II* Gaveston, considering how to bend the pliant king as he wishes, plans Italian masques, and pages, clothed or unclothed, to represent nymphs, satyrs, Diana and Actaeon.[34] At Pentecost, says Julia to Silvia, in *The Two Gentlemen of Verona*,

> When all our pageants of delight were play'd,
> Our youth got me to play the woman's part . . .

> Madam, 'twas Ariadne passioning
> For Theseus' perjury and unjust flight;
> Which I so lively acted with my tears . . .

And that marvelous evocation of a purely romantic mood, the allusion to Dido with a willow in her hand, is so un-Virgilian that Shakespeare is thought to have had Ovid's or Chaucer's Ariadne in mind. Probably he did, but may he not also have recalled some Dido of "Pentecost"? One has only to think of *A Midsummer Night's Dream* to see how apparently heterogeneous elements could be wrought into a harmonious whole, to understand the potency of the tradition which romanticized classical figures and stories in a way that no reading of the classics could "correct."[35]

These few references must serve to indicate the highly romantic influence of tapestries, pageants, and plays upon Elizabethan concep-

33. Baskervill, pp. 483–84.
34. *Works of Marlowe*, ed. T. Brooke, p. 315. One line in this passage, "Crownets of pearle about his naked armes," is recalled in *Hero and Leander*, i.375–76.
35. In connection with the play of Pyramus and Thisbe may be mentioned a border-piece used by Tottel, a "double-timed" picture of the lovers in modern costume. See R. B. McKerrow, "Border-pieces used by English Printers before 1641," *Library*, Fourth Series, V (1924–25), 17–18.

tions of mythological figures. Writing at such a time, the authors of mythological poems could hardly sit down to their desks without being consciously or unconsciously affected by the mixture of classical, romantic, pastoral, and folk motives which, for generations of spectators in both palace and market place, had been the accepted and very acceptable rendering of classical story. In view of such facts Spenser's frequently "Gothic" treatment of myth appears more natural and intelligible, and, in general, the reading of Elizabethan mythological poems may leave one less surprised at finding alien elements than at not finding more of them.

III. THOMAS LODGE

In the evolution of the mythological poem Lodge's *Scillaes Metamorphosis* or *Glaucus and Scilla* (1589) has an importance independent of intrinsic merits.[36] Apart from his real titles to fame Lodge has long enjoyed a certain eminence as one of the chief of the light-fingered Elizabethan gentry who pillaged foreign authors to adorn their country, their mistresses, and themselves. As earlier pages have made very clear, what the mythological poem needed if it was to rise above feeble paraphrases and moralizations of Ovid was the influence of continental art and style, and above all, of course, something nearer poetic genius than an earnest desire to write or to edify. These desiderata Lodge supplied, after a fashion.

In Ovid, Lodge's main source, Scilla, while bathing in her favorite pool, is seen, loved, and pursued by Glaucus, who tells how he was changed into a sea-god, and urges his suit. But Scilla flees again, and Glaucus in anger betakes himself to Circe, begging that the nymph may, in Golding's words, be made partner of his smart. Circe's obliging offer of herself as a substitute being rejected, she mixes a "grisly jewce" which, when dropped into Scilla's pool, transforms the damsel into the traditional monster. Glaucus "wept therat," and Scilla remained to wreak her spite on passing mariners.[37]

Ovid's hundred and forty-three lines are metamorphosed by Lodge's magic into nearly eight hundred. The poet is wandering near the Isis, lamenting misfortunes which, we later infer, are those of one crossed in love. Glaucus comes out of the water, lays his head upon the knee of the poet (who had sat down under a willow), and they mingle their tears. Glaucus offers comfort in several stanzas on

36. *Works of Lodge*, ed. Gosse, Hunterian Society, Vol. I.
37. *Metam.* xiii.900 ff., xiv.1 ff.; Golding, ed. Rouse, pp. 272 ff.

mutability in nature and life.[38] A band of nymphs appear from the water and dance about the disconsolate pair. Glaucus again becomes vocal, on the subject of nature's sympathy, and we have the not wholly Ovidian situation of a Greek sea-god, lying beside an Oxford stream, with his head on the knee of Thomas Lodge, complaining of love with citations from Ariosto. Fifteen stanzas of lamentation have their effect upon Glaucus, and he faints. Urged by the sympathetic nymphs, he recovers and launches on his story.

We have now reached the point where Ovid begins. In his tale the heroine, when seen by Glaucus, merely *sine vestibus errat*. Lodge gives one of those luscious catalogues of feminine beauties which were to be extensively cultivated in the next decades; the convention was medieval, but Renaissance poets made it much warmer and more anatomical.[39] Glaucus proceeds with the story of his love and Scilla's proud disdain until he is again overcome. The nymphs raise a pretty litany to Venus, and a few lines will show, in their delicate allusiveness and sensuous rhythm, how far the Italianate style has gone beyond the jigging verses of earlier Ovidian poems:

> Borne of the Sea, thou Paphian Queene of loue,
> Mistris of sweete conspiring harmonie:
> Lady of Cipris, for whose sweete behoue
> The Seepeheards praise the youth of Thessallie:
> Daughter of Ioue and Sister to the Sonne,
> Assist poore Glaucus late by loue undone.

In answer to the prayer Venus appears with Cupid and gives another opportunity for luxuriant description. Cupid transfixes Glaucus with an arrow, and he starts up, completely cured of his infatuation. In the midst of general rejoicing Scilla approaches, and is punished with a shaft from Cupid, whereupon she "gan claspe the Sea-god in her amorous armes." Nine stanzas describe her unavailing attempts to win the love of disdainful Glaucus. With a shriek she flies out to sea, and the company prepare to follow, including the narrator, who rides with Glaucus on a dolphin. While Scilla proclaims her sorrows

38. The theme was a commonplace, but Lodge may have had in mind the passage in *Metam.* xv which was one of Spenser's sources in *Mutability*.

39. The Renaissance catalogue is based on patterns ranging from the *Song of Songs* (chapter 4) to some Anacreontics. On Boccaccio's use of it, see Symonds, *Italian Literature* (1909), I, 98 ff. Thomas Watson, one of the many English practitioners, says that he imitated Aeneas Sylvius (later Pope Pius II) and Ariosto (*Poems of Thomas Watson*, ed. Arber, p. 43).

there appear Fury, Rage, Despair, Woe, and Wan-hope, who bind
her to the rocks, and she undergoes a metamorphosis. Glaucus and
the rest repair to Neptune's bower to celebrate the happy event, and
the poet accompanies them, but sits apart to

> write this storie
> With many a sigh and heart full sad and sorie.

Finally Glaucus conveys him on the useful dolphin back to where he
was at first,

> Willing me let the world and ladies knowe
> Of Scillas pride,

and the moral is enforced

> That Nimphs must yeeld, when faithfull louers straie not.

Lodge has been justly credited with introducing into English a new
genre, the minor epic in which a classical subject is treated in a romantic manner. But if we look at the poem from the dubious vantage
point of the last chapter we may also say that Lodge was only developing a form and subject already common in Elizabethan verse, that
Glaucus and Scilla was not so much the first poem in a new genre as
one of the last in an old one. It is less a minor epic than a love-complaint, and its pedigree takes us as far back as the Theocritean idyll
of Polyphemus and Galatea.[40] Lodge of course owed more to French
and Italian writers than to the classics.[41]

The relationship between *Glaucus and Scilla* and Elizabethan lyrics
is concealed by the poem's abundant draperies, but the beginning and
end hint at a broken heart. We have observed the Elizabethans' fondness for recounting briefly the story of an Ovidian lover and then ap-
plying it to their own case. Lodge keeps his professed, one might say

40. See Lodge's lyric on this theme in *Rosalynde* (*England's Helicon*, ed.
H. Macdonald, p. 61).

41. Since *Glaucus and Scilla* is immediately followed by a short piece,
Glaucus Complaint, and since his other work shows thefts from Ronsard, Lodge
must have known Ronsard's *Complainte de Glauce a Scylle Nimphe* (*Œuvres*,
ed. Laumonier, II, 57; ed. Marty-Laveaux, II, 285). Although the French
poem is brief its general tone is like that of *Glaucus and Scilla*; in fact Lodge
seems to echo it in several places. Lodge may also have read Ronsard's *Le
Ravissement de Cephale* (Laumonier, II, 133 ff.; Marty-Laveaux, II, 329 ff.),
which treats the pursuit of a reluctant man by an amorous goddess.

professional, pangs in the background, and the mythological example is greatly elaborated, but the poem has an evident connection with the orthodox formula. Indeed it might almost be regarded as a sonnet sequence strung on a mythological thread.[42] The style also is in harmony with the amatory tradition; it is a mosaic of Petrarchan conceits.

On one side then Lodge's theme is related to the sonneteering tradition; for centuries the coy dame had been, despite her proud virginity, the mother of a vast amount of poetic invention. But courtship of a disdainful mistress who in turn pleads in vain opens up other literary vistas. It was not a mere accident that such a subject should have been chosen for the first Italianate mythological poem. Amorous and argumentative women were familiar in all kinds of fiction, from Achilles Tatius to Sidney's *Arcadia*, in Ovid's *Heroides* and *Metamorphoses*. The reversal of the rôle of wooer had been common in English, from *Robin and Makyne* to courtly ballads in *A Handful of Pleasant Delights*.[43] Though *Robin and Makyne* is remote in treatment from Lodge, it indicates the genus if not the species to which *Glaucus and Scilla* belongs. Both in subject matter and mode of handling Lodge's poem is related to the Italian pastoral. "In fact the idea of a Nemesis overtaking the disdainful nymph or shepherd is the fundamental theme of the Italian pastoral, though the tragedy is generally averted by his or her ultimate yielding." [44] Lodge's wide read-

42. The full title of the first edition was:
"Scillaes Metamorphosis: Enterlaced with the unfortunate loue of Glaucus. Whereunto is annexed the delectable discourse of the discontented Satyre: with sundrie other most absolute Poems and Sonnets.
Contayning the detestable tyrannie of Disdaine, and Comicall Triumph of Constancie: Verie fit for young Courtiers to peruse, and coy Dames to remember."
Many of the short pieces in the volume are in the same key as the moans of Glaucus.

43. In one pair of poems we have "The scoffe of a Ladie" and "An answer as pretie to the scof of his Lady"; the wooer, repulsed, scoffs in his turn, "being glad he went without her" (*Handful*, ed. Rollins, pp. 12–15). Another and fragmentary piece, one of the many imitations of Elderton's "Pangs of Love and Lovers' Fits," uses the story of Narcissus' disdain of love and his fate to show that the cold mistress may become the vain suitor (*ibid.*, pp. 29 ff., 96–97).

44. V. M. Jeffery, *MLR*, XIX (1924), 180. Miss Jeffery gives examples from Guarini, Tasso, etc. Cf. F. W. Moorman, *William Browne* (1897), p. 31; W. W. Greg, *Pastoral Poetry and Pastoral Drama, passim*; Hector Genouy, *L'élément pastoral dans la poésie narrative et le drame en Angleterre, de 1579 à 1640* (1928).

ing in continental literature precludes any doubt of his acquaintance with foreign pastorals, but for an illustration of his theme and manner it is enough to cite Peele's *Arraignment of Paris*. Parts of that work are closer to *Glaucus and Scilla* than are any of the mythological narratives so far considered.[45] Lodge's pattern in the main resulted from a combination of the stock theme and style of Italian pastoral with the stock conventions of love poetry. The marriage could not be regarded as altogether eugenic, and most of the English mythological poems which followed bore obvious marks of heredity.

The outline of *Glaucus and Scilla* will have made clear its formal defects. Indeed, of it and a number of its descendants one might use that celebrated dictum of an agonized aesthete, "The two countesses had no outlines at all, and the dowager's was a demd outline." The poem has its skeleton framework, but otherwise, to quote the author,

> Discourse was steeresman while my barke did saile,
> My ship conceit, and fancie was my bay . . .

Incongruities of costume and allusion have been partly indicated; not the least remarkable is the combination of an Ovidian metamorphosis with figures from medieval allegory.

But the poem as a whole is not medieval, except in the large sense that most of its Italianate elements have a medieval origin. If set beside Peele's *Tale of Troy*, published in the same year, *Glaucus and Scilla* shows the break with the English and medieval manner. Instead of a sketchy chronicle of many events we have eight hundred lines made out of one bare circumstance. Instead of the more or less bald narrative and plain diction of Peele and the other writers discussed in the last chapter, we find that Lodge loads every rift with ore, or at least pyrites, in the form of amatory rhetoric and description, of Italianate language both luscious and precious. If in this poem a man capable of lovely lyrics seldom rose above facile prettiness, and often sank below it, he did show the way to the stronger poets who were to follow. Except in parts of *The Shepheardes Calender* English poetry had as yet nothing so smooth and warmly pictorial as this:

> He that hath seene the sweete Arcadian boy
> Wiping the purple from his forced wound,
> His pretie teares betokening his annoy,
> His sighes, his cries, his falling on the ground,

45. *Works of Peele*, ed. Bullen, I, 46.

> The Ecchoes ringing from the rockes his fall.
> The trees with teares reporting of his thrall:
>
> And Venus starting at her loue-mates crie,
> Forcing hir birds to hast her chariot on;
> And full of griefe at last with piteous eie
> Seene where all pale with death he lay alone,
>   Whose beautie quaild, as wont the Lillies droop
>   When wastfull winter windes doo make them stoop:
>
> Her daintie hand addrest to dawe her deere,
> Her roseall lip alied to his pale cheeke,
> Her sighes, and then her lookes and heauie cheere,
> Her bitter threates, and then her passions meeke;
>   How on his senseles corpes she lay a crying,
>   As if the boy were then but new a dying.

We may as we go on in this book be surfeited with honey, whereof a
little more than a little is by much too much, but, unless the reader has
skipped most of chapter three, he should be convinced that the earlier
Elizabethan verse was in need of some refining.

CHAPTER V
Spenser

Although Spenser has no single poem that belongs to our genre—unless the *Cantos of Mutability* may be so regarded—*The Faerie Queene* is such an endless gallery of mythological and usually allegorical or symbolic paintings that a chapter, however inadequate, must be given to a subject that requires a book. Much has been written, and much remains to be written, about a poet whose capacious receptivity is equaled only by his originality and by his own influence on English poets. No estimate can be made here of his debts to particular authors, though some of these are touched upon. Spenser is a supreme exemplar of a main theme of this book, the way in which ancient, medieval, and modern elements come together; and in *The Faerie Queene* they create a world, a world which exists in some fashion even in the minds of people who have not read the poem.

While Spenser's classical mythology is inseparable from his whole mythic creation, there is much more open use of mythology than we can take account of, so that we must generally neglect the veiled use of it. Some recent interpretations of Spenserian figures and themes, while diverse (and suggestive) in their conclusions, seem to have in common a tenuous relation both to the poem and to mythological data and logic. *The Faerie Queene* is assuredly complex and subtle in its presentation of characters and religious and ethical ideas in action; yet, if we work from the equation "A = B = Anything," our understanding is doubtfully clarified. This chapter, accordingly, will stay on firm ground, whatever the loss in imaginative range.

I

Nowadays, especially in the United States, if a poet is "literary" and writes in the consciousness of a great tradition, his work, if not absolutely blasted as "derivative," is likely to be eyed askance. As Fielding would say, all the young critics of the age, the clerks, apprentices, etc., call it traditional and fall a-groaning. The important question is whether the poet is the master or the servant of tradition. Renaissance poets, good or bad, seldom desired or received a higher tribute than the epithet "learned." The association of learning and poetry was no novelty; we meet it in ancient Alexandria and Rome and in the Middle Ages. But in the Renaissance the union became especially close and self-conscious, and it was productive of both good and ill. Elizabethan critics, distressed by the "fardles" of broadsides on sale in St. Paul's churchyard, lamented the degradation of poetry, and urged, wisely enough, that poets should elevate their art through study, discipline, imitation of the ancients and the best moderns. Learning was a wall that the profane rabble of poetasters could not scale. Here, it may be repeated, we have a main reason for the wholesale "plagiarism" that confronts us everywhere in Renaissance writing. Spenser, justly hailed by his own and later ages as the much-desired regenerator of English poetry, was learned both in his rich assimilation of imaginative literature of the past and in his very deliberate following of critical precept. He was a royal borrower, and why not? He was linking English poetry with the European tradition; he was re-creating in English the themes and devices consecrated by centuries of poetic handling. If in one sense his work is a mosaic of traditional materials, in another it is greatly original; for to almost everything he appropriated he gave his own interpretation and coloring.

A no less essential part of the task which Spenser set himself is revealed in the fact that at every turn we find him working in the light of the best critical opinion of his age. From the theory and practice of pastoral to the theory and practice of the heroic poem he is aware of what Italians and Frenchmen have been doing. Yet he was not at any time merely an imitator. Though the Pléiade turned away from medieval literature, except as a source of words, Spenser in *The Shepheardes Calender* proudly announces discipleship to Chaucer. His own critical utterances are mostly lost, but we have such things as the letter to Ralegh, and anyhow his creative work affords sufficient proof of a substantial if eclectic artistic theory. The "dewe obseruing of Decorum euerye where," which E. K. praised as one of the chief virtues of the new poet, has been well emphasized by Mr. Renwick as a dominant principle in all Spenser's work.[1] In his various modes of writing, not merely in the shorter pieces but within *The Faerie Queene*, Spenser's choice and variation of style, partly suggested by the model of the moment, are governed by the principle—a not too rigorous principle—of congruity. Spenser rather than Ben Jonson is

1. W. L. Renwick, *Edmund Spenser* (1925), p. 74.

the first modern English poet in whom critical theory supports and
controls imaginative expression.

On the other hand the mention of Ben Jonson along with Spenser
indicates the distance between them, between the dim figure of the
poet of the half-medieval English Renaissance and the substantial
personality of the first thoroughgoing neoclassicist. Spenser is not of
our world, Jonson is, though Spenser's junior by only twenty years.
The mold of Jonson's thought and expression was formed mainly by
the ancients, whom he knew so familiarly, and by the Dutch Latinists
of his own day, and he owed something to the classicist strain in Sidney; the medieval tradition, however, and the modern literature of
Italy and France counted for little. And the fruits of Jonson's relatively pure classicism—the word "relatively" is emphatic—are obvious in almost all his work, from his theory and practice of comedy
to the clear-cut symmetry and diction of his lyrics. With Spenser, on
the contrary, the medieval tradition and the critical and creative literature of modern Italy and France counted for much more than the
classical, and his classicism was rather an acquisition than a mental
habit. Living in a time when the omnivorous assimilation of the earlier
Renaissance was only beginning to come under theoretical discipline,
Spenser was neither medieval nor modern. Certainly he had a unified
religious and humanistic vision and a theory of poetry, and he created
a language as well as a world. But his wide-ranging imagination absorbed or invented the most heterogeneous materials, and he seems to
treat them, if not in really contradictory ways, at least with very different degrees of both sympathetic involvement and sophistication. He
remains the nostalgic panegyrist of an imagined chivalry, the bold
satirist of ugly actuality, cosmic philosopher and pastoral primitivist,
ardent lover and half-mystical Neo-Platonist, didactic moralist and
sensuous painter, Calvinist preacher and Catholic worshiper. To ask
"Which is Edmund Spenser?" would be to misunderstand the spirit
of an age when, in life no less than in literature, a man could be all
these at once.

II

Although it is a textbook commonplace that Spenser's poetry gathers
many-colored threads from ancient, medieval, and modern worlds
into one shimmering web, scholars nowadays speak less certainly than
they once did of his familiarity with ancient literature. While his acquaintance with medieval and Renaissance writing has been extended,

his supposed classical learning has been reduced here and there. We do not speak of Spenser's Platonism as if it came from the fountainhead, for there is hardly any evidence that he knew Plato at first hand. Doubtless, like most men of his time, he read Ficino and similar authors, and slighted the Greek. At any rate the so-called Platonism which runs through so much of his work, and constantly kindles his idealistic nature, is thoroughly of the Renaissance.[2] It has been proved that the ethical scheme of *The Faerie Queene* is based directly upon Aristotle; it has also been proved that it is not based upon Aristotle. Again, for Spenser as for most men of his age, Aristotle meant not so much the body of writings that we know as the numerous strata of medieval and Renaissance commentary; and his name might be attached to pagan doctrines of morality implicit in the Christian tradition.

Or there is *The Shepheardes Calender*. A critical legend, started by E. K. and repeated with embellishments by later generations, has found Greek influence in Spenser's pastorals. But it has been conclusively shown that "direct Greek influence on the *Calender*, if it existed at all, was negligible"; that Spenser's chief models were Marot and the poets of the Pléiade, along with Chaucer and Mantuan; and that even Virgil's influence "seems to have been slight, indirect, and distorted."[3]

These are some instances of the way in which Spenser's direct debt to classical, especially Greek, literature has been shrinking. Few modern readers have brought to Spenser the classical equipment of J. W. Mackail, and Mackail has said that "even for traces of any influence on him from Homer, from the Greek lyrists, or from Attic tragedians we may search through him in vain."[4] The exceptions that can be lodged against that statement seem to be relatively few.

On the other hand, as I have remarked, Spenser's debt to medieval and Renaissance literature has been steadily illuminated and extended. Such facts are no reflection upon the genuineness of the poet's wide culture, but they do involve a shift of emphasis. The process of investi-

2. The latest and fullest study of the whole subject is Robert Ellrodt, *Neoplatonism in the Poetry of Spenser* (Geneva, 1960). Cf. M. Evans (Bibliography, V).

3. M. Y. Hughes, "Spenser and the Greek Pastoral Triad," *SP*, XX, 187; *Virgil and Spenser* (1929), p. 307.

For Spenser's classical knowledge and sources in general, see the Variorum Edition and H. G. Lotspeich (Bibliography, V), and Starnes and Talbert (*ibid.*, "General").

4. *The Springs of Helicon* (1909), p. 98.

gation, still far from complete, has not been mere barren source-hunting; it has helped to clarify our understanding of Spenser's art and thought, to root him more solidly in his own age. Closer scrutiny of dozens of Renaissance figures, along with fuller knowledge of the Middle Ages and the medieval tradition, has exploded the older conception of the Renaissance as a sudden awakening, a complete break with the medieval past. The Elizabethan author, as we have frequent occasion to observe, was, in his treatment of mythology and his general mental habit, nearer 1400 than 1700. Spenser would have been more at ease with Chaucer than with Dryden.

Though internal evidence is our only guide to the sources of Spenser's mythology in general, the glosses of the *Calender* provide a suggestive basis of concrete fact. A gloss on *March* begins: "Flora, the Goddesse of flowres, but indede (as saith Tacitus) a famous harlot . . ." But Tacitus does not say so; the information comes, probably by way of Cooper's *Thesaurus*, from the *De Genealogia Deorum* of Boccaccio, who got it from Lactantius.[5] On *July*, E. K. refers to Diodorus Siculus for the story of "the hyl Ida," but Spenser is following Mantuan, who reflects a medieval tradition based on Ezekiel.[6] An example of allegory is the note on *March* which relates the story of Achilles' heel (and assigns it to Homer!). The exposition, derived ultimately from Fulgentius, is that, since the heel is connected by veins and sinews with the genitals, "by wounding in the hele, is meant lustfull loue." It is significant, though not in the least surprising, that we find two young men, fresh from the university, accepting very mixed mythology with no more hesitation than was shown by medieval writers. They have of course a wider acquaintance with ancient literature, but they are often inaccurate, and their allusions are mainly to Latin authors. In addition to examples cited already—in addition also to many correct references—there are items attributed to Hesiod, Plato, Theocritus, Virgil, Ovid, Mantuan, that cannot be found in modern texts. All these straws indicate how the wind blows, and the impression given by Spenser's first book is not essentially altered by study of his later work.

When we move on to *The Faerie Queene* and other poems we accumulate a list of "errors" in mythology not remarkable in a voluminous Elizabethan poet, yet rather damaging to any exaggerated estimate of the solidity of Spenser's classical learning. Some of these may be ascribed, like our own, to slips of memory or "Ignorance,

5. Starnes and Talbert, pp. 44–45.
6. Lotspeich, pp. 71–72.

Madam, pure ignorance"; besides, as Gascoigne said, poetic license is a shrewd fellow and some "errors" may have been deliberate. Further, Spenser, who more than most poets instinctively saw all myth and poetry as one body of high and significant revelation, was no more troubled than Chaucer by the modern pedantry that distinguishes ancient myth (which itself underwent endless variations) and later accretion. We may be surprised to read that Hercules took the distaff in hand "for Iolas sake" instead of Omphale's, but in *Gerusalemme Liberata,* in one of the cantos Spenser drew upon for the Bower of Bliss, we find Iole and the distaff; she had appeared more than once in Boccaccio's Italian works.[7] The Elizabethans, despite their generally superior knowledge of Latin and sometimes Greek authors, were very often content, like their medieval predecessors, to gather their mythological nosegays from the nearest conservatory. What was much more important, the mythographers, as we have seen, were not merely convenient dictionaries of reference; their allegorical interpretations, their conception of myth as the root of all poetry, were of prime attractiveness and value, not least to an imagination so richly creative and strongly ethical as Spenser's. His desk evidently held well-thumbed copies of Boccaccio's *De Genealogia Deorum* and Natalis Comes.[8]

III

In approaching the question of Spenser's artistic handling of myth we may ask how far the medievalism apparent in matters of fact extends to spirit and mode of treatment, and how far he moves toward neoclassical fashions.

Ornamentation—which is not merely that—ranges from allusions, similes, periphrases, to narratives or pictures occupying a number of stanzas. Like bookish poets before and after him, Spenser used the names of classical divinities instead of the natural phenomena they represented, and such allusions in him, as in Shakespeare, were often conventional and colorless. Yet, artificial as these stereotypes are, in the better poetry of the sixteenth century they may be more or less saved by a touch of freshness, of unspoiled gusto, which we miss in later times when the flowers had gone to seed. So we may enjoy Spenser's

7. *F.Q.,* V.v.24; *G.L.,* XVI, 3.
8. See Lotspeich's introduction and individual entries.

As gentle Shepheard in sweete euen-tide,
When ruddy Phoebus gins to welke in west,

more than Gray's similar but shopworn phrasing,

In vain to me the smiling mornings shine,
And redd'ning Phoebus lifts his golden fire.

The first English heroic poet could not fail to employ the detailed simile sanctioned by poetic precedent and critical doctrine. The long and unclassical catalogue of Belphoebe's charms of person and dress ends with a pair of similes of which the first may be compared with its source in Virgil's picture of Dido:

Such as Diana by the sandie shore
Of swift Eurotas, or on Cynthus greene,
Where all the Nymphes haue her unwares forlore,
Wandreth alone with bow and arrowes keene,
To seeke her game. . . .

The mildly and vaguely sensuous adjectives, "sandie," "swift," "greene," "keene," are characteristic Spenserian additions.[9] Once at least he anticipates Milton's manner of introducing a comparison:

Not that great Champion of the antique world,
Whom famous Poetes verse so much doth vaunt,
And hath for twelue huge labours high extold,
So many furies and sharpe fits did haunt,
When him the poysoned garment did enchaunt
With Centaures bloud, and bloudie verses charm'd,
As did this knight twelue thousand dolours daunt.

This gives a vague glamorous sense of heroic and poetic tradition; it has nothing of the immediacy and force of Milton's allusion to the same incident.[10] Ancient epic similes, however, were drawn less from mythology than from nature and familiar experience, and the majority of Spenser's are of this sort. Whichever they are, his similes, compared with Milton's, lack salience, although in their context they may be functional and satisfying, and sometimes they have a uniquely Spenserian tenderness and beauty.

The decorative circumlocution we think of as an eighteenth-century

9. *F.Q.*, II.iii.31; cf. *Aen.* i.498 ff.
10. *F.Q.*, I.xi.27. The Miltonic lines (*P.L.*, ii.539–46) are quoted below on page 292.

disease, but the rash had appeared long before. Du Bellay described the art of periphrasis with a fullness of detail which suggests that he believed himself to be inaugurating a fashion new in France. It is more graceful, he says, to write "the thundering father" for Jupiter, "the virgin huntress" for Diana; instead of the prosaic "from east to west" let us have "From those who first see Aurora blush to where Thetis receives in her waves the son of Hyperion." [11] But this trick was not merely a result of the classical measles of the Renaissance; it had never been absent from the European tradition since Roman times and was a "color of rhetoric" highly esteemed in the Middle Ages. We remember how Chaucer launches a bubble of high-flown style and with a quiet wink punctures it before proceeding:

> Til that the brighte sonne loste his hewe;
> For th'orisonte hath reft the sonne his lyght,—
> This is as muche to seye as it was nyght.[12]

Renaissance critics and poets, molding classical examples into sacred law, allowed no Chaucerian instinct for simple directness to stand in the way of ornate amplitude, and in this as in other matters they went beyond their Roman models; both ancient and modern excesses were to receive attention from Scarron and Butler. This reminder of the pedigree of circumlocution concerns some of Spenser's successors rather more than Spenser himself, though he has a good many examples. One was in the last quotation above, and it has something of the Miltonic function of elevating its subject and placing it in the stream of history. An example of a different kind—nearer the medieval and Chaucerian habit of setting the time in astronomical or astrological terms—opens Spenser's second canto:

> By this the Northerne wagoner had set
> His seuenfold teme behind the stedfast starre,
> That was in Ocean waues yet neuer wet,
> But firme is fixt, and sendeth light from farre
> To all, that in the wide deepe wandring arre:
> And chearefull Chaunticlere with his note shrill
> Had warned once, that Phoebus fiery carre
> In hast was climbing up the Easterne hill,
> Full enuious that night so long his roome did fill.[13]

11. *La défense et illustration de la langue française*, ed. L. Séché (1905), pp. 152–53. Cf. Boileau, *L'art poétique*, iii.165 ff.

12. *Franklin's Tale*, *C.T.* V (F), 1016–18.

13. *F.Q.*, I.ii.1. Cf. the very different picture quoted below at the beginning of section vi, page 106.

Spenser might have said, "It was now morning," but the loss would have been great; the stanza in both substance and tone is a miniature of macrocosmic order, touched, in the middle line, by his characteristic sympathy for human distress. Most of Spenser's several dozen periphrases are statements of time—the majority occur in the first two books, where the action is more closely knit—and their mythology is warmer and more romantic than Chaucer's. Of the small change of the neoclassical treasury—"Venus' train" and the like—he has little, though he was a pioneer in using, in their literal sense, words derived from Latin.

IV

One concrete approach to Spenser's ways of handling myth is provided by his use of Homer, Virgil, and Ovid.

It is clear that he knew, or had known, some Greek, but, like many another busy man, he evidently did not keep it up. Modern scholarship has discounted the claims once made for his knowledge of Homer. We remember Achilles' heel, and when the poet burns

> To heare the warlike feates, which Homere spake
> Of bold Penthesilee,

we may conclude that his Homer has not been opened very lately. The most obviously Homeric part of *The Faerie Queene*, the voyage to the Bower of Bliss, does derive ultimately from the *Odyssey*, but, although that canto is a gulf of greediness in the matter of sources, the text of Homer was not necessarily one of them.

At any rate Spenser is quite un-Homeric in his treatment of Homeric material—as of course any poet should be, since mere imitation would be fatal. His ethical emphasis, his conception of Agamemnon and Ulysses as, in Homer's intention, "a good gouernour and a vertuous man," is Renaissance orthodoxy, but it explains the way—a far from ignoble way—in which Homer and much other classical matter are reinterpreted. Explicit moral and allegorical teaching, which turns characters and incidents into symbols, at once separates Spenser—and such a devotee of Homer as George Chapman—from the forthright objectivity, simple realism, and unobtrusive morality of Homer. So the girdle of Aphrodite, becoming the girdle of Florimell, becomes also, by way of folklore and Renaissance Platonism, a test for distinguishing true from spurious beauty. The golden chain of the

Iliad is associated with Philotime in the cave of Mammon as a symbol of avarice and ambition; thus Natalis Comes interprets it.[14] The meaning of the golden apples in the same canto is explained by Comes, who makes the apples of the Hesperides symbols of wealth, "which is given to men almost as a touchstone by which to test their souls."[15] The episode of Circe, though perhaps felt by Homer as partly didactic, becomes much more so when it provides the thematic quest and the climax of a book devoted to temperance. Thus Spenser regularly alters the spirit of what he borrows, and so far as these items are concerned he needed no more of Homer than he could find, translated and moralized, in Comes and other higher critics—not to mention the adaptations of Circe in Ariosto and Tasso, which were molded into still more usable shape.

Most sixteenth-century poets were likely to assimilate Virgil much more fully than Homer. But Virgil's or any great poet's deepest influence upon another is hardly demonstrable, and the most palpable parallels between Spenser and Virgil are not very satisfying as evidence. The influence of the *Eclogues* we have already seen to be "slight, indirect, and distorted." The *Georgics* left no or almost no trace in Spenser. He was attracted by the *Culex* and the *Ciris*, a fact which suggests the Alexandrian taste of the Renaissance rather than an instinct for the mature and true Virgil. *Virgils Gnat*, the paraphrase of the *Culex*, is of interest mainly as a biographical puzzle. Though the *Ciris* as a whole is unattractive, Virgil depicts the anxious care of the old nurse with homely pathos and dramatic truth of detail, and Spenser, in presenting Britomart and Glauce, follows so congenial a model with tender feeling.[16]

There remains the *Aeneid*. E. K., in pointing out that the new poet was treading the path of Virgil and others in beginning with pastoral, had established him as "the English Maro." The identifica-

---

14. *F.Q.*, II.vii.46–48; Comes, ii.4 (Padua, 1616, p. 72). See C. W. Lemmi, *PQ*, VIII, 277. Chapman, that great borrower from Comes, has the same interpretation in his *Hymnus in Noctem* (F. L. Schoell, *Études sur l'humanisme continental en Angleterre*, p. 35).

A. C. Hamilton (*The Structure of Allegory in The Faerie Queene*, 1961, pp. 116 ff.) sees an imitation of the *Iliad* in the first half of Guyon's story, of the *Odyssey* in the second half. One may be quite unconvinced by the parallels imposed upon the text—a kind of reinterpretation to which Mr. Hamilton is given.

15. *F.Q.*, II.vii.54 (quoted below in section vi, page 107). I have quoted part of Lemmi's translation of Comes (vii.7, p. 385).

16. *F.Q.*, III.ii. Cf. especially stanza 47 and *Ciris*, 340 ff.

tion, accepted by admirers, was confirmed when, in the opening lines of *The Faerie Queene,* Spenser echoed *Ille ego qui quondam gracili modulatus avena*—though it was the voice of Ariosto that promised to sing "of Knights and Ladies gentle deeds."

The chief Virgilian item in Spenser's first book is the Red Cross Knight's encounter with the bleeding tree, whose story of Duessa fails to warn the untried Christian soldier. While there are some Virgilian touches, the incident is closer to Ariosto's version than to the tale of Polydorus. It is also closer to Ariosto in spirit, for Ariosto, though enjoying the thing simply as another marvel, makes use of it in his most elaborate allegory, the series of episodes which show the temptations confronting the temperate man.[17] In the second book Spenser's description of the dying Amavia is partly modeled on the suicide of Dido, but Amavia is not a grand heroine, she is an intemperate and fatal excess of "spirit"; her story may be based on Ariosto, though it is given a sterner meaning.[18] In the second canto of the same book Medina entertains Guyon, and her desire to hear of his adventures corresponds to that of Dido—except that "the mean" has no heart to be captured by a guest. In the *Aeneid* the hero's story is the structural device that follows the initial plunge *in medias res;* but Guyon has no epic narrative to recount, and Spenser seems merely to have taken over a bit of technique for which he had no real use.[19] In the third canto Braggadocchio, who is compounded out of Ariosto's braggarts, and his man Trompart encounter the dazzling Belphoebe. The meeting recalls that of Aeneas, Achates, and Venus, and Trompart even echoes the words of Aeneas, but Spenser's scene is partly burlesque. Here as elsewhere Belphoebe has some kinship with the Virgilian Venus, but the description of her is based mainly on Ariosto's Alcina, with Platonic additions taken perhaps from the Clarice of Tasso's *Rinaldo*.[20] Venus does not praise the arduous life of seekers after honor; the theme was a poetic and especially a pastoral commonplace and one very welcome to Spenser.[21] Of course it fits

17. *F.Q.,* I.ii.30–32; *Aen.* iii.27 ff.; *O.F.,* vi.27. On this and other items see the Variorum commentary and M. Y. Hughes, *Virgil and Spenser.*

18. *F.Q.,* II.i.38–40. See S. J. McMurphy, *Spenser's Use of Ariosto for Allegory,* pp. 25–26.

19. Hughes, p. 331.

20. H. H. Blanchard, "Imitations from Tasso in the 'Faerie Queene,'" *SP,* XXII (1925), 205–07.

21. Greenlaw (*MLN,* XLI, 325) traced Spenser's forty-first stanza to Hesiod's *Works and Days,* 287 ff.; the parallel had been noticed by C. A. Elton in his translation of Hesiod (2nd ed., London, 1815, p. 37). Since

Belphoebe's primary role of Diana, the virgin huntress.

Chaucer, in outlining the *Aeneid* in the *Hous of Fame,* greatly slighted the epic story in order to make Dido a romantic and pathetic heroine. Spenser's outline, in the ninth canto of the third book, does not even name her, and one stanza takes Aeneas from Troy to Latium. His reason was doubtless the desire to relate the Trojan founding of Rome to the Trojan founding of Britain.[22] Such a patriotic motive was common enough, but Spenser's general lack of interest in the Trojan war is rather odd, since in his age it was the most popular of classical themes. At any rate in this summary he turns Virgil to quite un-Virgilian account (as Virgil had done with what he inherited).

Finally we may notice the parallels between the underworld of Virgil's sixth book and Spenser's partial imitations, which are no less than three. The first passage is the description of "Plutoes house."[23] When we remember Virgil's compassionate scenes—

> matres atque viri defunctaque corpora vita
> magnanimum heroum, pueri innuptaeque puellae—

we can hardly be stirred to any kind of emotion by Spenser's shades:

> The trembling ghosts with sad amazed mood,
> Chattring their yron teeth, and staring wide
> With stonie eyes; and all the hellish brood
> Of feends infernall flockt on euery side. . . .

In the whole passage he is apparently content to make over Virgilian items in the spirit of Ovid, Seneca, and Virgil's youthful *Culex.* If Spenser is showing the inadequacy of paganism by a deliberate parody of Virgil at Virgil's best, we may be left more conscious of poetic inadequacy than of the fatal defects in pagan notions of the curing of sin.[24] Much the same contrast holds between Virgil's personified ab-

Spenser was apparently acquainted with a Latin version of Hesiod (J. W. Bennett, *American Journal of Philology,* LII, 1931, pp. 176 ff.), Hesiod may be the source. Mr. Blanchard recorded parallels in Boiardo and Tasso (*PMLA,* XL, 832–34). Cf. Seneca, *Hipp.,* 483 ff.; the first scene of Tasso's *Aminta;* and *Pastor Fido* (1590), iv.6 (ed. Brognoligo, p. 147; trans. Fanshawe, ed. 1676, p. 135).

22. Hughes, p. 336.

23. *F.Q.,* I.v.32–35. The Virgilian lines quoted are *Aen.* vi. 306–07. Cf. the remarks on Sackville above, page 62.

24. A. C. Hamilton (see note 14 above), pp. 70–71: "Clearly Spenser means

stractions and those of Spenser's second account of the underworld, that of the cave of Mammon.[25] Virgil's list embodies his profound sense of the human condition; though Spenser's canto as a whole is one of his impressive achievements, his abstractions are mostly unrealized "emblems," theatrical properties. Again there are a few faint hints of Virgil, but the passage in tone and details reminds one of Theseus' account of the underworld in *Hercules Furens*.[26] Spenser's third adaptation of the Virgilian underworld is equally frigid.[27] Whether or not Spenser felt the quality of Virgilian compassion— and we can hardly think he did not feel it—perhaps a sixteenth-century sense of sin and hell made it imperative to arouse more fear than pity; but the result was not fearful.

Thus Spenser's chief imitations of Virgil are quite external. There are certain general resemblances: both poets embody their deepest thoughts about life in the material of romantic legend, and both use it to glorify their country and the ruling house. But these things belong to the Renaissance conception of the heroic poem, and Spenser's treatment of national history is very different from Virgil's. The two poets differ likewise in workmanship. With some reservations it may be said that while Virgil has the grandeur of generality Spenser is minute and circumstantial, and where Virgil is concentrated and suggestive Spenser is diffuse and transparent. As Dryden finely remarked, Virgil has the art of "expressing much in little, and often in silence"; that can sometimes be said of Spenser at his best, but, like most poets of his age, he seldom leaves anything unsaid. Of course Spenser has his own peculiar virtues which are not in Virgil.

to parody Virgil. . . . Spenser parodies the classical account precisely because it is itself a parody of the Christian statement."

For the list of mythological sinners in stanza 35, cf. Ovid, *Metam.* iv.457 ff. (and *Metam.* x.41 ff., *Ibis*, 173 ff.) ; Seneca, *Herc. Fur.*, 750 ff. (in the Elizabethan version, Tudor Translations, I, 33) ; *Culex*, 231 ff. Such lists, derived ultimately from the *Odyssey*, xi.576 ff., lost their human quality when they became mythological trappings. Cf. Thomas Watson, Sonnet lxii. The list in Lucretius (iii.978 ff.) is "moralized" with all its author's passionate sympathy for mankind.

25. *Aen.* vi.273 ff.; *F.Q.* II.vii.21–22.

26. "Strife" comes perhaps from Chaucer's "Contek, with blody knyf and sharpe manace" (*Knight's Tale*, 2003). "Payne" is akin to the *frendens Dolor* of Seneca; "Shame" also resembles Seneca's *Pudorque serus conscios vultus tegit* (*Herc. Fur.*, 692–93). In the Elizabethan version this phrase is rendered "And shame to late doth hide his face that knowes what crimes it hath" (Tudor Translations, I, 31). "Fear," in this and a later passage (*F.Q.* III.xii.12), recalls the medievalized "Dread" of Sackville's *Induction*.

27. *F.Q.*, IV.i.20 ff. See Hughes, pp. 379–80.

One large question can be asked, though hardly answered. We cannot tell how much Spenser's high seriousness owes directly to Virgil. His survey of epic heroes in the letter to Ralegh is, however, enough to show his acceptance of the didactic and allegorical conception of the *Aeneid* which had flourished in the Middle Ages and was reinforced rather than weakened by Renaissance commentators.[28] This not altogether un-Virgilian view was more of an asset than a liability; it meant a partly Christianized classicism that was earnest, alive, and fruitful, not merely literary. But it might mean also some narrowing and codifying of Virgil's large and sad uncertainties. Spenser is nearest to Virgil not when he is borrowing something, but when, contemplating the ruthless course of time and change, he feels the pagan *lacrimae rerum* and the Christian *contemptus mundi* and utters a longing cry for the changeless stability of heaven.[29]

V

Spenser would not be an Elizabethan if he had not felt the charm of Ovid's sensuous grace and brightness, the stimulus of his inexhaustible invention; but of course he is seldom purely or merely Ovidian. As in the Middle Ages, Ovid lent himself readily to a tale of courtly love. Paridell's seduction of Hellenore owes something, as the names suggest, to the letters of Paris and Helen in the *Heroides;* and Spenser's half-courtly *fabliau* ends with the transformation of Hellenore's husband into the creature "Gelosy," an incident more grimly memorable than Ovid's metamorphoses.[30] As we should expect, it was mainly the *Metamorphoses* that Spenser drew upon; the myths were infinitely adaptable to his various purposes and Ovid's pictorial habit was even more congenial to him than to a multitude of other Renaissance poets. (What attracted the young Donne was Ovid's amatory attitudes in the *Amores*.) For the very first adventure of the knight of holiness Spenser converts an Ovidian forest into a Wood of Error—and carries the not wholly instructive tree-list along with it.[31] There is no better proof of Spenser's liking for the

28. See Mr. Hughes' final chapter.

29. *F.Q.*, VII.viii.1–2. The stanzas are quoted near the end of this chapter.

30. *F.Q.*, III.ix–x. See also R. E. N. Dodge, *PMLA*, XII, 201–02; S. J. Mc-Murphy, p. 33; Hughes, *Virgil and Spenser*, pp. 333, 339.

31. *F.Q.*, I.i.7–9; *Metam.* x.86 ff. For the convention of the list of trees see below, Chap. VIII, note 17. M. Evans (see Bibliography) takes Spenser's trees as symbolizing the seductive distractions of everyday life; but some of the trees have no function at all.

Metamorphoses than his inventing myths on the Ovidian pattern, and
no better proof of his Elizabethan character than his often giving
them an allegorical application.[32] Ovidian rhetorical devices also left
their mark.

One elaborate example of the purely pictorial is the description of
Europa in *Muiopotmos:* twenty lines that start from two small bits
of Ovid seem to gather in other sources as well, Moschus, Horace,
perhaps Achilles Tatius, and become a tapestry more finely woven,
more Alexandrian and Italianate, than Ovid.[33] A shorter example of
the process is Spenser's treatment of the House of Sleep. Chaucer, following Ovid at a distance, is plain and "primitive":

> Beste, ne man, ne noght elles,
> Save ther were a fewe welles
> Came rennynge fro the clyves adoun,
> That made a dedly slepynge soun. . . .[34]

Between Chaucer and Spenser, Poliziano and Ariosto and such
"translators" as Anguillara have handled the theme, and Spenser is
neither plain nor primitive; he weaves a hypnotic spell:

> And more, to lulle him in his slumber soft,
> A trickling streame from high rocke tumbling downe
> And euer-drizling raine upon the loft,
> Mixt with a murmuring winde, much like the sowne
> Of swarming Bees, did cast him in a swowne:
> No other noyse, nor peoples troublous cryes,
> As still are wont t' annoy the walled towne,
> Might there be heard: but careless Quiet lyes,
> Wrapt in eternall silence farre from enemyes.[35]

32. E.g., *F.Q.*, I.vii.4; II.ii.7.

33. *Muiopotmos*, 277 ff.; *Metam.* ii.873–75, vi.103 ff.; Moschus, *Id.* ii;
Horace, *Odes*, I.ii.33–34 (lines quoted by both Comes and Cartari in their accounts of Venus); Achilles Tatius, tr. Gaselee (Loeb Classical Library), p. 9.
For a long quotation from this last passage, see below, Chap. VI, note 13.
Cf. Lucian, *Dialogues of the Sea-Gods*, xv (tr. Fowler, I, 105–06); *Aen.*
v.822–26.
In *F.Q.*, III.xi.30, the picture of Europa is for once slighter than Ovid's. The
line "The huge seas under her t'obay her seruaunts law" may have been suggested by Moschus but is given an Ovidian "turn."

34. *Book of the Duchesse*, 159 ff. Cf. *Hous of Fame*, i.66–80. The Ovidian
passage is *Metam.* xi.600 ff. For traditional treatments of the theme see A. S.
Cook, *MLN*, V, 9 ff.

35. *F.Q.*, I.i.41. See Poliziano, *La Giostra*, ii.22 ff. (the lines are translated
in Cook); *Orlando Furioso*, xiv.92 ff.; Anguillara, *Metamorfosi* (1575), p.
201[v].

The formal description of a series of mural paintings or tapestries had behind it a long tradition, to which Ovid contributed much. The several examples in Chaucer are familiar, and there are innumerable others in medieval literature, especially court-of-love poems and romances.[36] The Italian poets of the Renaissance gave the convention a new warmth and lusciousness. How much of Spenser's mythological painting was inspired by actual tapestries or pictures we cannot say, but his set descriptions are regularly executed in the spirit of the tapestry worker.[37] The grand example is of course the pictures showing the power of Cupid which hang in the palace of the enchanter Busyrane. Spenser starts, like many other poets, from the list of Jove's amours in Ovid, but he multiplies and greatly expands Ovid's brief allusions. For the stanza on Leda quoted below Ovid supplies only this hint: *Fecit olorinis Ledam recubare sub alis.*[38] Similarly Ovid has *Aureus ut Danaën . . . luserit,* while Spenser builds up a stanza. Spenser's picture-making is less heady and energetic, less economical, too, than Marlowe's in *Hero and Leander,* but in its softer way it is no less warmly voluptuous; of course Spenser's motives are different.

Another example of Spenser's exuberant expansion is the pageant —how his spirits rise when he has a processional in hand!—in the second of the *Cantos of Mutability.* In Ovid Phaethon's arrival at the palace of the sun gives occasion for a brief but suggestive picture of the scene:

> purpurea velatus veste sedebat
> In solio Phoebus claris lucente smaragdis.
> A dextra laevaque Dies et Mensis et Annus
> Saeculaque et positae spatiis aequalibus Horae
> Verque novum stabat cinctum florente corona,
> Stabat nuda Aestas et spicea serta gerebat,
> Stabat et Autumnus calcatis sordidus uvis
> Et glacialis Hiems canos hirsuta capillos.

Shakespeare adapts the last line in an Ovidian way:

> And on old Hiems' thin and icy crown
> An odorous chaplet of sweet summer buds. . . .[39]

---

36. F. Hard, *SP*, XXVII, 163; E. B. Fowler, *Spenser and the Courts of Love* (Menasha, 1921).
37. Hard, *loc. cit.*, 162 ff.
38. Note 44. See *F.Q.*, III.xi.32, and *Metam.* vi.109.
39. *Metam.* ii.23 ff.; *Midsummer Night's Dream*, II.i.109–10.

That is not Spenser's way. With this and a similar list in Ovid's fifteenth book in his mind he creates the sumptuous pageant of the seasons, months, and the rest. Mutability, in calling forth the pageant, is seeking to prove that all things are subject to her; but, except as the idea of change is implicit in the succession of seasons and months, the emblematic pictures do not in themselves point up the theme. Though there are numerous classical allusions, Ovid is left far behind; as for unclassical allusions, the stanza on "iolly Iune" brings in folk players, bargemen, and apparently courtiers ("that ungracious crew which faines demurest grace"). "The symbolic figures of the months are, as Ruskin showed, the traditional figures illuminated in mediaeval Books of Hours, and the reader is reminded often, in such passages as the Masque of Cupid, not only of court masques which Spenser may have seen, but of the woodcuts of the *Hypnerotomachia Poliphili* and those in the old editions of Petrarch's *Trionfi*." [40]

VI

We have met already some mixing of classical and non-classical elements, but this is so typical of the Renaissance imagination and of Spenser in particular that we may look at a wider range of examples.

One familiar but often arresting kind of fusion brings together the classical and the Biblical. Within the compass of the *Shepheardes Calender* Pan is at various times Henry VIII, the pope, and Christ (as in Marot's pastoral poems he is both God and Francis I); if the mixture casts back to Petrarch's allegorical eclogues, it also looks forward to Hippotades, Camus, and the Pilot of the Galilean lake. Of course such things are a commonplace in Renaissance art of all kinds; the comprehensive unity of all truth and beauty permits the most diverse and flexible combinations. Thus Spenser's loveliest description

40. Renwick, *Spenser*, p. 119. See *Stones of Venice* (*Works*, ed. Cook and Wedderburn), II.vii.52–53. For the resemblance between Spenser's descriptions and figures in pageants, see above, page 83, and H. R. Patch, *MLN*, XXXIII, 177; C. R. Baskervill, *SP*, XVII, 19 ff.; R. Heffner, *SP*, XXVII, 142 ff.; and, in general, R. Withington, *English Pageantry* (2 vols., Harvard University Press, 1918–20).

For Ovidian influence on *Mutability*, see W. P. Cumming, *SP*, XXVIII, 241 ff. Anguillara, in his translation of the *Metamorphoses*, expands Ovid's description of the palace of the sun, giving a stanza to each of the seasons and more to Time.

of the dawn blends classical myth and the imagery and language of
the nineteenth Psalm:

> At last the golden Orientall gate
>   Of greatest heauen gan to open faire,
>   And Phoebus fresh, as bridegrome to his mate,
>   Came dauncing forth, shaking his deawie haire:
>   And hurld his glistring beames through gloomy aire.
>   Which when the wakeful Elfe perceiu'd, streight way
>   He started up, and did him selfe prepaire,
>   In sun-bright armes, and battailous array:
> For with that Pagan proud he combat will that day.[41]

Here there is no incongruity; Hebraic and classical images are fused
in the alembic of a Renaissance imagination. And the pure natural
light of the sun dawns above the false glitter of the House of Pride
to which, forgetful of his quest, the knight of holiness has been led.
Everywhere Spenser freely mingles fictitious and historical, Hebraic
and classical. The well of life which renewed the strength of the
Red Cross Knight—that is, the sacrament of baptism—excels, as well
it may, "Silo" and Jordan, Bath, "the german Spau," Cephisus and
Hebrus. The hill from which the same Christian soldier surveys "the
new Hierusalem" is

> like that sacred hill, whose head full hie,
> Adornd with fruitfull Oliues all arownd,
> Is, as it were for endlesse memory
> Of that deare Lord, who oft thereon was fownd,
> For euer with a flowring girlond crownd:
> Or like that pleasaunt Mount, that is for ay
> Through famous Poets verse each where renownd,
> On which the thrise three learned Ladies play
> Their heauenly notes, and make full many a louely lay.[42]

---

41. *F.Q.*, I.v.2. Cf. Psalm xix.5; "In them hath he set a tabernacle for the
sun: which cometh forth as a bridegroom out of his chamber, and rejoiceth
as a giant to run his course."
    The same combination appears in another place where the decorative im-
pulse subserves the poet's deepest personal ardor and reverence (though the
necessary shift from Phoebus to Phoebe mars the astronomical logic):

> Loe where she comes along with portly pace
> Lyke Phoebe from her chamber of the East,
> Arysing forth to run her mighty race. . . .

Cf. *Comus*, 95–101.
    42. *F.Q.*, I.x.54.

This instinctive fusing of apparently alien elements is not a mere matter of random or irreverent allusion, it is central in Spenser's sensibility and artistry.

To the casual reader *The Fairie Queene* may seem a tissue of decorative episodes and quite often, without closer scrutiny, we may think that the poet has forgotten his serious purpose in the elaboration of sensuous detail. In the account of Mammon's temptations of Guyon, Spenser has in mind the familiar three tests of folklore and Satan's three temptations of Christ; this is one of the two passages Milton referred to when he called Spenser "sage and serious," "a better teacher than Scotus or Aquinas." Here if anywhere Spenser is in a soberly didactic mood, and this is the scene of the final temptation:

> The Gardin of Proserpina this hight;
>   And in the midst thereof a siluer seat,
>   With a thicke Arber goodly ouer dight,
>   In which she often usd from open heat
>   Her selfe to shroud, and pleasures to entreat.
>   Next thereunto did grow a goodly tree,
>   With braunches broad dispred and body great,
>   Clothed with leaues, that none the wood mote see
> And loaden all with fruit as thicke as it might bee.
>
> Their fruit were golden apples glistring bright,
>   That goodly was their glory to behold,
>   On earth like neuer grew, ne liuing wight
>   Like euer saw, but they from hence were sold;
>   For those, which Hercules with conquest bold
>   Got from great Atlas daughters, hence began,
>   And planted there, did bring forth fruit of gold:
>   And those with which th' Eubœan young man wan
> Swift Atalanta, when through craft he her out ran.
>
> Here also sprong that goodly golden fruit,
>   With which Acontius got his louer trew,
>   Whom he had long time sought with fruitlesse suit:
>   Here eke that famous golden Apple grew,
>   The which emongst the gods false Ate threw;
>   For which th' Idæan Ladies disagreed,
>   Till partiall Paris dempt it Venus dew,
>   And had of her, faire Helen for his meed,
> That many noble Greekes and Troians made to bleed.[43]

43. *F.Q.*, II.vii.53-55.

After these lines, laden with glamorous images of beauty, we may not remember that the knight of temperance is winning a hard victory over avarice and ambition and we may have no ear for the groans of Tantalus and Pilate. But such a reaction would miss the subtle and pervasive suggestion that these are images of specious beauty or at best of earthly love and vanity.

The *locus classicus* is of course the Bower of Bliss (Milton's other passage). The groundwork of the whole second book is the ethical psychology of Plato and Aristotle and Christian writers. The groundwork of this final episode is the story of Circe, though there is far less of Homer than of the allegorical tradition that interpreted the myth as the battle between flesh and spirit. Spenser, like Milton in *Comus*, is showing the conquest of sensual appetite by the virtuous will; but while Milton's Lady is invulnerable, Spenser's hero is not quite so. When the sirens sing

> O turne thy rudder hither-ward a while:
> Here may thy storme-bet vessell safely ride;
> This is the Port of rest from troublous toyle,
> The worlds sweet In, from paine and wearisome turmoyle,

it is no wonder that Guyon's senses are "softly tickeled," and that a little later he slackens his pace to gaze at the wanton damsels in the pool. But these are only realistic admissions of human frailty. Critics in the romantic tradition, misled by inadequate apprehension of appearances, could see Spenser letting a really voluptuous imagination have free rein. This wholly mistaken notion was happily killed by C. S. Lewis in his *Allegory of Love*. He showed with what subtlety Spenser worked cumulative variations on two main motives: the contrast between the simple purity of nature and the diseased luxuriance of artifice, and the contrast between healthy love and the insatiable lust of the eye. The interweaving of these motives makes the Bower a beautiful nursery of sterile corruption. In destroying it Guyon is no rigorous puritan; it is not the kind of place that could be "reopened under new management."

This is not to say that Spenser's senses are not richly responsive to physical beauty, but his tone varies with his purpose. In the first canto of the third book he wishes to suggest the sensuality of the Castle Joyous and gives five luscious stanzas to tapestries in which Venus, like Acrasia, gluts her eyes on Adonis; in the Gardens of Adonis, the scene of wholesome fecundity, the love of Venus and Adonis is the union of matter and form. Once in a while the distinction between good and evil may seem less clear-cut. We touched before on Spenser's expansion of Ovid in the mythological tapestries which "shew Dan Cupids powre and great effort." These pictures hang in the mansion of the evil enchanter, Busyrane, that foe of chastity; but profane love may seem to lose half its evil by losing all its grossness when it appears in tapestries depicting Europa on the bull's back, Danae in her tower, and many more.

> Then was he turnd into a snowy Swan,
> To win faire Leda to his louely trade:
> O wondrous skill, and sweet wit of the man,
> That her in daffadillies sleeping made,
> From scorching heat her daintie limbes to shade:
> Whiles the proud Bird ruffing his fethers wyde,
> And brushing his faire brest, did her inuade;
> She slept, yet twixt her eyelids closely spyde,
> How towards her he rusht, and smiled at his pryde.[44]

Never on Olympus did Jove's exploits receive such mild censure. But Spenser is not escaping from the *utile* into the *dulce;* the conception of love in such a picture is judged and placed by the tone and the context and by our recollection of Britomart or Una or the *Epithalamion.*

One very different, indeed unique, item must be mentioned, Sir Calidore's vision of the Graces. Wandering one day beyond the pastoral community, he hears "a shrill pipe" and "many feete fast thumping th' hollow ground"—Spenser's natural magic does not forbid homely realism—and then the knight, who is no example of the lust of the eye, beholds such a sight

> That euen he him selfe his eyes enuyde,
> An hundred naked maidens lilly white,
> All raunged in a ring, and dauncing in delight.[45]

This is pure, unearthly beauty; the dancing maidens are as sexless as lilies waving in the wind. In the center of the ring are the three classical Graces, and Colin Clout's Rosalind, and the symbolic relation of the Graces to Courtesy is duly expounded.

This item leads into a world or otherworld traditionally blended

44. *F.Q.,* III.xi.32.
45. *F.Q.,* VI.x.10 ff. See the Variorum commentary and Edgar Wind, *Pagan Mysteries* (Bibliography, "General").

with that of classical myth, the Celtic (if the word may be used in a broad sense). We remember the medieval *Sir Orfeo* and the *Merchant's Tale*, in which Pluto and Proserpine are the king and queen "of Fayerye." In such blending of the classical and the fairy world Spenser is pre-eminent over his contemporaries in degree, not in kind. Philomela, says Ovid, was more beautiful than *naidas et dryadas*, and Golding renders "fairies." [46] Nashe as a matter of course links the sprites of English folklore with the woodland divinities of "idolatrous former daies and the fantasticall world of Greece." [47] Reginald Scot catalogues all kinds of "bugs" ranging from centaurs to Tom Thumb, and quotes a decree of a General Council about women who profess to "ride abroad with Diana, the goddess of the Pagans, or else with Herodias." [48] But we need only think of the name of Oberon's wife, Titania, who fell in love with Bully Bottom.

Naturally, then, in *The Faerie Queene* we find Celtic motives woven into the narrative texture and into the allegory. Sometimes they proclaim their origin, sometimes they have become almost unrecognizable through combination with other material; yet always they contribute their peculiar quality of strangeness added to beauty. Spenser's second book draws more from the classics than any other, and expounds the classical virtue of temperance in terms of the classical divisions of the soul, but even here the three chief adventures involve Celtic elements. The wanton Phaedria is a lady of the lake and not merely an adaptation of Tasso's Armida (who belongs anyhow to the same romantic sisterhood). The *Odyssey* is romantic enough, but it is not such a repository of wonders, such an *omnium gatherum*, as Spenser's twelfth canto. Here we have matter from modern books of travel, from Celtic *imrama*, from Mandeville and possibly Lucian's *True History*; Ovidian and Homeric myths and an apparent recollection of Christ calming the waters; strange beasts from Gesner and from Plutarch the hoggish Grill (to whose stubborn individuality the irrational part of one's soul accords a degree of respect); the guide Reason from Ariosto, music and enticing damsels from Tasso. . . .[49]

46. *Metam.* vi.452–53; Golding, ed. Rouse, p. 130, line 579. In translating the *Culex* Spenser gives "many Fairies" for *naidum coetu*. See M. W. Latham, *The Elizabethan Fairies* (Columbia University Press, 1930).

47. *Works*, ed. McKerrow, I, 347.

48. *The Discovery of Witchcraft* (ed. 1665), bk. vii, c. 15, p. 85; bk. iii, c. 16, p. 36 (on Herodias, cf. Chambers, *The Mediaeval Stage*, I, 109). Scot expatiates on the text that "the gods of the Gentiles are Devils."

49. For the influence of Comes' interpretations see Lemmi, *PQ*, VIII, 270 ff.; Lotspeich, pp. 21, etc. For some of the other items mentioned, see Lois

Or, if we think of the Cave of Mammon mainly in terms of Spenser's *chiaroscuro* effects, or of the ethical psychology of Aristotle and Plato, we may remind ourselves of other elements:

The old man who guards a fairy hill is a stock character; sometimes he is a *leprechaun*, who guards a treasure that he tries to hide when he is caught by a mortal; sometimes he is a fairy king. Again, the idea that to touch any object in the Underworld will necessitate remaining in the power of the fairy owner is not only a part of the Proserpina myth, but of Celtic folk tradition generally. The very nature of Guyon's temptation: the offer of riches, love, fame, is in the story of Murrough. Guyon's sight of souls suffering the tortures of hell, which seems to owe something to Dante, is analogous to the legends about magic islands converted into places of eternal punishment. But the most significant detail is that of the apples. Since Warton's time the relation between Spenser's account of the Garden of Proserpina and Claudian's *De Raptu Proserpinae* has been recognized. In this we have the famous golden bough. But while Warton sees in the silver stool "a new circumstance of temptation," he does not explain it. In Celtic tradition resting beneath an apple tree subjected one to danger from fays. Lancelot, for example, is sleeping under an apple tree when he is seized by fays and carried into captivity. Ogier comes to an orchard, eats an apple, and is soon in the power of Morgain. Avalon is "apple land." [50]

Spenser's Celtic lore may not have embraced all these items but he must have known some.

In the "Gardens of Adonis," and on a larger scale in the *Cantos of Mutability,* Spenser employs classical myth in a way that is more symbolic than allegorical, though it springs from the allegorical or "parabolic" habit of mind. The earlier passage, the sixth canto of the third book, begins with the miraculous conception of Belphoebe and Amoret. Then we have Venus searching for Cupid, a theme that Renaissance poets loved to play with. [51] Venus encounters Diana, who is in that extreme dishabille so common among Spenserian ladies.

Whitney, *MP*, XIX, 143 ff.; E. Greenlaw, *SP*, XV, 105 ff.; S. J. McMurphy, p. 28; Ariosto, *O.F.*, x.43 ff.; R. M. Durling (Bibliography, chap. V).

50. E. Greenlaw, *SP*, XV, 111. Stanzas describing the Garden of Proserpina are quoted earlier in this section.

51. Spenser's handling of the theme again illustrates his taste. He had probably read Moschus at some time (see E. K.'s gloss on *March*), but he follows rather the embroidering of Moschus in the prologue of Tasso's *Aminta* (J. D. Bruce, *MLN*, XXVII, 183–85). For imitations of the idyll of Moschus in ancient and modern poetry see James Hutton, *American Journal of Philology*, XLIX (1928), 105–36, and J. G. Fucilla, *ibid.*, L (1929), 190–93, and *Classical Philology*, XXVI (1931), 135–52.

During the hunt for Cupid the two infants, Belphoebe and Amoret, are found, and one is taken by each goddess, to be reared according to their respective standards.

Then comes the "scientific" part of the canto, the description of the Gardens of Adonis where Venus dwells. "A thousand thousand naked babes" are in this garden; some are clothed in flesh and sent to live in the world; after a time they return to be "planted" in the garden, and, in forgetfulness of their mortal life, they grow again during "some thousand yeares." These souls grow in the same way as animals and plants, under the care of nature and the porter, "Old Genius." In the wide womb of the world there lies

> An huge eternal Chaos, which supplyes
> The substances of natures fruitfull progenyes.

> All things from thence doe their first being fetch,
> And borrow matter, whereof they are made,
> Which when as forme and feature it does ketch,
> Becomes a bodie, and doth then inuade
> The state of life, out of the griesly shade.
> That substance is eterne, and bideth so,
> Ne when the life decayes, and forme does fade,
> Doth it consume, and into nothing go,
> But chaunged is, and often altred to and fro.

> The substance is not chaunged, nor altered,
> But th' only forme and outward fashion . . .

Even here Spenser has Ovid in mind, though it is Ovid versifying Platonic ideas.[52]

52. *Metam.* xv.252–60. See J. W. Bennett, "Spenser's Garden of Adonis," *PMLA*, XLVII, 66–67. The canto is a repository of such a complex mass of traditional ideas concerning otherworld paradises, chaos, creation, mutability, etc., that a glance at Mrs. Bennett's learned discussion will explain why my few paragraphs can merely indicate the general nature of Spenser's mythological-metaphysical symbolism. Greenlaw's argument for Lucretian influence has been discredited, by Mrs. Bennett and others.

Since Du Bartas was a favorite of Spenser's, we might notice a passage in Sylvester which illustrates the prevalence of some ideas regarding form and matter (ed. Grosart, I, 28, lines 164 ff.) :

> Yet think not that this Too-too-Much remises
> Ought into nought: it but the Form disguises
> In hundred fashions, and the Substances
> Inly, or outly, neither win nor leese.

Cf. *ibid.*, lines 219 ff.:

> Here's nothing constant: nothing still doth stay;

Of this continual renewing of life the great enemy is Time, who mows down "the flowring herbes and goodly things"; but for Time the garden would be a cloudless paradise. Yet even Time cannot destroy a covert on a hill where Venus lives eternally with Adonis,

> for he may not
> For euer die, and euer buried bee
> In balefull night, where all things are forgot;
> All be he subiect to mortalitie,
> Yet is eterne in mutabilitie,
> And by succession made perpetuall,
> Transformed oft, and chaunged diuerslie:
> For him the Father of all formes they call;
> Therefore needs mote he liue, that liuing giues to all.

> There now he liueth in eternall blis,
> Ioying his goddesse, and of her enioyd:
> Ne feareth he henceforth that foe of his,
> Which with his cruell tuske him deadly cloyd:
> For that wilde Bore, the which him once annoyd,
> She firmely hath emprisoned for ay,
> That her sweet loue his malice mote auoyd . . .

Thus Spenser sets forth the idea of permanence underlying eternal flux. The theme is presented first in the concrete manner of a Platonic myth, then generalized in abstract terms, and finally embodied in the myth of Venus and Adonis. The myth which, in connection with the Castle Joyous, had been erotic here becomes metaphysical: Venus is matter, Adonis is form, and their perpetual love represents the perpetuity of life.[53] In this canto Spenser does not seem to be greatly troubled—apart from the activities of Time—since he has found at least an imaginative reconciliation between the fact of change and the desire for stability; and, though as a whole the myth

---

> For, Birth and Death have still successive sway.
> Here one thing springs not till another die:
> Onely the Matter lives immortally . . .
> Change-lesse in Essence; changeable in face. . . .

53. For one illustration of Spenser's symbolism one might quote Pico della Mirandola: "Venus is said to be born of the Sea; Matter the Inform Nature, whereof every Creature is compounded, is represented by Water, continually flowing, easily receptible of any form" (*A Platonick Discourse upon Love*, tr. Thomas Stanley, II.xiii, *Poems*, 1651; *Poems and Translations of Thomas Stanley*, ed. G. M. Crump (Clarendon Press, 1962), p. 211. Cf. Leo Hebraeus, *Dialoghi d'Amore*, ed. Caramella, pp. 131–32.

is given in naturalistic terms, there is a reminder (stanza 34) that the great process has divine sanction.

For a still more elaborate and a more deeply troubled answer to the question of change and permanence we must turn to the *Cantos of Mutability,* which were first published in 1609 and were evidently Spenser's last composition.

A writer in the Elizabethan age had more than ordinary reason for being drawn to such a theme. During the century religion and politics had frequently changed their complexion over night, with a loss of benefices and heads. The block on Tower Hill was the very altar of Mutability. And if mutability in life and fortune was at once theatrical and commonplace—the Elizabethans never wearied of moralizing on both aspects—the inner life also, for thoughtful men, was becoming less stable and secure. From wicked Italy a dozen varieties of skepticism or atheism had been spreading over Europe. The reading of Lucretius, Cicero, Lucian, helped to revive and fortify medieval heresies. For the dominant philosophy of the Middle Ages God's world had been intelligible; the later sixteenth century was beginning to see the outlines of a problem which, in the seventeenth, was to be crystallized by the new science, namely, the problem of knowledge. While mathematical concepts of the universe lay beyond Spenser's horizon, it was plain to him and others of his time that orthodoxy in religion and ethics was being challenged, not by isolated rebels, but by strong groups of Renaissance thinkers, with compromising support from Renaissance pagans. The current of atheism—a rather crude and compendious term—was more or less subterranean in England, but its presence may be inferred from the frequent denunciations of it, and from the feeling aroused against such scapegoats as Marlowe and Ralegh.

One treatment of atheism and its usual companion, naturalistic ethics, is of special interest in relation to *Mutability.* Sidney's revised *Arcadia* was, like *The Faerie Queene,* by Elizabethan standards a "heroic poem," and into it the ideal knight, courtier, poet, statesman, Christian, put his most serious thoughts on such subjects as government, ethics, and religion. Thus the wicked queen Cecropia urges the maiden Pamela to enjoy the flower of her youth, since youth is made for love. When Pamela cites the injunctions of religion, Cecropia replies that religious restraints are foolish bogies in a world governed by chance. Pamela, whose motives are more exalted than those of her namesake, is stirred to a passionate affirmation of belief in the divine ordering of the world and a passionate denial of the contrary doctrine.[54] Spenser's *Mutability* is concerned with the divine government of the world, and one might predict that, nourished in the same tradition as Sidney, Spenser would make substantially the same answer; though the downright Pamela-Sidney does not, like Spenser, feel the inward pangs of a divided response. But we had better look at the poem.

Spenser's presentation of the idea of eternal flux seems to be based mainly on the fifteenth book of the *Metamorphoses*. His fable, a largely original offshoot of the story of war between gods and Titans, apparently combines suggestions from Ovid and Natalis Comes.[55] We are told that the Titaness Mutability, having brought all earth under her control, conceives the ambition to rule heaven as well. She mounts up to the circle of the moon, and her attempt to thrust Cynthia from her throne leads to Jove's calling a celestial council. While the gods confer, Mutability appears among them. We may note two characteristically Spenserian details, testimonies—one homely, one exalted in style—to his unfailing sense of the power of beauty: beholding even their enemy's face, the gods "Stood all astonied, like a sort of Steeres," and Jove's hand is stayed, "Such sway doth beauty euen in Heauen beare." Challenging Jove's right to rule, Mutability appeals to Nature, and Jove reluctantly grants that the case shall be heard before Nature, on the top of Arlo hill.

Now, with an apology for abating the sternness of his style, Spenser digresses in order to weave myth about the names of Arlo hill and "my old father Mole." Since we have not taken time to consider Spenser's original myths—apart from *Mutability* itself—we may notice this one. In old times in Ireland Cynthia and her nymphs used to delight in Arlo and its streams, where they bathed. The rustic god Faunus, desiring to "see her naked mongst her Nymphes," persuaded one of them, Molanna, to enable him to gratify his wish, and promised in return that he would make Molanna beloved of Fanchin. Faunus gazes to his satisfaction,

54. *Arcadia*, ed. A. Feuillerat (1912), pp. 402–10; E. Greenlaw, "Sidney's *Arcadia* as an Example of Elizabethan Allegory," *Kittredge Anniversary Papers*, 1913; "The Captivity Episode in Sidney's *Arcadia*," *Manly Anniversary Studies*, 1923; L. Whitney, "Concerning Nature in *The Countesse of Pembrokes Arcadia*," *SP*, XXIV, 207 ff.; R. B. Levinson, "The 'Godlesse Minde' in Sidney's *Arcadia*," *MP*, XXIX (1931), 21–26.

55. W. P. Cumming, *SP*, XXVIII, 241 ff.; Comes, ii.1, vi.20 (ed. 1616, pp. 38, 53, 341); Lotspeich, pp. 85, 111, etc.

> But breaking forth in laughter, loud profest
> His foolish thought.

The goddess and her attendants find him, and, dressing him in a deerskin, pursue him with their hounds. Molanna they stone, but, through Faunus' aid, her stream is united with that of Fanchin. Diana "thence-forth abandond her delicious brooke." The story of course starts from the myth of Actaeon, to which Spenser alludes, and at the end recalls the union of Alpheus and Arethusa; it reminds one also in part of Marlowe's episode of Mercury and the country maid. Spenser's invented or adapted myths usually have an allegorical purpose, but it is hard to find one here, and the tone of the digression is certainly out of key with the prevailing seriousness of *Mutability*. But Spenser's code of poetic decorum, though active, is not ours, and such apparent incongruities are everywhere in *The Faerie Queene*; witness the difference between the search of Venus for Cupid and the account of perpetual creation and destructive Time in the "Gardens of Adonis."

Returning to his "greater Muse" in the seventh canto, Spenser tells of the assembly at Arlo hill; the setting is in the tradition of the medieval courts of love. Mutability pleads that all things are under her control. Vegetation flourishes and dies. Men slay animals, and themselves experience change in age and fortune and mind. The elements are perpetually changing. Then the Titaness calls forth as witnesses the seasons, months, and the rest of the figures which make up one of Spenser's finest pageants. When these have gone by the plaintiff urges that all are subject to her, and that Time preys upon all. Jove replies that he controls Time. Mutability declares that the gods— Cynthia, who is a byword for changeableness, Mercury, Jove himself —are subject to change and motion. Nature, after reflection, gives her verdict:

> I well consider all that ye haue sayd,
>   And find that all things stedfastnes doe hate
>   And changed be: yet being rightly wayd
>   They are not changed from their first estate;
>   But by their change their being doe dilate:
>   And turning to themselues at length againe,
>   Doe worke their owne perfection so by fate:
>   Then ouer them Change doth not rule and raigne;
> But they raigne ouer change, and doe their states maintaine.

Cease therefore daughter further to aspire,
    And thee content thus to be rul'd by me:
    For thy decay thou seekst by thy desire;
    But time shall come that all shall changed bee,
    And from thenceforth, none no more change shall see.
So was the Titaness put downe and whist,
    And Ioue confirm'd in his imperiall see.
Then was that whole assembly quite dismist,
And Natur's selfe did vanish, whither no man wist.

For his answer to the question of the one and the many, the question whether unity lies behind the eternal flux, Spenser, in the true
vein of Renaissance reconcilers, seeks a compromise. That compromise
is half "scientific," half Christian. All things work out the law of
their being, not in the naturalistic sense but under divine control; and
then will come eternity when all shall be changed for the last time.
Yet the doctrine of evolution under Providence, however traditional,
does not seem to have wholly quieted Spenser's distress, however devout a Christian he was. After Nature's orthodox verdict comes a
personal reaction, in two stanzas that are the voice of an infant cry-
ing in the night:

When I bethinke me on that speech whyleare,
    Of Mutability, and well it way:
    Me seemes, that though she all unworthy were
    Of the Heav'ns Rule; yet very sooth to say,
    In all things else she beares the greatest sway.
Which makes me loath this state of life so tickle,
    And loue of things so vaine to cast away;
    Whose flowring pride, so fading and so fickle,
Short Time shall soon cut down with his consuming sickle.

Then gin I thinke on that which Nature sayd,
    Of that same time when no more Change shall be,
    But stedfast rest of all things firmely stayd
    Upon the pillours of Eternity,
    That is contrayr to Mutabilitie:
For, all that moueth, doth in Change delight:
    But thence-forth all shall rest eternally
    With Him that is the God of Sabbaoth hight:
O that great Sabbaoth God, graunt me that Sabaoths sight.[56]

56. F.Q., VII.viii.1–2.

Keats, writing in an era of Revolutionary optimism, made the defeat of the Titans by the gods a symbol of progress (though his main theme was more personal and less cheering); but in the late sixteenth century the theory of progress was only coming to birth. From a world of medieval fixities Spenser contemplates the spectacle of ceaseless change and he cannot suppress the instinctive and age-old feeling of *contemptus mundi*. For all the differences in substance and manner, there is a general parallel between *Mutability* and Donne's *Anniversaries*. Though Spenser has not lost his awareness of beauty, he longs for release from the fallen world.

A partly similar dichotomy appears elsewhere in Spenser, for example, in the *Fowre Hymnes*. Although the Renaissance religion of beauty achieved its culmination in mystical union with the divine essence, most adherents lingered on the lower rungs of the Platonic ladder, satisfying their sense of poetry with mystical rhapsodies and their other senses with mundane mistresses. Scholars have disagreed on whether Spenser's two later hymns are a continuation or a repudiation of the first two. In the first two, following Castiglione in part, Spenser touched two or three of the orthodox stages in the Platonic ascent from the love of woman to absolute love and beauty. But those two could never lead on to Spenser's third hymn with its devout account of Christ and the redemption of man, which belongs to a different order of vision and experience. Spenser was neither a mystic nor a pseudomystic but an evangelical Christian with a Platonic ethical strain. So in the eighth canto of the second book of *The Faerie Queene* there is a point beyond which the moral reason cannot go, and Guyon is protected, when the palmer is helpless, first by an angel and then by Arthur, the instrument of God's providence.[57] And in *Mutability*, as we have seen, the metaphysical doctrine of permanence behind the flux is inadequate reassurance, and Spenser turns away from earth to the hope of heaven.

It is at such moments, surely, that Spenser's inmost self is stirred. The mood may be more intelligible if we remember Chaucer's recoil not merely from the passions he had so subtly delineated in *Troilus* but from all earthly love. Or there is Sidney's "Leave me, O love which reachest but to dust. . . ." It does not mean that Chaucer and Sidney and Spenser can permanently renounce the joys of earth, can deny for good the rights of half their nature, but that, in mo-

57. On this and many related questions, see A. S. P. Woodhouse, "Nature and Grace in the *Faerie Queene*," *ELH*, XVI (1949), 194–228.

ments of profound revulsion, all things seem dross except God. Such moments of course are rare; these poets' names suggest delight in all that the world can give. But we are in no doubt concerning the orthodox normality of Chaucer's religious faith and that of Sidney and Spenser was more active and intense. Yet only in a Renaissance poet, and only in Spenser among English poets, could we have a poem about the government of the universe based on a classical myth, in the setting of a medieval court of love in Ireland, including the mishaps of a mythological Peeping Tom, and ending with a heartfelt prayer to "that great Sabbaoth God."

It would be hard to find in *The Faerie Queene* two consecutive cantos that give a wider and finer display of Spenser's particular gifts. Few readers are likely to dissent from Courthope's judgment that *Mutability* is "both in conception and execution, the most sublime part" of the poem. It is, to be sure, the Elizabethan, not the Miltonic, sublime. When sources range from Ovid to Alanus de Insulis, and mood and style from the celestial to the earthy, when the poet pauses in his search for unity to paint gorgeous pictures of diversity, the total effect is almost kaleidoscopic.

One can hardly summarize a chapter that is itself a partial summary. Of Spenser's general cultural debt to the classics it is really impossible to say much, for such things do not always yield the "evidence" beloved of scholars. At the same time it is clear that a study of classical influences much fuller than this sketch includes would not make a rounded and just estimate of Spenser and his place in poetry. Spenser without the classics would be different, but his main outlines would be little changed; Spenser without medieval and modern literature would be inconceivable. To borrow a paragraph from Courthope:

Spenser's genius is inspired almost exclusively by the Middle Ages. The chivalrous matter of his poems is mediæval: so is his allegorical spirit: so is his quasi-archaic diction. Enthusiastic admirer of the classics as he is, all that he really draws from them is a frequent allusion to the tales of Greek mythology, and a certain concinnity in the metrical combination of words and phrases, which he imitates from the style of the Latin poets. The structure of his composition is in every sense of the word "romantic." [58]

58. *History of English Poetry*, III, 134. The romantic quality of Spenser was admirably treated in an essay by E. E. Stoll in his *Poets and Playwrights* (1930). For a brief but suggestive note on medievalism in Spenser's treatment of myth, see Mr. Osgood's *Boccaccio on Poetry*, p. xxxix.

There are very few passages in Spenser's work of which one can say, "Here he is writing like a classical ancient." Classical influence on him is much more indirect than direct. In the main it reaches him as already transmogrified, romanticized, by medieval, Italian, and French writers. Such classical "impurity" is of course the note of his age.

Spenser's treatment of myth, then, is largely colored by the medievalism apparent in his fable, in his narrative and descriptive technique, in his own thought and feeling, and by the theory and practice of continental literature of the sixteenth century. Myths are retold with Italian sensuousness, and allegorized with medieval seriousness. Spenser's romantic-didactic conception of poetry led him, as it led others, to borrow material from some ancients, to alter its form and spirit for his own purposes. "He shows no suspicion of Malherbe's rule, that if you borrow from the classics you must adhere rigidly to the traditional story or characteristics; that a dead mythology admits of no development; that to add new stories or new features only emphasizes the decorative, fantastic character of your material." [59] Nor did his borrowings from the classics teach him, any more than they taught most of his fellows, the lessons of form, selection, precision, restraint. It is needless to add that if he had learned those lessons he could not have written *The Faerie Queene.*

59. Sir H. J. C. Grierson, *The Background of English Literature* (London, 1925), p. 17. See Ferdinand Brunot, *La doctrine de Malherbe* (Paris, 1891), pp. 168–70.

CHAPTER VI

Marlowe: *Hero and Leander*

All the best qualities of the Italianate Ovidian tradition are embodied, and transcended, in *Hero and Leander*. It is equally true that the poem exhibits in high relief all the vices of the tradition. Yet it remains for us the most beautiful short narrative poem of its age, and for Marlowe's contemporaries and followers the causes of our partial dissatisfaction did not exist. It was immensely admired before and after its formal publication, and was enthusiastically quoted and plagiarized for two generations.[1] In the heyday of the mythological poem men recognized that Marlowe had done superbly what many were trying to do, and that by imitating him—whose faults were more easily matched than his virtues—they might excel themselves.

Hero and Leander was entered in 1593, but apparently not published until 1598. The date of composition is not absolutely certain. It has been generally assumed that the poem was Marlowe's last work, and that its completion was prevented by his sudden death. Blount's dedication seems to say as much, but inferences from that strange document are doubtful.[2] While research has complicated problems to such a degree that even guesses are hazardous, the notion of a date earlier than 1593 does not seem untenable.[3] Marlowe's treatments of classical matter, the *Ovid, Dido* (most of it, at any rate), the lost version of Colluthus ascribed to him, are assigned to his bookish days at Cambridge (not wholly bookish, as we know

---

1. Allusions of the period 1593–98 are mentioned below. Later allusions which occur in the material treated in this book are listed in the index. See Tucker Brooke, "The Reputation of Christopher Marlowe," *Transactions of the Connecticut Academy of Arts and Sciences*, XXV (1922), 347–408; my note on the influence of *Hero and Leander, MLN*, XLII, 211; and the notes in L. C. Martin's valuable edition of Marlowe's poems (1931).

2. See Boas, *Marlowe and His Circle* (1929), pp. 130–32.

3. See L. Chabalier, *Héro et Léandre* (1911). Mr. Martin (pp. 3–4) states the problem without attempting to decide; decision is of course impossible.

now), or a shortly subsequent period.[4] Might not his enthusiasm for
Musaeus belong to the same time?

Internal evidence is conflicting and dubious. Parts of the poem
show Marlowe's mastery of image and phrase at their impetuous best;
other parts show an indifference to form and a fondness for puerile
conceits which, in any age but the Elizabethan, would suggest the
yeasty and uncontrolled imagination of youth. The translation of
Ovid's *Amores*, which has its warm and felicitous lines, is accepted
as an early work, yet its erotic tone is reflected in *Hero and Leander*,
even to the extent of numerous verbal correspondences. On the other
hand Marlowe has a way of echoing himself.[5]

Moreover, a classical poem was, and continued to be, an early
rather than a late episode in an Elizabethan dramatic career. And, in
comparison with Marlowe's best plays, *Hero and Leander*, for all its
wealth of sensuous beauty, is spiritually poor, "a pretty piece of
paganism," if the rather priggish phrase be allowed. Could it be the
last and crowning work of a man who had entered into the agonized
soul of Faustus? It is almost as if Shakespeare, after writing *King
Lear*, had turned to *Venus and Adonis*—however inferior that poem
is to Marlowe's. Yet literary history does record such disconcerting
things, and in the Elizabethan age glorification of the senses was no
mere phase of adolescence. Again, *Hero and Leander* seems a kind
of inevitable fragment. What we have seems no prelude to catastrophe, Hero and Leander are not star-crossed lovers; the poem in
its total effect is an almost unclouded celebration of youthful passion
and fullness of physical life. These various facts and speculations prove
nothing one way or the other, but in the absence of positive testimony
it seems possible to query the accepted date.

The numerous allusions to the poem, or imitations of it, between
1593 and 1598 show the influence it exerted even while circulating in
manuscript; no allusion earlier than 1593 has been found.[6] We must

4. In his edition of Marlowe (1910) Brooke regarded the *Lucan* as an
early effort, but in his later edition of *Dido* (page 51) he links it and *Hero
and Leander* as productions of the poet's last months. His reasons, as he kindly
informed me, are, in brief, the apparent maturity of style and the fact that
the *Lucan*, a fragment also, was entered in September, 1593, along with *Hero
and Leander*.

5. For instance, Brooke remarks of *Dido* that parallels "are found most
copiously in *Tamburlaine* and the translation of Ovid's Elegies, but some of
the most striking link this play with such late works as *Edward II* and *Hero
and Leander*" (*Dido*, p. 117).

6. A microscope reveals a few slight resemblances in phrasing between the

assume that Shakespeare had early knowledge of it, since both *Venus and Adonis* (1593) and *Lucrece* (1594) contain many obvious parallels. Traces of the poem appeared in Drayton's *Peirs Gaveston* (1593) and *Heroical Epistles* (1597), while his *Endimion and Phœbe* (1595) revealed its large debt in both style and details. In his *Cephalus and Procris* and *Narcissus* (1595) [7] Thomas Edwards not only made a direct acknowledgment to Marlowe but borrowed from his poem in dozens of passages. Dunstan Gale's *Pyramus and Thisbe,* the dedication of which is dated 1596, imitated Marlowe's description of Hero.[8] "About 1596 Richard Carew in a letter on the 'Excellencie of the English tongue' linked Shakespeare's poem [*Venus and Adonis*] with Marlowe's 'fragment,' and credited them jointly with the literary merit of Catullus." [9] The fifty-fourth sonnet of Bartholomew Griffin's *Fidessa* (1596) has two clear references.[10] Thus the fragment was uncommonly well known among the literary before it was published.

Marlowe chose a theme that had long been popular. Musaeus enjoyed a special fame among writers of the sixteenth century because he was regarded as the earliest of Greek poets, a contemporary of Orpheus. In addition to the immediate appeal of a tragic story of romantic love, the somewhat unclassical quality of the Greek poem commended itself to Renaissance taste. There were many modern versions of Musaeus, ranging from translation to free redaction, such as those of Bernardo Tasso, Baldi, Marot, Boscán. A multitude of readers knew the story through the letters in the *Heroides*. In England there were countless allusions to the tale, but no English translation of Musaeus except one that Abraham Fleming said he had published.[11] In 1592 Abraham Fraunce remarked that "Leander and Heroes loue is in euery mans mouth," and proceeded to draw, as

poem and Daniel's *Complaint of Rosamond* (1592), but they may be quite accidental. Anyhow such things would prove nothing as to priority.

7. Entered on October 22, 1593 (*Stat. Reg.*, ed. Arber, II, 639). Edwards is noticed in the Appendix, under 1595.

8. See the Appendix, under 1596.

9. Lee, *Life of Shakespeare* (New York, 1929), p. 142, note; G. G. Smith, *Elizabethan Critical Essays*, II, 293.

10. Lee, *Elizabethan Sonnets*, II, 292. In addition to the above items, Nashe's *Jack Wilton* (1594) possibly borrowed the description of Hero's extraordinary buskins: see *H. and L.*, i.31 ff.; *Works of Nashe*, ed. McKerrow, II, 283–84. (Cf. Sidney's *Arcadia*, ed. Feuillerat, 1912, p. 92; Browne, *Brit. Past.*, Bk. ii, Song 3, ll. 504 ff.; Drayton's *Minor Poems*, ed. C. Brett, p. 175, ll. 249 ff.) See the "stolne remnants" from Marlowe in Matthew's poem in *Every Man in his Humour* (Herford and Simpson, *Ben Jonson*, III, 249, 365).

11. See the Appendix, under 1577.

Fulgentius had done a thousand years before, the allegorical lesson that the extinguishing of Hero's torch means the decay of lust, and "Leander tossed with the colde storme of old age, is at last drowned." [12] This is not quite Marlowe's reading of the tale.

A few parallels that have been observed between Marlowe and Tasso, Marot, and Boscán, are weak and negligible. He depended mainly of course upon Musaeus (probably in a Greek-Latin edition), but the original contains about three hundred and forty lines, the English fragment over eight hundred. Marlowe omits a number of things, such as the business of the torch, and adds a great many—the long descriptions of Hero, Leander, the temple; the episode of Mercury, the country maid, and Cupid; the first meeting of the lovers in the tower; the account of Leander's behavior in Abydos, and his swim. Everything drawn from Musaeus is much expanded, especially the enamorment and the ensuing dialogue, and the union of the lovers.

When one turns from Musaeus to Marlowe one is conscious of a not always agreeable sophistication of the story. A main reason, Ovidian influence, will be noticed later. A possible minor one might be found in the half-prurient tone that characterizes Greek romances and a good many Renaissance pastorals. Leander's ignorance of the rites of love reminds one of the idyllic innocence of Daphnis.[13] Some lines in the description of Leander's swim might have been inspired by Greek romances, such as that of Achilles Tatius, but perhaps there is no need of going so far afield for an element in Greek civilization which the Italian Renaissance had made its own. The general influence of these romances upon the sensuous and pictorial elements in Renaissance literature has already been observed, and their pictures of physical and artistic beauty sometimes suggest Marlowe's opulent brush.[14]

12. *Third part of the Countesse of Pembrokes Ivychurch*, p. 46. Fraunce, by the way, quotes from Boscán's version.

13. *Daphnis and Chloe* was translated by Angel Day in 1587, from the French of Amyot. See the reprint by Joseph Jacobs (London, 1890), pp. 33–34, 135. Day, however, following Amyot's example, omits the somewhat protracted business of Daphnis' erotic curiosity.

14. A couple of specimens may be quoted:
"Hir lockes dispersed on hir shoulders, in colour like the burnisht yellow of the finest gold, made hir to appeare as one of the nymphs, whom Iupiter erst fauored, or Apollo with ardent flames whilom eagerly pursued." *Daphnis and Chloe*, p. 20.

"The virgin sitting upon his back, not after the maner of horsmen, but both her legs being fitly laid downe on his right side, with her left hand held

Much that is remote in spirit from Musaeus may be traced to the *Amores* of Ovid, which Marlowe had translated without any loss of warmth. In addition to the development of Ovidian suggestions, something over two dozen lines are more or less made up of verbal reminiscences.[15] Most of these are found in the speeches of Leander; others, drawn from Ovid's most candid accounts of amorous afternoons, contribute to the final picture of Hero "all naked to his sight displayd." There is no need of emphasizing the Ovidian character of Leander's wooing and its fruition, and the Greek maiden of Musaeus does not emerge unsullied from association with Corinna. Further, in contrast with Marlowe's detailed story of two meetings and a delayed climax, Musaeus has a reticent account of one. Taking the physical ardors and satisfaction for granted, the Greek poet, with the tragic issue in mind, concentrates on the pathos of a furtive union that lacks the wedding rites hallowed by tradition. His lovers are so truly in love that there is simple acceptance on both sides, yet their helplessness and their approaching fate are suggested by the darkness of the lonely tower, the absence of processional torches and nuptial hymns. Though Marlowe's treatment of young love rises far above the level of a casual encounter with Corinna, its substance and dominant tone would seem, as I have said, to make an inadequate prelude to the tragic operation of fate.

his horne . . . her breast to her privy parts was attired with a vaile of lawne, the rest of her body was covered with a purple mantle, all the other parts were to be seene, save there where her garments covered . . . her tender brests seemed to swel, throgh the midle of which went down a faire narrow way most pleasant & delightfull to the beholders: with one hand did she holde his horne, with the other his taile, but yet so that the attire of her head covered with a scarf cast over her shoulders, was held on fast against the force of the wind, which did so beat on her bosom, that every where it seemed to swell. She thus sitting on the bull, was caried like a shippe, her scarfe serving in stead of a sayle. Round about the bull Dolphins floted about, and sported at their loves in such sort, as that you would thinke, you saw their verie motions drawne." Achilles Tatius, *Clitophon and Leucippe*, trans. William Burton, 1597, ed. S. Gaselee and H. F. B. Brett-Smith (Blackwell, Oxford, 1923), p. 3; and see page xxx.

There is no need of recording here a number of miscellaneous details that Marlowe might have borrowed from various sources. (See Mr. Martin's notes and my note in *PMLA*, XLIV, 760 ff.) For Hero's second reception of Leander (ii.235 ff.) one need not seek models—Ovid and Marlowe's imagination were enough—but, if only as a confirmation of the feminine psychology, one might refer to the story of Jupiter and Danae in Caxton's *Recuyell* (ed. Sommer, I, 129). Cf. Harington's *Orlando Furioso*, first published in 1591 (ed. 1607, p. 238, st. 58–59).

15. The passages are quoted in *PMLA*, XLIV, 760 ff.

The episode of Mercury and the country maid is quite Ovidian in spirit, recalling as it does the many tales of amorous gods. In the Ovidian tradition too, though with the added glow of Renaissance painting, are the abundant mythological decorations. While Musaeus has only one epithet for the temple, Marlowe lets himself go in this purple patch:

> So faire a church as this, had Venus none,
> The wals were of discoloured Iasper stone,
> Wherein was Proteus carued, and o'rehead,
> A liuelie vine of greene sea agget spread;
> Where by one hand, light headed Bacchus hoong,
> And with the other, wine from grapes out wroong.
> Of Christall shining faire the pauement was,
> The towne of Sestos cal'd it Venus glasse.
> There might you see the gods in sundrie shapes,
> Committing headdie ryots, incest, rapes:
> For know, that underneath this radiant floure
> Was Danaes statue in a brazen tower,
> Ioue slylie stealing from his sisters bed,
> To dallie with Idalian Ganimed,
> And for his loue Europa bellowing loud,
> And tumbling with the Rainbow in a cloud:
> Blood-quaffing Mars heauing the yron net,
> Which limping Vulcan and his Cyclops set:
> Loue kindling fire, to burne such townes as Troy,
> Syluanus weeping for the louely boy
> That now is turn'd into a Cypres tree,
> Under whose shade the Wood-gods loue to bee.

Such set pieces of mythological painting are conventional, as we have seen, in medieval pictures of temples and courts of love, but Marlowe's treatment is not Chaucer's. He is making use of at least two passages in the *Metamorphoses* that Spenser also adapted—the pictures of Jove's amours woven into Arachne's web, and the description of the palace of the sun [16]—although these are only a starting point. Marlowe's vivid glow and energy outdo Ovid.[17]

16. *Metam.* vi.103 ff., ii.1 ff.

17. The Leander-Hero epistles in the *Heroides* also afforded some hints, such as the rather absurd allusion to an interchange of letters, and certain details for the long and florid account of Leander's swim. From the same source evidently comes Hero's nurse, who is barely mentioned in Musaeus (*Her.* xix.25, 45). For other similarities in detail, cf. Marlowe, ii.150 ff., and

Although we cannot survey the classical matter in Marlowe's plays, a sketch of Ovidian elements in *Hero and Leander* may permit a glance at the great speech of Faustus uttered when he has one bare hour to live. "He prays that this final hour may be but

> A year, a month, a week, a natural day,
> That Faustus may repent, and save his soul.
> *O lente, lente currite noctis equi.*

Here too his mind goes back to the past; he is quoting Ovid, the prayer of a lover in his mistress's arms that the horses of the chariot of the night may move slowly across the sky. There is a grim irony in the application of it here; it is the agonized cry of the sensualist who had claimed Helen for his paramour." [18] But time will not stand still. There comes the overwhelming vision of Christ's blood streaming in the firmament, and as his fear and torment increase Faustus calls upon mountains and hills to fall upon him and hide him from the heavy wrath of God. He is quoting again, not Ovid this time, but the Bible. While one cannot properly compare works of different scope and intention, yet there is a scale of values, and those who entertain Swinburnian sentiments toward *Hero and Leander* might, after reading *Doctor Faustus,* recognize the gulf between major and minor poetry.

The Greek poem, as Symonds said, unites classic form with the warm autumnal tint of decadence.[19] It is a miniature epic, admirably proportioned, without superfluous details. There is scarcely a jarring note; characters, setting, motives, are in harmony. The story is not told with classic bareness of style, yet, compared with Marlowe's version, it seems almost Sophoclean, and its relative simplicity and naturalness are its strength. It is highly pictorial, but the pictures have the plastic clarity of figures on a Grecian urn, figures of young lovers remembered from an antique world, at once sculptural and timeless, human and of yesterday. What one feels is the beauty and pathos of the story as a story.

Among the virtues of Renaissance writing form is not generally reckoned, and the formless unrestraint of Marlowe's poem one might

---

Her. xviii.47–48, 53; Marlowe, ii.205, and *Her.* xviii.49; *Marlowe,* ii.206, and *Her.* xviii.84.

18. Percy Simpson, "Marlowe's *Tragical History of Doctor Faustus,*" *Essays and Studies by Members of the English Association,* XIV (1929), 26.

19. *Studies of the Greek Poets* (ed. 1893), II, 346–47.

think obvious if so much critical opinion had not spoken otherwise. Swinburne set the fashion, in his eulogy of a work that "stands out alone amid all the wide and wild poetic wealth of its teeming and turbulent age, as might a small shrine of Parian sculpture amid the rank splendour of a tropic jungle." [20] Oliver Elton, comparing the fragment with Drayton's *Endimion and Phœbe*, praises "the lucid glow, as of a burning alabaster lamp of Greek design, that fills *Hero and Leander;* there alone was the secret of satisfying form, pure amid its richness." [21] Miss Ellis-Fermor, in her sympathetic and sensitive study of Marlowe, writes of "added gravity of form," of "Hellenic security and repose in the mood," and again of "Hellenic repose, security, and formal excellence." Miss Ellis-Fermor also remarks that "heavy ornament and rich irrelevant imagery conceal for a while the slenderness and the ephemeral quality of the emotions." [22] How heavy ornament and rich irrelevant imagery contribute to Hellenic formal excellence does not appear. If Musaeus reminds one of a Grecian urn, not a little of Marlowe is suggestive of Cellini's salt-cellars, and to speak of form is to speak of what is not. Ovid was a brilliant maker of pictures, as Marlowe and his fellows well knew; it was not always remembered that he was in the main a swift and straightforward story-teller. *Hero and Leander,* it might be said, is like *The Eve of St. Agnes,* narrative poetry of a kind that makes its own laws, but Marlowe lacks Keats's sustained perfection of detail, his perfect harmony of tone. He does surprise by a fine excess, yet he was an Elizabethan, and his excess is frequently cloying. Marlowe seems resolved to gather up all pictorial conventions that tradition supplied and excel all predecessors in the luxuriant handling of them. When he describes Hero's dress, including the singing buskins, he forgets that he is writing about a young woman, he is showing what rich effects an unrestrained pen can create. Musaeus, as we observed, bestows one adjective upon the temple; Marlowe gives an exuberant series of mythological pictures. A hundred lines are occupied with a somewhat incoherent tale of Mercury, Cupid, and the Destinies; its relevance is fanciful, but it furnishes occasion for more sensuousness.

In general Marlowe's crowding images are drawn from art and fancy rather than nature. The fact itself is not damaging, the meretricious character of many images is. We do not like the incessant con-

20. Introduction to Chapman's *Poems and Minor Translations* (1875), p. lix.
21. *Michael Drayton* (1905), p. 63.
22. *Christopher Marlowe* (1927), pp. 124–139.

ceits; Cupid turns Hero's tears into pearls and winds them on his arm, Neptune's mace returns to strike the hand that threw it. One exceptional and vivid little scene from nature is this:

> Far from the towne (where all is whist and still,
> Saue that the sea playing on yellow sand,
> Sends foorth a ratling murmure to the land . . .

But such lines provoke the question why, in the long account of Leander's swim, there is such a lack of feeling for the sea. Though the passage has its beautiful bits, the general impression is of Leander gliding over waves of mythological tapestry. The human values of the story suffer from the cumulative effect of artifice in description and narrative. They suffer also from the excess of rhetorical speech-making. Leander's plea is so long and subtle that one forgets, because Marlowe himself does, that he is a flesh-and-blood lover; he becomes the mouthpiece for the *suasoria* of a naturalistic philosopher of love. Thus for all the picture-making we seldom really see the lovers—indeed, despite the prevailing sensuousness we are not sure that they have bodies and faces—and for all the expression of feeling we seldom really feel with them. We have to turn to Musaeus for the dignity, humanity, and pathos of the story.

Anachronisms never troubled an Elizabethan poet, and, in plays of vivid characterization, they do not trouble us. But when, along with slight and shadowy characters, we have sixteenth-century dress and manners introduced into a Greek story, the total effect is discordant. Marlowe's Greek maiden does not need to wear gloves, for neither sun nor wind would injure her hands. Her admirers, finding their love scorned, write sharp satires. She faints, and, revived by a kiss, "away she trips." Leaving the temple, she drops "her painted fanne of curled plumes," [23] "thinking to traine Leander therewithall."

> He being a nouice, knew not what she meant,
> But stayd, and after her a letter sent,
> Which ioyfull Hero answerd in such sort,

23. Cf. Peele, *Arraignment of Paris* (Bullen, I, 12):
> Fair Venus of sweet violets in blue,
> With other flowers infixed for change of hue;
> Her plumes, her pendants, bracelets, and her rings,
> Her dainty fan, and twenty other things,
> Her lusty mantle waving in the wind,
> And every part in colour and in kind.

As he had hope to scale the beauteous fort,
Wherein the liberall graces lock'd their wealth . . .

As M. Chabalier says, it is obvious that Marlowe, writing in the spirit of his time, gives to the idyll of Hero and Leander the character of an affair of gallantry between a gentleman and lady of the court.

   This external impression of artifice and unreality is heightened by the inconsistent behavior of the hero and heroine. In the lines just quoted Leander, for all his amatory lore, shows himself a novice.[24] Though a master of Ovid's *Amores* and a learned enemy of virginity, the young man, at the first meeting in the tower,

> Long dallying with Hero, nothing saw
> That might delight him more, yet he suspected
> Some amorous rites or other were neglected.

He is supposedly a strong and bold swimmer, but many of the descriptive lines have a taint of effeminacy. Hero's diverse qualities are likewise hard to reconcile. The Hero of Musaeus is really virginal, and she is overcome by nature rather than persuasion. Marlowe's Hero is at times an artless virgin, at times—as we have seen in the business of fainting and dropping a fan—a sophisticated coquette. The first enamorment (lines 158–98) is admirably simple and direct in feeling; then Leander's casuistry begins and feeling is obscured. Between passages which show Hero's newborn love, in spite of religious and maidenly scruples, achieving an innocent avowal, come these lines of hers:

> A dwarfish beldame beares me companie,
> That hops about the chamber where I lie,
> And spends the night (that might be better spent)
> In vaine discourse, and apish merriment.

The parenthetical phrase belongs to Mrs. Pinchwife rather than Hero; Marlowe has forgotten his character and cannot resist inserting a sentiment of his own. The addition of Ovidian wine to the crystal water of Musaeus is not altogether fortunate. Hero and Leander are different persons at different times, because the author wishes to run the whole gamut of erotic emotions, from reverent adoration to voluptuous abandonment—somewhat as Beaumont and Fletcher disregard

---

24. The mingled boldness and shyness of the Leander of Musaeus is natural, not exaggerated.

consistency of character in order to extract the maximum of theatrical effect from every situation.

Hero and Leander has often been linked with *Romeo and Juliet* as a story of pure and ardent love finding a pure and ardent consummation. But there are essential differences in conception and treatment. Shakespeare's lovers, like those in the Greek poem, are consistent, natural, healthy. Their love, not of course because it enjoys benefit of clergy, is deep, intense, complete. The love Marlowe represents is satisfying on its own level, but it does not go beyond a rapturous exaltation of the senses, the kind of experience from which the mature Donne generally turned away. Marlowe's preoccupation with the primary phases of love makes the emotional world of his poem infinitely smaller and poorer than that of Shakespeare's play. Nor is he conscious of any lack; there is no striving for the

> One thought, one grace, one woonder at the least,
> Which into words no vertue can digest.

In Musaeus and in *Romeo and Juliet*, moreover, the theme is treated with complete sincerity and pity, and the reader's emotions are simple, direct, homogeneous. Marlowe has no such emotional integrity. Preserving at times the sincerity and pity which the subject demands, he brings into the poem almost mocking comments. He can write thus:

> And like a planet, moouing seuerall waies,
> At one selfe instant, she poore soule assaies,
> Louing, not to loue at all, and euerie part
> Stroue to resist the motions of her hart.
> And hands so pure, so innocent, nay such,
> As might haue made heauen stoope to haue a touch,
> Did she uphold to Venus . . .

And then he can laugh at Hero's confusion and perplexity, and her latest actions, inspired by mingled eagerness and fear, are treated with half-cynical acknowledgment of the power and cruelty of Cupid:

> Loue is not ful of pittie (as men say)
> But deaffe and cruell, where he meanes to pray.[25]

25. Cf. *Pastor Fido*, iii.6, ed. Brognoligo, p. 106. The lines are thus rendered by Fanshawe (ed. 1676, p. 99):
> [Love] . . . is at first
> Weak and raw, but when 'tis nurst,
> Fierce and cruel.

The account of Leander's inexperience is partly sensuous, partly ironi-
cal. There is mirth of a sort in the tale of Mercury. Such touches of
irony or bitterness are doubtless not too serious, as Miss Ellis-Fermor
says, but they are there, and their slight yet recognizably acidulous
taste does act as "a cooling card." Of course it may be said that
Marlowe is expressing a realistically complex view of love; but even
a complex view should have its own harmony—as it does in Marvell.

If passion is for the most part inadequately represented it is never-
theless intended to be consuming; the outer world of order and
convention fades away, for each lover is the other's world. The
powers Marlowe recognizes are beauty and love. In being beautiful
and in loving Hero and Leander fulfill the law of their nature, the
one law that is supreme. They themselves are not responsible.

> It lies not in our power to loue, or hate,
> For will in us is ouer-rul'd by fate.

But though fate is thus invoked as the cause of love, the conception of
fate as foredooming lovers, which is so essential to the story, Marlowe
scarcely does more than play with. There are slight hints in the first
sestiad (which we forget in the intoxication of the second), but in
general, instead of the ever present consciousness of tragic destiny that
Shakespeare gives us, or Chaucer in *Troilus,* we have the mingled
conceits and satire of the tale of Cupid, and briefer but not less trivial
allusions to the part played by the gods.

Although the poem celebrates the union of two inexperienced lovers
the philosophy of love, expressed and implied, is in accord with the
doctrines of Renaissance naturalism. Leander pleads for chaste love,
not the plurality of loves of many fellow rebels, but he uses the stock
arguments in attacking conventional notions of virtue, honor, virginity,
as sterile and negative:

> This idoll which you terme *Virginitie,*
> Is neither essence subiect to the eie,
> No, nor to any one exterior sence,
> Nor hath it any place of residence,
> Nor is't of earth or mold celestiall,
> Or capable of any forme at all.
> Of that which hath no being doe not boast,
> Things that are not at all are neuer lost.
> Men foolishly doe call it vertuous,
> What vertue is it that is borne with us?

Much lesse can honour bee ascrib'd thereto,
Honour is purchac'd by the deedes wee do.
Beleeue me Hero, honour is not wone,
Untill some honourable deed be done.

The positive, realistic spirit of the Renaissance, which in politics is
called Machiavellian, becomes in the sphere of sexual morality an
antipathy to traditional restraints, to anything that curbs the impulses
of nature. Many Elizabethan writers give expression to it, but usually
in order to add triumphant counter-arguments.[26] It crackles, along
with other ingredients, in the pregnant pot of Donne, who, like Jean
de Meun and many successors, celebrated the Arcadian license of the
golden age when no one suffered from Christian monogamy and
monotony.

26. In Daniel's *Complaint of Rosamond* (1592) "a seeming Matrone, yet a
sinfull monster" uses the customary arguments to work upon the heroine
(*Poems,* etc., ed. A. C. Sprague, p. 47, ll. 267 ff.):
> Pleasure is felt, opinion but conceau'd,
> Honor, a thing without us, not our owne . . .

The debate is a common theme in pastorals. See the opening pages of Tasso's
Aminta, or these passages from Guarini's *Pastor Fido* (ed. Brognoligo, pp. 19,
31; trans. Fanshawe, pp. 13, 26):
> For as the Iron, of it self too rough,
> And of a harsh unmalleable stuff,
> Softned with fire, and gentler metal, strength
> From weakness gathers, and becomes at length
> Fit for the noblest use: so hearts untam'd,
> (Which their own stifness often breaks) enflam'd
> With generous Love, and with his sweets allay'd,
> Are clearer, apter for great Actions made . . .

> What's beauty (tell me) if not view'd? or view'd,
> If not pursu'd? or if pursu'd, pursu'd
> By one alone? Where Lovers frequent are,
> It is a sign the party lov'd is rare,
> Glorious and bright.

Some other examples of naturalistic arguments more or less akin to Leander's
are: Seneca, *Hippolytus,* ll. 435 ff.; Pettie's *Petite Pallace,* "Germanicus and
Agrippina"; Sidney's *Arcadia,* ed. Feuillerat (1912), pp. 402–10; Gabriel
Harvey, *Letter-Book,* ed. Scott, pp. 86–87; Warner, *Albion's England,* bk. v,
c. 24 (1589), Chalmers, IV, 565 (quoted in *PMLA,* XLIV, 762); *The
Faerie Queene,* II.vi.15, and elsewhere; Drayton, *Heroical Epistles* (see below,
page 165); S. Brandon, *The Virtuous Octavia,* 1598, Malone Society Reprints, ll. 891 ff. (Brandon seems to have some echoes of Sidney); Heywood,
Troia Britanica (1609), canto 2, st. 53–54 (see below, page 194). Of course
the theme is often touched by the sonneteers.

> Who e'r rigg'd faire ship to lie in harbors,
> And not to seeke new lands, or not to deale withall?
> Or built faire houses, set trees, and arbors,
> Only to lock up, or else to let them fall?
>> Good is not good, unlesse
>> A thousand it possesse,
>> But doth wast with greedinesse.

The youthful Donne's seriousness is mingled with wit. Not so Leander's, which echoes Ovid, but adds a note of high romantic eloquence:

> A stately builded ship, wel rig'd and tall,
> The Ocean maketh more maiesticall:
> Why vowest thou then to liue in Sestos here,
> Who on Loues seas more glorious wouldst appeare?
> Like untun'd golden strings all women are,
> Which long time lie untoucht, will harshly iarre.

This, and much more, is not the speech of a simple Greek youth to a simple maiden, but the rhetoric of an emancipated young poet of the Italian Renaissance who tramples underfoot the puritan, bourgeois standards professed by his countrymen. And the Elizabethan *enfant terrible* did not live down his *Poems and Ballads* in the elderly and suburban decorum of Putney. *Hero and Leander* is, in Swinburnian phrase, a love song of earth. The poet who dramatized his thirst for knowledge and power had also before him the vision of Helen,[27] and in *Hero and Leander* he showed the same egoism, on a smaller stage, seeking and enjoying possession of beautiful bodies and beautiful things.

With intoxicating rhythms and pictures in one's ear and eye one cannot draw up a profit-and-loss account of virtues and defects. The latter have been given rather disproportionate space partly because they are ignored or minimized in the conventional eulogies, partly because *Hero and Leander,* the best Elizabethan poem of its kind, shows so

---

27. The vision remains no less dazzling though a source has been suggested, Lucian's *Dialogues of the Dead,* xviii (trans. Fowler, I, 137):

Hermes. This skull is Helen.

Menippus. And for this a thousand ships carried warriors from every part of Greece . . .

The parallel was pointed out by F. Tupper, *MLN,* XXI, 76; and E. H. W. Meyerstein, *TLS,* March 22, 1928, p. 221.

I might add the quite irrelevant query whether the famous "pampered jades of Asia" might have been sired by Golding's "pampred Jades of Thrace" (ed. Rouse, p. 186, l. 238).

clearly the fundamental weaknesses of the whole genre. But the faults are mainly those of the age, the beauties are Marlowe's own, and they are obvious to anyone whose senses are not dead. Marlowe's energy divine makes the poem read as if it had been written at a breath. Thronging images are poured out with the prodigality that marks a master who has no need to husband a slender stock. Everything in the poem, good or bad, is tinglingly alive.

> But far aboue the loueliest Hero shin'd,
> And stole away th' inchaunted gazers mind,
> For like Sea-nimphs inueigling harmony,
> So was her beautie to the standers by.
> Nor that night-wandring pale and watrie starre
> (When yawning dragons draw her thirling carre
> From Latmus mount up to the glomie skie,
> Where crown'd with blazing light and maiestie,
> She proudly sits) more ouer-rules the flood,
> Than she the hearts of those that neere her stood.

But quotation can only suggest a quality which pervades and vivifies the whole.

Marlowe's unique magic is best appreciated if one thinks of the mythological poems which had been written during the preceding generation. Mythological allusion, moreover, had been used copiously but seldom with distinction. Marlowe, to a degree that few poets have excelled, made classical myths his own. Shelley could live in a myth, but his mythological beings were all air or water, his Pan was not rude and shaggy. Marlowe really sees Diana in the sky, and under the sea sweet singing mermaids sporting with their loves, and on the earth goat-footed satyrs and up-starting fauns. Such things are not merely bookish allusions taken out of Ovid. Further, Marlowe, like Spenser, invents myths of his own. Too often they are bad conceits, but sometimes they are not:

> Hero the faire,
> Whom young Apollo courted for her haire,
> And offred as a dower his burning throne,
> Where she should sit for men to gaze upon.

The tasteless conceits in fact are inseparable from Marlowe's peculiar gifts. His imagination inhabits a brave new world, in which it is bliss to be alive, and to be young is very heaven; his vision is not merely

fresh but extravagant. He must sing of the body electric with an un-
tamed splendor of the senses and of language. When he pillages Ovid
to describe the beauty of his lovers he combines literary sophistication
with a kind of primitive spontaneity.[28]

If the indescribable beauty of bodies and things compels the use of
mythological parallels, for indescribable emotions Marlowe resorts, a
few times, to the very opposite kind of figure, the scientific and "metaphysical." [29] One such image has been quoted already—Hero, with
conflicting emotions in her soul, is "like a planet, moouing seuerall
waies"—and it is one of the most memorable parts of the poem. However vivid the mythological pictures, they seem merely pictures when
set beside a couple of lines in which, for a moment, a metaphysical
image gives an intensity and depth of emotion that is nowhere else
approached:

> She trembling stroue, this strife of hers (like that
> Which made the world) another world begat
> Of unknowne ioy.

The last hundred lines of the poem certainly carry sensuous rapture
above the fleshliness of the *Amores*, yet, as one comes on the words
quoted, in the midst of a tissue of Ovidian motives and sensations, one
wonders what miracle Marlowe might have achieved if he had been
able to approach Musaeus directly, to create and sustain the note of
simple and genuine passion. But when one thinks of what even
Elizabethan poetry would be without *Hero and Leander*, perhaps the
fragment is miracle enough as it is.

28. To mention a detail of mythology, the drowning of Narcissus (i.74)
is unclassical, but the tradition goes back to the Middle Ages (*Histoire
littéraire de la France*, XXIX, 499). Some random references are these: Villon,
Ballade contre les mesdisans de la France; Lydgate, *Reson and Sensuallyte*
(*E.E.T.S.*, ll. 3850, 4258) ; *Handful of Pleasant Delights*, ed. Rollins, pp.
29 ff.; John Clapham's Latin *Narcissus* (1591); *Albion's England*, bk. ix,
c. 46 (Chalmers, IV, 609); Lodge, *Phillis* (1593), Sonnet xxxiv; *Phœnix
Nest*, ed. Rollins, pp. 81, 91. Lodge and one of the *Phœnix Nest* authors were
translating Ronsard (Marty-Laveaux, I, 12); see Rollins, p. 181. Shakespeare's allusions to Narcissus' drowning (*V. and A.*, l. 161; *Luc.*, l. 265)
might have been suggested by Marlowe or the general un-Ovidian tradition.

29. Miss Elizabeth Holmes called attention to the presence of metaphysical
imagery in *Hero and Leander* as well as in Elizabethan drama (*Aspects of
Elizabethan Imagery*, 1929, pp. 22 ff.).

Some later discussions of the poem are cited in the bibliography for this
chapter.

CHAPTER VII

Shakespeare: *Venus and Adonis* and *Lucrece*

Swinburne declared in his emphatic way that *Hero and Leander* was a model of what a young poet should write on such a subject, *Venus and Adonis* a model of what he should not write. Coleridge, on the other hand, in the fifteenth chapter of *Biographia Literaria* saw Shakespeare's two narratives as poems which, though immature, displayed the potential strength of his dramatic genius in his choice and detached presentation of non-personal subjects and in versification, language, and imagery. Various recent critics have found in *Venus and Adonis* highly symbolic and metaphysical patterns. Elizabethan readers saw no such matter; they ranked *Hero and Leander* and *Venus and Adonis* in the same category as spicy erotic poems. Historically, they are the twin peaks of the Ovidian tradition in England. Whether or not *Venus and Adonis* rises still higher into a cloudy Platonic heaven, this chapter will stick largely to some indisputable ways in which the poem reflected, confirmed, or modified the developing convention.

I. Venus and Adonis

Venus and Adonis was entered in April, 1593, and published shortly afterward. There is no need of considering the old theory that the poem had been written years before, since there is no evidence in favor of such a speculation and very much evidence against it. The obvious facts are that the mythological poem was beginning to be fashionable and that the young playwright, in a theatrical off-season, decided to try the new recipe.

There is no reason to think that Shakespeare borrowed from any Italian source. The citations of Sir Sidney Lee and others only help to show, what is important enough in itself, that certain motives and methods of treatment were common property among Renaissance poets. It is hardly necessary to ransack continental authors to find a source for the sunny atmosphere of *Venus and Adonis,* or for such a conceit as the boar's wanting merely to kiss the youth, which was a commonplace of sixteenth-century verse.[1] Shakespeare's appropriation, if direct, of Ronsard's lines,

> Les Muses lierent un iour
> De chaisnes de roses, Amour,[2]

does stimulate one to look further, especially in Ronsard's version of the story of Adonis. This is quite different in conception from Shakespeare's, but there is, as Sir Sidney Lee observed, a similarity in tone and temper, though perhaps no more than natural coincidence.[3]

The chief items in Shakespeare's debt to Ovidian material are set forth in every edition of the poems and may be briefly summarized.[4] From the tenth book of the *Metamorphoses* he takes the central figures and something of the general background; from the eighth book the description of the boar, which reveals verbal echoes of Golding.[5] Since the Adonis of Ovid and common tradition is not a reluctant lover, it has generally and reasonably been assumed that Shakespeare

1. The conceit had lately appeared in English in the *Sixe Idillia* of 1588 (see above, page 54). It occurs also in a French translation by Saint-Gelais (*Œuvres,* Paris, 1873, I, 127) and in Latin in *Adonis Theocriti, ex Gallico Sangelasii* (Gruter, *Delitiae C. Poetarum Gallorum,* Part II, Sec. 1, p. 470); and in Minturno's *De Adoni ab apro interempto* (Gruter, *Delitiae CC. Italorum Poetarum,* II, 924).

2. These lines had already been cited and turned into English by that indefatigable borrower, Thomas Watson (*Poems,* ed. Arber, Sonnet lxxxiii, p. 119):

> The Muses not long since intrapping Loue
> In chaines of roases linked all araye.

Shakespeare's much finer phrase, "Leading him prisoner in a red-rose chain" (l. 110), admirably suggests the tone of a mass of amatory and mythological verse of the Renaissance. For Ronsard's poem see *Œuvres,* ed. Marty-Laveaux, II, 360; and Lee, *French Renaissance in England,* p. 221.

3. *Œuvres,* IV, 26 ff. Passages illustrating the similarity are collected in my note in *PQ,* VI, 300; one is quoted below, note 8. Lee's parallels with other French poets seem quite fanciful.

4. The fullest accounts of sources and themes are in H. E. Rollins and T. W. Baldwin (see Bibliography).

5. This useful boar also contributed, apparently, to Spenser's dragon (L. Rick, *Ovids Metamorphosen,* p. 58), though Whitney Wells showed the dragon's kinship with medieval monsters (*MLN,* XLI, 1926, 143 ff.).

partly modeled his characters on the wanton and dominating Salmacis and the shy young Hermaphroditus, as these appear in Ovid's fourth book.[6] The somewhat similar story of Narcissus and Echo may also have been in the poet's mind; but more will be said of Adonis a little later. This outline gives an exaggerated notion of the actual amount of matter taken over from Ovid, for, in proportion to the length of Shakespeare's poem, it is really slight.

A few not insignificant details of probable Ovidian coloring may be added. When we read

> Look, how a bright star shooteth from the sky,
> So glides he in the night from Venus' eye,

we may be justifiably content to praise a vivid original image. But we may also remember these lines from Golding's second book:

> But Phaeton (fire yet blasing stil among his yellow haire)
> Shot headlong downe, and glid along the Region of the Ayre
> Like to [a] Starre in Winter nightes (the wether cleare and fayre),

or this,

> There glyding from the sky a starre streyght downe too ground was sent.[7]

There may be a similar mingling of common observation and bookish or pictorial reminiscence in the description of Venus running:

> And as she runs, the bushes in the way
> Some catch her by the neck, some kiss her face,
> Some twine about her thigh to make her stay . . .

There is a hint of this in Ovid's first book, in the words of Apollo to the fleeing Daphne, and more than a hint in the picture offered to Christopher Sly:

> Or Daphne roaming through a thorny wood,
> Scratching her legs that one shall swear she bleeds;

6. On the resemblances between Adonis and Hermaphroditus see Pooler's edition of the poems, pp. xxxi–xxxii.

7. Golding, ed. Rouse, p. 49, ll. 404–06; p. 294, l. 978; *V. and A.*, ll. 815–16. See above, chapter III, note 17.

> And at that sight shall sad Apollo weep,
> So workmanly the blood and tears are drawn.[8]

The most attractive passage of any length in *Venus and Adonis* is the account of the hunted hare, a very English vignette in this conventional Arcadia. Reading it we may say, with Bagehot, that we know Shakespeare had been after a hare. But recollections of Warwickshire seem to be mixed with recollections of Ovid. Poor Wat in desperation

> sometime sorteth with a herd of deer;
> Danger deviseth shifts; wit waits on fear.

Ovid, describing the pursuit of Daphne by Apollo, has an elaborate simile of a hare and hound, which ends with a typical Ovidian line, *Sic deus et virgo est, hic spe celer, illa timore.*[9] Shakespeare's phrase is an evident attempt to rival in English the antithetical brevity of the Latin.[10]

This particular example suggests the importance of Ovid as one source of a conspicuous element in the style of *Venus and Adonis,* that is, the antithetical pattern of lines and phrases. Here are some of the more obvious instances in the first fifty lines:

> Hunting he lov'd, but love he laugh'd to scorn.

> Saith that the world hath ending with thy life.

> But rather famish them amid their plenty.

> Ten kisses short as one, one long as twenty.

8. *Taming of the Shrew,* Induction, ii.59 ff. Cf. Ronsard's poem on Adonis (*Œuvres,* IV, 34):
> Furieuse d'esprit, criant à haute vois,
> Ie veux escheuellée errer parmy les bois,
> Pieds nuds, estomac nud: ie veux que ma poitrine
> Se laisse esgrafiner à toute dure espine,
> Ie veux que les chardons me deschirent la peau.
Of course the idea is in Bion.
9. *Metam.* i.539; cf. Golding (p. 34, ll. 659–60):
> So farde Apollo and the Mayde: hope made Apollo swift,
> And feare did make the Mayden fleete devising how to shift.
10. With *V. and A.,* ll. 681 ff. and 703 ff., compare Golding's lines about the hound of Cephalus (pp. 156–57, ll. 1014–17):
> And like a wilie Foxe he runnes not forth directly out,
> Nor makes a windlasse over all the champion fieldes about,
> But doubling and indenting still avoydes his enmies lips.
See also Pooler's notes on the Shakespearian lines.

He red for shame, but frosty in desire.

Backward she push'd him, as she would be thrust,
And govern'd him in strength, though not in lust.

It is hardly too much to say that the whole fabric of the poem is woven of antitheses, as if Shakespeare had fallen in love with one of Ovid's tricks and worked it to death. The central antithesis of subject, between the warm goddess and the cold youth, is reflected in line after line that breaks more or less clearly into two parts containing opposed ideas. The use of the antithetical formula is marked enough in narrative and descriptive passages; it is, as one would expect, still more persistent in the speeches. One must allow of course for the Petrarchan and euphuistic delight in logical and verbal antitheses, but eager first-hand imitation of Ovid evidently counted a good deal. When one compares *Venus and Adonis* with the work of Lodge and Spenser it is plain that, while Shakespeare exploits Italianate conventions, his taut style is different in texture from the smooth velvet of Italianate verse.[11]

To say that *Venus and Adonis* reveals hardly a trace of direct foreign influence is not of course to say that apart from Ovidian elements it is an original poem. Even in the plays Shakespeare was seldom an innovator; his way was to accept the current fashion and excel in it. His first narrative poem, naturally, is almost wholly conventional, an exhaustive collection of traditional motives and devices, though he appropriates them, and plies his nimble wit in embroidering them, with as much zest as if they were his own jerks of invention. Shakespeare breathed the same air as other men, and his scent for popular formulas was unusually keen and prophetic. The luxuriant Italianate manner had been naturalized in England, and no immediate foreign contacts were necessary. Not only was every poetical device at hand, there was also Elizabethan fiction. If in Shakespeare's poems action bears to rhetoric much the same proportion as bread to sack in Falstaff's bill, we may remember the technique of Pettie, Lyly, and Greene in their prose tales.

Shakespeare's representation of a chaste youth solicited by an amorous woman had precedents not only in Ovid but in the pastoral tradition derived partly from Ovid. The vain pursuit of a woman by a man or of a man by a woman was, as we have seen in connection with

---

11. This poem, like the plays, shows that Shakespeare was familiar with both Ovid's Latin and Golding's English. See Rollins, Baldwin, and Bullough (Bibliography, below).

Lodge, the stock situation of the Italian pastoral. The conventions had now become familiar in English, and *Venus and Adonis*, like the other mythological poems, makes use of them (though it stands somewhat apart on account of its more direct imitation of Ovidian style). There must be an obstacle somewhere in such stories of love; if Adonis were as willing as Barkis, and Venus equally laconic, what would become of the poem? As for Shakespeare's choice of the more piquant of the two standard situations, it offered some obvious advantages. Since it appears virtually certain that he had read *Hero and Leander*, he might have felt as Rossetti did about *The Raven*—that, as Poe had said all that could be said on one aspect of the theme, *The Blessed Damozel* would take the other side. Anyone who knew Leander's plea could hardly avoid the conviction that the subject must be freshened by reversal of the parts.

For the particular conception of a reluctant Adonis there were suggestions at hand also. There is a faint hint of initial coyness in the Adonis of Spenser:

> Then with what sleights and sweet allurements she
> Entyst the Boy, as well that art she knew,
> And wooed him her Paramoure to be.

Further, Spenser's picture of Venus watching Adonis bathe suggests a mild combination of the story with that of Salmacis and Hermaphroditus.[12] Less vague are two songs of Greene's quoted by all the editors, which show that the notion of a chaste Adonis was current; they appear in *Perimedes the Blacke-smithe* (1588) and *Never Too Late* (1590). Marlowe's allusions to Venus and "proud Adonis" is sufficiently different from Shakespeare's conception to suggest independent use of a non-classical variant. Thus Shakespeare had only to look about him to find hints for a cold Adonis.[13]

12. *F.Q.*, III.i.35–36.

13. Adlington's *Golden Asse* (ed. Seccombe, 1913, p. 48) has the phrase "as the proude yonge man Adonis who was torne by a Bore"; the epithet does not seem to be the common one for Adonis. There is a hint of a chaste Adonis in Servius on *Ecl.* x.18 (ed. Thilo and Hagen, III.i, pp. 121–22). It will be remembered that the Venus of Lyly's *Sapho and Phao* (1584) is decidedly aggressive.

For later combinations of Venus and Adonis with Salmacis and Hermaphroditus (*Taming of the Shrew*, Induction, ii.52–55; *Passionate Pilgrim*), it is enough to refer to some discussions in editions of Shakespeare's poems, such as those of Pooler (pp. xxx–xxxi), Carleton Brown (pp. xxi ff.), Feuillerat (pp. 185–86); and Chambers, *William Shakespeare*, I, 547–48. Chettle's poem is mentioned in the Appendix, under 1600.

Shakespeare was obviously indebted to Lodge's languidly pretty *Glaucus and Scilla,* both in the central theme and in details, such as the popular sixain stanza and the likewise popular "echo" device. Lodge's purple patch on Venus and Adonis, which was quoted above, is enough to indicate not only the degree to which Shakespeare caught the Italianate style, but the extent of his rhetorical originality and vigor. In all points, form as well as detail, Shakespeare greatly bettered his instruction.[14]

Shakespeare doubtless knew at least two treatments of Adonis in Spenser; a few lines from one passage have already been quoted. Spenser's symbolic adaptation of the myth in the sixth canto of the third book is quite remote from Shakespeare's, for Shakespeare's attitude toward his material is simply that of a Renaissance Ovid; his Venus and Adonis are symbolic only in the sense that they and everything connected with them are manifestations of physical beauty. The pictorial warmth and richness of Spenser's work in general must have affected Shakespeare, as such qualities affected most poets of the day, but *Venus and Adonis* has a distinct hardness and precision of line which is not Spenserian. Whatever Italian Shakespeare picked up, he does not, even at his most florid, write like Spenser and others to whom the soft fluidity of Italian verse was both more familiar and more congenial.[15]

---

14. Pooler, pp. xvi–xvii, gives the chief parallels between Shakespeare and Lodge.

15. Spenser's *Astrophel* was published in 1595, though probably written some years earlier. The passage on Adonis (ll. 151 ff.) is somewhat akin to Shakespeare, but still closer to Lodge and continental imitations of Bion.

Another luxuriant handling of the story appears in Fraunce's *Third part of the Countesse of Pembrokes Ivychurch* (1592). Since the book is rare I may quote some lines:

> Sometimes downe by a well with Adonis sweetly she sitteth,
> And on Adonis face in well-spring louely she looketh,
> And then Adonis lipps with her owne lipps kindely she kisseth,
> Rolling tongue, moyst mouth with her owne mouth all to be sucking,
> Mouth and tong and lipps, with Ioues drinck Nectar abounding.
> Sometimes, louely records for Adonis sake, she reciteth;
> How Læander dyde, as he swamme to the bewtiful Hero,
> How great Alcides was brought from a club to a distaffe . . .

> Sometimes unto the shade of a braunched beech she repaireth,
> Where sweete bubling brook with streames of siluer aboundeth,
> And faire-feathred birde on tree-top cherefuly chirpeth;
> There her voyce, which makes eu'n Ioue himselfe to be ioying,
> Unto the waters fall, and birds chirpe ioyfuly tuning.

Venus is here presented as the wooer. In particular one may compare the fourth and fifth lines of the quotation with *V. and A.,* ll. 541 ff., and l. 572, "Such

The influence of Marlowe the dramatist upon Shakespeare was so strong that it affected the structure, characterization, and style of some of the earlier plays. The influence of *Hero and Leander* upon *Venus and Adonis,* however, is both obvious and superficial. Some apparent resemblances are only characteristics of the mythological genre. What seem to be demonstrable borrowings, though numerous, are mainly incidental and external, and Shakespeare, for good or ill, subdues them to his own style and mode of treatment. Many passages in the Marlowesque plays one might assign to Marlowe; there are few bits of *Venus and Adonis* that could be mistaken for quotations from *Hero and Leander.*

Conceits of course everyone delighted in, but Shakespeare's, especially those of the myth-making sort, sometimes resemble Marlowe's. Mythological allusions were also common property, and Shakespeare, like his fellows, took them indifferently from Ovid and from modern sources.[16] Since Shakespeare's plays are full of mythological allusions,[17] and since these were a conventional element in the mythological poem as established by Lodge and Marlowe, it may be observed that such allusions in *Venus and Adonis* are relatively scanty and unadorned. If in this respect Shakespeare departed from the convention he was evidently following Lodge and Marlowe—and Ovid— when he scattered aphorisms and epigrams through an erotic poem. The amorous arguments of Venus recall Leander's and those of the *Sonnets,* where the theme of procreation is decidedly more pertinent than in the mouth of the undomestic goddess.[18]

The differences between Marlowe and Shakespeare are no less obvious, and more important, than the resemblances. Hero and Leander,

---

nectar from his lips she had not suck'd"—which, to be sure, is not beyond Shakespeare's unaided imagination. One may note, with the same reservation, Shakespeare's "Ten kisses short as one, one long as twenty" (l. 22), and Fraunce's

> Thinking euery howre to be two, and two to be twenty,
> Til she beheld her boy . . .

16. For instance, though Shakespeare knew Ovid so well, he was content to take over, perhaps from Marlowe, the non-Ovidian drowning of Narcissus. See above, chapter VI, note 28.

17. In addition to the older discussions of mythology in the plays there are the brief but suggestive remarks of George H. W. Rylands in his *Words and Poetry* (1928), pp. 87 ff., 135 ff. See some items in the Bibliography.

18. Parallels between *Hero and Leander* and Shakespeare are recorded in various editions, e.g., Pooler (pp. xxii ff.).

For echoes of Ovid in Shakespeare's poems (and Sonnets), see T. W. Baldwin.

despite Marlowe's inconsistencies of characterization and excess of decoration, win our sympathy; there is warmth and something of natural passion. Shakespeare, dealing with an unattractive pair who are more remote from humanity, fiddles on the strings of sensuality without feeling or awakening any such sympathy, without even being robustly sensual. Marlowe has too many merely pretty lines, but generally he is strong, masculine, swift; Shakespeare is much more content with prettiness, and the poem, though far from languid, is sicklied o'er with effeminacy. Many lines in *Hero and Leander* glow with a beauty that might be called haunting if the word were not overworn; the reader of *Venus and Adonis* is chiefly impressed by the astonishing skill of phrase and rhythm—

> Which bred more beauty in his angry eyes.

> Leading him prisoner in a red-rose chain.

> Full gently now she takes him by the hand,
> A lily prison'd in a gaol of snow.

But when one thinks of "Love's not Time's fool," not to mention the plays, one is made aware of the fatal lack of emotion. Finally it is noteworthy, in a poem which is a tissue of bookish conventions, that Shakespeare's best bits of imagery are fresh pictures of nature. Marlowe's images are almost wholly a fusion of art, literature, and imagination.

Incongruity of costume we have already observed as a normal element of mythological poems as well as other types of Renaissance writing, and Shakespeare of course does not depart from the mode. When Venus approaches Adonis and "heaveth up his hat," and at other times, we have a suspicion that we are witnessing an Arcadian encounter between a scantily clad Maid of Honor and, say, the Earl of Southampton in a rare moment of satiety.[19] Indeed if one considers the opportunities offered by Shakespeare's subject, and the popularity of voluptuous anatomical catalogues, in which even the sober Sidney and the philosophic Spenser and Chapman indulged, Shakespeare's neglect of "the nude" is somewhat remarkable. This is

19. In his first *Elizabethan Journal* (London, 1928, pp. xii, 236) Mr. G. B. Harrison gives a reproduction of a tapestry that depicts Venus and Adonis in the dress of the period, and remarks: "This, rather than the more fleshly kind of painting, was the Elizabethan conception of Venus. The connection between tapestry pictures and such narrative poems as *Venus and Adonis* and *Hero and Leander* is close." Cf. the quotation from Peele, above, chapter VI, note 23.

another respect in which Shakespeare is closer to Ovid—the Ovid of the *Metamorphoses,* that is—than to the Italianate fashion.[20]

The Shakespeare of the mature plays is greatest perhaps in his power over words; he uses language as if it were his own creation and he alone understood its infinite capacities. In the poems there are few traces of such concentration and suggestion; the words mean what they say, and this is not much. Only a few times in *Venus and Adonis* is there a slight break in the flat, two-dimensional surface, when the poet works in a natural image from his own observation, the dive-dapper, the snail, the gentle lark, the dew-bedabbled hare, and such fresh glimpses of something real, welcome as they are, heighten the total effect of artifice. In them, however, we do have a faint promise of the real Shakespeare, the poet who can see and feel and communicate what he sees and feels. On the other hand the auctioneer's description of the horse, which, since Hazlitt, has so often been put beside the passage on the hounds in the *Midsummer Night's Dream,* shows the difference between the minute, self-defeating realism of the tyro and the swift, suggestive strokes of the master. The horse embodies all the good points prescribed in Elizabethan treatises on the animal, and remains a catalogue; we see, hear, touch, and smell the hounds.

The living things described in the poem are not all creatures of the English countryside. We know that the man who wrote of the lark ascending, or of "poor Wat," had been in the fields as well as in his study. We know that the same man fully shared the taste of his age when we read this:

> To see his face the lion walk'd along
> Behind some hedge, because he would not fear him;
> To recreate himself when he hath sung,
> The tiger would be tame and gently hear him;
> If he had spoke, the wolf would leave his prey,
> And never fright the silly lamb that day.
>
> When he beheld his shadow in the brook,
> The fishes spread on it their golden gills . . .

Even if such a string of fancies be half humorous—and Venus' lamentation is not especially merry—it reminds us that Shakespeare not

---

20. There are to be sure such lines as 233 ff., which are sensual enough, but their indirectness is far from the set description. Ll. 397 ff. have been related to the poem in *The Phœnix Nest* cited above, chapter IV, note 12.

only laughed at euphuism but practiced it with some relish. The poem everywhere shows that its author lavished artistic labor upon it, in a sense put himself into it, yet perhaps nothing proves more clearly what a circumscribed self it was than the fact that the creator of this polite lion behind an English hedge was shortly to create another kind of polite lion for Snug the joiner. But every age, our own included, has its stylistic tricks which lose their charm for posterity.

The Elizabethans generally anticipated Wilde in believing that nothing succeeds like excess, and if we dislike their rhetorical extravagance it is after all no great price to pay for their unique virtues. Their exuberant excesses were the natural overflow of tremendous energy in an era of uncertain taste and an intoxicated delight in words. In the plays Shakespeare never entirely outgrew his love of rhetoric, though his critical powers ripened with his other faculties and enabled him to satirize flamboyance. In *Venus and Adonis* he seems quite satisfied and happy in seriously exploiting the popular conceits, decoration, rhetorical wooing, rhetorical declamation. In the speeches of Venus we have the arguments of an Ovidian lover combined with the strained fancies of a sonneteer, moral aphorisms, and, even from Adonis when he finds his tongue, some of the paradoxes on the nature of love so dear to Elizabethan writers,[21] all worked out with an inexhaustible ingenuity that compels a kind of admiration. The poem is indeed a bible for lovers. To quote one allusion out of many, a character in a play of 1640 longs for "the book of *Venus and Adonis* to court my mistress by."[22] And when speaking of rhetoric one must notice Venus' apostrophe to Death, which is thoroughly of the Renaissance and also thoroughly medieval.[23]

F. T. Prince, the latest editor of Shakespeare's poems, finds *Venus and Adonis* "a complete artistic success, despite some flaws or weaker passages," and sees its "imaginative unity"

in its view of elemental and human passions as a feast for the mind and the spirit: as sometimes moving, and sometimes amusing, but always offering an absorbing living spectacle. This is the indulgent mood of Shakespeare's comedies, with their delight in human energies and emotions, their keen savour of everyday life mixed with abundant poetry, and their undertones of deeper seriousness.

21. For these paradoxes see lines 649 ff., 793 ff., 1137 ff. Since almost every Elizabethan indulged in at least one such series it is needless to give references. Miss Jeffery comments on the habit (*John Lyly*, pp. 82, 123).
22. Pupillus in Lewis Sharpe's *The Nobler Stranger*.
23. Cf. the address to Death in the *Philomena* (above, page 10).

He also sees a unique fusion of "romance and humour" and "sympathetic irony" in the presentation of Venus.[24] Professor Prince, as both a poet and a scholar, is the best kind of judge, but one may be unable to go along with such a favorable view. Also, Professor Prince makes no reference to numerous critics of recent years who have reinterpreted the poem in various ways that go well beyond Coleridge. For example, Adonis represents the destruction of beauty by evil, or an incapacity to respond to the ideal of Platonic love and beauty, or a rational and ethical rejection of lust (Venus having the several corresponding roles, earthy or transcendental); and the poem as a whole is a tragic parable of the fall of man or a farcical comedy or several things between. The fact that Elizabethan readers were apparently unaware of all these themes does not of course prove that they are not there. Yet the multiplying of such contradictory interpretations may suggest, if not that the vagaries of current symbolical criticism are limitless, at least that Shakespeare's intention, whatever it was, does not come through very clearly. If *Venus and Adonis* were plainly nothing more than a two-dimensional tapestry, all would be well, in a limited way. But for a sensual orgy it is too intellectual and serious, for a metaphysical fable it is too Ovidian. We observed partly similar discords in *Hero and Leander*, but in *Venus and Adonis* they are more central. The poem seems to waver between cool rhetorical contrivance and impassioned engagement, although the author seems to feel himself in complete and assured control of his direction and tone.

II. LUCRECE

Having produced an erotic poem much to the taste of Southampton and the emancipated in general, Shakespeare paid his debt to morality and the non-emancipated by celebrating, in the following year, the most famous of all martyrs of chastity. Although *Lucrece* contains few indications of intense feeling in the author, when he comes later to conjure up the sinister specters of night no image is more vivid in his memory than that of Tarquin's ravishing stride. However, the poem seems to be quite as deliberate a literary exercise as *Venus and Adonis*, and the reversal of the theme and the graver style need not imply anything in the way of apology. Almost any Elizabethan could write a sensuous mythological poem once; he could hardly do it twice. *Lucrece* is not a sensuous mythological poem, and, if less attractive

24. *The Poems* (Arden Edition, 1960), pp. xxv–xxxii.

than its predecessor, it is in some respects much more ambitious.

As before Shakespeare greatly embellishes the original tale. Here he seems to have followed Livy in the main, with supplementary details from Ovid and others.[25] A number of details point to knowledge of Chaucer's story in the *Legend of Good Women*, such as Tarquin's definite threat to kill one of Lucrece's slaves and not merely a slave, and the carrying of her body to Rome. There are perhaps verbal reminiscences in the words "stalk" and "dishevelled." Lucrece's golden hair and the simile of the wolf and the lamb are found in Ovid, Chaucer, and Gower. In Chaucer—and Gower—Lucrece swoons, though not in the classical sources.[26] The brief reflections in Chaucer on Tarquin's violation of chivalry might have suggested a text for the long debate in Shakespeare.

In addition to elaboration of the story proper there are the Trojan scenes in the painting which the distraught Lucrece was able to study so minutely. The classical model for the episode was Aeneas' scrutiny of the pictures in Dido's temple, and the Shakespearian de-

---

25. Livy, i.57–59; Ovid, *Fasti*, ii.685 ff. For an analysis of sources see T. W. Baldwin (Bibliography).

Livy and Ovid Shakespeare evidently read in Latin, and it has commonly been said that he did not use Painter's paraphrase of Livy's story. In the poem itself I observe only one hint to the contrary; while Livy (c. 59) has *Brutus castigator lacrimarum atque inertium querellarum*, Painter's phrase is "childishe lamentacions," and Shakespeare (ll. 1825, 1829) has "such childish humour" and "lamentations." The prose argument, however, offers more evidence. Here Lucrece "dispatcheth messengers, one to Rome for her father, and another to the camp for Collatine." Ovid has only the word *evocat* (ll. 815–16), and Livy (c. 58) has *eundem nuntium*. Chaucer and Gower say nothing of two messengers. Painter writes: "Lucrece sent a post to Rome to her father, and an other to Ardea to her husbande." Bandello speaks of two messengers, but there is no reason to think that Shakespeare knew his version. (W. Marschall gives not very cogent parallels to prove that Shakespeare used Bandello; see *Anglia*, LIII, 1929, pp. 102–22.) In Shakespeare's poem there is only one messenger. There are in the argument a few other possible traces of Painter, for example, Shakespeare's "late in the night . . . amongst her maids," and Painter's "late in the night . . . amonges her maydes." While using Livy's text for the poem, Shakespeare might have turned to the convenient Painter for the argument.

26. Cf. Chaucer, ll. 1815–18; Gower, *C.A.*, vii.4986–89; Shakespeare, ll. 1261–67. Gower is commonly ruled out of the list of sources (see Pooler, p. lvi), but one slight detail may be mentioned. In Shakespeare (l. 170) Tarquin, having risen from bed, sets forth "Throwing his mantle rudely o'er his arm." There seems to be no such action in any version except Gower's (ll. 4964–65):

And thanne upon himself he caste
A mantell . . .

scription is based on the second book of the *Aeneid*. We have, however, such un-Virgilian details as these:

> Here one man's hand lean'd on another's head,
> His nose being shadow'd by his neighbour's ear;
> Here one being throng'd bears back, all boll'n and red;
> Another smother'd, seems to pelt and swear . . .

A combination of separate incidents in one picture was of course traditional in poetry; the shields of Achilles and Aeneas (the latter of which Sackville had imitated) were illustrious precedents. But the multitude of scenes that Lucrece described, along with such concrete pictorial items as those just quoted, lend color to Sir Sidney Colvin's conjecture that Shakespeare had in mind one of the common tapestries depicting the Trojan story.[27]

The sources so far mentioned have to do more with plot and detail than with the general mode of treatment, and that, as scholars have long recognized, owes much to Daniel's *Complaint of Rosamond* (1592).[28] The story of Lucrece could not very well be told in the manner of *Venus and Adonis,* and for a tragedy of guilt and innocence and sorrow Shakespeare found a partial model outside the mythological convention. *Lucrece* belongs with *Rosamond* in the category

---

27. "The Sack of Troy in Shakespeare's 'Lucrece' and in Some Fifteenth-Century Drawings and Tapestries," *A Book of Homage to Shakespeare* (1916), pp. 88 ff. Cf. W. Marschall, "Das Troja-Gemälde in Shakespeare's „Lucrece," " *Anglia*, LIV (1930), 83–96; and M. F. Thorp, *PMLA*, XLVI (1931), 687 ff.

While there is a clear connection, whether satirical or not, between the player's speech in *Hamlet* and Marlowe's *Dido* (see Brooke's edition of *Dido,* page 160), *Dido* may be related to the Trojan scenes in *Lucrece.* Several phrases have to do with Sinon:

Dido (p. 154, l. 144): A man compact of craft and perjury. Cf. *Aen.* ii.195.

Lucrece (l. 1517): False-creeping craft and perjury.

Dido (p. 155, l. 153): Phrygian shepherds. Cf. *Luc.,* l. 1502; *Aen.* ii.58–59.

Dido (l. 161): O, th' enchanting words of that base slave.

Luc. (l. 1521): whose enchanting story.

In *Dido* (p. 159, l. 242) Pyrrhus in killing Priam is described as "treading upon his breast," a detail not in Virgil. In *Lucrece* (l. 1449) Priam's body "bleeding under Pyrrhus' proud foot lies."

On the whole question see Else von Schaubert, "Die Stelle vom „Rauhen Pyrrhus" (Hamlet II, 2, 460–551) in ihrem Verhältnis zu Marlowe-Nashes „Dido," zu Seneca, etc.," *Anglia*, LIII (1929), 374–439.

28. See especially Pooler, p. xlviii.

of "complaints." Both poems are in rhyme royal, which was regarded by Elizabethan critics as especially suited to serious themes. The opening lines of *Rosamond* indicate the poem's relation to the *Mirror for Magistrates* and the medieval tradition:

> Out from the horror of infernall deepes,
> My poore afflicted ghost comes heere to plaine it . . .[29]

Rosamond tells how she, a virtuous maiden, was corrupted by "a seeming Matrone," the character of whose arguments we noticed already in connection with Leander's.[30] Rosamond's detailed analysis of the inner conflict that preceded her surrender to Henry, and her moralizing on the consequences of sin, gave an obvious cue for Shakespeare's psychological handling of his story. One particular incident Shakespeare turned to account. Rosamond describes a casket sent to her by her lover; the pictures engraved on it, showing the suffering victims of amorous Neptune and Jove, forecast her own sorrows, as Paris and Sinon and the Trojan scenes remind Lucrece of hers. In execution the poem represents the middle level of the well-languaged but somewhat prosaic Daniel; it is much simpler and quieter in style than Shakespeare's piece, which is scored for the brasses rather than the wood winds.[31]

Lucrece differs from *Venus and Adonis* in attempting to deal dramatically and realistically with a tragic situation involving two "historical" persons. The versions of the story that Shakespeare knew are very brief compared with his eighteen hundred and fifty-five lines, and, while the action is spun out as much as possible, the great additions are the long passages of dramatic or rhetorical moralizing. He does try to enter into the feelings of the characters, though his love of rhetoric runs away with his sense of drama. The conflict in Tarquin's mind when he sets out for Lucrece's room occupies nearly two hundred lines of soliloquy and description; like the villains of the plays he leaves nothing unsaid in the way of self-condemnation. Lucrece,

---

29. *Samuel Daniel: Poems,* etc., ed. A. C. Sprague (1930), p. 39.
30. See above, chapter VI, note 26, page 133.
31. Daniel in turn seems to have been inspired by *Lucrece* to amplify and heighten rhetoric in his own poem. See the long addition made in the revised version of 1594 (Sprague, pp. 198 ff., especially ll. 99 ff., 113 ff.).
Various minor obligations to other contemporaries need not be recorded, though some are mentioned later. Shakespeare again derives ornamental details from *Hero and Leander,* but, the tone of the poem being so different, they are of no great account.

when awakened, marshals orderly arguments in about eighty lines. Later, after a few hundred lines of rhetoric, she exclaims, with justice:

> In vain I rail at Opportunity,
> At Time, at Tarquin, and uncheerful Night . . .

Declamation roars while passion sleeps. The description of the Trojan scenes and Lucrece's reflections thereupon involve a further smoke of words, to the extent of about two hundred lines.

Dramatic realism is likewise defeated by the incessant conceits. Shakespeare, in trying to be both serious and decorative, can fall between two stools. When Tarquin arrives on his evil errand, three stanzas are given up to the "silent war of lilies and of roses" in the face of his hostess:

> This heraldry in Lucrece' face was seen,
> Argu'd by beauty's red and virtue's white:
> Of either's colour was the other queen,
> Proving from world's minority their right:
> Yet their ambition makes them still to fight;
>   The sovereignty of either being so great,
>   That oft they interchange each other's seat.

Granting of course that the conceited style was instinctive with most Elizabethans as it cannot be with us, one discerns in this baffling tissue of ingenuities only a clever brain, not a quickened pulse. So too when Tarquin gazes at his prospective victim we have such a conceit as this, in Marlowe's worst vein:

> Her lily hand her rosy cheek lies under,
> Cozening the pillow of a lawful kiss;
> Who, therefore angry, seems to part in sunder,
> Swelling on either side to want his bliss.

As often in the early plays, the author has quite forgotten the situation; he is holding the subject at arm's length, turning it round, saying as much as he can about every side of it. Almost every line gives evidence of a self-conscious pride in rhetorical skill. The antithetical pattern of *Venus and Adonis* appears again. Shakespeare rejoices in matching Ovid:

> Quid, victor, gaudes? haec te victoria perdet.
> A captive victor that hath lost in gain.

A Tarquin who "justly thus controls his thoughts unjust" is too cool, his creator too epigrammatic, for the matter in hand.

In addition to the usual gnomic lines [32] we have an extraordinary profusion of proverbs, singly and in series, after the style of the euphuists in verse and prose. *Venus and Adonis* had its heaped-up illustrations, but the quantity of them in *Lucrece* helps to give the poem an old-fashioned air. Says Tarquin to Lucrece, in words feverish with desire:

> I see what crosses my attempt will bring;
> I know what thorns the growing rose defends;
> I think the honey guarded with a sting . . .

And, justly controlling her just thoughts, Lucrece replies:

> Mud not the fountain that gave drink to thee;
> Mar not the thing that cannot be amended;
> End thy ill aim before thy shoot be ended;
> He is no woodman that doth bend his bow
> To strike a poor unseasonable doe.

Accompanied by such antiphonal wisdom, rape becomes ritualistic.

The mere bulk of Lucrece's declamation after the event demands that something be said of it. Having tried his hand at oratory in *Venus and Adonis*, Shakespeare liked it well enough to provide Lucrece with a whole series of apostrophes. They have undeniable force, but the effect is like that of Senecan declamation, like an explosion in a vacuum. The apostrophe to Time may have been inspired by contemporary poets, but it has a literary pedigree that goes back to Ovid's *Tristia*.[33] The apostrophe to Night is likewise conventional in style and subject matter, but it bears a special resemblance to a speech that Spenser puts in the mouth of Arthur.[34] Sir Sidney Lee remarked that

---

32. Not being versed in Baconian literature, I do not know if an obviously Baconian line (353) has been observed: "Thoughts are but dreams till their effects be tried." Cf. *Of Great Place:* "For good thoughts (though God accept them) yet towards men are little better than good dreams, except they be put in act."

33. *Luc.*, ll. 939 ff.; *Tristia*, IV.vi.1 ff. See Watson, Sonnets xlvii, lxxvii, and Giles Fletcher, *Licia*, Sonnet xxviii.

34. *Luc.*, ll. 764 ff.; *F.Q.*, III.iv.55–59. The details are given in *PQ*, VI, 301. Cf. Drayton, *Ideas Mirrour* (1594), Sonnet xlv. In Chaucer's *Troilus and Criseyde* (iii.1429 ff., 1450 ff.) are apostrophes to night and day, for which both Ovid and Boccaccio have been suggested as sources (E. F. Shannon, *Chaucer and the Roman Poets*, pp. 133 ff.). See below, chapter X, notes 5 and 6.

Lucrece's address to Opportunity "seems an original device of Shake-speare." The matter at least is proverbial; in fact most of it is con-tained or suggested in the comment on *Nosce tempus* in Taverner's *Proverbes or Adagies, gathered out of the Chiliades of Erasums.*[35] This trick of apostrophe, inherited from the more rhetorical Roman writers, was one of the most important devices of rhetoric in the Middle Ages, and Lucrece's declamations are of obvious medieval flavor.[36]

With all its Renaissance trappings *Lucrece* is thoroughly in the medieval tradition. On the other hand, with its undramatic drama, its endless rhetorical digressions, it reads at times like an unconscious burlesque of Elizabethan plays. There are a few really dramatic touches, such as parts of Tarquin's behavior, and especially the sympathetic maid and the "sour-fac'd groom." This "homely villein," who, summoned to act as Lucrece's messenger, "curtsies to her low," receives only a few phrases, but he is almost as real a person as either of the principals. These various bits are slighter and paler than the pic-tures of the lark and the hare in *Venus and Adonis*, but they are similarly out of key. They introduce an air of truth and actuality into a would-be dramatic but quite bookish poem, and they are too few to do more than heighten the artificial unreality of all the rest. For all its seriousness of theme and intention *Lucrece* is as soulless as the earlier poem, and much more wearisome.

Thus for a modern reader it remains a museum piece. Both it and *Venus and Adonis* lack the headlong poetic vitality of *Hero and Lean-der;* they lack also the charm and sweetness of most of Drayton's *Endimion and Phœbe.* But there is no doubt that the rising dramatist knew what the public wanted; we may recall the familiar words of that useful index of taste, Francis Meres. *Venus and Adonis,* said the

---

35. Ed. 1552, fol. xxiv. The comment is quoted in *PQ*, VI, 302. Cf. Spenser's Occasion (*F.Q.*, II.iv.4). Spenser's emblematic personification, which is as old as Phaedrus, is born of the same habit of mind as Shakespeare's apostrophe.

36. "Third in importance among the devices of amplification may be placed apostrophe, with its rhetorical colours *exclamatio, conduplicatio, subiectio,* and *dubitatio.* It would be difficult to exaggerate the importance of apostrophe in medieval literature. Addresses to persons living or dead, present or absent, to personified abstractions, and even to inanimate objects are to be found in almost every composition with any pretensions to style from the eleventh century onward; and a special form, the *Complainte,* developed into one of the most widely cultivated types of literature." J. M. Manly, "Chaucer and the Rhetoricians," *Proceedings of the British Academy,* XII (1926), p. 104.

With the speeches of Lucrece compare those of the ravished woman in Nashe's *Jack Wilton* (ed. McKerrow, II, 293–94).

more exacting Gabriel Harvey, pleased the younger sort, *Lucrece* (and *Hamlet!*) the wiser sort. Both poems were abundantly praised; it is not every poet who can contrive to be both the Swinburne and the Patmore of his generation. But, from the testimony of editions and allusions, the wiser sort, as usual, appear to have been a minority, and for the next generation at least *Venus and Adonis* was linked with *Hero and Leander* as the amorist's *vade mecum,* equally popular in study, boudoir, and brothel.

CHAPTER VIII

Drayton: Giles and Phineas Fletcher: William Browne

I. MICHAEL DRAYTON

Drayton's *Endimion and Phœbe* (1595) was not reprinted, apart from excerpts in *England's Parnassus*, until the third quarter of the nineteenth century, and no popular edition was available until 1925.[1] Thus belatedly was rescued a poem which was in the anomalous situation of having been read only by a handful of specialists and yet thought worthy of a page in the *Cambridge History of English Literature*.[2] Skeptics for whom this last item is an imperfect guarantee of merit can test critical opinions for themselves. The poem has a further interest in that Keats used the same Platonic "plot" in *Endymion*, though it appears very unlikely that he could have seen Drayton's rare book.

Surveying Drayton's voluminous output, from the unreadable *Harmony of the Church* (1591) to the lovely *Muses Elizium* (1630), one may grant that he seldom sings because he must. Yet this most industrious of poets took up one fashion after another, eclogues, sonnets, mythological poems, historical chronicle, heroic ballad, fairy poetry, and the rest, and he gained respectable rank in all forms, unique excellence in some. His writing mirrors the poetic history of a whole period. His first work, as Fuller said of Sternhold and Hopkins, contains more of Jordan than of Helicon, while his last has the charm and lightness, if not the flawless detail, of Herrick. And between these he had done all manner of good things; even *Polyolbion* has rewards for the well-girt reader.

The strength of *Endimion and Phœbe* does not lie in its narrative structure. Indeed most mythological poems recall Bayes's exclamation, "Plot stand still! why, what a devil is the plot good for, but to bring in

1. Ed. J. W. Hebel. See also the *Works*, I and V, 19–22.
2. IV, 180.

fine things?" Yet Drayton has a story. Endymion is a devout servant
of the goddess, who returns his love, though she has not yet confessed
it. In the guise of a mere nymph she appears to him at the river side
and makes love. Loyal to his goddess, the youth rejects her, and prefers to go on fishing. The supposed nymph again pleads in vain, then
returns to Latmus. But now Endymion, overcome in spite of himself, feels a new passion. At night, sitting near his flock, he utters an
amorous plaint. With the dawn Phoebe glides down from her crystal
chair, "longing to see her sweet Endimion." She finds him asleep, and
after her nymphs have danced in, with garlands, and danced out
again, she wakens him. Endymion, "not knowing yet great Phœbe
this should be," tells of his ardent love. Phoebe now pretends to be
coy, but after further protestations from her lover she reveals her
identity, and avows that she has long loved him. Wrapping him in a
fiery mantle she carries him through the air, so that he learns the
mysteries of the heavens. Set down on earth again, Endymion is endowed with new powers and finds all nature ready to serve him. The
rest of the poem describes the gorgeous mythological pageantry that
attends his wedding and deification—not without further discourses
on the trinal triplicities of the heavenly hierarchy. Then Endymion
is transported to Latmus to remain, "ever beautifull and yong," the
goddess' paramour.

The various disquisitions on the heavenly mysteries with which the
narrative is interlarded, and which a modern reader is inclined to
skip, have a real relation to the main theme. For Drayton stands quite
apart from the fleshly school in his conception, although he writes in
the decorative manner. He pictures no erotic delights, and chooses a
subject that allegorical interpreters had long understood as a symbol
of high contemplation.[3] As J. W. Hebel said, Drayton "presents in
concrete story the 'way of love' of traditional Platonism. Endimion
reluctantly comes to love material beauty in Phœbe disguised, whom
he supposes to be a nymph 'of fayre *Floras* trayne,' only to discover to
his happiness that the nymph is absolute beauty, Phœbe herself. Then,
just as the Platonist is led on by love for beauty, Endimion is whisked

---

3. Cf. Fulgentius, ii.19; Natalis Comes, iv.8. Drayton might have got most
of his titles for Diana (p. 43) from Comes (iii.15–18; iv.1). The opening
glosses on Chapman's *Hymnus in Cynthiam* (nearly all of the glosses on the
poem are derived from Comes) give six of the titles. A passage (based on
Comes) near the end of Chapman's poem sets forth the Platonic conception
of Endymion and Diana (*Poems and Minor Translations*, 1875, p. 16; *Poems,*
ed. P. B. Bartlett, pp. 41–42).

away to the heavens where Phœbe imparts to him the 'heavenly secrets.' Thus love has

> impt the wings of his desire,
> And kindled him, with this cœlestiall fire." [4]
> Thence gathering plumes of perfect speculation,
> To impe the wings of thy high flying mynd,
> Mount up aloft through heauenly contemplation,
> From this darke world, whose damps the soule do blynd . . .

Platonism was such common property that it is needless to seek a definite source for Drayton's ideas, but one may illustrate them by glancing at a versifier who enjoyed extraordinary popularity in England for two generations, Du Bartas. In 1584 King James published his translation of *Uranie,* and from that date onward almost every other year witnessed further renderings.[5] Drayton dedicated his *Moyses* (1604) to Du Bartas and his English translator, though Upham remarks that at that time he possibly knew both original and translation chiefly by repute; in some later work there is evidence of knowledge. But he might have known Du Bartas as early as 1594–95; so conscientious and idealistic a writer as Drayton, and one so sensitive to changes in poetic taste, would surely not be backward in welcoming such a remarkable portent. At any rate it is permissible to observe some similarities without offering them as arguments for influence.

The story of Endymion and Diana, as traditionally Platonized, virtually endows Diana with the attributes of Urania. In *Uranie* the goddess appears, like Drayton's Phoebe, in an azure mantle; we have planetary lore, and the suggestion of a journey above the poles to learn heavenly secrets and absorb the divine fire of poesy.[6] There are frequent resemblances between Drayton and portions of the "first week" of Du Bartas,[7] both in descriptive details and in the abundant matter on such topics as the zodiac, the nature of the elements, the

4. Cf. Spenser, *Hymne of Heavenly Beautie,* ll. 134 ff.:
5. See the table in Upham, *French Influence in English Literature,* p. 152.
6. See Arber's reprint of *The Essayes of a Prentise* for King James's translation and the French original, or *Works of Joshuah Sylvester,* ed. Grosart, II, 3. Sylvester's version was apparently first published in 1605.
The Urania of Du Bartas and the Platonized Phoebe of Drayton are sisters, or at least cousins, of Spenser's "Sapience." The medieval character of Phoebe's habiliments may be illustrated by comparison of Drayton (pp. 44–45) with Alanus de Insulis, *The Complaint of Nature* (trans. D. M. Moffat, New York, 1908, pp. 7 ff.).
7. The dates of various sections of Sylvester's version defy the bibliographer, "yet partial translations by him began appearing in print that same year

relations of Phoebus and Phoebe, the influence of the planets and the moon in particular, the aspirations of the flesh-imprisoned soul toward heavenly truth, voyages through the air in quest of these cosmic secrets.[8] While such ideas were not novel, the mention of Du Bartas at least emphasizes the change of spirit that Drayton wrought in his mythological poem; one would not look in the Protestant epic for illustrations of *Hero and Leander* and *Venus and Adonis*.

Since Drayton was an inveterate imitator it might be expected that he had some model for his central device, Phoebe's appearing in disguise as a rival to herself. But no source has been found, and I have come upon nothing more than hints of a similar situation.[9] One is in an Italian poem, *L'Endimione*, by Francesco Ellio, though in general this piece is different from Drayton's.[10] Diana, inspired by Venus and Cupid with love for Endymion, and much disturbed in consequence, descends to Latmus. Laying aside her divine splendor she appears as a nymph with purple buskins and hair adorned with myrtle. She gazes at Endymion as he sleeps, and talks of her love until he awakes. In language modeled on the much-imitated meeting of Venus and Aeneas, Endymion asks if she is nymph or goddess, and how she came there. Diana avows her love, and then her divinity. Further, there is the Homeric *Hymn to Aphrodite*, which tells how the goddess of love, who controlled even the gods, conceived a passion, through the agency of Zeus, for the mortal youth, Anchises. She appeared to him as a nymph, and did not reveal her identity until their union was consummated. Both these stories stop short of Drayton's plot. There is always the possibility, though it does violence to scholarly instincts, that Drayton himself "thought of Mr. Pickwick."

Instead of reviewing one another's works Elizabethan poets, with their deficient ethical sense, indulged in imitation or plagiarism, and no more than other men could Drayton ignore the existence of *Hero and Leander* and *Venus and Adonis*.[11] Indeed he had given testimony

[1591], and by his own statement these pieces existed in fragmentary form long before they were printed as a collected whole" (Upham, p. 157).

8. For these aërial journeys cf. Drayton, pp. 36–39, and Sylvester, ed. Grosart, I, 31, ll. 409 ff.; 79, ll. 842 ff.

9. The Platonic possibilities of Lyly's play involve two distinct persons, Tellus and Cynthia.

10. The only text I have seen is that in G. Bidelli, *Gl'idillij di diversi ingegni illustri* (Milan, 1618); whether Ellio's poem had appeared before I do not know.

11. While Drayton does not mention Marlowe and Shakespeare he honors Lodge with an over-generous tribute. The influence of *Glaucus and Scilla* had been swallowed up in that of its greater successors, and it is hard to isolate any

of his appreciation already. In *Peirs Gaveston* there are several certain imitations of *Venus and Adonis*—the earliest known—and a possible reminiscence of *Hero and Leander*.[12] Though Drayton did not in *Endimion and Phœbe* include Marlowe among his teachers, he made ample recompense many years later, in the briefest and best eulogy the poet has ever received. In those famous lines the memory of Marlowe raises Drayton's writing above its normal level, and his inspiration is potent in *Endimion and Phœbe*. There are obvious borrowings, like this:

> The shag-haird Satyrs Mountain-climing race,
> Have been made tame by gazing in his face.
> For this boyes love, the water-Nymphs have wept
> Stealing oft times to kisse him whilst he slept:
> And tasting once the Nectar of his breath,
> Surfet with sweet, and languish unto death . . .[13]

Throughout the poem, except in the learned parts, are equally clear echoes or imitations of Marlowe's mythological conceits, descriptive details, gnomic lines. The sensuous pictures of Endymion and Phoebe would not be what they are but for Leander and Hero. The similarity in style, however, only emphasizes the difference in spirit between the two poems. The love which in Marlowe is final, the sweet fruition of

---

special proofs of it in *Endimion and Phœbe*. The dance of the nymphs, though a common device, may be related to a similar incident in Lodge, and perhaps Endymion's change of heart was derived from Lodge also (Hebel, p. xi). Phœbe's assertion (p. 16) that she was "Begot by Pan on Isis sacred flood" recalls the scene of Lodge's poem, "nere to Isis floud." The description of the Muses as "heaven-inspired Babes of memorie" (p. 47) evidently comes from another poem of Lodge's in the *Scilla* volume, *In commendation of a solitarie life,*

> See where the babes of memorie are laid
> Under the shadow of Apollos tree.

Cf. *Britannia's Pastorals* (Bk. i, Song 5, l. 283): "O come, ye blessed imps of Memory."

12. J. W. Hebel, *MLN*, XLI, 248–50. *Peirs Gaveston* was entered on December 3, 1593, and "evidently published soon after."

The thirty-eighth sonnet of *Ideas Mirrour* (1594) has these lines:

> If chaste and pure deuotion of my youth,
> Or glorie of my Aprill-springing yeeres,
> Unfained loue in naked simple truth . . .

The phrasing, however, is as close to Marlowe's *Ovid* as to *Hero and Leander* (*Works of Marlowe*, ed. Brooke: *H. and L.*, i.207–08; *Elegies*, i.3, ll. 5–6, 13–14). Cf. *The Faithful Shepherdess*, II.iv.9–10.

13. P. 12.

an earthly crown, in Drayton is the first step toward the mystical apprehension of truth. But Drayton was no mystic, and the heavenly
secrets prove less memorable than the lovers' ecstasy.

More important than actual imitation of Marlowe is the pervasive
influence that gives "air and fire" to long stretches of original writing, that inspires the creation of more purely sensuous beauty than
Drayton was to achieve again until his last book. More than one passage might have come out of *Hero and Leander,* and it would be
severe to dismiss such things as merely derivative, for not every poet
can write like Marlowe by taking thought.

> She layd Endimion on a grassy bed,
> With sommers Arras ritchly over-spred,
> Where from her sacred Mantion next above,
> She might descend and sport her with her love,
> Which thirty yeeres the Sheepheards safely kept,
> Who in her bosom soft and soundly slept;
> Yet as a dreame he thought the tyme not long,
> Remayning ever beautifull and yong,
> And what in vision there to him be fell,
> My weary Muse some other time shall tell.

"This," said Oliver Elton, very moderately, "is nearer the manner
of the dead shepherd than much of the *Endymion* of Keats." [14] Drayton's loving study of Marlowe is evident not only in substance and
style, but also in rhythm. Instead of using the sixain of Lodge and
Shakespeare he follows Marlowe in electing the couplet, and his handling of it, as extracts will already have suggested, is close to Marlowe's. If Drayton's lines do not attain the impetuous rush of their
model they are sufficiently swift, strong, fluent, and varied in movement, equally remote from the rocking-horse couplets of the eighteenth century and from the wayward meanderings of Hunt and the
youthful Keats.

The influence of *Venus and Adonis* is less significant and appears
mainly in Phoebe's wooing of the reluctant Endymion. But even here
the spirit of Drayton's work is different, for Phoebe's vein of badinage
sets her apart from the feverish Venus. [15]

14. *Michael Drayton* (1905), p. 65.
15. One may wonder if the odor of unsanctity which clung to Marlowe's
name, and which quickly attached itself to *Venus and Adonis,* deterred the
more chaste and idealistic Drayton from mentioning these creditors in his postscript and thereby formally linking his Platonic poem with the two notorious
erotic pieces.

Drayton pays tribute to Spenser, and with reason. But in discussing a genre devoted to sensuous word-painting one cannot readily isolate special influences. Some of Phoebe's speeches to Endymion remind one of Spenser as well as of Shakespeare.[16] Further, while Marlowe has almost no natural scenery, and Shakespeare has a few bits of fresh observation, Drayton indulges in luxuriant landscapes in which literary convention and the authentic countryside are pleasantly mixed. Only quotations, for which there is no space, would make clear how his Elizabethan gusto gives charm to his catalogues of pastoral properties, and how he appropriates and embroiders Spenser. The picture of Mount Latmus is closely modeled on the Gardens of Adonis, with further details from the Bower of Bliss.[17]

By this time, having indicated the nature if not the full extent of Drayton's borrowings from others, one may ask if the poet had any capital of his own. The answer of almost any reader must be that he had a good deal. For though the mythological poem in its very nature

16. *E. and P.*, pp. 19–20; *V. and A.*, ll. 1093 ff. (quoted above, page 146); *F.Q.*, I.vi.24–26.

17. *F.Q.*, III.vi.42–45, and II.xii.71. This last bit of Spenser is of course adapted from Tasso.

Since Drayton has two tree-lists (pages 10, 20), and since we meet the convention elsewhere, I might make a catalogue of tree-lists somewhat fuller than any I have seen:

Ennius, *Annales* (ed. Vahlen, 1903, ll. 187–91; ed. E. M. Steuart, 1925, bk. vi, frag. 9, p. 26); Virgil, *Culex*, l. 123; *Georg.* ii.12, 65, 442; *Aen.* vi.179; Ovid, *Metam.* x.86; Seneca, *Oed.* 532; Lucan, *Phars.* iii.440; Statius, *Theb.* vi.90; Claudian, *De Raptu Proserp.* ii.107; Joseph of Exeter, *Bellum Troianum*, i.505 (see above, page 5); *Roman de la Rose*, ll. 1338 ff. (1355 ff. in Chaucerian version); Boccaccio, *Teseide*, xi.22–24; Chaucer, *Parl. Foules*, 176 (based on Joseph of Exeter), and Knight's Tale, A 2920–24; Tasso, *G.L.*, iii.75; Sidney, *Arcadia* (original version), ed. Feuillerat (1926), pp. 83–84; Spenser, *F.Q.*, I.i.8–9 (based on Ovid and Chaucer; see above, chapter V, note 31); Robert Chester, *Loves Martyr*, ed. Grosart, pp. 95–96; *Works of Joshuah Sylvester*, ed. Grosart, I, 45; Hugh Holland, *Pancharis* (see the Appendix, under 1603); William Browne, *Britannia's Pastorals*, Bk. i, Song 2, l. 353; Patrick Hannay, *The Nightingale* (*Minor Caroline Poets*, ed. Saintsbury, I, 622; see the Appendix, under 1622); W. Basse, Eclogue ix (ed. Bond, pp. 253–54).

Such lists are naturally more or less alike, and Drayton knew more than one, from Spenser's backward. But it may be remarked that his Larix and Teda (p. 20) are in the *Hypnerotomachia* (trans. of 1592, pp. 77, 239, in reprint of 1890); and cf. Sylvester, *loc. cit.*

By way of a botanical conclusion to this note it may be added that "lunary," which Drayton mentions (page 12), occurs repeatedly in Lyly, in *Endimion* and elsewhere.

is highly "literary," *Endimion and Phœbe* as a whole has a distinct character which is not that of Marlowe or even Spenser. The characters remain phantoms, and, in such a cool silvery tale, we are content that they should. There is no disconcerting admixture of sophistication or realism in the treatment of Drayton's Platonic lovers. The poem certainly does not possess intensity, yet it accomplishes what it sets out to do with charm and color and sweetness.

With much that is conventional the mythological background combines numerous bits of pastoral description which, to be sure, are partly conventional also, but are partly fresh and English. Sprays of roses and sweet eglantine; the nightingale, ousel and mavis caroling, the joyful lark stretching her wing, the cock playing "hunts-up" for the day star; the shepherd singing, piping a roundelay, fishing by a river side; dew falling upon flowers and pastures; fountains bubbling over silver sand—such things make a pastoral scene that is more than bookish.[18] We hear of the good old game of barley-break, played by satyrs on Latmus; of sports on shearing day; of shepherds telling stories—an Ovidian story in particular—as they sit by their folds; of naked fairies dancing the "heydegies." The mixture is at least as much English as mythological, but the youthful world of the poem has a harmony of its own.

Of course *Endimion and Phœbe,* like most poems of the kind, is rather too facile, and, if not invertebrate, has not a back strong enough to bear the load of Drayton's beloved "nines and threes," the business of the celestial hierarchies inherited from Dionysius the Areopagite. Nor do such stout bags of astrological ballast facilitate the ascent to the Platonic heaven. But, as we often have occasion to remember, even the greatest Elizabethans are subject to what for us are lapses in taste and literary tact; they display a medieval readiness to tell all they know up to the date of publication, and poets as well as prose men do not hesitate to incorporate footnotes in the text.[19]

Drayton showed originality chiefly in abandoning half-realistic

18. For a random bit of pastoral-mythological extravagance, the promise to turn sheep's fleece into gold, cf. Drayton, p. 19, and Peele's *Arraignment of Paris* (Bullen, I, 28–29).

19. Cf. Gabriel Harvey: "Other commend Chawcer, & Lidgate for their witt, pleasant veine, varietie of poetical discourse, & all humanitie: I specially note their Astronomie, philosophie, & other parts of profound or cunning art. Wherein few of their time were more exactly learned. It is not sufficient for poets, to be superficial humanists: but they must be exquisite artists, & curious uniuersal schollers" (*Gabriel Harvey's Marginalia,* ed. G. C. M. Smith, pp. 160–61).

eroticism for idealistic symbolism. Poets could hardly go beyond *Hero and Leander* or *Venus and Adonis,* they could only imitate, and they did. But if that type of mythological poem had become sterile, the symbolic was not. Though the minor writers of the next generation tried to work the vein of Marlowe and Shakespeare, modern poets have generally been of Drayton's mind.

We do not know why *Endimion and Phœbe* was not reprinted. Drayton did, unhappily, rewrite the poem and published the new version in 1606 as *The Man in the Moone.* It is about half as long as the original and not half so good. The piece opens with a shepherd feast in honor of Pan—a suggestion that Keats turned to account. After the festival the shepherds call on one of their number to while away the time by telling a story in the moonlight. The story is that of Endymion and Phoebe.

One large addition is a description of the pictures on Phoebe's mantle, which occupies over seventy lines; it was perhaps inspired by Chapman's lines on Hero's wondrous robe, though Drayton's realistic picture of the stormy sea and the inland birds is quite different.[20] Hero's buskins may be responsible for the similar tasteless extravagance of Phoebe's equipment. The central idea of Drayton's earlier piece, Phoebe's appearing as a nymph and winning Endymion's love away from herself, is dropped. Instead the goddess merely visits the youth and gives him a long account of her life and divine powers; the planetary lore is not dropped, though it is somewhat altered. Endymion finally becomes the man in the moon and accompanies Phoebe on her celestial circuit. The rest of the poem, about forty lines, is given up to rather clumsy satire; the man in the moon sees the doings of men on earth which remain hidden from their fellows. The poem is dull, with little left of the charm of the first version, but it is, as Hebel remarked, "one of the interesting examples of Drayton's quick change from the Spenserian to the Jacobean manner." The mood of Lodge, Marlowe, and Shakespeare was mainly serious, though Marlowe's digression on Cupid and the destinies, with its somewhat incoherent satirical strokes, anticipated the later style. After about 1600 there is an obviously growing taste for humor or satire in the treatment of mythology, and such qualities, when they appear, generally deflate Elizabethan rhetoric. The older tradition continued to attract the majority, but even the mythological poem could not escape the realistic tendencies, especially conspicuous in the drama, which marked the turn of the century.

20. Chalmers, *English Poets,* IV, 418–19; *Works,* II, 577–79.

A few words may be added concerning some other works of Drayton's, first of all *England's Heroical Epistles* (1597), his most popular production. These pairs of letters exchanged between famous lovers, Rosamond and Henry, Queen Isabel and Mortimer, and the rest, are of course modeled on the *Heroides*. The influence of Ovid appears not only in the general conception but also in the rhetorical, somewhat declamatory style, and in turns and antitheses which, along with the neat closed couplets, suggest a later age.[21] To the example of Ovid also may perhaps be attributed the restrained handling of mythological allusions, which are mostly sparing of sensuous decoration. A few reminiscences of Marlowe and Shakespeare occur. Here, for instance, are some familiar lines of *Hero and Leander* converted into an Augustan couplet:

> Thus still we strive, yet overcome at length,
> For men want mercie, and poore women strength.[22]

The orthodox naturalistic arguments against chastity are employed in the epistle of John to Matilda (and in the *Legend of Matilda*).[23] King Henry writing to Rosamond echoes the words of Venus to Adonis:

> If I were feeble, rheumatike, or cold,
> These were true signes that I were waxed old. . . .

> The Tent my Bed, no Pillow but the Ground. . . .[24]

But such items are significant mainly in emphasizing how far Drayton has moved from the Italianate manner.[25]

21. For example, these two bits (*Works*, II, 133, 140):
    Punish my Fault, or pittie mine estate,
    Reade them for Love, if not for Love, for Hate. . . .

      Put on with Boldnesse, and put backe with Feares.
On the development of the heroic couplet see R. C. Wallerstein, *PMLA*, L (1935).

22. Chalmers, IV, 91; Works, II, 258; *H. and L.*, ii.291–96. Drayton alludes to Hero and Leander soon afterward (Chalmers, p. 92; *Works*, p. 261).

23. See above, chapter VI, note 26.

24. *Works*, II, 142. Cf. *V. and A.*, ll. 108, 133 ff.

25. The Italianate manner appears in the catalogue of mythological pictures in the Tower of Mortimer which is one of the oases in *The Barons' Wars* (1603). Here are Phoebus clipping Hyacinth, Io gazing at herself in the water, etc. (Chalmers, IV, 51–52; *Works*, II, 110 ff.).

Polyolbion, with its innumerable nymphs, we must pass by, though we may

One last poem may be mentioned, *The Quest of Cynthia* (1627), which marks still another stage in Drayton's treatment of myth. The style and details are Elizabethan—at least once he echoes *Endimion and Phœbe* [26]—but the spirit is not. To borrow the suggestive summary of M. Legouis, the poet

se montre suivant la déesse à travers les campagnes dans lesquelles ses pas divins ont laissé des traces charmantes, mille fleurettes épanouies sous ses pieds. Il arrive enfin jusqu'à elle et ils décident de vivre ensemble une vie d'amour et d'innocence. Cynthie symbolise ici la nature. C'est déjà un thème lakiste, mais revêtu de fantaisie élisabéthaine.[27]

II. GILES AND PHINEAS FLETCHER

A marked characteristic of the later English Renaissance, especially notable in Spenser, is the mingling, in entire good faith, of religious earnestness and pagan sensuousness. When we reach Milton we find the same essential elements, combined, however, in very different proportions, and pagan opulence is decidedly subdued. Of the transition from the tone of Spenser to that of Milton no poem is more typical than Giles Fletcher's *Christ's Victorie and Triumph* (1610). The very title of that uneven but often beautiful work indicates a shift of emphasis; here we have set forth, not the attributes of a Renaissance gentleman, from holiness to courtesy, but only the Christian story of redemption. Yet the cross is almost hidden behind the luxuriant draperies; the path to Calvary is roses, roses, all the way. Medieval theology is presented in Italianate style.

---

remember Drayton's fond cherishing, in the first Song and elsewhere, of the legend of Brute, "which now the envious world doth slander for a dreame." The envious world, in the person of the learned Selden, amiably proceeded, in his Illustrations to the poem, to demolish "the Arcadian deduction of our British monarchy."

26. *Quest of Cynthia:*
> As when she from the water came,
> Where first she touch'd the molde,
> In balls the people made the same
> For Pomander, and solde.

Cf. *E. and P.*, p. 17:
> The place wherein my bare feete touch the mold,
> Made up in balls, for Pomander is sold.

27. E. Legouis & L. Cazamian, *Histoire de la littérature anglaise* (Paris, 1925), p. 293. On Drayton's *Muses Elizium*, which perhaps ought properly to be noticed here, see below, page 230.

But the sumptuousness is not wholly Italianate, it too is partly medieval. Here is one stanza from the long description of Mercy:

> Her upper garment was a silken lawne,
> With needle-woorke richly embroidered,
> Which she her selfe with her owne hand had drawne,
> And all the world therein had pourtrayed,
> With threads, so fresh, and lively coloured,
>   That seem'd the world she newe created thear,
>   And the mistaken eye would rashly swear
> The silken trees did growe, and the beasts living wear.[28]

The first line seems to echo a line in Marlowe's description of Hero, and the last lines suggest Ovid's story of Arachne or the many imitations of it. We meet so many elaborately attired divinities and especially so many garments with embroidered pictures that, whatever their differences, they have a family resemblance—we may remember Marlowe's Hero, the embroidered mantle of Chapman's Hero, the resplendent goddess of Drayton's *Endimion and Phœbe,* and the mantle described in *The Man in the Moone*—but Fletcher's Mercy is closest perhaps to Nature in Alanus de Insulis, an author to whom he might have been led by Chaucer or, more probably, by the reference in Spenser's *Mutability*.[29]

Fletcher's Christ in the wilderness might be another Leander or Endymion, Narcissus or Hermaphroditus, with his black hair in short curls, and "His cheekes as snowie apples, sop't in wine." [30] Such a

28. *Poetical Works,* ed. F. S. Boas, I, 31, st. 53.

29. H. M. Belden, "Alanus de Insulis, Giles Fletcher, and the 'Mutabilitie' Cantos," *SP,* XXVI, 131 ff. Belden also argued plausibly for the general influence of *Mutability* on Fletcher's case presented in the court of heaven. Whether or not there is influence, there is an interesting contrast; Spenser's vehicle is a mythological story, with the Titaness Mutability as plaintiff, while Fletcher is religious rather than philosophical and has such figures of medieval allegory as Justice, Mercy, Repentance, Faith. Cf. Courthope, *History of English Poetry,* III, 126, 134.

As for the figure of Mercy and her mantle, Belden's argument for Alanus seems probable enough, but he does not take account of the descriptive convention, of which some modern instances are given above.

30. P. 42, st. 8, 11. The simile is not novel, of course, but one may compare some lines about Hermaphroditus as they appear in Golding (ed. Rouse, p. 90, ll. 405–06):

> For in his face the colour fresh appeared like the same
> That is in Apples which doe hang upon the Sunnie side.

Cf. *The Purple Island* (Boas, II, 169, st. 84).

Christ may well attract mythological allusions. Like Golding and others before him Fletcher finds that "obscure fables of the Gentiles" embodied Biblical truth:

> Who doth not see drown'd in Deucalions name,
> (When earth his men, and sea had lost his shore)
> Old Noah; and in Nisus lock, the fame
> Of Sampson yet alive; and long before
> In Phaethons, mine owne fall I deplore:
>> But he that conquer'd hell, to fetch againe
>> His virgin widowe, by a serpent slaine,
> Another Orpheus was then dreaming poets feigne.[31]

Only in the all-reconciling imagination of the Renaissance could "the second Adam" become a second Orpheus.

Of the general influence of Spenser upon Fletcher nothing needs to be said here, since the subject is familiar enough, and some particular imitations are obvious; for instance, the Bower of Vain-Delight is modeled on the Bower of Bliss.[32] Of their mingling of medieval allegory with Renaissance paganism some illustrations have been given, and Fletcher, incidentally, is more medieval than his master. One more characteristic combination cannot be passed over. We noticed before the unconscious ease with which Spenser linked in a double simile the Mount of Olives and the mount of the Muses. We need not then be astonished at Fletcher's picture of Christ's ascent into heaven:

> The rest, that yet amazed stood belowe,
> With eyes cast up, as greedie to be fed,
> And hands upheld, themselves to ground did throwe,
> So when the Trojan boy was ravished,
> As through th' Idalian woods they saie he fled,
>> His aged Gardians stood all dismai'd,
>> Some least he should have fallen back afraid,
> And some their hasty vowes, and timely prayers said.

> Tosse up your heads ye everlasting gates,
> And let the Prince of glorie enter in . . .[33]

---

31. P. 59, st. 7. Gavin Douglas speaks of Christ as "that hevinlie Orpheus" (Smart, II, 18, ll. 9–10).

32. P. 49, st. 39 ff.

33. P. 78, st. 14–15. Cf. *Faerie Queene*, III.xi.34. The sensuous expression of religious feeling in the first half of the seventeenth century needs no illustra-

Christ and Ganymede!

In 1628 appeared a mythological poem entitled *Brittain's Ida*, with the name of Spenser on the title-page. The virtually conclusive internal evidence in favor of Phineas Fletcher's authorship was confirmed some years ago by Miss Seaton's discovery of a manuscript containing *Brittain's Ida*, under the better and presumably correct title *Venus and Anchises*, along with five other pieces known to be Fletcher's and a hitherto unknown *Epithalamium*.[34] Since *Venus and Anchises* is one of the more attractive exemplars of the Spenser-Marlowe-Shakespeare tradition, it is satisfactory to have it definitely established in the Fletcher canon. The date of composition is uncertain.[35]

Fletcher was not the only Jacobean cleric whose "looser merriment" proved embarrassing. The mythological mode encouraged an erotic warmth which even a free-spoken age did not associate with the cloth, and a respectable country parson might be quite ready in 1628 to let the attribution to Spenser pass unchallenged.[36] Whatever his later qualms Fletcher felt none in writing the poem; it is an untroubled banquet of sense. The opening stanzas tell us that the young

tion. It is enough to recall the name of Crashaw, or, as a less familiar instance, Benlowes' very Italianate description of Theophila, "the soul" (*Minor Caroline Poets*, I, 355).

34. *Venus and Anchises*, etc., ed. E. Seaton, 1926.

35. It is safe to assume with Miss Seaton that so voluptuous a poem was written before Fletcher commenced his ministry (about 1616), and Miss Seaton (page xxxix, note 2) would date it "probably soon after 1603." Something can be said for a later date. Adolescent eroticism was not in that period confined to a man's early twenties. Miss Seaton observes that most of Fletcher's poetry centers around 1610, at any rate belongs to the decade 1605–15; further, she shows that the quite warm *Epithalamium*, which she regards as more mature work ("probably before 1611"), "has closer correspondences with *Venus and Anchises* than with any other poem." In addition to these general considerations, which are not unfavorable to a later date than Miss Seaton's, the first line of the third stanza seems a probable echo of a line in Spenser's *Mutability* (1609). Spenser (vi.36) has "Of Arlo-hill (Who knowes not Arlo-hill?)"; Fletcher says "In Ida vale (whoe knowes not Ida vale?)." Such repetition of a name was a not uncommon device (cf. *Shep. Cal., August,* l. 141), but I do not recall examples of the formula's being used with place names. We have just noticed Giles Fletcher's probable borrowing from *Mutability* in a poem published in 1610. Of course both brothers might have read Spenser in manuscript. But it is not impossible that *Venus and Anchises* was written in 1609–10.

36. There may be an acknowledgment of the poem, along with a farewell to the scenes and the writings of his youth, in the last lines of *Non invisa Cano*. See Miss Seaton, pp. xxiii, xxix, xxxi, 32, and Boas' edition, II, xxi, note.

poet Thirsil, sitting beside the Cam, began to sing of "fayre Eliza." The poem proper occupies fifty-nine eight-line stanzas, and is only a series of voluptuous pictures. Anchises, since he is most familiar to us in Virgil, we think of as an epic parallel to Mr. Wemmick's Aged Parent; here, naturally, he is a youth, and his beauty and pastimes are described at length. One day, tired of hunting, he wanders in the grove of Venus. Hearing music come from a bower, he creeps up to it, and beholds Venus, whose bodily beauties are catalogued, in the traditional manner, in about a hundred lines. Fainting with delight, Anchises sinks down, and Venus, awakened, revives and comforts him. Not at all offended by his evident adoration, the goddess equips him with bow and quiver like another Love. He utters his passion in solitary laments. But when opportunity prompts a more open declaration, and he entreats a kiss, his gracious divinity leads the novice on to a happy consummation. Anchises now lives in joy, but he is one of those who kiss and tell, and Jove sends his lightning. The poet, says the final stanza—for again we have the old personal note—would not blab if he received such favors from his love.

The union of Venus and Anchises is treated, as we have noticed in connection with Drayton, in the Homeric *Hymn to Aphrodite*. Fletcher takes over little except the names. Anchises is mentioned as "a lowlie swaine," "not noblie borne," but otherwise the original story, with its epic dignity and restraint, is forgotten. Motives, character, situation, are altered in accordance with the Italianate convention.

By this time, indeed earlier, the "lacteall path" of that convention was too well worn to leave very distinct traces of individual influences, apart from actual verbal clues. In style, contrasted with the onward movement and energy of Marlowe and Shakespeare, the softness of Fletcher's "sugered streames" is nearer to that of Spenser, or even Lodge. *Venus and Anchises* has more virility than *Glaucus and Scilla*, but Fletcher, like Lodge, has a notable relish for feminine endings (especially those in *ing*), and, like Lodge also, he places his mythological tale in a personal framework. The poem is full of conceits and antitheses which are more akin to those of the Elizabethan Petrarchists than to Ovid's. Miss Seaton records a number of parallels with Sidney's *Arcadia*, and one may add that, however conventional the anatomical catalogue, Fletcher's description of Venus bears some resemblances to Zelmane's song in praise of Philoclea.[37]

37. *Arcadia*, ed. Feuillerat (1912), pp. 218 ff. Miss Seaton (page 106) notices one parallel, but there are others. Koeppel (*Anglia*, XI, 362) quoted Tasso in connection with stanza 28.

Fletcher with his economical habits offers an especially good illustration of the close affinity between the pastoral and the mythological poem. As Miss Seaton observes, the seventh eclogue, "though less directly personal in subject, is in tone and treatment so close to *Brittain's Ida* as to read almost like a first draft of its descriptive passages," and the third "also has close correspondences with the long poem."[38] For instance, Fletcher divides between Mira and Stella of the eclogues a good many of the bodily beauties (and metaphors) that appear in the picture of Venus.[39] For Fletcher as for many predecessors the pastoral and mythological worlds were identical, and the artificial tone, setting, themes, and pretty diction appropriate to one kind of writing were equally appropriate to the other.[40]

The general situation of Venus and Anchises bears some obvious resemblance to that of Venus and Adonis, though the bashfulness of Anchises is caused by lack of confidence rather than lack of ardor, and it soon disappears. Anchises is a shepherd, but also, like Adonis, a huntsman who pursues the hart and the tusked boar. Like some Ovidian youths he disdains the attentions of affectionate nymphs. Fletcher's Venus, like Shakespeare's, is the wooer, but she has no need of Shakespearian eloquence. In teasing Anchises for asking too little she displays, moreover, a slight but sufficient degree of humor, and her tone of banter, like that of Drayton's Phoebe rather than the rhetoric of Shakespeare's tempestuous and perspiring goddess, helps to keep the poem's fleshliness wholesome.

There are incidental traces of *Hero and Leander*.[41] The chief item is Fletcher's use of a titbit for the erotic palate, Leander's ignorance of what might follow kisses.[42]

The "garden of delight," where Anchises discovers Venus in her bower, we have visited before, and the song that Anchises hears is on a not unfamiliar text:

38. P. xli.

39. Cf. Boas, II, xvii, 217, and Seaton, st. 21, 23, 27, 28.

40. One might quote Chapman's fine eulogy of *The Faithful Shepherdess*, which, he says,

> Renews the golden world, and holds through all
> The holy laws of homely Pastoral,
> Where flowers, and founts, and nymphs, and semi-gods,
> And all the Graces find their old abodes.

41. Cf. "His lovelie limbs . . . Were made for playe" (st. 4), and Marlowe, i.88; "Night is Loues holyday" (st. 12), and Marlowe, i.191. The idea of this last phrase was of course common. Further, cf. "Too foolish is the man that starves to feed his treasure" (st. 16), and Marlowe, i.243.

42. St. 56, 59. Cf. Marlowe, ii.61 ff., 68–71.

Then while thy time affordes thee time & leasure
Enioye while yet thow mayst thy life's sweet pleasure.

Whether the scene is taken directly from Tasso [43] or from Spenser's imitations of Tasso, or from both, does not greatly matter. The differences, however, are significant. Tasso's picture is highly sensuous, but Armida is a wicked enchantress to be shunned. The episodes of Phaedria and Acrasia's Bower of Bliss, in both of which we have a similar setting and lyrics, are of course, the second especially, among Spenser's most purple passages; [44] but the knight of temperance breaks away from the wanton lady of the lake and destroys Acrasia's bower. Fletcher uses the same material in order to conduct his hero, not without envy, to the acme of sensual delight.

When a poet has gone on a moral holiday and created a piece of voluptuous tapestry, one need not shake a moralistic finger. At the same time such a poem as Fletcher's provides a fair test for readers who find all or most of Spenser in his picture-making and are skeptical of his didactic seriousness. *Venus and Anchises,* considered simply as poetical writing, is inferior to the Spenserian cantos, yet not so much inferior that they cannot be compared. In point of sensuousness they are pretty much on a level, but *Venus and Anchises,* however pleasant a concoction, is, after all, empty, and Spenser is not. Fletcher's cake is all icing.

One illustration of Fletcher's flexibility of mind (as well as economy) cannot be passed over. He has no less than four versions of Boethius' tale of Orpheus and Eurydice.[45] The paraphrase in *A Father's Testament* is the closest to Boethius, and the last lines are these:

This Fable looks to thee, who tir'd with night
Desir'st to draw thy soul to life, and light
On that Eternal Sun set, fasten, fix thy sight.

43. Koeppel, *Anglia,* XI, 361–62.

44. *F.Q.,* II.vi and xii. The songs occur at vi.15 and xii.74 respectively. One of Spenser's most Spenserian lines in the song of the mermaids (II.xii.32) is this: "Here may thy storme-bet vessell safely ride." In Fletcher (st. 58), Anchises, having boldly entered "Loves highway," goes further and at length arrives "Where safe from storme the love beate vessell rides."

45. One is a chorus to the fourth act of *Sicelides.* Another, in the fifth canto of *The Purple Island,* follows a discourse on the tongue and its office. A third appears among *Poeticall Miscellanies.* The fourth is mentioned in the text. See *Works,* ed. Boas, I, 246; II, 66 ff.; II, 243–44; II, 336–37; and see remarks and notes, II, viii, xii, 364, 366.

> If you turn back on hellish Shades to pore,
> Thou ever losest what thou wan'st before:
> Thy soul more barr'd from Heav'n, in hell implunged more.[46]

The versions in *The Purple Island* and the *Poeticall Miscellanies* end on a similar note. Not so the chorus in the *Sicelides;* indeed one asks what Boethius is doing in that galley, in a labyrinth of pastoral love affairs. This is the conclusion, not quite in harmony with Boethius:

> Thus since love hath wonne the field,
> Heaven and Hell, to Earth must yeeld,
> Blest soule that dyest in loves sweete sound,
> That lost in love in love art found.
> If but a true-loves joy thou once doe prove,
> Thou wilt not love to live, unlesse thou live to love.

This last line (with its suggestion of the *Pervigilium Veneris*) is also the last line of the song that lures Anchises to the bower of Venus.[47]

We shall not linger over *The Purple Island,* which, though it appeared in 1633, was written earlier.[48] Inspired by one of Spenser's most instructive cantos, and by Sylvester,[49] it dresses medieval conceptions in the colors of the Renaissance. Even in the midst of his anatomical explorations Fletcher sometimes remembers that he is a poet, but the mythology shares the general characteristics already indicated; what is central and all-sufficing in *Venus and Anchises* is here peripheral and decorative. The conclusion of the poem, an epithalamium on the union of Christ and the church, is an especially good example of the way in which the devout ardors of both the Fletchers received, quite naturally, the most sensuous expression. It is not the least medieval of their qualities, though it can be found in religious poetry of all ages.

46. Cf. Boethius, *De Consolatione Philosophiae,* bk. iii, met. 12.

47. The *Sicelides* as a whole I pass by, partly because I am not dealing with drama, and partly because I find it unreadable. It involves Ovidian and kindred stories, more or less modified, such as that of Glaucus, Circe, and Scylla. Some episodes appear to be related to Browne's *Britannia's Pastorals* (Boas, p. xviii, note 1).

48. Miss Seaton (page xl, note) supposes that it was "begun about the same time as *Christ's Victorie and Triumph,* published in 1610 (cf. Canto i, st. 59)." Cf. Boas, II, vii.

49. Upham, *French Influence,* pp. 199–201.

III. WILLIAM BROWNE

The pastoral poetry of William Browne, so easy to read and so easy to forget, has its mild and individual charm, but it concerns us because it embodies some general tendencies in the use of mythology which pass from the age of Spenser to the age of Milton. Whereas poets of the breadth and depth of Spenser and Milton re-create tradition, a writer of Browne's slender talent only reflects it. I am speaking of course of his mythological incidents and allusions, in which he follows the Renaissance tradition, and in general it is not these but the more original and attractive parts of his work that sustain his poetic reputation.

The first book of *Britannia's Pastorals* appeared in 1613, when Browne was presumably twenty-two, and the second book in 1616.[50] The plot makes that of *The Faerie Queene* appear neat and compact, and I shall not try to follow its mazes; it is not Browne's main concern. Of the endless episodes involving shepherds and nymphs a number can be called mythological, but the motives had been handled so often in Renaissance pastorals, foreign or English, that their original character is obscured. For instance, the shepherds Remond and Doridon are in search of Fida, who has vanished; they come upon blood —of a hind—and see the collar of Fida's companion, and Remond is sure that Fida has been slain. It is the situation of Pyramus and Thisbe, but Browne is thinking less of Ovid than of Spenser's story of Florimell,[51] and perhaps *Aminta*.

In the third Song of the second book is the half-Spenserian, half-Ovidian tale of two streams, Walla and Browne's beloved Tavy. Tavy, waiting for Walla, is deaf to the solicitations of other nymphs; after singing in her honor he learns that she has been pursued by a satyr. We are told of the pursuit and of Walla's prayer to Diana; when the satyr follows her into the cave where she has sought refuge she prays again, to the nymph Ina, to transform her into any shape. She is changed into a spring, which drowns the satyr, and flows to join her lover. Tavy arrives, to hear of her fate and to grieve. The story is a mosaic of pastoral and mythological themes and conventions.[52]

50. Quotations are from the edition in the Muses' Library. The fullest discussion of Browne, which I have made use of, is that of F. W. Moorman (1897).

51. *F.Q.*, III.vii–viii; Browne, Bk. ii, Song 2, ll. 349 ff.

52. "The metamorphosis of Arethusa pursued by Alpheus, of Ambra by Om-

In addition to such more or less mythological tales there are end- less decorative allusions. Like Spenser, Browne is fond of stating the: time of day in this manner:

> Now great Hyperion left his golden throne
> That on the dancing waves in glory shone,
> For whose declining on the western shore
> The oriental hills black mantles wore . . .

But Spenser might not approve of the conceit. Browne is given rather more than Spenser to the ornamental periphrasis; Hippolytus is "he whose chastity made him a star." We have a good deal of "fiery Titan," "radiant Phoebus," and the rest of the mythological slang which tells us that the bookish view of nature is established, and which, of course, appears in most writing of the time, including Shakespeare's plays, but the character of Browne's material makes it conspicuous in him. In similar style he writes not only of honest sheep but of "fleecy train" and "bleating charge," of the sea and also of the "liquid plain." Homely observation and bookishness may be mingled in the same picture, and the genuine exposes the counterfeit. Yet the bookish elements are by no means all counterfeit or disagree- able:

> This swain, entreated by the mirthful rout,
> That with entwined arms lay round about
> The tree 'gainst which he lean'd, (so have I seen
> Tom Piper stand upon our village green,
> Back'd with the May-pole, whilst a jocund crew
> In gentle motion circularly threw

---

brone, of the nymphs by the satyrs of the *Salices*, or as frescoed on the temple of Pales in the *Arcadia*, the loves of Mulla and Mollana in Spenser, and the mythological impersonations of the *Polyolbion*, find, as it were, a meeting- place in Browne's lay of Walla" (W. W. Greg, *Pastoral Poetry and Pastoral Drama*, p. 137).

While one constantly meets Ovidian themes more or less disguised by the pastoral convention, Browne does occasionally recount a classical myth without changing the names. The story of Cephalus and Procris receives two dozen lines (toward the end of the fourth Song in the first book). The last three hundred lines of the fragmentary third book are devoted to Cupid and Psyche. Reminiscences of Adlington show that Browne had a text before him, but of course he wandered from the original tale. He added a pastoral episode, and a description of Psyche's beauties which alone fills a third of the piece. The story has hardly got under way when it ends with the suggestion that Psyche's love- liness is painted with "Caelia" in mind.

> Themselves about him), to his fairest ring
> Thus 'gan in numbers well according sing:

> Venus by Adonis' side
> Crying kiss'd, and kissing cried,
> Wrung her hands and tore her hair
> For Adonis dying there.[53]

The lyric takes us back to the songs of Greene, though Browne is lighter and more sophisticated in tone.

In describing persons Browne makes abundant use of mythological parallels and conceits, fanciful and extravagant in the Elizabethan manner. Phoebus looked on the bright eyes of Walla

> And by their radiance was the god struck blind,
> That clean awry th' ecliptic then he stripp'd
> And from the milky way his horses whipp'd;
> So that the Eastern world to fear begun
> Some stranger drove the chariot of the sun.[54]

Mythological comparisons are used singly and in series. Now and then the effect is happy; more often, since Browne lacks Marlowe's gift of phrase, it is little better than boyish pedantry. Sometimes there are verbal echoes of Marlowe; for instance the four lines on Leander's dangling tresses and the golden fleece are twice imitated, the heady wine of the original becoming somewhat pale and diluted.[55]

Browne imitates other motives and devices that Marlowe had made popular, arguments against virginity,[56] gnomic lines,[57] myth-making.[58] The influence of Marlowe of course cannot always be isolated from that of Marlowe's disciples. The following passage might be said to be compounded, with variations, from *Hero and Leander,* *Venus and Adonis,* and *Endimion and Phœbe:*

53. Bk. ii, Song 2, ll. 95 ff.
54. Bk. ii, Song 3, ll. 800 ff.
55. Bk. i, Song 1, ll. 255 ff., 481 ff.
56. Bk. i, Song 1, ll. 634 ff.; Song 2, ll. 570 ff.; Bk. ii, Song 3, ll. 939 ff.
57. Bk. i, Song 1, ll. 77–78; Song 3, ll. 289–90; and *passim.* One example may be quoted: "True loue is mute, and oft amazed stands" (Marlowe, i.186); "But love surpriz'd the hart, the tongue is dumbe" (Drayton, *E. and P.,* p. 20); "Love often makes the speech's organs mute" (Browne, Bk. i, Song 2, l. 549).
58. For example, Bk. i, Song 2, ll. 411 ff. (see just below); Bk. ii, Song 1, ll. 211 ff.; and see the lines about Walla quoted above.

Narcissus' change sure Ovid clean mistook,
He died not looking in a crystal brook,
But (as those which in emulation gaze)
He pin'd to death by looking on this face.
When he stood fishing by some river's brim,
The fish would leap, more for a sight of him
Than for the fly. The eagle, highest bred,
Was taking him once up for Ganymede.
The shag-hair'd satyrs, and the tripping fawns,
With all the troop that frolic on the lawns,
Would come and gaze on him, as who should say
They had not seen his like this many a day.
Yea, Venus knew no difference 'twixt these twain,
Save Adon was a hunter, this a swain.[59]

These lines, and thirty more that continue the formula, are, in substance, diction, rhythm, closer to Drayton than to anyone else. The lavishly "conceited" description of Walla, part of which has been quoted, is likewise in the vein of Drayton. Indeed Drayton is for Browne "our second Ovid." His soft, flowing sweetness was more congenial than the energy of Marlowe; congenial too were Drayton's idealism and his combination of pastoral, mythological, patriotic, and fairy lore. But such generalities call up the greater name of Spenser, whom Browne loved especially to praise, and among whose disciples he is regularly listed. Some Spenserian qualities in Browne's treatment of mythology we have noticed, and the influence of Spenser is often merged with that of a fellow Spenserian like Drayton.

Browne's references and quotations show his considerable learning. He cites not merely the ancient authors commonly read, but some of the less familiar, such as Apollonius Rhodius, Pausanias, Silius Italicus.[60] The chief classical influence is that of Ovid. The adaptation of Ovidian tales to pastoral uses has been touched on already. The allegorical figure of Limos, in the second book, is mainly compounded out of Ovid's *jejuna Fames* and Erysichthon, and the episode perhaps owes something to Dante.[61] There are many Ovidian details as well.

59. Bk. i, Song 2, ll. 411 ff.
60. Without casting unjust slurs upon Browne's scholarship one may illustrate the way in which abstruse erudition could travel about. For the Fates as sisters of Pan Browne cites "Pronapis in suo Protocosmo" (Bk. ii, Song 4, l. 888). Abraham Fraunce had quoted the same authority for a full account of creation and the birth of Pan, the Fates, and other deities, and he took it all from Leo Hebraeus. See the Appendix, under 1592.
61. Moorman, pp. 52–55. On Lyly's use of the Ovidian episode and probably Boccaccio also, see V. M. Jeffery, *John Lyly*, pp. 87–88.

No poet of the time knew country life better than Browne, or took more pleasure in describing what he saw with his own eyes, yet he testifies to the power of literary tradition when he paraphrases the elaborate simile of hare and hound that occurs in the tale of Apollo and Daphne [62]—the simile that Shakespeare remembered in his picture of poor Wat.

Browne's elaborate account of the golden age necessarily embodies many of the features sanctified by Ovid and his numerous successors, but he has less familiar details too. His people are not vegetarians, and instead of idleness we have "Labour the salad that their stomachs bred." The customary praise of rural innocence and simplicity leads to satire on modern extravagance, and, what is more novel, to praise of communism, an idea drawn apparently from Don Quixote's discourse to the goatherds.[63] But for a number of the less traditional details Browne seems to be chiefly indebted to Chaucer's *Former Age*.

The mention of Chaucer reminds us of Browne's unusual knowledge of medieval literature; his special interest in Occleve is well known. Both directly and as a Spenserian he has affinities with medieval allegory and satire. Then, although he knows Camden and Selden, he is too proud of the glories of Elizabethan England to pass over the story of "mighty Brute" and "the brave issue of the Trojan line." [64] He praises Robert of Gloucester, and other early bards who had sung of Brute,

> Striving in spite of all the mists of eld,
> To have his story more authentic held.[65]

And, though he quotes Homer in Greek, he tells of a nymph who meets Thetis singing a lay that she had learned from "a skilful swain," Joseph of Exeter.[66]

With the best of Browne's work, the fresh and loving observation of rural scenes and manners, we have not been much concerned; we have rather, not quite fairly, been indicating unhealthy symptoms of

62. Bk. ii, Song 3, ll. 1133 ff. It may be added that our country dweller, unlike his illustrious and skeptical namesake, accepts the tradition concerning the legs of the badger (Bk. i, Song 4, ll. 91 ff.).

63. Bk. ii, Song 3, l. 425; *Don Quixote*, bk. ii, c. 3. Shelton's translation appeared in 1612. See Moorman, pp. 59 ff.

64. Bk. ii, Song 1, ll. 93, 105. Browne quotes "Galf. Monum."

65. Bk. ii, Song 4, ll. 241–42.

66. Bk. ii, Song 3, l. 628. The reader is directed to Selden's notes on *Polyolbion*.

pseudo-classicism. But it is not insignificant that a writer of Browne's quality, an ancestor of a long line of genuine poets of nature, should so readily take the literary coloring of the Renaissance pastoral. Sometimes he looks at nature and man for himself, still oftener he looks through a mythological haze. The results of the latter process are as yet seldom unpleasant, but mythology is on the way to becoming a nuisance.

Browne's classicism is of the external kind and quite impure. He is half medieval in his mixtures of classical and unclassical matter, in his rather wooden allegory, in the nature of his satire, in his wayward narrative style. In these respects, and in his combination of moral seriousness and sensuousness, he is of course a Spenserian. Though less warm and luxuriant than Spenser, Browne can enjoy pictorial beauty for its own sake, as, for example, in the well-known lines on the maiden undressing which caught the eye of a greater artist. Or, again like a mild Spenser, he can present temptation with more pretty paganism than Miltonic severity would allow, as when a nymph tries to seduce Tavy from his loyalty to Walla.[67] But neither seriousness nor sensuousness in Browne has much vitality.

67. Bk. ii, Song 3, ll. 953 ff.

CHAPTER IX

Minor Writers

The line of more or less Spenserian poets discussed in the last chapter has anticipated chronology, and we must return to the period following *Hero and Leander* and *Venus and Adonis*. Those two poems, along with the general influence of Spenser, had established the popularity of the Italianate mythological narrative, the Renaissance epyllion, and young men who were in the movement eagerly worked the new vein. The sensuous and pictorial manner conquered the bald and moral,[1] and it was a tune that every warbler soon had by heart.

The two best minor poems in the new convention, *Endimion and Phœbe* and *Venus and Anchises*, have already been noticed, and the present chronicle is of rather small beer. Indeed an unfriendly critic, observing the brief prime and the protracted decadence of the Renaissance genre, might say with Rosalind, "You'll be rotten ere you be half ripe, and that's the right virtue of the medlar." For signs of quick-coming decay were visible even in *Hero and Leander* and *Venus and Adonis*, fresh and youthful in many ways as those poems were. But a number of minor writers justify attention because of either modest poetical merit or historical interest. Of course only a select few can be mentioned here. In addition to poems of the new style, such as Marston's dubious *Metamorphosis of Pygmalion's Image*, the *Salmacis and Hermaphroditus* ascribed to Beaumont, and Barksted's *Mirrha*, we shall take account of some other authors, Davies, Heywood, Basse, and Bosworth, who must be labeled miscellaneous.

I. John Marston

Between 1593 and 1598 appeared about fifteen mythological poems of various kinds, most of them touched with Italianate color-

---

1. A goodly number of old-fashioned poetasters remained unconquerable, as the Appendix testifies.

ing, and some, like those of "T. H." (presumably Thomas Heywood), Barnfield, Drayton, Thomas Edwards, following closely the style of the acknowledged masters.[2] A mythological tale being the fashionable exercise for a young man who wished to commence author, the most unlikely persons tried their hand at it. One of these was John Marston. *The Metamorphosis of Pygmalion's Image* was published, along with "certain satires," in 1598.

In prefatory verses "To his Mistress" the poet declares

> My wanton muse lasciviously doth sing
> Of sportive love, of lovely dallying,

and he proceeds, in the manner of so many earlier amatory pieces, to identify himself with Pygmalion, at least to the extent of hoping for a similar consummation.[3] The poem itself is written in the popular sixain stanza. Only the beginning and end are at all close to Ovid, and the embellishments are largely of the kind promised in the verses quoted. The statue is made in the second stanza, and many stanzas are devoted to Pygmalion's raptures of admiration. Bodily beauties are itemized with conventional completeness, and the ensuing dalliance is described with more than conventional detail. The poem has something of the smoothness that is characteristic of the genre, but is quite lacking in charm or beauty.

There is less interest in the piece itself than in the question of the author's motive. Following the narrative are lines in the crabbed style of the satires, "The Author in praise of his precedent Poem," which repudiate any serious intention in

> The Salaminian titillations,
> Which tickle up our lewd Priapians.
> Is not my pen complete? Are not my lines
> Right in the swaggering humour of these times?

In the sixth satire of *The Scourge of Villanie* Marston gives a good many lines to *Pygmalion's Image,* maintaining that it was written as a burlesque:

> Curio, know'st my sprite?
> Yet deem'st that in sad seriousness I write
> Such nasty stuff as is *Pygmalion?*

2. For a full record of imitations of Marlowe or Shakespeare or both see the index. The series begins with the recently discovered *Oenone and Paris* of 1594, by "T. H."

3. *Works of Marston,* ed. Bullen, III, 251 ff.

Scholars in general have not accepted this declaration "in sad seriousness."[4] I am inclined to believe it. Morse Allen, who is not, remarks that "we feel that he himself while writing was never emotionally carried away; the poem is always cold and intellectual." Cold and intellectual sensuality is certainly favorable to the notion of satire. The authorities of London, like modern scholars, did not perceive an adequate satirical intention, but it has always been the fate of irony to be misunderstood; one might invoke the somewhat greater names of Defoe, Swift, Burke. Besides, Marston had a heavy hand, and a burlesque of erotic poetry needs a light touch. The extravagances of the sonneteering craze had been laughed at in Davies' *Gulling Sonnets,* and to a literary aspirant of strongly satirical bent the vogue of the sensuous mythological poem might well seem to invite an ironic piece of studied excess.[5]

But there are more than general reasons for accepting Marston's statements. If one comes to the poem after *Hero and Leander* or *Venus and Adonis* one perceives a real difference in tone. There are bits of satire, about papists and busk-points, which are echoed in the formal satires.[6] There is an undercurrent of mockery and jocularity that runs from the prefatory verses "To his Mistress" through the poem itself. To cite only an instance or two:

> And therefore, ladies, think that they ne'er love you,
> Who do not unto more than kissing move you . . .

> And now, O now, he finds how he is graced
> By his own work! Tut! women will relent
> When as they find such moving blandishment.[7]

There is no space for illustrating further a quality that seems evident enough. It may be said that Marston's indecency is hardly that of a

4. E.g., Grosart, Bullen, Winckler (*John Marston's litterarische Anfänge,* 1903, p. 38); Morse Allen, *The Satire of John Marston,* 1920, pp. 88 ff. Marston's poem is referred to as a satire by Mr. G. Kitchin, though he does not discuss it (*Survey of Burlesque and Parody in English,* 1931, p. x). Two recent critics, G. Cross and A. Caputi, accept Marston's satirical intention (see Bibliography). Cf. *Poems of John Marston,* ed. A. Davenport (Liverpool University Press, 1961).

5. In the opening lines of his second satire Marston apparently refers to the poem when he speaks of having "even now lisp'd like an amorist," and of being himself "not immaculate." But the former phrase does not necessarily disprove a satirical purpose, and the latter is too vague to have any force.

6. Cf. pp. 254–55, 357.

7. Ll. 119–20, 172–74.

reforming satirist. But, as his satires show, Marston, like many another censor of society, derived a vicarious gratification from detailed
accounts of the vices he attacked, and, as I have said, he had a heavy
hand.

A burlesque would naturally glance at the most popular poems of
the type. Allen observes that Marston later hinted, without actually
asserting, "that the *Pygmalion* contained definite hits at contemporary poetry. These have been sought for, of course vainly, by modern critics." [8] But the echoes of Marlowe seem fairly audible. To
quote only the head and tail pieces, in "To his Mistress" we have this:

> Thy favours, like Promethean sacred fire,
> In dead and dull conceit can life inspire.

Marlowe had written

> Whose liuely heat like fire from heauen fet,
> Would animate grosse clay, and higher set
> The drooping thoughts of base declining soules.

In "The Author in praise of his precedent Poem" Marston asks

> Do not I flatter, call her wondrous fair,
> Virtuous, divine, most debonair?

Marlowe's oft-echoed lines are these:

> But you are faire (aye me) so wondrous faire,
> So yoong, so gentle, and so debonaire.

Marston more than once sneers at lovers who pule "Aye me." [9]
There are other more or less evident allusions to *Hero and Leander*,
or echoes of its phrasing, which may be thought sufficient to prove a
satirical purpose, but they are too numerous to be quoted.[10]

8. P. 92.
9. *Scourge*, vi.18; viii.33, 52. Cf. Drayton's sonnet "To the Reader," 1599
(ed. Brett, p. 28). In Marston's second satire in the same book there is a very
palpable hit at Marlowe:
> Here Jove's lust-pander, Maia's juggling son,
> In clown's disguise, doth after milkmaids run.
10. The more tangible correspondences are these:

MARSTON	MARLOWE
L. 19	ii.317, 324
Ll. 38–39	i.21–22

II. Francis Beaumont (?): Salmacis and Hermaphroditus

Salmacis and Hermaphroditus (1602) was published anonymously at first, but in editions of 1640 and later the name of Francis Beaumont was attached to it. Our knowledge of booksellers' methods, the fact that Beaumont must have been eighteen or thereabouts, and differences in style and temper between this poem and the dramatist's undisputed writings, have generally inclined scholars to think that Beaumont was not the author. On the other hand it has been argued that the piece is not beyond the capacity of a precocious Elizabethan young man, that it shows characteristics of Beaumont's mature style which, though not marked, may be set over against the alleged differences. The mythological poem of the age was to a large degree *sui generis*, and if *Hero and Leander* and *Venus and Adonis* were anonymous one might hesitate to assign them to the authors of *Doctor Faustus* and *Hamlet*. *Salmacis and Hermaphroditus* is superior to most of its fellows in the Marlowe-Shakespeare tradition, and one would like to identify the writer, but the evidence is vague and not conclusive either for or against Beaumont.[11]

Ll. 78, 80, 84, 91 (on the dumbness of the statue)	i.186 (and Hero's prolonged silence)
Ll. 117–18	ii.51 ff.
Ll. 134–35	i.299 ff.
L. 149	ii.153
L. 155	ii.248
Ll. 219–20	ii.255–57, ii.67 ff.

There are not many tangible links between *Pygmalion* and *Venus and Adonis*. Pygmalion's protracted dalliance and the statue's silence remind one of the relations between Shakespeare's pair (cf. Marston's "dull image," l. 78, the couplet quoted above from "To his Mistress," and "image dull and dead," *V. and A.*, l. 212). There is a fairly clear echo in the epilogue, though one need not take Labeo as Shakespeare:

> So Labeo did complain his love was stone,
> Obdurate, flinty, so relentless none.

Cf. *V. and A.*, ll. 199–200. See Chambers, *William Shakespeare*, II, 195.

For notes on Marston's poem in relation to Shakespeare's plays, see Root, *Classical Mythology in Shakespeare*, p. 103; C. Winckler, *Englische Studien*, XXXIII (1904), 216; C. Fries, *ibid.*, XXXIV, 445; H. C. Lancaster, *SP*, XXIX (1932), 233.

11. Quotations are from the text in the *Shakespeare Society's Papers*, III (1847), 98 ff. The poem is also in Chalmers, VI, 210 ff., and was edited by G. Jones (London, 1951). To mention only two discussions, G. C. Macaulay opposed the attribution to Beaumont (*Francis Beaumont*, London, 1883, pp.

"My wanton lines doe treate of amorous loue," the poet begins, and the promise is amply fulfilled. Skipping fancy expands the Ovidian tale to something over nine hundred lines. Diana, we learn, had resolved to slay the youth whose attractions kept her nymphs from hunting, but she herself fell a victim, and instead of an arrow she bestowed a kiss.

> Then the boy ran; for (some say) had he stayd,
> Diana had no longer bene a mayd.

Further mythological inventions are employed to describe his beauty. Ovid's account of the lad's explorations is paraphrased, but the poet breaks off to indulge in a long and luscious account of Salmacis. She was loved by Jove, who promised to make her a star, but Salmacis-Pamela would not yield until her suitor gained the consent of Astraea. Jove then sought Astraea's court, which was not unlike that of Elizabeth:

> But there was such a busie rout before,
> Some seruing men, and some promooters bee,
> That he could passe no foote without a fee;
> But as he goes, he reaches out his hands,
> And payes each one in order as he stands;
> And still, as he was paying those before,
> Some slipt againe betwixt him and the dore.

Jove finds Venus pleading against Vulcan, and, after he has won Astraea's consent to the elevation of Salmacis, he is overtaken by Venus, who urges him to bring no more wantons to heaven. Unsuccessful, Venus, by her own unfailing method, persuades Vulcan to refuse to supply Jove with thunderbolts, and the two go to Jove's palace and threaten him until he agrees to give up Salmacis, though he makes her twice as beautiful as before.

The poet returns to Ovid, but not for long. A mere chance encounter between hero and heroine is not enough, the gods must take a hand. Bacchus saw and loved the nymph, but Apollo

> kept her from the sweets of Bacchus bed,
> And 'gainst her wil he sau'd her maiden-head.

21, 197 ff.), while C. M. Gayley considered the case against Beaumont not proven (*Beaumont the Dramatist*, New York, 1914, pp. 38 ff.). See Hallett Smith (Bibliography, "General").

Bacchus complained to Mercury (whose character and functions are described) and Mercury stole the wheels from Apollo's chariot. Apollo offered to show Salmacis the most beautiful youth that ever was if she would obtain the wheels again . . . But it is needless to go through the whole piece. The conclusion, though freely handled, is necessarily closer to Ovid.

The probability that the author did not use a foreign redaction of Ovid is perhaps strengthened by the fact that, although he does not often follow the Ovidian story, he reproduces phrases from Golding. *Venus and Adonis* doubtless influenced the choice of subject and to some degree the general tone, but there is very little specific borrowing; the most obvious bit occurs in the amorous pleading of Salmacis.

Much stronger is the influence of Marlowe, as it is in most of these poems. Those three purple patches in the first part of *Hero and Leander*, the descriptions of the maiden, the youth, and the temple, are clearly imitated. Indeed the picture of Astraea's throne is almost plain theft:

> Then she descended from her stately throne,
> Which seat was builded all of iasper stone,
> And o're the seat was paynted all aboue,
> The wanton unseene stealths of amorous Ioue.
> There might a man behold the naked pride
> Of louely Venus in the vale of Ide . . .[12]

Then in the episode of Bacchus and Salmacis there are parallels, partly verbal, with both the meeting of Hero and Leander in the temple and the incident of Mercury and the country maid; this last item may also have suggested the bargain between Apollo and the nymph. The amorous arguments of Salmacis are conventional, of course, but it was Marlowe who had chiefly made them so, and enough of Marlowe's phrasing is echoed to leave no doubt. In short, there are few pages which do not show the stamp of Marlowe, in mythological descriptions, conceits, invented episodes, gnomic lines.[13]

12. P. 107. Marlowe's lines on the temple are quoted above, page 126.

13. To mention some items of probably more remote origin, the business of Venus and Vulcan recalls Venus' persuading Vulcan to make arms for Aeneas. The author may have known Homer; at any rate he knew "the rosie fingred morne." The incident of Bacchus and Salmacis may have been adapted from the story of Bacchus and Ariadne. Finally, although there were accounts of deities in current handbooks and elsewhere, the description of Mercury (pp. 114–15) suggests a partial paraphrase of Horace's tenth ode.

The poem is written with fluent ease. In spite of the excessive play of fancy and memory the narrative is clear and rapid. There is no straining after effect. Epithets are mostly conventional, but quite adequate for the plane on which the story is conceived, and the imagery, though luxuriant, is always definite. The writer works the voluptuous vein with relish, of course, but he is not at all possessed by his theme. His cool, genial detachment appears in occasional touches of humor. For a further instance, one couplet, in the account of the story told by Jove to Astraea, pleasantly vivifies the amiable and elderly rake:

> But a faire Nymph was bathing when he waked,
> (Here sigh'd great Joue, and after brought forth) nak'd.[14]

III. William Barksted

A mythological poem less lively than *Salmacis and Hermaphroditus,* but not without some gleams of poetry, was the *Mirrha* (1607) of William Barksted, the actor.[15] Ovid tells the story of Myrrha's passion for her father in two hundred and twenty lines; Barksted's version runs to almost nine hundred, and not only the general texture but the added episodes illustrate his debt to the popular models. After some stanzas on Orpheus and his power of song we are told that the lovely and innocent Myrrha, a servant of Vesta, was one of a number of maidens who gathered to hear Orpheus sing. The bard falls in love with Myrrha and urges his suit, while she appeals to her vows of virginity. This romantic and un-Ovidian incident occupies more than a hundred lines. The story proper then follows Ovid, apart from details and an episode or two.[16] To mention another item, which is a reminder of the close relations between the mythological narrative and the pastoral, Myrrha has an encounter with a satyr, and Diana, angry at the profanation of her grove, transforms the satyr into a poplar, which hangs down its head for the loss of Myrrha.

14. P. 108.
15. Ed. Grosart, 1876. The full title is *Mirrha The Mother of Adonis: or Lustes Prodegies.* See *Metam.* x.298 ff.
16. For example, Myrrha carries on a sort of dialogue with her father's picture. Further, near the end of the tale a myth of Hebe is introduced; Jove's handmaiden had spilled nectar in heaven and it fell down, enriching Panchaia "with odorous smell." Cf. the end of E. K.'s gloss on Spenser's eclogue for November. Though the handbooks tell of Hebe's falling while she waited on Jove, I have not noticed a source for the spilling of nectar.

The conclusion of the story, except for the length of Myrrha's final prayer, is Ovidian.

Phrases scattered through the Ovidian portions of the poem show Barksted's dependence on Golding. The commendatory verses of Robert Glover allude to *Venus and Adonis*, and Barksted himself, in declining to carry his tale beyond the birth of Adonis, ends with a compliment to Shakespeare. The popularity of Shakespeare's poem had suggested a related theme, and Barksted frequently imitates the phrasing and rhythms.

But, though *Mirrha* is commonly referred to as one of the progeny of *Venus and Adonis*, Barksted's chief debt is to Marlowe. The en-amorment of Orpheus and Myrrha is closely modeled on the meeting of Hero and Leander, as even my brief outline will have indicated, and the fact is made doubly sure by such lines as these:

> My heart is the true index of my tongue.
> And by my naked wordes you may discouer,
> I am not traded like a common Louer . . .

> With this, she turnd her blushing head aside,
> & vail'd her face with lawne, not half so white . . .

The decorative digression on Hebe recalls Marlowe's incident of Mercury and the country maid; indeed Barksted has it in mind when he writes "Women are enuious, where they long for nectar." Marlowe's trick of the ætiological conceit was learned by Barksted as well as by others:

> Then blusht he [the sun] first, and backward would
>   ha fled
> And euer since in rising hee's still red.

Aphoristic or gnomic lines, like mythological conceits, by this time were a trick of the trade, and every imitation of Marlowe and Shakespeare had made them commoner; Barksted of course has his share of them.[17]

Although Barksted borrows and imitates so freely, and in general falls far below his masters, he has a few lines that neither Marlowe nor Shakespeare would have disowned. For instance, he probably re-membered Shakespeare's line about the boar—"His eyes like glow-

17. Barksted's *Hiren* (1611), which tells the story, taken probably from Painter, of Mahomet and his fair captive, lies outside of our range. It also re-veals some traces of Marlowe and Shakespeare.

worms shine when he doth fret" [18]—but he amplified and improved the image:

> As glow wormes adde a tincture to the night,
>   Glimmering in pallid fire, upon some greene,
> mixt with the dew, so did her eyes appeare.

That fine phrase, "glimmering in pallid fire," indeed describes the reflection, in Barksted and some other small poets, of the Elizabethan glow and voluptuousness of style.[19] And Barksted would be less obscure if he had written more lines like these:

> Night like a masque was entred heauens greate hall
>   with thousand torches ushering the way.

The personifying habit fostered by mythology was not always a vice.[20]

18. Cf. Lyly, *The Woman in the Moone* (Bond, III, 271):
    And yet as bright as Glow wormes in the night,
    With which the morning decks her louers hayre.

19. Gosse, *Jacobean Poets* (New York, 1894), p. 112.

20. These last lines also occur near the end of Marston's *Insatiate Countess* (ed. Bullen, III, 243), which is thought to have been revamped by Barksted. One may be allowed to add that a line of English verse can hardly fail of rhetorical effect if it has "thousand" as the second and third syllables. Thus Golding rises (ed. Rouse, p. 92, ll. 544–45):
    A thousand wayes, a thousand gates that alwayes open stand,
    This Citie hath.
And this bit of Ovid recalls the famous lines which show that Nat Lee was not always mad or bad (*Oedipus*, Act V; *Works*, 1772, I, 343):
                                    Thou Coward yet
    Art living, canst not, wilt not find the Road
    To the great Palace of magnificent Death;
    Tho thousand Ways lead to his thousand Doors,
    Which Day and Night are still unbarr'd for all.
    Another item of interest in connection with *Mirrha* is the fact that one stanza echoes some lines in *Measure for Measure:*
    And like as, when some suddaine extasie,
      seiseth the nature of a sicklie man,
    When hee's discernd to swoune, straite by and by
      folke to his helpe confusedly haue ran,
    And seeking with their art to fetch him backe:
      so many throng, that he the ayre doth lacke.
Cf. *M. for M.*, II.iv.25 ff. In the Cambridge edition of the play (pp. 132, 118) Dover Wilson, without alluding to Barksted, observes that ll. 25–30, "which have been generally taken as a complimentary reference to King James's hatred of crowds, read like a later addition."
    I have not seen three eclogues by Lewis Machin which were appended to

Before going on to two late representatives of the Ovidian tradition, James Shirley and Cowley, we may look at the less readily definable work of Davies, Heywood, Basse, and Bosworth. If Richard Brathwait's poetical quality at all corresponded to the bulk of his mythological writing he would demand consideration here also, but as it is I hesitate to release him from the cave of dullness; the curious, if such there be, will find brief notices there—in the Appendix, that is—from 1611 onward.

IV. Sir John Davies

Mythology has appeared in many strange guises, but perhaps few stranger than the "suddaine, rash, half-capreol" of Sir John Davies' wit, *Orchestra, or A Poeme of Dauncing* (1596). When Homer sang of Ulysses and Penelope, he forgot, it seems, "one thing most worthy his eternall song," the courtly love proffered to the queen by "Antinous that fresh and iolly knight." [21] This story Davies' light and graceful muse is called upon to tell.

On a festive evening in the palace, when Phemius recites tales of Troy, and Penelope, endowed by Pallas with new beauty, comes in to hear him, Antinous asks her to dance. Her avowed ignorance of the art leads Antinous to commence a long discourse on dancing, which—like Browne's quincunx—appears to be the central principle of the universe. Creation itself, the distribution of the four elements "by Loue's perswasion," are part of the eternal rhythm. The conventional Platonism of these stanzas reminds one of the opening lines of a poem published in the same year, Spenser's first *Hymn;* one is reminded too, as the dance of planets and elements proceeds, of the arguments of Spenser's Titaness, Mutability. Earth alone stands still, though some say it is the earth that moves.[22] Flowers wave in the

---

Mirrha; two of them dealt with Apollo and Hyacinth, in the approved idyllic-erotic manner (see W. W. Greg, *Pastoral Poetry and Pastoral Drama*, p. 116). To Barksted has been attributed a poem of 1617, a "tragicall narration of Virginias death," which was added to a version of Juvenal's tenth satire "as an illustration of the preceding reflections on the curse of beauty" (R. W. Bond, *Works of W. Basse*, p. xlii; see Brydges, *Restituta*, I, 41; H. R. Palmer, pp. 66–67). I have not seen the piece.

21. *Complete Poems of Sir John Davies*, ed. Grosart (1876), I, 161 ff. The poem was entered in 1594. It was edited by E. M. W. Tillyard (London, 1945) and further discussed in his *Five Poems 1470–1870* (1948). Bullen noticed Davies' borrowings from Lucian (*Some Longer Elizabethan Poems*, pp. vii–ix).

22. St. 51.

wind, birds skip from bough to bough, everything in the world is dancing—"Learne then to daunce, you that are Princes borne."

Mythology contributes all manner of examples, at least when reinterpreted. Whatever lewd wits may say, the net that held Venus and Mars together was only the embrace of dancers. But for dancing and the sound of timbrels the infant Jove would have perished. Proteus —as Lucian had said—was a versatile dancer. Caeneus and Tiresias, who were reputed to have changed their sex, sometimes took the woman's part in dancing. Did Venus change herself to a fish? No, she "did daunce with slyding easines." Dancing, in short, is

> The faire caracter of the World's consent,
> The Heau'ns true figure and th' Earth's ornament.

Penelope ventures to cite instances to the contrary, but Antinous goes on to praise "that true Loue which Dauncing did inuent" in Platonic language:

> Life's life it is, and cordiall to the heart,
> And of our better part, the better part.

He longs to convince her, and in answer to his prayer Love appears, with a mirror, the sight of which fills Penelope with winged thoughts —for Vulcan had wrought in it

> Our glorious English Courts diuine image,
> As it should be in this our Golden Age.

Orchestra illustrates the readiness with which a man of the Renaissance turned to mythology for the embellishment of serious as well as fanciful ideas, in this case the Platonic conception of world-order, a conception alive in English from Sir Thomas Elyot's *Governour* to Milton's "starry dance." [23] *Nosce Teipsum* (1599) is of course wholly serious. Neither *Orchestra* nor the *Epigrams* nor the early misadventures of the genial but choleric lawyer would prepare us for one of the few elaborate philosophical poems in English. With Davies' ideas, and his debts to Primaudaye and Mornay, we are not concerned, but we may notice that even in a treatise on the soul and immortality he does not abandon myth. Some of his adaptations are

23. See John M. Major, "The Moralization of the Dance in Elyot's *Governour*," *Studies in the Renaissance*, V (1958), 27–36.

traditional, others perhaps original. "Fond fruitlesse curiositie" seeks "in bookes prophane . . . for knowledge hid."

> What is this knowledge but the sky-stolne fire,
> For which the thiefe still chain'd in ice doth sit?
> And which the poore rude Satyre did admire,
> And needs would kisse but burnt his lips with it.[24]

· Io, transformed into a cow, was horrified at the sight of herself in the water; so man's soul, when its innocence is spotted with sin, cannot bear to contemplate itself. But it is needless to enumerate examples. The allegorical allusions, in a poem of such a character, have a degree of subtlety lacking in Golding and his predecessors, yet they belong to the same tradition.

V. Thomas Heywood

The sheer industry of Thomas Heywood appalls a faint-hearted modern reader. As if it were not enough, according to his own famous statement, to have had either an entire hand, or at the least a main finger, in over two hundred plays, he produced monstrous non-dramatic works the mere transcription of which would, one might think, occupy a life of penal servitude.

Heywood has been accepted as almost certainly the "T.H." whose *Oenone and Paris* (1594) was the first full-length imitation of *Venus and Adonis*.[25] It is indeed so close an imitation, and we have

24. *Poems*, I, 17. The reference to Io is on p. 21.

25. The poem was elaborately edited by J. Q. Adams (Folger Shakespeare Library, 1943).

One need only mention Heywood's formal translations of the *Ars Amatoria* and *De Remedio Amoris*. The former went through at least eight editions, the last appearing in 1705; the version of the *De Remedio* seems to have been lost, or at any rate not identified. While the translation is not distinguished, it shows, along with Heywood's letters of Paris and Helen—and one may add Drayton's *Heroical Epistles*—the importance of Ovidian elegiacs in molding the closed couplet.

Heywood charged one Austin—justly, it would appear—with feloniously appropriating his translations. See the Appendix, under "H. A.," 1613, and the article by A. M. Clark there cited. See also Clark's "A Bibliography of Thomas Heywood," *Oxford Bibliographical Society Proceedings and Papers*, Vol. I, Part 2 (1925), pp. 97 ff. For critical comments on the works of Heywood noticed here, see Clark's *Thomas Heywood* (1931).

Heywood had more than his share of trials at the hands of pirates. To the third edition (1612) of *The Passionate Pilgrim* Jaggard, who had published looked at so many, that, having noted its chronological primacy, we may turn to a later and much longer work.

In 1609 appeared *Troia Britanica,* a poem of about thirteen thousand lines, mainly in the *ottava rima* that Harington and Fairfax had made popular. Apart from episodical digressions, the subject matter of the "xvii. seuerall Cantons" is chiefly the story of Troy, from the time of chaos and creation to the fall of the city; the last two cantos bring Brute to England and chronicle the English kings down to James. The title and scope of the book are significant enough, and its medieval character is further illustrated in Heywood's choice and handling of sources.[26]

The dedication mentions Homer and Virgil as authorities, but one's anticipations of classical orthodoxy are not altogether fulfilled, since not much use is made of either. The fifteenth canto follows the Virgilian account of the fall of Troy, though un-Virgilian details are included. The *Iliad* seems to contribute a few bits, such as the death of Patroclus and Thetis' procuring new arms for Achilles. The treatment of this last incident shows Heywood's eclectic method. The visit of Thetis to Hephaestus is Homeric, her speech is not; she returns to Achilles with a helmet, gorget, "vaunt-brace," and other pieces; the description of the shield, much briefer than in Homer, retains a few items, names the signs of the zodiac, and, instead of the matchless vignettes of scenes of peace and war, gives allegorical figures of the seasons.[27]

Some knowledge of Homer does not necessitate the abjuring of Dares. "The description of the Troians be according to Dares the Troian, who liued in the warres of Troy, and writ their utter subuersion." [28] Indeed, as the example of Warner might lead one to expect, Heywood's main source is Caxton's *Recuyell,* though he does not emphasize the fact; like medieval authors, he prefers ancient names. Throughout the book he offers a bewildering array of authorities; how many are taken over from other compilations one can-

---

Troia Britanica, added from that work the Ovidian epistles of Paris and Helen and passages from the other Ovidian translations which Heywood had incorporated in his notes.

26. See J. S. P. Tatlock, "The Siege of Troy in Elizabethan Literature," *PMLA,* XXX, 683 ff.

27. Canto xiii, pp. 339 ff.

28. Pp. 192–93. But the account (pp. 175 ff.) of Priam and his family is much more detailed than in Dares (c.12), and seems to be taken, along with the ascription to Dares, from Caxton (ed. Sommer, pp. 543–44). Dictys is also cited (e.g., p. 333).

not inquire. Thus in his opening pages on the creation, where Caxton fails him, Heywood invokes such various opinions as those of Thales, Moses, Polydore Vergil, Hesiod, Pherecrates, Trismegistus, Marsilio Ficino, Tibullus, to mention only a few.[29]

The source next in importance to Caxton is Ovid. Heywood's ninth and tenth cantos are largely taken up with translations of the epistles of Paris and Helen. In the notes especially are incorporated passages translated from the *Ars Amatoria*, such as the tales of Cephalus and Procris and Bacchus and Ariadne. Incidents like the quarrel between Ajax and Ulysses, and many details, come from the *Metamorphoses;* yet the story of Callisto, as we have observed, elaborates the vivacious realism of Warner.[30] Nothing can be said of Heywood's other sources, for he ranges far and wide, but it may be added that his account of a feast given in Troy to the Greeks is indebted to Greene's *Euphues his Censure to Philautus*.

Troia Britanica is obviously a medieval chronicle, not an epic, but it is quite readable. Heywood is an adequate story-teller, and his digressions and topical allusions are not dull. Thus in the fourth canto remarks on the birth of Venus lead, very logically, through stanzas on religious sects to the character of the Brownist or puritan whose

> phrase is, Verily; By yea and nay,
> In faith, in truth, good neighbor, or good brother,
> And when he borrowes mony, nere will pay.

Modern heroes, Howard, Grey, Norris, Sidney, and others are celebrated as equal to the Greeks and Trojans. Jason and Hercules took Troy as Drake and Essex took "Cales." Ancient villains have also

29. An instance may be given of the circuitous route by which knowledge traveled. In the thirteenth canto (p. 333) Hector and Ajax interchange as gifts a sword and a girdle; the sword became the instrument of Ajax' suicide, the girdle was used to tie Hector's body to Achilles' chariot. Although Heywood has a quotation from Aeschylus (in Latin), and one from Euripides (Greek and Latin), such things are almost certainly taken from handbooks, and he would be quite unlikely to know the *Ajax* of Sophocles (ll. 661, 817, 1029). But he would have found the facts about the gifts in Hyginus (*Fab.* 112); Servius (on *Aen.* iv.496); or in Whitney's *Choice of Emblemes* (1586), p. 37.

30. See above, page 66; Heywood, pp. 36 ff. Heywood provides Jupiter with the conventional arguments against virginity. Cf. Warner, bk. v, c. 24 (Chalmers, IV, 565; the passage is quoted in *PMLA*, XLIV, 762); Marlowe, Shakespeare, and others. On the use of these arguments in the Jupiter-Callisto episode in *The Golden Age*, see R. G. Martin, *MLN*, XXXIII (1918), 23 ff., though Martin does not take account of Warner.

modern parallels; as a prelude to Sinon's betrayal of Troy, we hear of Dr. Parry, Babington, Guy Fawkes. Finally, for a specimen of Heywood's poetical quality we might take from a passage about the Gorgons some lines on the idea of people all over the earth being suddenly turned to stone. We have here, not Keats's bold lover, to be sure, but still something like poetry:

> Another digging as the Queene came by,
> Stoopes stil with one Hand boue the other placst,
> The right foot fixt, the left aduanced hie
> To driue the dull Spade in, another facst
> the Gorgon-monster, as his loue past by,
> Who spreads his amorous armes t'infould her wast:
>   and smiling in her face, his Image stands,
>   Laughing with halfe-shut eyes, & broad-spread hands.[31]

Heywood, like Boccaccio, based his hopes of fame not so much on his imaginative creations as on his encyclopedic compilations of historical and biographical anecdote. It is hard to think of any story about women, good or bad, divine or human, that Heywood omitted from Γυναικεῖον.[32] From planning to printing the work occupied seventeen weeks, says Heywood; well might he exclaim *Laus Deo!* It was modeled on the collections of ancients like Valerius Maximus and Aelian, and the numerous miscellanies of the Renaissance. However much Heywood took directly from such favorites as Ovid and Plutarch, he took still more from preceding compilers, especially Ravisius Textor.[33]

To return, for a moment, to Heywood's verse, *Pleasant Dialogues and Dramma's* (1637) contained, in dramatic form, a few selections from Erasmus' *Colloquies,* Ravisius Textor, the *Metamorphoses,* and

---

31. Canto v, p. 111.

32. Γυναικεῖον or *Nine Bookes of Various History Concerninge Women* (1624). See Clark, *Thomas Heywood,* pp. 91 ff.; and R. G. Martin, "A Critical Study of Thomas Heywood's *Gunaikeion," SP,* XX, 160 ff. Martin shows (pp. 180 ff.) that Heywood "had at best but a distant bowing acquaintance" with Greek. Greek authors are regularly quoted in Latin.

33. In his *Exemplary Lives* (1640) Heywood chose nine female worthies to parallel the traditional nine—Deborah, Judith, Esther, Boadicea, Penthesilea, Artemisia, "Elphleda," wife of Æthelred of Mercia, Margaret, wife of Henry VI, and Elizabeth. Around these were grouped countless other tales of famous women, for such a compiler must needs be thrifty. A loose adaptation of this book, called *Female Excellency,* was issued in 1688 by Nathaniel Crouch; see Louis B. Wright, *RES,* IV (1928), 137.

fifteen of Lucian's mythological dialogues.[34] The work as a whole is decidedly heavy, but the Ovidian episodes of Jupiter and Io, Apollo and Daphne, are treated with some original touches in the vein of pastoral masques. Heywood is a too pedestrian and loosely girt Landor to achieve "Hellenics." [35]

VI. WILLIAM BASSE

William Basse is remembered chiefly for his epitaph on Shakespeare. He wrote pastorals which pleasantly mingle fresh rural impressions with Ovidian myth, and his mythological fancies received elaborately playful expression in *Urania. The Woman in the Moone.*[36] Although Basse is grouped with disciples of Spenser, this poem belongs rather with miscellaneous works. It was first dedicated to Prince Henry, who died in 1612, and, in the opinion of Basse's editor, was written some years before that date. A doubtful earlier limit might be found in the second stanza:

> For when Endymion once in Latmos slept
> The Moone (some say) came downe and kis'd him there,
> Erronious Fame reports that she hath kept
> Him euer since within her spotlesse Sphere.
> And of this falshood, so profusely blowne,
> The generall tale of Man i' th' Moone is growne.

While the tale was common, and the allusion is vague, the lines do suggest Drayton's *The Man in the Moone* (1606), which, as a partly satirical treatment of the myth of Cynthia, might have helped to inspire Basse.[37]

34. Reprinted by W. Bang, *Materialien* (1903). Heywood had drawn upon Lucian before (Martin, p. 167; Clark, *Thomas Heywood*, pp. 157–59).

35. Heywood of course was not unaware of Spenser, Marlowe, and Shakespeare; the last two are praised in the roll-call of poets in the *Hierarchie of the Blessed Angells* (a eulogy of Spenser is quoted by F. F. Covington, *MLN*, XLI, 1926, 386–87). Clark (p. 56) has rightly called attention to Spenserian influence in *Troia Britanica*. For some echoes of *Venus and Adonis* in Heywood see R. G. Martin, *MLN*, XXXIII, 23 ff. In *Pleasant Dialogues* we have at least one trace of Marlowe—"Women by nature are ambitious"—though the idea had become proverbial (p. 159, l. 5359; *H. and L.*, i.428). But the influence of Shakespeare and Marlowe seems very slight.

36. *Poetical Works*, ed. R. W. Bond (1893), pp. 267 ff.

37. Might the choice of Ethiopia for his scene have been suggested by Jonson's *Masque of Blackness* (1605)? And see below for a possible reference to *Mutability* (1609).

Urania offers a new theory about the face in the moon. Disgusted with sinful humanity Jove sends down to earth as investigators "two handsome youthfull Gods." These envoys, carefully observing "ioyes, woes, wants, wealthes, sinnes, service," find themselves in Ethiopia, then inhabited by people "white & fayre." Being entertained by the loveliest woman in the land, the two gods, disguised as mortals, fall in love with her, and make rapid progress in courtship. Jove's commission is forgotten, though they have visited all nations except

> some base Americans
> That know not Ioue, and Ioue cares not to know.

Their hostess loves them equally, and bestows her favors without prejudice. When the two lovers, to forward their suit, reveal their divinity, the crafty woman extracts from them the secret which enables them to reach heaven, a place she has longed to see. She mounts on unfamiliar wings.

> Her sprawling heeles, in stead of wonted molde
> Kick Cedars tops.

The young gods pursue her, but in vain,

> For in this Charme did such a vertue lye,
> Those that could fastest speake, could fastest flye.

Passing celestial sentinels with their "harquebushes," she arrives in the Olympian hall. Jove summons an assembly to decide what shall be done with the interloper, since this female Tomlinson is "nor fit for heau'n nor (from heau'n) fit for earth." It is settled that she shall lodge in the moon.[38]

Cynthia is more annoyed at being saddled with a companion than she had been at the slanderous tale of there being a man in the moon, but she bows to Jove's desire. In a rage, however, she dashes around her circuit at great speed, outstripping the other planetary gods, and

38. This disturbing invasion of heaven by a woman might have been inspired, humorous though it is, by the enterprise of the Titaness in Spenser's *Mutability*—which itself has touches of something like humor. And these lines (page 294) seem a not improbable allusion to Spenser's work:

> They saw that she was none of Titan's race
> Who by pretence of eldership layd clayme
> And title to expulsed Saturne's place;
> For they long since by Ioue were overcame . . .

> Rattles her tedious guest, to make her bones
> And well knit joynts to totter in her skin,
> To turne her maw or shake th' ambitious dame
> Downe from her seate to earth from whence she came.

The tedious guest, unperturbed, sits in the moon's windows, "Dressing her dainty browes from Morne to Noone." The exasperation of Cynthia leads her to exercise her divine powers in various ways upon all terrestrial things, especially upon women, whom she afflicts

> With fancyes, frenzies, lunacyes, with strange
> Feares, fashions, factions, furyes, & affections . . .[39]

Yet, since Basse would not be a misogynist, his mildly satirical extravaganza ends with praise of womanly virtues.

Following the narrative comes a piece of over eighty lines, "This Story Morallized," which Basse's editor, from its style, supposed to be a later addition.[40] A friend, says the author, demanded allegory, since fictions without a moral are mere fables. Here as elsewhere Basse seems to be skeptical, but he consents to expound a moral. The woman, "Mind," sought celestial knowledge; her deserting the gods who helped her showed ingratitude; their passion typified the supremacy of love . . . But Basse's heart seems to have been mainly in the telling of his tale. He may not have genius, but he has geniality, a quality not too common in mythological poems to be despised.

There is much more narrative than picture-making, and descriptions, instead of being warm and luscious, are in the cooler style of Drayton. The transition from the Elizabethan to the Jacobean manner is most obvious in the prevailing mock-heroic and satirical tone, though the satire is only a flavor. The passion for beauty, the intoxication of the senses, which inspired poems so various as *Hero and Leander,* *Venus and Adonis, Ovid's Banquet of Sense,* has given way, even in poets writing partly in the older vein, to an attitude of ironic and humorous detachment. Since, however, we read the earlier poems and do not read the later ones, the change is not entirely a gain.

39. The influence of Lyly's *The Woman in the Moone* is obvious here (*Works,* ed. Bond, III, 287–88; see also p. 237).

40. At the beginning of the third canto the woman is said to represent "Mind," though her lively adventures somewhat obscure the symbolism.

VII. William Bosworth

A chapter much concerned with the influence of *Hero and Leander* cannot pass by the exuberant *Arcadius and Sepha* of William Bosworth. Though written apparently in 1626, when the author was nineteen, the poem did not reach print until 1651.[41]

One can hardly even summarize this wayward romance of sixty-four pages, for the chief story, of the love of Arcadius and Sepha, is not always lucid, and there are five or six inset tales of some length. Sepha falls in love at the first sight of the gallant Arcadius and yearns for a return of affection. On her way to a temple she encounters a band of satyrs and fauns who dance around her as their queen. One of these tells a story of Bacchus and Diana: Bacchus proposes to build in a region frequented by Diana, and in the battle which ensues between the two divinities the maiden Antigone is killed.

There follows—according to the chronology of events it should precede—the story of Haemon and Antigone. A reader who expects something Sophoclean is quickly undeceived. Haemon, stricken by Cupid, sees and loves the sleeping Antigone, who, awakened, first prays to Diana and then arranges to meet Haemon the next night. But she is killed and he, keeping tryst, writes an elegy and kills himself on her tomb. His blood is turned into a columbine, his body to a marble statue. Sepha, whom we may have forgotten, goes on her way to the temple, and Arcadius rides by her without a word; one cannot help thinking of Lavinia and Aeneas in the *Roman d' Eneas*. She reads on Diana's altar

> Those that Idalia's wanton garments wear,
> No sacrifices for me must prepare.

She faints. Then comes a story of Eramio and Amissa. In the second book Sepha revives, at the embrace of Arcadius, and as they walk home together he tells the story of Sappho and Phaon. Sepha is offended by her lover's allusion to "Venus' pleasures" and goes to her tower, but when she sees him below, apparently dead, she runs out and kisses him. Arcadius revives, Sepha avows her ardent love—not without a prudential reference to Hymen—and Arcadius goes home elated.

We are now reminded of the original narrator, Epimenides, and he

41. Saintsbury, *Minor Caroline Poets*, II, 523 ff.

tells of the love of Delithason and Verista, a story which Verista, dying, told to him. Then Epimenides, coming upon two knights in combat, had gone away with the survivor, Arcadius. The two were entertained by Sepha in her tower. A jealous suitor attacked the wedding party and Arcadius was killed. Sepha, after fleeing into a wood,
returned to find her lover dead. She killed herself, and the ever help-
ful Epimenides cremated both bodies; a phoenix arose from the ashes
of the star-crossed lovers. Finishing his tale, Epimenides dies.

Even this outline suggests some influences which Bosworth's editor, "R. C.," indicates in his preface—Ovid, Marlowe, Sidney. To
the first are indebted "the high, the fluent, and the pathetic discourses
of his lovers," and the metamorphoses. "The strength of his fancy,
and the shadowing of it in words, he taketh from Mr. Marlow in his
Hero and Leander . . . You shall find our Author everywhere in
this imitation." "The weaving of one story into another" Bosworth
had learned from Sidney. And "his making the end of one verse to be
the frequent beginning of the other, (besides the art of the trope)
was the labour and delight of Mr. Edmund Spencer." Ralegh and
Sir Kenelm Digby, says R. C., called Spenser the English Virgil, and
in these devices Bosworth imitated both the ancient and the modern
poet.

R. C. indicates some aspects of Ovidian influence, and there are
others, both in situations and in details. But classical figures may, as
in medieval romance, become quite unrecognizable. Here are some
lines concerning an old lover of Sappho's, as reported by Arcadius,
who is himself the son of Capaneus, one of the seven against Thebes:

> This done, I saw a knight of courage bold,
> Cloth'd all in argent armour, strip'd with gold . . .
> . . . . "Discourteous knight," he said,
> "Dost not repent thee that thou hast betray'd
> That honour'd lady?" [42]

The young poet, whether in the main plot or the inset tales, does not
really try to create a mythological world. Classical and mythological
figures are introduced into a pastoral and romantic Arcadia, to become bright threads in a fanciful decorative pattern. The author enjoys writing pretty words about pretty things, and denatured characters from ancient story are among the prettiest things available.

The influence of *Hero and Leander*, as R. C. says, is everywhere.
One could cite many passages that testify to a study of Marlowe both

42. P. 577.

loving and inadequate, but this will serve to illustrate the difference
between, as it were, an Elizabethan Keats and Leigh Hunt:

> Then to the altar went he, where he pray'd,
> While Sepha, overcome with passion, said,
> So loud that he might hear, "Were I the saint
> To whom he prays, sure I would hear his plaint." [43]

Spenser was more than a model of style. Sepha and the satyrs, for
example, remind us of Una; but what in Spenser has allegorical significance is in Bosworth only another ornamental episode. So too, as a
young man in love with poetry, he responds to the romantic and
sensuous elements in the *Arcadia,* not to the serious and didactic.
Finally, the poem may be linked, though not in the way of "influence," with *Glaucus and Scilla,* for, despite its length and intricacies,
it is in structure a personal love-complaint; we learn the fact at the
beginning, and completely forget it until the end. Although the poem
is so largely a mosaic of imitations, the author's Elizabethan enthusiasms give it enough freshness and charm to carry one through
a single reading at least.[44]

VIII. James Shirley

In 1646 Shirley published *Narcissus, or, The Self-Lover,* a poem
that had been entered in 1618.[45] Although he was born in 1596
Shirley is often spoken of as the last Elizabethan dramatist, and
Narcissus was one of the last specimens of the conventional Elizabethan mythological poem.

The Ovidian story is expanded to the length of about a hundred
and thirty six-line stanzas. The incidents are not essentially altered,
except that Echo, through the compassion of Juno, is endowed with a
voice, and she makes fluent and passionate use of it. The amplification
is all in the way of descriptive detail and speeches; a third of the poem
consists of dialogue and soliloquy. The Shakespearian epithet in the
first line—"Fair Echo, rise, sick-thoughted nymph, awake" [46]—announces a debt to *Venus and Adonis* that increases as the poem pro-

43. P. 570. Cf. Marlowe, i.177 ff.
44. I may mention inevitable but insignificant allusions to *Venus and Adonis,*
pp. 533, 569.
45. Of the 1618 edition no copy has survived. For the text see Dyce's edition of Shirley (1833), VI, 463 ff., and *Poems of James Shirley,* ed. R. L.
Armstrong (New York, 1941).
46. Cf. *V. and A.,* l. 5.

ceeds. Shirley makes a good deal of Narcissus as a huntsman, like Adonis, and, as usual, the most obvious imitation is in the woman's wooing of the man. There are abundant conceits in the vein of Shakespeare and his fellows. The customary gnomic lines are lacking. Hitherto we have found that almost any poem that bore traces of *Venus and Adonis* revealed the stronger influence of *Hero and Leander*. *Narcissus* is an exception, for it seems to contain no suggestion of Marlowe, though there is an echo of the lyric which, along with *Hero and Leander,* sustained his reputation in the seventeenth century.[47]

The poem is smooth and fluent, but the mannerisms of *Venus and Adonis* without its impetuous verve had been staled by custom. While there are no special felicities, here is a stanza that begins well:

> No portion of a bird's forsaken nest
>   Fell from the boughs to interrupt the calm;
> No wither'd leaf did in his fall molest
>   The stillness of it, smooth as settled balm,
> But crystal less transparent: such a mirror,
> So form'd, could only shew disdain his error.

One may remember that the man who commenced his career with this thin and facile Elizabethan piece did not abandon Ovid. Over a generation later came *The Contention of Ajax and Ulysses,* with the great lyric on a deeper but still Elizabethan note.

IX. ABRAHAM COWLEY

While a mythological poem had long been for young authors the correct door through which to enter the literary world, no one made his début at quite so early an age as Abraham Cowley. His *Tragicall Historie of Pyramus and Thisbe* was first published in 1633, but it had been written five years before, when the author was ten years old.[48] If less ambitious and sophisticated than the "novels of the nursery and poems of the pram" which the twentieth century has witnessed, Cowley's poem is precocious enough—not to mention the more elaborate romance, *Constantia and Philetus,* composed at the mature age of twelve.

47. P. 478: Yet these but shadows of the mirth we'll prove,
        If thou wilt stay, and be thy Echo's love.
48. *Essays, Plays and Sundry Verses,* ed. A. R. Waller (1906), pp. 31 ff.

In addition to a lyric and an epitaph, of eight lines each, *Pyramus and Thisbe* contains thirty-five stanzas of rather odd form (*abaabb*). The lyric, which Thisbe sings while waiting under the mulberry tree, and the epitaph, are original ventures. Otherwise the story is a free redaction of Ovid, and the treatment shows some acquaintance with the conventions of the mythological genre. There is not much in the pictorial manner, but we have the conceits and gnomic lines so popular in this kind of writing. Near the beginning Cowley introduces an un-Ovidian motive; Venus, envying the lovers' beauty, has Cupid transfix them with his darts.[49]

A schoolboy's verses usually possess the merit of indicating his favorite authors. We have Cowley's testimony to his early love of Spenser, but there is hardly anything clearly Spenserian in this piece.[50] There is a reference to *Venus and Adonis* in *Constantia and Philetus*, and probably Cowley knew the poem when he wrote his *Tragicall Historie*. Such lines as these seem to have a Shakespearean ring:

> Thus Beautie is by Beauties meanes undone,
> Striving to close these eyes that make her bright.[51]

Cowley may well have read Ovid in Latin, but he was more familiar with Golding than perhaps his "very loving Master" of Westminster would have thought desirable. In fact he sometimes follows Golding when Golding does not follow Ovid.[52]

It is not unfitting that this chapter should end, allegorically as it were, with the Ovidian exercise, the belated Elizabethan imitation, of a small boy, and that boy Abraham Cowley. The mythological

49. Such a motive is not uncommon in mythological poems, but it may be observed that Dunstan Gale made use of it in his long poem on Pyramus and Thisbe. See the Appendix, under 1596.

50. Commenting upon the prosody A. H. Thompson remarked that "Spenser's successors, rather than Spenser himself, appear to have been Cowley's model" (*Cambridge History of English Literature*, VII, 62). See A. H. Nethercot, *Abraham Cowley* (New York, 1931), pp. 10–11.

51. More definite, though the figure itself is common, is the resemblance between Cowley's "Like as a Bird which in a Net is tane" (st. 4) and Shakespeare's "Look! how a bird lies tangled in a net" (l. 67).

52. Golding and Cowley speak of Thisbe's not looking back as she runs away; both render *alto pulvere* as "subtle sand"; in both Thisbe beats her breast and tears her golden hair, while in Ovid she does not beat her breast and her hair is not golden.

Some details also suggest that Cowley may have known Brathwait's long tale of Pyramus and Thisbe (see the Appendix, under 1615).

poem of the Renaissance was an unconscionable time a-dying, and, with very few exceptions, it did not attract the important poets of the early seventeenth century. Marlowe had carried the Ovidian and Italianate tradition as far as it could go, and most of his successors could only try to imitate his incidents, his rich mythological descriptions, his rhetorical tricks. They followed Marlowe and Shakespeare rather than Drayton, who, whatever his faults, had inaugurated a kind of poem more fruitful and less easily exhausted than the merely erotic and decorative minor epic.

Yet these minor epics were only one manifestation of the mythological impulse, and if we think not merely of them but of allusions in almost the whole body of Elizabethan poetry, from Shakespeare and Spenser down, we shall not underestimate the beauties that the Ovidian tradition carried with it. Whether of gold or gilt, there they are, a sumptuous tapestry. On the other hand, while it is quite unfair to judge of a tradition from one brief illustration of one particular vice, a single example will remind us of certain weaknesses, of the leveling tendencies, which could develop within the Renaissance convention. Here are three generations of a popular conceit:

> I sawe Phœbus thrust out his golden hedde,
>   upon her to gaze:
> But when he sawe, how broade her beames did spredde,
>   it did him amaze.
> He blusht to see another Sunne belowe,
> Ne durst againe his fyrye face out showe:
>   Let him, if he dare,
>   His brightnesse compare
> With hers, to haue the ouerthrowe.[53]

> At which the Sunne his glorious face did hide,
>   Each Planet pulleth in his golden head,
> The other stars out of the heauens glide:
>   And Cynthia from her siluer Palace fled,
> The night is robbed of her wonted light,
>   Each thing turn'd dark that formerly was bright.[54]

> And though the shady gloom
> Had given day her room,
>   The sun himself withheld his wonted speed;

53. Spenser, *Shep. Cal., April.*
54. *The Scourge of Venus* (1613), ed. Grosart, p. 30. The poem goes under the initials "H. A.," but the author is unknown. See the Appendix, and above, section V, note 25.

And hid his head for shame,
As his inferior flame
    The new-enlighten'd world no more should need:
He saw a greater sun appear
Than his bright throne or burning axletree could bear.

Granted that the three extracts may be ranked in a foreordained order, do they show the differences in quality that one might expect to find among Spenser, an anonymous scribbler, and Milton? To abuse the old phrase again, one touch of Renaissance nature makes the whole world kin.

The stream of Ovidian tradition dried up, for the main current of poetry had been moving along a deeper channel. When the young Cowley was writing his romantic little tales a revolt against the normal Elizabethan spirit and style, a revolt starting from Chapman and Donne, had been in progress for over a generation, and later Cowley himself was to be regarded as the high priest of the new cult. But we may remember that metaphysical poetry also expired, and that the Ovidian mythology of the Renaissance was to be revived and invested with altogether new splendor by Milton. So sinks the day-star in the ocean bed . . .

CHAPTER X

Chapman

If any proof were needed that the classic artist is born and not made it might be found in the work of George Chapman. A man of vigorous and independent mind and character, with a high and serious conception of the function and craft of poetry, endowed with more than a spark of the true poetic fire, and, finally, possessed by a religious adoration for Homer—such a man, one might think, would stand forth as a modern embodiment of authentic classicism. Yet Chapman has been a byword for every kind of Elizabethan vice of thought and expression.[1] Of late, however, critics, following eagerly where Mr. Eliot leads, have been praising him, sometimes apparently reading him. He has taken rank as a metaphysical poet of importance; and, since he has not been conveniently anthologized and since he propounds an earnest moral philosophy, there is less danger than in the case of Donne that his vogue will become an uncritical cult.

The mere possession—one hesitates to say "exposition"—of a philosophy of life and literature is not in itself enough to set Chapman apart from his fellows; we have happily got beyond the notion that the Elizabethans were eternal children. Chapman's ethical ideas sometimes approach Spenser's, his faith in culture sometimes reminds us of Daniel, but his style is equally remote from the warm, melodious

1. For a compendious account of a reader's first sensations one cannot do better than quote Swinburne, though Swinburne also praised Chapman well. He speaks of the shock given to one's taste by the poet's "crabbed and bombastic verbiage, the tortuous and pedantic obscurity, the rigidity and the laxity of a style which moves as it were with a stiff shuffle, at once formal and shambling; which breaks bounds with a limping gait, and plays truant from all rule without any of the grace of freedom; wanders beyond law and straggles out of order at the halting pace of age and gravity, and in the garb of a schoolmaster plays the pranks of a schoolboy with a ponderous and lumbaginous license of movement, at once rheumatic and erratic" (Introduction to *Poems and Minor Translations*, 1875, p. xxi).

Quotations from this modernized edition have been retained, corrected in places from the standard *Poems*, ed. P. B. Bartlett (New York, 1941).

fluidity of the one and the pure, rational soberness of the other. What distinguishes Chapman, and Donne, as metaphysical poets is, in Mr. Eliot's pregnant words, "a direct sensuous apprehension of thought, or a re-creation of thought into feeling." [2] Donne's work, though circulating privately, had more influence than Chapman's, but Chapman's published poems were the first open revolt against orthodox or conventional canons of Elizabethan taste. The limitations of our subject forbid any attempt at a rounded estimate of Chapman, in which *The Tears of Peace* would be central, and perhaps compel attention mainly to his weaknesses, but these are at any rate the weaknesses of gnarled and knotted muscles, not of flaccidity and anæmia. Who touches Chapman touches a man, though an uncouth one, a brine-encrusted Odysseus over whom Athene has not yet shed her luminous grace.

In 1594 appeared *The Shadow of Night,* comprising a *Hymnus in Noctem* and a *Hymnus in Cynthiam,* with prose glosses appended. The first paragraph of the dedication to Matthew Roydon indicates the prevailing character of Chapman's mythology:

> It is an exceeding rapture of delight in the deep search of knowledge . . . that maketh men manfully indure the extremes incident to that Herculean labour: from flints must the Gorgonean fount be smitten. Men must be shod by Mercury, girt with Saturn's adamantine sword, take the shield from Pallas, the helm from Pluto, and have the eyes of Græa (as Hesiodus arms Perseus against Medusa) before they can cut off the viperous head of benumbing ignorance, or subdue their monstrous affections to most beautiful judgment.

The allusions, and their significance, Chapman takes from Natalis Comes.[3] Wisdom, he proceeds, is not easily wooed and won, nor does she stoop to the profane rabble—no Renaissance poet is more disdainful of the vulgar than Chapman—but visits only those who approach her "with invocation, fasting, watching; yea, not without having drops of their souls like an heavenly familiar." The words recall some famous utterances of Milton's, with a difference.[4] This arduous ideal,

2. *Homage to John Dryden,* p. 29.
3. This chapter is constantly indebted to M. Schoell's *Études sur l'humanisme continental en Angleterre* (1926). For the item in question see page 179; and Comes, vii.11 and 12.
4. Chapman's "heavenly familiar" reminds one too of the Shakespearian interest of these poems, and of Chapman's evident dislike of Ovidian eroticism. Some critics have seen him as the rival poet of the *Sonnets,* the cloudy preacher

which Chapman never wearied of proclaiming, is set forth in these early Hymns with an enthusiasm that leaves few lucid intervals in the tangle of allegory and allusion. Yet beauty does peep through the blanket of the dark.

Grasping our golden bough, which will prove to be M. Schoell, we plunge into the shadows. To begin with a bit of arithmetic, these two Hymns, of over nine hundred lines, contain matter taken from Natalis Comes which fills about two hundred, and almost all of the learned glosses are from the same source. Chapman thinks of the day as the nurse of evil, an idea that leads to satire, and of the night as the mysterious source of good and spiritual strength; the conception, so different from the rhetorical denunciation of night that we met in Shakespeare and Spenser,[5] is correspondingly more difficult to render. To mention only one element of confusion, Chapman distinguishes between the creative aspect of night and "this horrid step-dame, blindness of the mind," which he compares to a Gorgon.[6] The Calydonian boars that ravage the fields represent the chaos that followed the reign of order. Amalthea, who befriended Jove and was translated to heaven, is an example of virtue rewarded. The ship of the Argonauts was also placed among the stars because it carried the heroes to and from Colchis. The story of Orpheus reveals the power of wisdom in civilizing men.

> And that in calming the infernal kind,
> To wit, the perturbations of his mind,
> And bringing his Eurydice from hell

---

whose nocturnal visitations seem to draw Shakespeare's good-natured chaff (Sonnet lxxxvi) :

> He, nor that affable familiar ghost
> Which nightly gulls him with intelligence . . .

In his second Hymn, Chapman, singing the praises of his Cynthia, "the forces of the mind," breaks off with what seems a clear allusion to the *pocula Castalia* of the Ovidian motto prefixed to *Venus and Adonis:*

> Presume not then ye flesh-confounded souls,
> That cannot bear the full Castalian bowls,
> Which sever mounting spirits from the senses,
> To look in this deep fount for thy pretences.

The change from "ye" to "thy" may be thought to indicate a not wholly general object of censure. Chapman's lines read like the protest of a mystic and moralist against a leader of the fleshly school.

5. See above, chapter VII, note 34, and note 6 below.

6. The idea of the "night of mind" is taken from Comes, iii.12 (Schoell, p. 180). Spenser may have used the same passage in Comes (Lemmi, *PQ*, VIII, 275).

(Which justice signifies) is proved well.
But if in right's observance any man
Look back, with boldness less than Orphean,
Soon falls he to the hell from whence he rose.[7]

"The golden chain of Homer's high device," Chapman continues,

Ambition is, or cursed avarice,
Which all gods haling being tied to Jove,
Him from his settled height could never move.[8]

These are some of the mythological allusions in the first Hymn, and they all come from Natalis Comes,[9] not, however, in their first simplicity, but colored by their passage through Chapman's prismatic mind. The glosses, as I have mentioned, are likewise taken from Comes, though he is named only once. In any case the borrowed matter suited Chapman's theory and practice of poetry, the enforcing of moral ideas with novel figures and applications. His consciousness of himself as a rebel addressing a chosen few appears again in the last paragraph of the gloss. He will not labor to justify his innovations, they must justify themselves to such as understand them; "for the rest, God help them, I cannot do as others, make day seem a lighter woman than she is, by painting her."

The *Hymnus in Cynthiam*, which is complementary to the first piece, continues to shadow forth the oppositions between day and night, sun and moon, vice and virtue, sense and reason, confusion and order, with all Chapman's love of personification, and with much borrowing from Comes. The dominant idea, quite un-Elizabethan, is the primitive mystery, the vast fecundity, of night. Both poems, or the two parts of one poem, have a pattern of emotion and association, not of daylight logic; they are, as Janet Spens observed, a dream-fugue.[10] The longest unit is an allegorical tale of the nymph Euthimya, created by Cynthia, who is transformed to a panther and pursued by hounds; we are given a list of the hounds' names, derived

7. Schoell, pp. 34–35. Cf. Phineas Fletcher's version of Boethius, page 173 above.

8. In Chapman's *Tragedy of Caesar and Pompey* (IV.v.128 ff.) the golden chain "becomes in Cato's argument for immortality and freedom a symbol of the power and tenacity of the soul" (Elizabeth Holmes, *Aspects of Elizabethan Imagery*, p. 78).

9. Schoell, pp. 180 ff.

10. "Chapman's Ethical Thought," *Essays and Studies by Members of the English Association*, XI (1925), 161. Cf. E. Holmes, pp. 80 ff.

from Comes' story of Actaeon. The hounds pursue the nymph vainly during the day, encountering hard obstacles, but at night the goddess blows retreat, and there is peace. Thus, according to Miss Spens, the poet's thoughts pursue poetry and, baffled in the daytime, win peace and inspiration with darkness. It would be more in harmony with the orthodox moralization of Actaeon to take the hounds as the "monstrous affections," the irrational senses and emotions, which day, the time of evil, starts into activity, to disturb the poetic soul, and which at night are subdued.[11]

Leaving the myth wrapped in the shadow of night Chapman soon devotes a dozen lines to an account, taken from Comes, of the temple of Ephesus. Comes, who seldom neglects to attach a moral, fails him here, and he expounds an allegory of his own, exhorting "Elysian ladies" to

> Build Cynthia's temple in your virtuous parts,
> Let every jewel be a virtue's glass.

He returns to Comes for the meaning of Ganymede's translation to the skies:

> His beauty was it, not the body's pride,
> That made him great Aquarius stellified.
> And that mind most is beautiful and high,
> And nearest comes to a Divinity,
> That furthest is from spot of Earth's delight,
> Pleasures that lose their substance with their sight,
> Such one, Saturnius ravisheth to love,
> And fills the cup of all content to Jove.

It helps us to measure both Chapman's moral earnestness and his tortured and eccentric style if we recall the same sentiment in a poet who at his best combined seriousness and wit with classic clarity:

> Earth cannot shew so brave a Sight
> As when a single Soul does fence
> The Batteries of alluring Sense,
> And Heaven views it with delight.

11. For Actaeon see above, chapter IV, note 1. The best analysis of *The Shadow of Night* is that of Roy Battenhouse, *SP*, XXXVIII (1941).

But the effect of the whole poem lies in suggestion and symbol rather than in the more definite and particular allegories. It is far from a good poem, yet it adds a poetic province to one's consciousness. Chapman's conception is, in a way, the exact opposite of Plato's myth of the cave. Instead of mounting from the contemplation of vain shadows to the dazzling light of day and reality, one is borne along on a deep and turbid stream of creation which, far below the realm of the sun, moves toward the immense and fertile womb of night.

Ovid's Banquet of Sense (1595) is also addressed to the sympathetic Roydon, and the dedication is a more elaborate and reasoned manifesto of Chapman's poetical ideals. He hates the profane multitude, and consecrates his "strange poems to those searching spirits, whom learning hath made noble, and nobility sacred." Poetry should not be "as pervial as oratory," or, one might add, as most Elizabethan writing (except Donne's). True poetry, true clearness, comes not from the easy presentation of an easy subject, but from the adequate rendering of a complex and difficult one. Deliberate and wanton obscurity is "pedantical and childish; but where it shroudeth itself in the heart of his subject, uttered with fitness of figure and expressive epithets, with that darkness will I still labour to be shadowed." [12]

The extraordinary poem can best be outlined by means of Chapman's argument:

> Ovid, newly enamoured of Julia, daughter to Octavius Augustus Cæsar, after by him called Corinna, secretly conveyed himself into a garden of the Emperor's court, in an arbour whereof Corinna was bathing, playing upon her lute and singing;
>
> *Auditus.* which Ovid overhearing was exceedingly pleased with the sweetness of her voice, and to himself uttered the comfort he conceived in his sense of Hearing.
>
> *Olfactus.* Then the odours she used in her bath breathing a rich savour, he expressed the joy he felt in his sense of Smelling.
>
> *Visus.* Thus growing more deeply enamoured in great contentment with himself, he ventures to see her in the pride of her nakedness; which doing by stealth, he discovered the comfort he conceived in Seeing, and the glory of her beauty.
>
> *Gustus.* Not yet satisfied, he useth all his art to make known his being there without her offence; or, being necessarily offended, to ap-

pease her, which done, he entreats a kiss, to serve for satisfaction of his Taste, which he obtains.

Tactus.   Then proceeds he to entreaty for the fifth sense, and there is interrupted.[13]

One might expect another *Venus and Adonis* or *Venus and Anchises,* but Chapman's poem is more of a treatise than a debauch. He starts from a point beyond where *Venus and Adonis* leaves off. Various as were the uses of classic story, no one but Chapman could have woven an abstruse and subtle treatment of the sublimation of the senses into a series of pictures marked by a voluptuousness at once lavish and dry. Like Spenser, Chapman has both a fear of the senses that compels a desire to master them, and also, as a poet, a fervent belief that the senses, bestowed by nature, by God, are a means through which man may rise above himself to a vision of ideal beauty. But whereas Spenser shows the ethical will overcoming sensual temptation or, in the *Fowre Hymnes,* turns from the religion of beauty to Christian faith, Chapman seems here to set aside his moral and religious conviction in the interest of an aesthetic philosophy. Even Donne, who can be Platonic and sensual and scholastic, is rarely all three at the same time.[14] As an aesthetic essay the poem is unique in more than one way, and it must embody the only appearance in literature of Julia or Corinna as ideal beauty, and of Ovid as a worshiper thereof. Julia is a world away from Drayton's Platonized Phoebe.

As poet, Chapman is most satisfying, not when he is most subtle, but when his metaphysical strings have just been touched into vibration, when the rich imagery of ordinary Elizabethan writing is quickened by a peculiar intensity. There are such phrases in these bits:

13. M. Schoell seems to have overlooked Chapman's apparent debt to his favorite, Ficino. See Ficino's discussion of "Ratio, Visus, Auditus, Olfactus, Gustus, & Tactus," in *Comm. in Convivium* (*Omnia Divini Platonis Opera,* Lyons, 1548), v.2, and cf. i.4.

14. Some lines in the poem recall a famous bit of Donne. Chapman writes (page 30):

> The sense is given us to excite the mind,
> And that can never be by sense excited,
> But first the sense must her contentment find,
> We therefore must procure the sense delighted,
> That so the soul may use her faculty.

Here Chapman is more logical than imaginative, and one misses the sudden lift that comes with Donne's "Else a great Prince in prison lies."

In a loose robe of tinsel forth she came,
Nothing but it betwixt her nakedness
And envious light. The downward-burning flame
Of her rich hair did threaten new access
    Of venturous Phaeton to scorch the fields . . .[15]

O Beauty, how attractive is thy power!
For as the life's heat clings about the heart,
So all men's hungry eyes do haunt thy bower.
Reigning in Greece, Troy swum to thee in Art,
    Removed to Troy, Greece follow'd thee in fears . . .

Herewith she rose like the autumnal star,
Fresh burnish'd in the lofty ocean flood,
That darts his glorious influence more far
Than any lamp of bright Olympus' brood . . .

Chapman published his continuation of *Hero and Leander* in 1598.
He confesses in his dedication to Lady Walsingham that he has been
"drawne by strange instigation to employ some of my serious time in
so trifeling a subiect, which yet made the first Author, diuine Musæus,
eternall." Several times he uses the apologetic words "trifling" or
"trifle," but, in respect of bulk at least, the reader is soon undeceived,
as he is after Chaucer's promise of "a litel thing in prose." The continuation extends to over fifteen hundred and fifty lines.

Chapman begins with an assurance of something "more graue and
hie," and his stern Muse will have none of the moral laxity that
Marlowe glorified. That part of him which is an artist, a lover of
life, tells how Leander, "Lord of his desires," throws into the
Hellespont "his Hero-handled bodie." The moralist reports that

                The God of gold of purpose guilt his lims,
                That this word guilt, including double sence,
                The double guilt of his Incontinence,
                Might be exprest . . .

There follows a sermon on the text

    15. P. 23. The last lines of the next stanza, when Corinna casts off her robe,
are these:
                Or as when Venus strived for sovereign sway
                Of charmful beauty in young Troy's desire,
                So stood Corinna, vanishing her tire.
The lines may or may not be an echo of Marlowe's "Where Venus in her naked
glory stroue . . ."

> Joy grauen in sence, like snow in water wasts;
> Without preserue of vertue nothing lasts.[16]

Part of it comes from Plutarch's *Amatorius*.[17]

While, at home, Leander revels in memories of Hero, of how "on his breasts warme sea she sideling swims," [18] divine music pierces his ear, and through the roof, with many-colored lights, descends the Goddess Ceremony, leading Religion. After the exposition of much involved symbolism we have a speech from the goddess which convinces Leander of his sin in the "plaine neglect of Nuptiall rites," a sin that he resolves to atone for at once. In Musaeus the personal integrity of the lovers is full justification, as, though to a less degree, it is in Marlowe; Chapman's introduction into a poetic world of everyday conventions, however disguised, may suggest, in Katherine Mansfield's phrase, "taking up that magical poem and putting it into a bodice and skirt." [19] Yet Chapman's seriousness, here and elsewhere, is not that of a mere precisian; he is a Christian humanist of the Renaissance who has a high philosophic belief in order.

Before analyzing Hero's emotions Chapman takes one of those flights that compensate for many tortured ideas, and his repudiation of Marlowe's attitude is less memorable than the lines in which he sends a winged message to the dead poet's "free soule":

> Then thou most strangely-intellectuall fire,
> That proper to my soule hast power t'inspire
> Her burning faculties, and with the wings
> Of thy unspheared flame visitst the springs
> Of spirits immortall . . .[20]

16. Cf. *Hymnus in Cynthiam*, ll. 401–03 (ed. 1875, p. 15). Quotations from *Hero and Leander* are from the text in Brooke's edition of Marlowe's works, pp. 513 ff. A full and illuminating study of Chapman's symbolism was given by D. J. Gordon in *English Miscellany*, ed. M. Praz, V (1954).

17. Schoell, p. 225.

18. Since echoes of Chapman in other poets are not common I might quote a possible one from the extraordinary Nathaniel Whiting (*Minor Caroline Poets*, III, 550):

> Long since did Hellespont gulp in Leander,
> When he presumed on naked breast to wander.

There is another reference to the story (and to *Venus and Adonis*) in the same writer (page 452).

19. *Letters* (London, 1928), II, 106.

20. The meaning of the whole passage is not entirely clear. The legend that Marlowe asked Chapman to finish his poem, a legend sufficiently incredible

We come then to

> Sweet Hero left upon her bed alone,
> Her maidenhead, her vowes, Leander gone.

She is besieged by "new come thoughts" as Cadiz was by princely Essex. She reflects, with scientific help from Plutarch,[21] on the contrast between her outer semblance and her inner knowledge. In sorrow over broken vows she puts on a black robe; her feelings becoming more intense, she strews the floor with her hair and tears her mantle. She swoons, and revives to encourage herself with a great deal of casuistry:

> Had I not yeelded, slaine my selfe I had.
> Hero Leander is, Leander Hero.

She and Chapman finally reach a compromise:

> Beautie in heauen and earth this grace doth win,
> It supples rigor, and it lessens sin.

The last lines of the sestiad, after a tissue of ratiocination too subtle to admit emotion, end with a warm simplicity worthy of Juliet:

> Deare place, I kisse thee, and doe welcome thee,
> As from Leander euer sent to mee.

The fourth sestiad opens with a description of Hero's priestly garments. The scarf alone takes nearly a hundred lines, for in it are embroidered not only Leander but allegorical scenes—a fisherman stung by a serpent, two foxes robbing a girl who sings instead of watching her vine [22]—which "shew what death was hid in loues disguise."

---

anyhow, was finally exploded by the discovery of the circumstances of Marlowe's death. And, as F. S. Boas remarks (*Marlowe and His Circle*, page 68), in his dedication to Lady Walsingham Chapman says nothing about personal intercourse with Marlowe. The words already quoted—"drawne by strange instigation"—together with the lines in the poem, imply the notion of "some telepathic agency, inciting him to complete *Hero and Leander*" (T. Brooke, *Life of Marlowe*, 1930, p. 79); see also Mr. Martin's *Marlowe's Poems*, page 12, and notes.

21. Ll. 238 ff. See Schoell, pp. 225–26.

22. Both scenes are adapted from the description of the engraved bowl in the first idyll of Theocritus. The allusion to "Arachnean ditties" suggests recol-

"Proceed we now with Heros sacrifice," says the poet, but soon makes a digression of some eighty lines concerning Leander's picture and the lessons Hero sees in it are more in the vein of Marlowe than of our moralistic Chapman—

> that what her hart
> Did greatest hold in her selfe greatest part,
> That she did make her god; and t'was lesse nought
> To leaue gods in profession and in thought,
> Than in her loue and life: for therein lies
> Most of her duties, and their dignities;
> And raile the brain-bald world at what it will,
> Thats the grand Atheisme that raignes in it still.

So Hero resolves on dissimulation, and we are assured that her sin was nothing compared with "those foule faults other Priests are in." Hero begins the sacrifice, but Venus appears with her swans and rebukes her. The swan "Leucote," provided with a voice by "the Goddesse Ecte," speaks up in Hero's defense. Fire from Venus' eyes kindles the sacrifice, and from the flame is created the maiden "Eronusis" or Dissimulation, a new and useful deity for maids and men. Venus departs, to the accompaniment of more unexpected mythology.

As if enough action had not already been invented, the fifth sestiad announces that

> Day doubles her accustomd date,
> As loth the night, incenst by fate,
> Should wrack our louers.

This long day Chapman undertakes to fill. Hero, "to shorten time with merriment," sends for two lovers, Alcmane and Mya, whom she had hitherto refused to marry. The wedding feast takes place, and in comes the nymph Teras. There follows the tale of Teras, about Hymen's winning of his bride, in nearly four hundred lines elaborated, with relative clarity of narration and symbolism, from the version in Cartari's account of Juno in his *Imagines Deorum*.[23] The marriage

lection of the Ovidian web, and other details recall the shield of Achilles. Chapman published his translation of that part of Homer in 1598.

23. The story was told by Servius (on *Aen.* iv.99) and Boccaccio, *De Genealogia Deorum* (book v), but D. J. Gordon (*MLR*, XXXIX, 280–85) showed that Chapman used Cartari; see also his later and fuller study of the whole poem cited above in note 16 and 24 below.

of the hero and heroine shows ardent love governed by decorum and arriving at a moral consummation.[24] The tale ends with a lyrical epithalamium that shows Chapman at his best:

> Come, come deare night, Loues Mart of kisses,
> Sweet close of his ambitious line,
> The fruitfull summer of his blisses,
> Loues glorie doth in darknes shine.
> O come soft rest of Cares, come night,
> Come naked vertues only tire,
> The reaped haruest of the light,
> Bound up in sheaues of sacred fire.

Elizabethan and metaphysical strength is refined by the clear flame of Catullus.[25] Teras goes away, amid sinister omens, and we have another ingenuous apology for the episode; since trouble awaits Hero, "I use digressions thus t'encrease the day."

In the sixth sestiad the kindly swan, Leucote, gains the consent of the Fates to restrain the winds, but the Fates are treacherous. Hero prepares her torch; "Her Torch and Hero, figure shew and vertue." At Abydos cattle are being slain for the marriage feast, and happy Leander does not know that he is as far short of his supposed felicity as a London gallant; the parallel leads on to a satirical sketch of "an affectate traveller" and further parallels. Such a passage, at such a point in the story, is an astonishing prelude to tragedy. But the conclusion, which makes some necessary use of the Greek poem, rises above its conceits and moral comments to a pitch of genuine feeling. The lovers then undergo an Ovidian metamorphosis.

This work of Chapman's has been outlined at some length because, though regularly printed with Marlowe's fragment, it is by nearly all readers regularly skipped. But no outline gives a notion of the amount of alien material thrown into it. Marlowe's eight hundred and eighteen lines carry the story as far as the two hundred and eighty-first line of Musaeus; Chapman's portion, of nearly sixteen hundred lines, corresponds to the remaining sixty-two lines of Greek. That Chapman is not a born narrator has been plain enough. The result of his ethical, argumentative, mythological, and other preoccupations is that Hero and Leander as characters soon cease to exist. After being abstractions

24. See Gordon, *English Miscellany*, V (1954), 43 ff., 78 ff.
25. Catullus, lxii. See J. B. Emperor, *The Catullian Influence in English Lyric Poetry, ca. 1600–1650* (1928), p. 43. The lines quoted are not among the specific parallels with Catullus.

for many hundreds of lines, despite occasional moments of vividness, they cannot at the end come to life sufficiently for us to feel greatly moved by their fate. In comparison with Chapman, at least, Marlowe's fragment seems a miracle of elemental simplicity of conception and treatment. But the faults of Chapman are not accidental. The poem is fully in accord with his theory, already encountered, that poetry should convey moral ideas, not in a bald, didactic manner, but indirectly, through novel figures, comparisons, symbols.[26] And certainly one is always conscious of a strong and original mind at work. Only Donne could be imagined as invoking these similes, to describe Hero in her black robe:

> No forme was seene, where forme held all her sight:
> But like an Embrion that saw neuer light:
> Or like a scorched statue made a cole
> With three-wingd lightning: or a wretched soule
> Muffled with endles darknes, she did sit.

Yet there is a very frequent failure to fuse the image or emotion and the thought, and, as regards the whole poem, there is an obvious lack of architectonic power. Too often the centrality of Chapman's poetic purpose is frustrated by the eccentric, tangential quality of his intellect, which appears in his conceits, myth-making, abstract images, mysterious or occult symbols, Neo-Platonizing, and his abundance of queer and strained diction. In him as in later poets of wit the desire to compel attention overreaches itself.

We may break the order of chronology to say a word here of Chapman's translation of Musaeus, which appeared in 1616. The dedication, addressed to Inigo Jones, has the customary references to modern barbarism and the taste of the few elect. Speaking modestly, "to the commune reader," of "that partly excellent Poem of Master Marlowe's" and his own translation, he declares that "the Works are in nothing alike; a different character being held through both the style, matter, and invention." He accepts the tradition, not yet banished by scholarship, that Musaeus "lived in the time of Orpheus." His notes show that as usual he had a Latin version as well as the Greek before him; even the text gives evidence of the help Chapman derived from the lexicon of Scapula (a work based on the great *Thesaurus* of Estienne).[27]

26. See Schoell, *passim*, and D. J. Gordon (note 24 above).
27. Schoell, pp. 156–57. For the text, see *Poems* (1875), pp. 93 ff.

Chapman's English is faithful in the main, though his characteristic turns of thought and phrase alter the texture a good deal. Musaeus
describes Leander thus:

Then came upon him astonishment, audacity, trembling, shame; in his
heart he trembled, and shame seized him at having been made captive: yet
he marvelled at the faultless form, and love kept shame away; then manfully
by love's guidance he embraced audacity, and gently stepped and stood before the girl.[28]

And this is Chapman:

Amaze then took him, Impudence and Shame
Made earthquakes in him with their frost and flame.
His heart betwixt them toss'd, till Reverence
Took all these prisoners in him; and from thence
Her matchless beauty, with astonishment,
Increased his bands: till aguish Love, that lent
Shame and Observance, licensed their remove;
And, wisely liking impudence in love,
Silent he went . . .

Simplicity is almost beyond Chapman's reach. So we have instead of
"as if angry," "put on anger's cloak"; instead of "my rich parents,"
"The noblesse of my birth-right's either friend." Leander, says
Musaeus, returned home "unsatisfied with a whole night of love";
Chapman strikes out a conceit that finely justifies itself—Leander
"breathed insatiate of the absent Sun." But in general Chapman's
alterations of phrasing are for the worse; the examples illustrate his
introduction of irrelevant and top-heavy metaphors and personifications into a narrative that demands clarity and directness.

The same processes are exhibited on a large scale in Chapman's
translation of Homer. Many a reader, led by Keats to the "pure
serene" of Chapman, has been repelled by the smoke of conceits that
obscures his very genuine fire and energy. No one ever loved Homer
more ardently and jealously than Chapman, and no one could be, at
times, less Homeric. The voice, quite often, is the voice of Jacob, the
flesh is the flesh of Esau. Extended consideration of the *Homer* does
not come into our plan, but a glance at its unclassical qualities will
help to round out this sketch. There is no need of repeating Arnold's

28. Translation of J. A. Symonds, *Studies of the Greek Poets* (1893), II,
349.

analysis of those qualities, but we may borrow one of his briefer illustrations. Out of this simple line of Homer, ἔσσεται ἦμαρ ὅτ᾽ ἄν
ποτ᾽ ὀλώλῃ Ἴλιος ἱρὴ, Chapman makes this:

> And such a stormy day shall come, in mind and soul I know,
> When sacred Troy shall shed her towers for tears of overthrow.

As Arnold says, Homer is "tormented"; Chapman cannot forbear to
interpose a play of thought between his object and its expression. Not
only does he make Homer conceited and metaphysical in style, he
often gives the text an explicit moral coloring from his own Platonic-
Stoic creed, usually in a phrase, sometimes at length. M. Schoell has
demonstrated that Chapman's critical comments owed much to
Spondanus (Jean de Sponde), whose edition of Homer he used, and
that his other great prop in his Homeric labors was the lexicon of
Scapula. Let us take one illustration, the episode of Nausicaa:

> Thus she spake, and called to her maidens of the fair tresses: "Halt, my
> maidens, whither flee ye at the sight of a man? Ye surely do not take him
> for an enemy? That mortal breathes not, and never will be born, who shall
> come with war to the land of the Phaeacians, for they are very dear to the
> gods . . ."

On the word ἀνὴρ (*Odyssey*, vi.201) Chapman has this note:

> ᾿Ανήρ, *virili animo præditus, fortis, magnanimus.* Nor are those affirmed
> to be men, *qui servile quidpiam et abjectum faciunt, vel, facere sustinent:*
> according to this of Herodotus in Poly. πολλοὶ μὲν ἄνθρωποι εἶεν, ὀλίγοι δὲ
> ἄνδρες. Many men's forms sustain, but few are men.

The note is part of Scapula's note. More astonishing is Chapman's
version of the Homeric passage:

> Thus, passing him, she to the virgins went,
> And said: 'Give stay both to your feet and fright.
> Why thus disperse ye for a man's mere sight?
> Esteem you him a Cyclop, that long since
> Made use to prey upon our citizens?
> This man no moist man is (nor watrish thing,
> That's ever flitting, ever ravishing
> All it can compass; and, like it, doth range
> In rape of women, never staid in change).
> This man is truly manly, wise and staid,

In soul more rich the more to sense decay'd,
Who nor will do, nor suffer to be done,
Acts lewd and abject; nor can such a one
Greet the Phæacians with a mind envíous,
Dear to the Gods they are, and he is pious . . .' [29]

This little sermon in eight lines inserted in the simple speech of Nausicaa, and quite foreign to Homer, is the commentary of Estienne and Scapula, which Chapman is not content to borrow for his notes but also weaves into his text! Elizabethan freedom in translation could hardly go further—and yet Chapman has a mystical reverence for Homer. He is also a poet, however, and does not always fall short of his divine original; Odysseus is cast up on shore weary and spent, for "the sea had soakt his heart through."

The last work of Chapman's that demands attention is a performance extraordinary in more ways than one, the *Andromeda Liberata* of 1614. In the first place it is a little disconcerting to find our grave and high-minded moralist celebrating that precious pair, the Earl of Somerset and the Countess of Essex, whose marriage, with its train of intrigue and murder and executions, was the scandal of the age, although, when Chapman wrote, the facts about the poisoning of Overbury had not come out. The long Epistle Dedicatory, which paraphrases Plutarch's *Moralia* [30] in several places, sets forth Chapman's usual doctrine of poetry and the soul, reason and sense, with much praise of the two embodiments of virtue whom he addresses, who have been assailed by slanderous tongues. The poem itself, of well over six hundred lines, tells the story of Perseus and Andromeda; of course the noble earl is the gallant rescuer and "this matchless virgin," Andromeda, is Lady Frances (one recalls the dubious findings of the jury of matrons impaneled in the case). The third of the *dramatis personae* is "the monstrous beast, the ravenous multitude."

The piece begins by denouncing "ungodly vulgars," then celebrates "all-creating, all-preserving Love." There follows a long description of Andromeda taken in part from Natalis Comes. [31] Next is a diatribe, partly adapted from Plutarch, against those whose evil minds, seeking evil, befoul the good. We then come to an account of Perseus which, like so much of Chapman, is both mystical and misty.

29. *Odysseys of Homer* (Temple Classics), vi.306–20; Schoell, pp. 153 ff.
30. Schoell, pp. 234 ff.
31. Schoell, pp. 195–96.

> The mind a spirit is, and call'd the glass
> In which we see God; and corporeal grace
> The mirror is, in which we see the mind.

This tenet of Renaissance Platonism is worked out at length. To the "form" of Perseus "his mind fit answer made" in sixty-one obscure lines, on the text "Beauty breeds love, love consummates a man." This whole passage, comprising the description of Perseus as a sort of god of love, and the speech of his "mind," is a paraphrase of two chapters of the fifth discourse (that of Agathon) in Ficino's *Commentarium in Convivium.*[32] The attributes of Perseus are those given by Marsupini, who takes the part of Agathon, to Love. The lines on the power of the planet Venus over Mars are taken from the second of the two chapters.

Perseus speaks at length on the nature of love, and on the "interchange" or reciprocity that subsists between "true lovers." That is, the woman beloved should return her lover's passion and yield to his embraces, otherwise she prevents the birth of children and is worse than a homicide, for "divine worth doth in generation shine." These specimens of amatory casuistry are taken from the eighth chapter of the second discourse (Pausanias, as interpreted by Antonio) in Ficino. As M. Schoell says:

> On peut imaginer combien surprenante semblable exhortation, issue du cerveau délirant d'un théologien encore médiéval, peut nous apparaître, ainsi placée dans la bouche d'un héros de la mythologie grecque! Mais Chapman ne s'est pas embarrassé de vains scrupules. Il a tout simplement traduit et incorporé le morceau, sans nous donner la moindre indication de source.[33]

Altogether Chapman's treatment of the myth, quite apart from its connection with Somerset and his wife, is remote from, say, Ariosto's adaptation, yet both are of the Renaissance.[34]

32. Chapman (ed. 1875), pp. 188–89, from "Perseus of Love's own form" to the end of the ensuing speech (lines 251–344). See Schoell, pp. 14 ff.

33. P. 14.

34. See above, page 71, for a reference to the allegorical interpretation of the myth derived by Harington from Leo Hebraeus.

A word may be added about the ill success of the poet's tribute to the royal favorite and the "innocent and spotless virgin." More tactful men than Chapman might have blundered, in treating such a theme at such a time, and he, having in his "innocency" used expressions which had been misapplied, felt moved to write a "justification" in prose and verse. "Bound to a barren rock" was infelicitous, whether with regard to Somerset or the notorious charges

Chapman's Platonism here is more casuistical and less fruitful than it can be elsewhere, and one might refer to some noble lines in a very different poem, *A Hymn to our Saviour on the Cross*. We have observed that Chapman's allegorical mythology carries with it a distaste for contemporary and conventional Ovidianism, and whereas Marlowe and Shakespeare might use Narcissus as a bit of ornament or as a warning to enjoy youth and love, Chapman, after Ficino, takes Narcissus' self-love as an example of the way in which the soul is softened and

> rapt (as with a storm)
> With flatteries of our base corporeal form
> (Which is her shadow) that she quite forsakes
> Her proper noblesse, and for nothing takes
> The beauties that for her love, thou putt'st on,
> In torments rarefied far past the Sun.[35]

Chapman is at once an orthodox and a notably individual exemplar of Renaissance humanism. His contempt for the unlettered crowd and his faith in culture and poetry are proclaimed with more than normal fervor. In his literary and philosophical creed he has partial affinities with Spenser, Samuel Daniel, Sir John Davies, Jonson, and the more gloomy Fulke Greville. In style he is somewhere between Greville and the Donne of the *Anniversaries*. Obviously Chapman did not learn much from the classics about clarity, selection, coherence, restraint; but then not all the classical poets had all these virtues, and Chapman's texture is not unlike that of Pindar or Aeschylus. He does at times fuse thought with emotion, but sometimes also he fails to remove the cumbrous scaffolding, the débris of bricks and mortar, that remain from his wasteful operations.

Chapman's obscurity is partly temperamental, partly deliberate. He is passionately resolved to forge and propagate a working philosophy of cultural enlightenment and moral discipline, and his abundant borrowings from ancient and modern humanists do not always readily blend. He draws much moral wisdom from Cicero, Seneca, Epictetus, Plutarch, but much comes also from Ficino, the fountainhead of

---

against Essex. No less suggestive was the word "homicide"; there was (or soon was to be) in London too much whispering about homicide of a kind less theoretical than Chapman's. On the whole a quaint incident!

35. *A Hymn* (p. 146). See Schoell, pp. 7–8; P. B. Bartlett, p. 446. The passage in Ficino had inspired some lines in the Narcissus of 1560 (above, III.i).

Renaissance Platonism, and the mythographer Natalis Comes. The inspiration of his central non-dramatic poem, *The Tears of Peace,* starts from Erasmus and the Hermetic *Poimander* translated by Ficino, and of course from Chapman's adored Homer. Notwithstanding his considerable debt to other writers and thinkers and some mental and stylistic vagaries of his own, Chapman is one of the most positive and authentic of Christian humanists. He wrestles with problems of the inner life and the good life in a way that makes the "atheism" of Marlowe and the dramatic libertinism of the young John Donne sound like the talk of clever schoolboys. Without disowning the senses, of which he is such a curious explorer, Chapman insists upon the necessity of man's dominion over experience, on control of the mutinous animal within. In his dedication of the *Odyssey* he contrasts Achilles with his ideal hero, Odysseus, in terms that sum up much of his ethical creed:

In one, predominant perturbation; in the other, overruling wisdom: in one, the body's fervour and fashion of outward fortitude to all possible height of heroical action; in the other, the mind's inward, constant and unconquered empire, unbroken, unaltered, with any most insolent and tyrannous infliction.

It has been observed that the principals of Chapman's tragedies tend to fall into one or other of these categories—although critics of the plays, commonly ignoring the personal testimony of the non-dramatic poems, make him an exponent of lawless passion and *virtù*.[36]

36. A corrective interpretation is *The Tragedies of George Chapman* (Harvard University Press, 1954) by Ennis Rees, who gives the best exposition of the poet-dramatist's humanistic creed.

CHAPTER XI

Lyrical Verse

Some mythological conventions in lyrics of the first two thirds of Elizabeth's reign have already been described. To turn to the period from about 1590 to 1680 and contemplate the immense body of lyrical verse, with the thousand or two mythological allusions embedded therein, is to recall Psyche's task of separating the seeds; and the parallel is not casual, for a good deal of the mythology is without distinction. We can only observe some examples of changing modes. Behind the general fashion of Renaissance classicism there was always, in good poets, an authentic impulse. In lyrics as in the plays of Shakespeare and others, mythology provided a language of mainly ideal symbols, a means of transcending the merely natural in nature and the merely human in man—that is, in lyrical verse, woman. That idealism did not entirely vanish even in the skeptical air of the Restoration.

One of the most famous Elizabethan allusions was quoted at the beginning of this book, but no excuse is needed for quoting the stanza again:

> Beauty is but a flower
> Which wrinkles will devour:
> Brightness falls from the air,
> Queens have died young and fair,
> Dust hath closed Helen's eye.
> I am sick, I must die.
> Lord, have mercy on us!

We do not think of the boisterous Thomas Nashe as an inspired poetic craftsman, but here the statement of the universal theme closes in by degrees from the magically suggestive generality of the third line to the death long ago of the supreme pagan incarnation of youth and beauty and love, and the lines end with a Christian prayer (in a season of the plague). This is not Renaissance classicism but the spirit of the medieval *Ubi sunt,* of Villon's *Ballade,* of Donne's meditation on eternity and the little lives of all the powerful kings and beautiful queens of this world.

A very different impulse, the didactic sobriety of Tudor humanism, had one of its last and finest expressions in Daniel's *Ulysses and the Siren* (1605).[1] This poem, like Daniel's other best work, creates its effect, not by winged words and rich overtones, but by moral elevation and straightforward purity of style. The story of Ulysses and the sirens, like that of Circe, probably had its didactic implications in Homer and at any rate was accepted allegorically by Cicero and Horace.[2] Daniel's lyrical statement of the rival claims of slothful ease and honorable toil recalls Belphoebe's answer to Braggadocchio and other eulogies of heroic effort in Renaissance literature. But Daniel's siren is no voluptuous Spenserian temptress like Phaedria or Acrasia; she is rather a disembodied attitude of mind, and her language is, so to speak, as manly as that of Ulysses. When Marvell comes to write *A Dialogue between the Resolved Soul and Created Pleasure,* he has no classical frame or reference and his echoes are Biblical.

Another kind of exalted idealism appears in the ritualistic poem almost certainly by Sir Walter Ralegh:

> Praised be Diana's fair and harmless light,
> Praised be the dews wherewith she moists the ground;
> Praised be her beams, the glory of the night;
> Praised be her power, by which all powers abound. . . .
>
> Time wears her not—she doth his chariot guide;
> Mortality below her orb is placed.
> By her the virtue of the stars down slide,
> In her is virtue's perfect image cast.
>
> A knowledge pure it is her worth to know;
> With Circes let them dwell that think not so.

Even if Diana is closely related to Queen Elizabeth, the poet's mythic imagination is at work. With the same qualification, the same thing may be said of Jonson's

1. One might contrast *Beware of Sirens* in *The Paradise of Dainty Devices,* ed. Rollins, p. 63. Master Bew quickly leaves Ulysses for his real subject, the sirens of the moment—"Thei sigh, thei sobb, thei prate, thei praie. . . ."

2. Cicero, *De Finibus,* v.18; Horace, *Epistles,* i.2.23. See Fulgentius, ii.11.

> Queen and huntress, chaste and fair,
> Now the sun is laid to sleep,
> Seated in thy silver chair
> State in wonted manner keep;
> Hesperus entreats thy light,
> Goddess excellently bright.

And, amid all the pretty fancies Cupid is dressed in, we seldom meet the cosmic conception that inspired Jonson's stanza in the *Haddington Masque:*

> At his sight the sun hath turned,
> Neptune in the waters burned,
> Hell hath felt a greater heat,
> Jove himself forsook his seat;
> From the center to the sky
> Are his trophies reared high.

In *Tottel's Miscellany* and its successors we noticed a plaintive amatory formula, and it did not quite die out in the seventeenth century. As late as Philip Ayres we find a piece, not much longer than its title, which takes us back to the early miscellanies—*Compares the Troubles which he has undergone for Cynthia's Love, to the Labours of Hercules.* We are not surprised to learn that it is translated from Guarini.[3] Mythology was abundant in the lesser Elizabethan sonneteers, but one may be forgiven for not lingering with them; one might, however, record Bartholomew Griffin's unique picture of the dawn:

> So soon as peeping Lucifer, Aurora's star,
> The sky with golden periwigs doth spangle.[4]

In other kinds of amatory verse Elizabethan idealism can be both serious and attractive. Robert Greene's Samela is within twenty-four lines likened to Diana, Arethusa, Aurora, Thetis, Venus, Juno, and Pallas, but the result is not childish or pedantic; Greene here "touches the brink of perfection in his own kind, in an atmosphere as clear and stainless as early morning in a garden." [5] The apt phrase suggests

3. Saintsbury, *Minor Caroline Poets,* II, 341; M. Praz, *MLR,* XXX, 429.
4. *Elizabethan Sonnets,* ed. Sir Sidney Lee, II, 288. But we cannot blame mythology, in view of Sylvester's notorious line, "And perriwig with wool the balde-pate Woods" (ed. Grosart, I, 124, line 187).
5. Elizabeth Holmes, *Aspects of Elizabethan Imagery,* p. 18.

the special quality of Elizabethan mythology at its best, and in the
nature of things such "naiveté" could not long endure in the Jacobean
climate, though increasing sophistication was not immediately fatal.
One notable opening is Thomas Campion's

> When thou must home to shades of underground,
>   And there arrived, a new admired guest,
> The beauteous spirits do engirt thee round,
>   White Iope, blithe Helen, and the rest. . . .

But the promise of these Roman lines, which echo Propertius,[6] is not
fulfilled; the poem dwindles into a trivial Petrarchan conceit. Something of the old spirit could animate the Scottish William Drummond, who was especially drawn to continental models: in the grand
manner and with more than his usual energy Drummond gave
mythic stature to his mistress in those highly wrought pieces,
"Phoebus, arise" and "Like the Idalian queen." The latter ends with
a conceit taken from Marino.[7]

But amatory verse shows a general movement away from Petrarchan attitudes toward more courtly and robust gallantry or more
purely bookish compliment, and in the process mythological allusion
loses more or less of its mythic quality, though grace and charm may
remain. An anonymous poet in 1606 begins a complaint with

> The Queen of Paphos, Erycine,
>   In heart did rose-cheeked Adon love. . . .[8]

Venus and Adonis furnishes the theme and an epithet which Shakespeare and Marlowe had made current; but the poet-lover, far from
being intense or disconsolate, is cool and sensible:

> Hence, groaning sighs! mirth be my friend!
> Before my life, my love shall end.

In the whole body of lyrical verse Cupid exceeds all other deities in
the frequency of his appearance—his nearest rival is his mother—
and under the dominion of the blind bow-boy goddesses become
nymphs or pretty mistresses, the gods elegant shepherds or admiring
courtiers. Mythology becomes almost mock-heroic in an elegant lyric

6. Loeb Classical Library, II.xxviiiA.
7. *Works*, ed. Kastner, I, 188.
8. *Elizabethan Lyrics*, ed. N. Ault (1925), p. 374.

by William Strode, one of the three or four most popular of the seventeenth century:

> I saw fair Chloris walk alone,
> Whilst feathered rain came softly down,
> And Jove descended from his tower
> To court her in a silver shower. . . .

Cleveland has a less elegant and more athletic vision:

> The sluggish morn as yet undressed,
> My Phillis brake from out her east,
> As if she'd made a match to run
> With Venus, usher to the sun.

But when, as in the often charming Randolph or the seldom charming Waller, a classical education runs to seed in trite or absurdly extravagant allusions, mythology is merely capitalized slang. In regard to the slightness of many lyrics we may remember that they often are real lyrics, that they may take a mythological name as a theme for musical variations, as in Strode's *When Orpheus sweetly did complain*.[9]

Quite often the graceful or playful diminution of mythological figures goes along with their being domesticated in the English scene. We may think of Spenser's March and April eclogues or of Milton's *Arcades* and *Comus* (not to mention his remarkable fifth *Elegy*), but the process had begun long before. In Caxton's semi-Ovidian *Methamorphose* we have Pan, in his contest with Apollo, "vauntynge hyme of the horne-pype of Cornewaylle."

> Pan's Syrinx was a girl indeed,
> Though now she's turned into a reed,

sings Lyly, and it is Pan's pipe that stirs the feet of

> Cross-gartered swains and dairy girls,
> With faces smug and round as pearls.

9. *Poetical Works of William Strode*, ed. B. Dobell (1907), p. 1; *Parnassus Biceps*, ed. G. Thorn-Drury (1927), p. 100. William Cartwright has a piece of over a hundred lines, a complaint called *Ariadne deserted by Theseus*, which, after Catullus and Ovid, is not very satisfactory, but it may have been better when sung to the music of Henry Lawes. See the editions of Cartwright by R. C. Goffin (1918) and G. B. Evans (1951); Milton's sonnet to Lawes; and J. B. Emperor, *Catullian Influence*, pp. 72–73.

Diana is quite at home in rural England. A tuneful moralizer in *England's Helicon* begins:

> Hey downe a downe did Dian sing,
>   amongst her Virgins sitting:
> Then loue there is no vainer thing. . . .[10]

In more serious mood, and with the delicate and deliberate precision of diction and movement that mark the disciplined classicist, there is Campion's familiar

> Hark, all you ladies that do sleep!
> The fairy queen Proserpina
> Bids you awake, and pity them that weep.

The infinite gradations in the process of Anglicizing myths are illustrated in the almost infinite number of translations and imitations of Anacreontic pieces, Greek idylls, and similar things, variations on the hue and cry after Cupid, Cupid stung by a bee . . . Italian and French models count more than ancient as a rule, but the pastoral-mythological lyric of the Renaissance is essentially international, and only a slight coloring is needed to make it seem English. As examples of the wide range of treatment we might take Giles Fletcher's *Dialogue betwixt two Sea Nymphs, Doris and Galatea, concerning Polyphemus*, which is derived from Lucian,[11] and the most popular lyric of the age, Marlowe's *Passionate Shepherd*. This we think of as the fine flower of Elizabethan pastoral song, yet the invitation to love goes back ultimately to the Ovidian and Theocritean story of Polyphemus and Galatea.[12] Naturalization of a mythological theme could hardly be carried further. Or one might mention a different kind of example from Caroline days; Sidney Godolphin gives an English tone to the myth of Cephalus and Procris by altering the names and making it into a pastoral "ballet." [13]

No poet is more English than Drayton, and in his *Muses Elizium* he domesticates mythology with an abundance of realism both homely and dainty.

10. Ed. H. Macdonald (1925), p. 123; ed. Rollins (1935), I, 121–22.

11. *Elizabethan Sonnets*, II, 63. While professing to translate from Lucian, Fletcher does not say that he is making use of the expanded Latin version of Johannes Secundus (D. Crane, *Johannes Secundus*, Leipsic, 1931, p. 53).

12. R. S. Forsythe, "*The Passionate Shepherd;* and English Poetry," *PMLA*, XL, 692 ff.

13. *Poems*, ed. Dighton (1931), p. 15; *Minor Caroline Poets*, II, 242.

Olympus and Parnassus seem to have poured forth their people, if we listen to their names only, upon the pages of his Elysium. But whatever they may be called, the most unmistakable English men and maids, hale and buxom, blithe and frolic, discover themselves in the faces and forms that bear these classic labels and attributes. Venus and Cupid, trespassing furtively in the Elysium from which they have been sternly excluded, become a merry English wife and her 'little lad'; they take ferry, and she chats gaily with the ferryman, who marvels at the 'little dapper elf,' 'half bird half boy,' and finds it passing strange 'to have a child have wings to fly, and yet want eyes to see.' Drayton, in some sense the 'brave heroic mind' *par excellence* among all the Elizabethans, dared these incongruities with impunity, such is the charm of the English freshness and homeliness which his magic throws upon the most exotic figures.[14]

Much of the same quality, refined by more fastidious craftsmanship in word and rhythm, is in that other belated Elizabethan, Robert Herrick. In his allusions, however, mythological figures become less alive and more literary than Drayton's:

> The passive Aire such odour then assum'd,
> As when to Jove Great Juno goes perfum'd.

The occasion is "Julia's unlacing her self," and though the reference may add a Junoesque cubit to Julia's stature, the queen of heaven loses some regality. Stories of Jove's amours are less than Olympian when told among maids under a tree, with talk of brides, posies for rings, and gloves and ribbons.[15] Indeed one title suggests the general character of myth when it is painted into Herrick's exquisite miniatures, *The Parcæ, or, Three dainty Destinies*. To read Herrick after Marlowe or Spenser is to turn from the Italian painters to Watteau. Yet in that pagan-Christian masterpiece, *Corinna's going a Maying*, the opening and later allusions link Corinna and other budding boys and girls with pagan ritual and cosmic process, and the epithet in the fourth line bridges the gap between Apollo and Aurora and the "sweet-Slug-a-bed":

> Get up, get up for shame, the Blooming Morne
> Upon her wings presents the god unshorne.
> See how Aurora throwes her faire
> Fresh-quilted colours through the aire. . . .

14. Herford and Simpson, *Ben Jonson*, II, 230.
15. *Poems*, ed. L. C. Martin (1956), p. 215.

So far we have been concerned with the orthodox Elizabethan tradition, and we may turn now to poets of the metaphysical line—although, as modern criticism recognizes, there is often no clear-cut division. The brevity of the sketch will be in accord with the relative scantiness of the material. The whole body of Donne's poetry contains much more mythological allusion than one remembers, but his best or best-known pieces have hardly any. Instead of warm and diffuse Italianate word-painting, Donne's mythology bears the individual stamp of his wit, realism, ratiocination, learning, concentration of feeling and expression, and sometimes deliberate harshness and ugliness. What his contemporaries would spread over a page he puts into a line and a half:

> And to make blinde men see,
> What things gods are, I say they' are like to thee.[16]

When in the *Second Anniversary* the soul in its progress mounts through the planets,

> Hee that charm'd Argus eyes, sweet Mercury,
> Workes not on her, who now is growne all eye.

The first line might occur in any Elizabethan poet, but not the second. Donne can make use of Phoebus, but what one remembers is "Busie old foole, unruly Sunne." Venus is not the lover of Adonis but the patroness of "Loves sweetest Part, Variety." Orthodox poets might treat Cupid as the sportive god of love in idleness, or even rail at him with affected anger, but they did not entangle him in such nets of witty or passionate reasoning as Donne creates.

While he can reflect Ovid's amatory attitudes,[17] he is no Renaissance Ovidian in sensibility or style. His fleshliness is at once too realistically concerned with immediate experience and too intellectually analytical to spend itself in voluptuous and idealized painting of the body. Elizabethan Ovidians were inclined to be, in Donne's phrase, all eye, and if we could imagine his eighteenth and nineteenth elegies as written by one of them, the poems would be a tissue of mythological pictures and parallels. All this is not to say that Donne's poetry is better than, say, that of Spenser, who, though less attractive to the general reader of the present day, is a bigger, more philosophi-

16. *Poems*, ed. Grierson, I, 124. The next quotation is from I, 257.
17. See J. B. Leishman, *The Monarch of Wit* (1951; rev. 1962).

cal, more complex, and more difficult poet; and when Donne writes in the traditional genre of the epithalamium, the uneven results, however original, are sorry affairs in comparison with Spenser's. On the other hand, although Donne is somewhat akin to Chapman in his argumentative, analytical, and knotty style, he has nothing of Chapman's coherent and urgent ethical creed or mythological symbolism.

Donne's sparing or "perverted" use of mythological allusion implies of course a conscious revolt against this as against other conventions. The significance of that revolt was set forth as it appeared to a partial disciple and some of Carew's lines bear directly upon the matter in hand. Now that Donne is gone, says Carew, other poets

> will recall the goodly exiled train
> Of gods and goddesses, which in thy just reign
> Was banished nobler poems; now with these,
> The silenced tales i' th' *Metamorphoses*,
> Shall stuff their lines, and swell the windy page,
> Till verse, refined by thee in this last age,
> Turn ballad-rhyme, or those old idols be
> Adored again with new apostasy.

It was time for revolt, but, as we shall see in a moment, Carew's own instincts did not work altogether in the spirit of this rebuke of tradition. All conventions, including that inaugurated by Donne, become thin and barren in time, and, whatever the vices of Renaissance Ovidianism, it contributed to a body of poetry that needs no defense. If we are rash enough to read, say, *England's Helicon* at a sitting, we may turn to Donne for something craggy to break our minds upon; but a continuous spell of Donne may breed a taste for *England's Helicon*—not to mention Spenser or Chapman. At any rate the monarch of wit did react powerfully against the idealistic and idyllic mythology of the Elizabethan lyrists and for the consequences we may take a brief glance at some of his more or less metaphysical descendants.

In the first place, there is much less mythology in lyrics of the seventeenth century than in those of the sixteenth. If we take Norman Ault's anthologies as representative, remembering that they are divided at 1620, not 1600, we find that allusions in the second volume are only about half as numerous as they are in the first.[18] In Sir

18. This rough estimate leaves out, in the second volume (pp. 246–49), a catalogue of some two score deities, a racy and jolly piece but awkward for the statistician. It is quoted from in the last paragraph of this chapter.

Herbert Grierson's and later anthologies of metaphysical verse mythology is very scarce; it occurs mainly in poems or poets not genuinely metaphysical, such as Milton's *Nativity* and Randolph. Much metaphysical poetry of course is religious, and although Spenser, the Fletchers, Milton, and others could use mythology freely in religious or didactic poems, it would be very incongruous in George Herbert, Crashaw, Vaughan, and Traherne.[19]

In spite of his praise of Donne's rejection of Renaissance classicism and mythologizing, Carew himself found his master's laws too hard. Even in his elegiac eulogy, along with classical references brought in for condemnation, he speaks of "the Delphic choir" and "thy Promethean breath." In general, Carew is not above mythological conceits; a fly that gets into his mistress' eye is scorched and drowned and falls like Phaethon. *On Sight of a Gentlewoman's Face in the Water* has only one explicit allusion, but the tissue of imagery is essentially mythological. The last two stanzas are these:

> But if the envious nymphs shall fear
>   Their beauties will be scorn'd,
> And hire the ruder winds to tear
>   That face which you adorn'd,
>
> Then rage and foam amain, that we
>   Their malice may despise;
> When from your froth we soon shall see
>   A second Venus rise.

Carew, a disciple of Jonson as well as of Donne, is far more traditional and less realistic than Donne, and here the symmetry of the logical and rhythmical pattern, the rhetorical energy, the artistic elevation of the imagery, achieve a kind of dignity which makes a trivial

19. A passage may be cited from one of Crashaw's best poems. In persuading the Countess of Denbigh to resolution in religion he speaks of the perversity of the soul that fights against its own instincts:

> What fatall, yet fantastick, bands
> Keep The free Heart from it's own hands!
> So when the year takes cold, we see
> Poor waters their owne prisoners be.
> Fetter'd, & lockt up fast they ly
> In a sad selfe-captiuity.
> The' astonisht nymphs their flood's strange fate deplore,
> To see themselues their own seuerer shore.

The simile of the water elucidates a difficult idea, but the nymphs are less essential; the addition of a mythological conceit is a touch of that decorative excess to which Crashaw was always liable.

theme worthy of the concluding allusion. So too in the opening line of Carew's most smoothly perfect lyric the name of Jove just serves to take us out of our world into the world of pure art and beauty. *A Rapture,* while perhaps partly inspired by Donne's outspoken elegies, is a half-metaphysical product of Renaissance pastoralism, in particular of that libertine pastoralism which had become almost a distinct genre. In spirit its mythological allusions, and its attack on conventional notions of honor and virtue, are more akin to, say, *Hero and Leander* than to Donne. Among the references to Venus' doves, Danae, Lucrece, Lais, Penelope, we may take this bit as an example of Ovidian myth adapted to the service of sexual license:

> Daphne hath broke her bark, and that swift foot
> Which th' angry gods had fasten'd with a root
> To the fix'd earth, doth now unfetter'd run
> To meet th' embraces of the youthful Sun.
> She hangs upon him like his Delphic lyre;
> Her kisses blow the old, and breathe new fire. . . .

With these lines we might compare the opening stanza of Cowley's *Ode upon Dr. Harvey:*

> Coy Nature, (which remain'd, though aged grown,
> A Beauteous virgin still, injoy'd by none,
> Nor seen unveil'd by any one)
> When Harveys violent passion she did see,
> Began to tremble, and to flee,
> Took Sanctuary like Daphne in a tree;
> There Daphnes lover stop't, and thought it much
> The very Leaves of her to touch,
> But Harvey our Apollo, stopt not so,
> Into the Bark, and root he after her did goe. . . .

The mythological parallel is worked out in all its demented intricacies for two dozen lines more. It was indeed time for Dryden. Yet Cowley's *On the Death of Mr. William Hervey* is almost wholly free from mythology, and is one of the genuine elegies in English.

Marvell, by far the best of the mainly secular line, combines metaphysical range and subtlety of thought and feeling with classical economy, ease, grace, clarity, and precision of style, and he draws strength and beauty from both liberal puritanism and the sensuous tradition of the Renaissance. Unlike other poets of his time and kind, he seems now and then to echo Spenser; one item, which of course is not merely Spenserian, is the use of Pan for Christ in the slight but serious pastoral, *Clorinda and Damon*. Marvell's occasional allusions to myth are in the main not fully representative of his powers, but they have their individual note. When in *The Gallery* the poet invites Clora to view his soul and the paintings there, he offers a picture of Italianate opulence but quite un-Italianate brevity and surprise:

> But, on the other side, th' art drawn
> Like to Aurora in the Dawn;
> When in the East she slumb'ring lyes,
> And stretches out her milky Thighs. . . .

In *The Nymph complaining for the death of her Faun* pastoral Ovidianism acquires poignant concentration:

> So weeps the wounded Balsome: so
> The holy Frankincense doth flow.
> The brotherless Heliades
> Melt in such Amber Tears as these.

But one mythological stanza of *The Garden* is, like the whole poem, finely and fully typical. The poem expresses a reaction against the kind of libertine pastoralism represented by Randolph and Carew's *Rapture,* and the usual erotic motive turns in this stanza into poetry and music:

> When we have run our Passions heat,
> Love hither makes his best retreat.
> The Gods, that mortal Beauty chase,
> Still in a Tree did end their race.
> Apollo hunted Daphne so,
> Only that She might Laurel grow.
> And Pan did after Syrinx speed,
> Not as a Nymph, but for a Reed.

Beside this light, swift complexity of suggestion may be set a couplet of Waller's from *The Story of Phoebus and Daphne, Applied* (the title recalls the old mythological love-plaint touched upon early in this chapter):

> Like Phoebus thus, acquiring unsought praise,
> He catched at love, and filled his arm with bays.

The conceit, drawn from Marino, appears also in Thomas Stanley and Ayres.[20] Finally, there is no better example of pregnant metaphysical suggestion made concrete and vivid by the mythological tradition than

> But at my back I alwaies hear
> Times winged Charriot hurrying near. . . .

These lines are a reminder that this sketch must be cut short, since we cannot, like Dr. Harvey, penetrate bark and root. Mythology in poetry owed much to the metaphysical strain. The flood of indiscriminate allusion and merely sensuous picture-making was checked. Such things ceased to be satisfying, even in lyrical verse, and mythological allusions, becoming fewer, became more concentrated and significant. Pictorial luxuriance was burned out by intellectual subtlety; the best poets as a rule declared war on the adjective and death to the optic nerve. When lyrics became vehicles for complex philosophic conceptions of the universe and man's place in it, the Elizabethan manner disappeared beyond recall. But even after the impulse had spent itself it left its mark on poets not especially philosophic. The classical and Renaissance Cupid is touched by some metaphysical vibrations even in the late Sir Charles Sedley and Aphra Behn:

> Love still has something of the sea
> From whence his mother rose. . . .

> Love in fantastic triumph sat,
> Whilst bleeding hearts around him flowed. . . .

Unhappily the lyrical mythology that passed into the eighteenth century—unless satirical or comic—was that of the main Renaissance tradition, devitalized, bookish, and bad.

This chapter, like the book itself, must end with an anticlimax, for in lyrics as well as other kinds of verse the humorous treatment of mythology becomes quite noteworthy toward the middle of the seventeenth century. Cleveland's *Mark Antony* (which has a Gilbertian last stanza) describes rustic dalliance, and the nymph's "amber tresses" make on the lover's arm a bracelet

> Gaudier than Juno wears whenas she graces
> Jove with embraces more stately than warm.

20. *Poems* (Muses' Library), I, 52; Marino, *Lira, parte prima, Trasformazione di Dafne in Lauro.* For Stanley and Ayres, see M. Praz, *MLR*, XX, 283, 426, and below, pages 247 and 249.

A quite infectious gayety inspired *The Hunting of the Gods* in the *Westminster Drollery* (1672). No serious poetical directory of Olympus rattles along at such a pace:

> To see club-footed old Mulciber booted,
>   And Pan promoted on Chiron's mare;
> Proud Faunus pouted, and Aeolus shouted,
>   And Momus flouted, but followed the hare.[21]

The same collection contains a piece, *The Moon's Love*, that is far removed from Drayton; Phoebus (or perhaps "the Day") appears in waistcoat of red, and as for the Moon—

> Such changes of thought in her chastity wrought,
>   That thus she besought the boy:
>   'O tarry and marry the starry Diana
>   That will be thy gem and joy!' [22]

Finally, we might take it as an allegorical piece of literary history that the mythology which appears in the *Covent Garden Drollery* (1672) is mostly concentrated in *Mad Tom of Bedlam*.[23] Not here does Mulciber fall from morn to noon, from noon to dewy eve—

> Mars with his Weapon laid about,
> But limping Vulcan had the Gout . . .

21. Ault, *Seventeenth Century Lyrics*, p. 248. The piece was written *ca.* 1650(?).

22. *Ibid.*, p. 368.

23. Ed. G. Thorn-Drury (London, 1928), pp. 41 ff. See the editor's note, p. 138.

CHAPTER XII

Translators

The study of formal translations is a huge subject by itself and one that cannot be treated in such a volume as this. But from the multitude of translations in the seventeenth century this chapter selects a few that may serve to illustrate some general tendencies in the treatment of myth and in poetic style, the changes in taste which lead from Chapman's *Homer* to Pope's, from the Elizabethan Phillida and Corydon to the Augustan Strephon and Chloe.

The Elizabethan translators as a rule thought more of matter than of manner.[1] But some of the later Elizabethans and Jacobeans began to concern themselves a little with the principles of translation, with the rights and the obligations of a translator. As the seventeenth century advanced and translators grew both more self-conscious and more confident in matters of technique, the theory of literal translation was increasingly condemned—not that it had ever been extensively practised. Denham and Cowley may stand as representatives of the prevailing view, though the former, as Dryden said, "advised more liberty than he took himself." The theory of translation is of course as relative as any other question of taste—witness the diverse character of the classic English versions of Homer—and the style that is one age's meat is another's poison. Drayton extols Sandys' translation of Ovid as superior in sweetness and grace to the original; Dryden declares that all or most of Ovid's poetic quality evaporated in Sandys' pedantic lines.[2] The obvious retort, and the true one, is that both were wrong.

The motives and aims of translators in the last three-quarters of the seventeenth century moved further and further from the patriotic and

1. On the theory of translation in the seventeenth century see F. R. Amos, *Early Theories of Translation* (1920), cc. 3–4, J. E. Spingarn, *Critical Essays of the Seventeenth Century*, I, xlviii ff., and books cited in the Bibliography below.

2. Drayton, *Epistle to Reynolds*, ll. 157 ff.; Dryden, Dedication to *Examen Poeticum* (*Poems of Dryden*, Oxford, 1913, pp. 425–26). Dryden makes some amends in the preface to the *Fables*.

didactic ideals of the Elizabethans. England and the English language no longer needed apology in comparison with foreign achievement. Then, instead of the relative homogeneity of Elizabethan social and cultural standards we have a reading public broken up into groups marked off from one another by differences in birth, breeding, politics, religion; instead of the Elizabethan effort to spread enlightenment by popularization of the classics we have translators appealing to a select class of educated readers who are the arbiters of taste. As the accompaniment of more sophisticated scholarship there is a more conscious attempt to appreciate and render the special quality of an author—although neoclassic translations, from Ovid or Homer, Horace or Virgil, seem to us to have a good deal of family likeness. Translation comes to be a gentleman's accomplishment, and, as such, confined mainly to Latin poetry; it is a specimen of polite learning, and of skill in English versification.[3]

The reaction against Elizabethan and metaphysical waywardness and irregularity made translation from the classics a welcome instrument of discipline. To the nineteenth century that refining process seemed to have destroyed the soul of poetry.

"It cannot be denied," Johnson ends, after weighing Waller piece by piece and finding him light currency, "that he added something to our elegance of diction, and something to our propriety of thought." How important this end seemed may be judged from the amount of the sacrifice that was cheerfully made to reach it. By the time it was fully attained the jettison of poetry had been so great that in the eyes of a new reaction a century later it seemed there was nothing left worth saving: "Is Pope," people began to ask, "a poet at all?"[4]

To the achievement of correctness the translating activity of the seventeenth century contributed not a little. Its object, as Mackail says, was to make the English language into a complete vehicle of poetical expression, and to unite English poetry with the main European tradition. The few translators discussed in this chapter belong to a transitional phase, and show the refining process going on. First

---

3. And thus we arrive at Sir Max Beerbohm's "Statesman of Olden Time, making without wish for emolument a flat but faithful version of the Georgics, in English hexameters"—a generic portrait true in everything but the last word.

4. J. W. Mackail, "Sir Richard Fanshawe," *Studies of English Poets* (1926), p. 44. At present the writing of Dryden and Pope is in no danger of being undervalued.

of all we may notice a representative of the old tradition, of post-Elizabethan style decorative, vigorous, uneven, "unrefined."

I. SHAKERLEY MARMION

No myth has been retold in English more elaborately than that of Cupid and Psyche, and the roll of poetic paraphrases opens not unworthily with the work of a man whose name alone is seductive. Readers who have lost their way in *Pharonnida* and the other labyrinthine romances which wind through the volumes of Saintsbury's *Minor Caroline Poets* may begin Marmion's *Legend of Cupid and Psyche* (1637) with the initial assurance that the poet relied more upon Apuleius than his own invention. Embroidery of course there is, but Marmion's version is not, like William Morris', oppressively luxuriant and sweet. At the beginning he amplifies the description of Psyche's beauty, not with the aid of the beloved catalogue, but, in what was also a Renaissance fashion, by invoking extravagant parallels.[5] Mythological conceits in general vary from a few lines to a page or more; we have inserted even a version of the ever popular "hue and cry after Cupid." In the Ovidian tradition of the Renaissance is the needlework on Cupid's quiver, though the picture-making is more restrained than in Marlowe or Spenser:

> Next Venus and Adonis, sad with pain,
> The one of love, the other of disdain:
> There Jove in all his borrow'd shapes was dress'd,
> His thefts and his adulteries express'd,
> As emblems of Love's triumph; and these were
> Drawn with such lively colours, men would swear,
> That Leda lay within a perfect bower,
> And Danaë's golden streams were a true shower.[6]

Marmion's additions are not usually extensive enough to impede greatly the course of the story, and his narrative manner is clear, fluent, effortless. Bridges' version of the myth is beautiful, much more exquisitely finished than Marmion's, but it is not free from the sophisticated simplicity that calls attention to itself. Marmion evidently had before him the prose of Adlington as well as the Latin of Apule-

---

5. *Minor Caroline Poets*, II, 11. Marmion's poem was edited with an elaborate commentary by A. J. Nearing (1944).
6. P. 29.

ius, and the fact reminds us that his language has Elizabethan color
and richness. To say that his taste is uncertain is only to say that he is
a poet of the early seventeenth century. The most generous of editors
has a sad footnote on the lines,

> Night and her husband came, and now the sport
> Of Venus ended, he began to snort.

When her nocturnal bridegroom flew away in anger, Psyche "hung,
as an appendix of his flight." But the general texture is smooth and
attractive. By the light of the lamp one can see

> The god of Love himself, Cupid the fair,
> Lie sweetly sleeping in his golden hair.

And there is the phrase that awakened Saintsbury's enthusiasm, in
Psyche's despairing outcry against Venus:

> What darkness can protect me? what disguise
> Hide me from her inevitable eyes? [7]

But Marmion merely had the wisdom—though not everyone would
have had it—to render literally the words of Apuleius, *Veneris in-
evitabiles oculos.*[8]

II. Translators of Virgil

Marmion, along with such men as Leonard Digges and Henry
Reynolds,[9] may stand as representative inheritors of the Elizabethan
tradition, by virtue of their poetic style, their mode of handling their
authors, and their allegorical interests or professions. For the sake of
a compact illustration of the change from the post-Elizabethan to the
Augustan manner we may consider briefly two versions of the fourth
book of the *Aeneid.* They are the work of two of the most engaging
figures of the period, Sir Richard Fanshawe (1608–66) and Sidney

7. P. 44. See also Saintsbury's introduction.
8. The translator does not neglect the allegory. Most of the exposition is a
paraphrase of Fulgentius, whether at first hand or not, and the argument, except for a phrase or two, follows the narrative given by Fulgentius. Marmion's
pleasure in story-telling does not seem to be much affected by his sense of
"more deep and weighty mysteries."
9. See the Appendix, under 1617, 1628, 1632.

Godolphin (1610–43). Fanshawe's was written about 1639–40,[10] Godolphin's doubtless near the same time, yet the two pieces seem to belong to different generations. It is not merely that Fanshawe uses the Spenserian stanza, Godolphin the heroic couplet; there is a real difference in taste. Even if Godolphin's work passed under the smoothing hand of Waller, it will still serve our purpose.[11]

Like all other translators these two fail to render the subtleties of Virgilian style, but the work of Godolphin is respectable, that of Fanshawe is often something more. The opening lines are as characteristic as any. This is Fanshawe:

> But she who Love long since had swallowed down,
> Melts with hid fire; her wound doth inward weep:
> The man's much worth, his nation's much renown
> Runs in her mind: his looks and words are deep
> Fixt in her breast: care weans her eyes from sleep.[12]

Here is plain, strong literalness mixed with strong but gratuitous and irrelevant metaphors such as Chapman so abundantly provides. Godolphin is "correct" and diffuse, and ends with a gratuitous antithesis:

> Meane while the Queene Fanning A secret Fyer
> in her owne brest, revolves her deepe desire
> shee oft reflects upon the princely grace
> of great Eaneas, and that Noble race

10. *The Fourth Book of Virgil's Aeneid on the Loves of Dido and Aeneas,* ed. A. L. Irvine (1924). It was published in 1648.

11. *The Passion of Dido for Æneas* was published in 1658 as "translated by Edmund Waller and Sidney Godolphin." In the 1664 edition of Waller's poems ll. 455–585 are ascribed to him. The remaining 114 lines of the 699 have not been claimed for either Waller or Godolphin. Dighton thinks it likely "that Sidney Godolphin translated the whole, and that Waller in preparing the poem for publication reworked the middle section to such an extent that he considered it his own" (*Poems of Sidney Godolphin,* ed. W. Dighton, 1931, pp. xxxix ff.). Waller's work is said to have been done in 1657. How far Waller may have revised the whole one cannot tell.

In connection with the style of Virgilian translations of this period, see the remarks on Denham's work in T. H. Banks's edition of Denham (Yale University Press, 1928), and the books of W. Frost and L. Proudfoot in the bibliography for this chapter.

12.   At regina gravi iamdudum saucia cura
         vulnus alit venis et caeco carpitur igni.
         multa viri virtus animo multusque recursat
         gentis honos: haerent infixi pectore vultus
         verbaque, nec placidam membris dat cura quietem.

> from whence he springs, her wounded fancy feedes
> on his discourse, his high Heroyike deedes
> his wordes, his lookes, her waking thoughts imploy
> and when shee sleepes, shee sees him with more joye,
> but seldome sleepes.

Many phrases illustrate the same qualities. *Degeneres animos timor arguit* Fanshawe is content to render "Fear shows ignoble minds"; "The mortall seede of men acknowledge feare" is Godolphin's inflated rhetoric. In the description of the fateful storm we have the contrast between Fanshawe's uncertain force and Godolphin's Augustan rotundity. The passages are too long for quotation, but they begin thus:

> Meanwhile loud thunder heaven's pavilion tears
> Making a passage for th' ensuing rain . . .

> Meane while the gathering clowdes obscure the Pole
> they flash out Lightnings and in Thunder Role.

"She calls it wedlock, gives her fault an honest name," writes Fanshawe soberly, for *coniugium vocat, hoc praetexit nomine culpam.* Godolphin prefers the grandeur of generality:

> but doeth excuse it with Chast Hymens name
> and lives exposd a theame to various fame.

The refining process is carried further with the picture of Atlas, where Godolphin simply omits the lines that Fanshawe renders thus:

> Thick on his aged back the snow doth lie,
> And down his dravel'd chin pour plenteous springs,
> His beard in icicles grows horribly.[13]

Uncertainty of taste is one part of Fanshawe's heritage. Venus says to Juno:

> And yet, perchance, you lying in his breast
> With a wife's rhetoric may his counsels sway;
> Then break the ice; I'll second the request.

13. *Aen.* iv.250–51:
> nix umeros infusa tegit, tum flumina mento
> praecipitant senis, et glacie riget horrida barba.

Godolphin, with unusual condensation, has "this in your prayers, who are his wife doeth lie." The best passage in Fanshawe's whole book is followed by a painfully Elizabethan rendering of

> Talibus orabat, talisque miserrima fletus
> fertque refertque soror.

He writes:

> This Dido spake. The sad ambassadress
> Carries her tears, and brings them back again
> (As brackish tides post from and to the main).

While Godolphin generally maintains a level of decorous evenness, Fanshawe rises with some power to the height of Dido's passion. Thus Godolphin (whose third line is almost in the other's manner):

> I'le follow thee, bee present in thy paine,
> and when cold earth shall this mixt frame devide
> my Ghost shall lacquey by thy frighted side,
> thou dearely shalt repent, the newse of this
> shall overtake my soule, and give it blisse.

Fanshawe's version is free, but his Dido speaks like a Fury:

> For when cold death shall part with dreary swoon
> My soul and flesh, my ghost, where'er thou be,
> Shall haunt thee with dim torch, and light thee down
> To thy dark conscience: I'll be Hell to thee,
> And this glad news will make Hell Heav'n to me.[14]

Best of all, for sustained dramatic vividness, is Dido's speech to Anna.[15]

Waller's section is too little distinguishable from Godolphin's to require special comment, but his rendering of one bit may be compared with Fanshawe's.

> . . . with that word
> he cuts the cable with his shyning sword,
> through all the Navy doeth like Ardor raigne

14. *Aen.* iv.384 ff.
15. *Aen.* iv.420 ff. The passage is quoted in J. W. Mackail's essay on Fanshawe (*Studies of English Poets*, p. 51).

> the[y] quitt the shoare, and rush into the Maine
> plac'd on their Barks, the lusty Trojans sweepe
> Neptunes smooth face, and cleave the yeelding deepe.[16]

The effect is of a most orderly tumult; and the first half of the last line is rather a petrified metaphor than a mythological conceit. Fanshawe's Trojans are really in a hurry:

> This said, whipt out his lightning sword, and strook
>   The fastening ropes. Like zeal his pattern bred
> In all. They snatch'd, they ran, the shores forsook,
> Their sails like wings over the waves were spread:
> They comb'd with oars great Neptune's curled head.

The vividness is a trifle marred by the last line, which out-Chapmans Chapman. But such things are only occasional lapses.

On the significance of Fanshawe's work I cannot do better than quote Mackail's comments regarding one passage:

> But it shows a gentleman's scholarship to perfection; for combined dignity and sweetness it is, I think, unsurpassed by what any other rendering of Virgil into English has achieved . . . There are traces still left here of the Elizabethan rhetoric, and of the post-Elizabethan mannerism; but both are becoming subdued and civilised, while still possessing the glowing colour and melodious phrasing of that great school of poetry. Just a little more, and Fanshawe would have attained what he and all his contemporaries were feeling after, the secret of a style which will never be obsolete.

III. Stanley : Sherburne : Ayres

Something may be said of a few minor poets united partly by personal ties, partly by the range of their translating activities. The most original writer of the group, and the germinal force in the matter of translation, was Thomas Stanley. He appears in some respects as a belated Elizabethan, though more scholarly and more "smooth and genteel"—to borrow the phrase of Anthony à Wood—and it is significant that in youth he was taught by William Fairfax, son of the translator of Tasso. With Stanley's original lyrics we need not linger,[17] but the scope of his translations reveals both his Greek scholar-

---

16. Dighton, pp. 54–55. Cf. *Aen.* iv.579–83. Only the last line need be quoted: *adnixi torquent spumas et caerula verrunt.*

17. See Saintsbury's *Minor Caroline Poets*, III, 95 ff.; *Poems and Translations of Thomas Stanley*, ed. G. M. Grump (Clarendon Press, 1962); on Stan-

ship and his unusual knowledge of Italian, Spanish, and French poetry of the sixteenth and seventeenth centuries.

The volume of 1651 contained *Anacreon. Bion. Moschus. Kisses, by Secundus. Cupid Crucified, by Ausonius. Venus Vigils, Incerto Authore.* Nearly one hundred pages following these translations were devoted to notes or "excitations," which contained also some illustrative versions from Ronsard, Marino, and others. A third section comprised translations thus listed on a separate title-page: *Sylvia's Park, by Theophile. Acanthus Complaint, by Tristan. Oronta, by Preti. Echo, by Marino. Loves Embassy, by Boscan. The Solitude, by Gongora.* At the end of the volume came the prose version of Pico's *Platonick Discourse upon Love.* The list of titles, ancient and modern, is briefer than comment would be, and it indicates Stanley's taste for delicately carved cherry stones. The mythology that appears in the English reflects the familiar characteristics of the originals. Within his range Stanley is an easy and elegant translator. His versions of the ancients are faithful enough; as regards the moderns, "unlike other translators Stanley almost constantly condenses his model." [18] In one piece of twelve lines, *Apollo and Daphne,* he combines conceits drawn from poems by Garcilaso de la Vega and Marino. This is the Marinesque ending:

> And though the conquest which he sought he miss'd,
> With that triumphant spoil adorns his brow.
> Thus this disdainful maid his aim deceives:
> Where he expected fruit he gathers leaves.[19]

From Stanley one may turn to his friend Sir Edward Sherburne (1616–1702), who was likewise a prolific translator from the classical and modern languages. After the death of the king whom he had served, Sherburne spent some time in reading French and Italian poets, profiting from Stanley's acquaintance with continental literature. But while Stanley's stronger individuality found expression in some original work (not to mention the *History of Philosophy*),

---

ley's sources, Crump's notes and the articles by M. Praz and Sir H. Thomas (Bibliography, below).

18. Praz, p. 281.

19. *Minor Caroline Poets,* III, 128–29; Praz, p. 283. See the couplet from Waller quoted near the end of the last chapter.

The myth of Europa, by the way, seems to have especially attracted Stanley. For his references to a number of versions see Thomas, pp. 191, 228–29, and Praz, p. 287.

Sherburne "is purely a translator," with hardly anything original to his credit.[20] Two of his longer translations, however, are of interest in connection with the mythological poem and also with the influence of translation in refining poetic style.

With occasional slight omissions and expansions Sherburne's *Salmacis* is a close paraphrase of Preti's *La Salmace,* and Preti had taken the usual liberties with Ovid.[21] Almost everything in Ovid's tale is adorned with fanciful and pictorial detail except, oddly enough, the account of the nymph's ecstatic embracing of Hermaphroditus. At the beginning Ovid's few lines about the boy's history are elaborated into a tissue of pretty mythological inventions. The Augustans would hardly have approved of this picture of a mountain:

> So far above the clouds his head doth rise
> That his green locks no summer dripping spies
> With rain, his face no winter does behold
> Mask'd with a snowy muffler 'gainst the cold.[22]

The translation of Colluthus, following the Greek, does not exhibit the conceits which the Ovidian tale owed to Preti. Some bits of description recall such poems as *Endimion and Phœbe*. The picture of Paris, if less beautiful than Tennyson's, is also less artificial:

> Low as his knee a mountain goat's rough hide
> Hung from his shoulders, flagging by his side:
> In's hand a neatherd's goad: such to the eye
> (As slowly to his pipe's soft melody
> He moves) appear'd the gentle Phrygian swain,
> Tuning on's reed a sweet, though rural strain.

Sherburne's oxen emit a bovine odor:

> His oxen, cloy'd with the rank grass, were laid,
> Stretching their fat sides in the cooler shade . . .

20. Praz, p. 290.

21. *Salmacis, Lyrian & Sylvia, Forsaken Lydia, The Rape of Helen,* etc., London, 1651. Sherburne is reprinted, with some omissions, in Chalmers, Vol. VI; since the original volume is not now accessible my quotations are made from Chalmers. Sherburne's poems have been edited by F. J. van Beeck (Assen, 1961).

22. Incidentally, the conclusion of the piece makes use of the personal motive which we have often met. Amintas tells the story to coy Iole,

> Then adds: "O thou more fair, in love more cold
> Than he! Heaven yet may make thee mine in spite . . ."

By way of measuring Sherburne's position we might observe how, in the eighteenth century, the oxen have learned deportment and become gentlemanlike:

> The herd full fed the fertile grass refrain,
> And scatter'd lay reclin'd upon the plain.[23]

Sherburne's couplets are smooth enough, but not quite regular. His diction in general retains a good deal of the older juice and sweetness, even though here and there, to mix metaphors, it reveals, if not a cloven hoof, just the tip of a patent leather shoe. But, from comparison with most translators of the eighteenth century, Sherburne, like many of his fellows, emerges without loss. Apart from any question of individual talent, they had a better medium at their disposal. It might be uncertain, it might be subject to Elizabethan lapses in taste, or even show traces of Augustan poetic diction, but it was not a uniformly glossy picture postcard.[24]

This sketch may be rounded out with a word concerning Philip Ayres (1638–1712), though his *Lyric Poems* were published as late as 1687, because he is related through his work, if not personally, with Stanley and Sherburne.[25] Two of Ayres's poems were mentioned in the last chapter and there is no need of adding much here, since his almost wholly lyrical pieces are drawn from the same general range of authors translated by his predecessors.[26] Saintsbury remarked upon his fondness for Greek—"the small Greek poets," as Ayres calls them—at a time when Latin was becoming more predominant than ever; and the same critic emphasizes Ayres's conservatism, his loyalty to "the tastes, the traditions, the style even to some extent, of the reign of Charles I." In *Endymion and Diana*, however, Ayres was far from loyal to the monster-spawning tradition of the earlier period, for the poem contains but thirteen eight-line stanzas, and, as the

23. From a version of Colluthus published in 1731 (*The Rape of Helen*, Brit. Mus., 11340.c.2).

24. Some of the notes that Sherburne appended to his translation are links with the past. Citing Fulgentius, he interprets the marriage of Peleus and Thetis as the union of earth and water. Dictys Cretensis is mentioned more than once.

25. M. Praz, *MLR*, XX, 419 ff.; H. Thomas, *Rev. Hisp.*, XLVIII, 243 ff., 311 ff. Ayres is reprinted in Saintsbury, II, 265 ff.

26. To mention one lyric on a classical theme, Thomas (p. 251) observes that *Leander drowned* was modeled on Garcilaso de la Vega's imitation of Martial. Cf. Praz, p. 429.

editor observes, is "the shortest of our 'Heroic' poems, but complete enough in its miniature." [27] For that virtue we may thank Alessandro Tassoni, whom Ayres duly acknowledges as his source. In conception the little piece is remote from Drayton or Keats. While Endymion sleeps on a bed of flowers, with Cupids playing around him, Diana comes and sees him. His beauty overcomes her virgin modesty, and she fondles him until he wakens. When he starts up she holds him back, and consents to his demand for a place in heaven. After a night of pleasure the goddess wishes she had not wasted so much time in hunting. The polished prettiness of the poem recalls the mythological paintings of the seventeenth century.

27. Saintsbury, II, 285. See Praz, p. 424.

CHAPTER XIII

Allegory and Anti-Pagan Sentiment in the Seventeenth Century

I

By this time allegory may seem to have become a King Charles's head in our Memorial, but a record of the treatment of mythology would be very incomplete if it left out of account the continued flourishing of allegorical ideas in the seventeenth, even in the eighteenth, century. Although some great and less great names appear in the list of orthodox believers, the story, as the seventeenth century advances, is one of decline and fall. What in the Elizabethan age had been orthodoxy, sometimes genuine, sometimes not, dwindles by degrees into a heterodoxy cherished by persons of slightly queer notions, Platonists and such. Yet the skeptical and scientific movement was very slow in undermining the allegorical tradition, and we may assemble enough testimonies to outline the gradual dissolution of the venerable doctrine. The result might cheer the ardent lover of truth, but it was more than coincidence that the decline of the allegorical and didactic conception of myth was accompanied by the loss of imaginative and spiritual values in poetry.

While Bacon labored to emancipate his age from medieval ways of thought he was so imperfectly emancipated himself that posterity is in doubt whether to call him medieval or modern. He is one of the conspicuous instances of the phenomenon we have often noticed, that Renaissance minds are (though free from vulgarity) like luxurious houses of the newly rich, with rooms incongruously furnished in the style of many periods. No room in the spacious mind of Bacon is more significant for our purpose than the *De Sapientia Veterum* (1609), a book expounding the allegorical meaning of thirty-one characters or stories from classical mythology.[1] In his preface Bacon manifests a little uneasiness when he anticipates the possible charge that he is entertaining himself with a toy, but he proceeds to argue on traditional grounds for allegory concealed in fable. If the ancients did not write thus with conscious purpose at any rate they were lucky in falling "upon matter which gives occasion to such worthy contemplations."

Bacon then expounds the myths, under such titles as "Cassandra, or Plainness of Speech"; "Narcissus, or Self-Love"; "Endymion, or the Favourite"; "Sphinx, or Science" . . . Outwardly, and often inwardly, the method is that of a thousand, or two thousand, years earlier, and it is true that Bacon "wasted much time and ingenuity in showing that some mute inglorious Newton has hidden the true principles of Natural Philosophy in the story of *Pan*, and that some prehistoric Clausewitz has embedded the rules of military strategy in that of *Perseus and Medusa*." [2] But the approach is not wholly medieval. The story of Cassandra and Apollo "seems to have been devised in reproof of unreasonable and unprofitable liberty in giving advice and admonition." The story of Typhon has to do with the variable fortunes of kings and rebellions against them. Narcissus, of course, represents self-love, but with a Baconian difference; the victim is averse to public business, and, secluding himself with a circle of admiring "echoes," he grows besotted and weak, fading away like flowers. The fates of Actaeon and Pentheus deal respectively with "the secrets of princes" [3] and "the secrets of divinity." Thus if we forget the myth involved we have virtually another series of civil and moral essays, with the same realistic grasp of human nature and affairs, the same practical and utilitarian motives. The interpretations of myth are generally of a corresponding character; in fact we meet some of them in the *Essays, Advancement of Learning,* and elsewhere.

A number of chapters are concerned with science.

1. *Works*, ed. Spedding (Boston, 1860), XIII, 75 ff. Cf. Bacon's discussion of "poesy parabolical" (Spingarn, *Critical Essays of the Seventeenth Century,* I, 7 ff.), and Lemmi, Rossi, and E. Sewell in the Bibliography below.

2. C. D. Broad, *Philosophy of Francis Bacon* (Cambridge University Press, 1926), pp. 26–27.

3. Cf. Natalis Comes, *"De Actæone"* (Padua, 1616, p. 546): "Significant præterea deuitandam esse omnibus curiositatem & earum rerum studium, quæ nihil ad nos pertinent, quoniam multis perniciosa fuit arcanorum consiliorum principum cognitio." See also *ibid.*, vi.24, p. 354.

Nor need we wonder that Pan's horns touch heaven; since the summits, or universal forms, of nature do in a manner reach up to God; the passage from metaphysic to natural theology being ready and short . . .

With regard to the audacity of Pan in challenging Cupid to fight, it refers to this,—that matter is not without a certain inclination and appetite to dissolve the world and fall back into the ancient chaos; but that the overswaying concord of things (which is represented by Cupid or Love) restrains its will and effort in that direction and reduces it to order.[4]

Cupid has lost his dominion over the heart; his character and activities have to do with "the natural motion of the atom." Bacon's adaptation of myths to the illustration of his scientific notions sometimes embodies the traditional lore of the mythographers, but a good deal of it seems to be original. Everywhere too he emphasizes the necessity, in the search for truth, of infinite patience, of single-hearted devotion to the cause. The seeker is Mercury restoring the sinews of Jupiter, Prometheus transmitting the torch of light, Oedipus wresting her secrets from the sphinx. The book was very popular, and not undeservedly. If it was not *L'Esprit des Mythes* it was in a sense *l'esprit sur les mythes*.

Ralegh's *History of the World* (1614) is, as Arnold easily demonstrated, less modern in its attitude than the work of Thucydides, for Ralegh starts from uncritical premises. But the early books of the *History*, with their medley of Hebraic and classical legend and medieval accretion, do not mark their author as behind the times. His view of myth is quite similar to that of George Sandys. Within the prescribed limits he is critical. He constantly relates Biblical and classical stories, trying to distinguish between fact and fiction. He accepts allegorized myth, and sometimes quotes Natalis Comes. As an example of rationalizing we might take this interpretation of the amorous activities of Jupiter:

And of these his several ravishments, betrayings, stealing away of men's wives, daughters, and sons, buying of virgins, and the like, came in all those ancient fables of his transformations into showers of gold, eagles, bulls, birds, and beasts; and of him and by him (in effect) all that rabble of Grecian forgeries.[5]

4. Pp. 95, 99. Cf. Natalis Comes, v.6 (p. 247): "Dicunt illum [Pan] fuisse cum Cupidine colluctatum ab eo victum, quia, ut diximus, amor & litigium principium fuisse rerum naturalium putata sunt."

5. *History* (1829), bk. i, c. 6, sec. 5 (II, 172–73). For some further items see the chapter on Milton.

Robert Burton, who read everything, of course read the mythographers, and he quotes such familiar ones as Fulgentius, Lilius Giraldus, Natalis Comes, Cartari. Lovers, he says,

become at last *insensati*, void of sense; degenerate into dogs, hogs, asses, brutes; as Jupiter into a Bull, Apuleius an Ass, Lycaon a Wolf, Tereus a Lapwing, Callisto a Bear, Elpenor and Gryllus into Swine by Circe. For what else may we think those ingenious Poets to have shadowed in their witty fictions and Poems, but that a man once given over to his lust (as Fulgentius interprets that of Apuleius, Alciat. of Tereus) is no better than a beast.[6]

In the preface to Γυναικεῖον (1624) Thomas Heywood sets forth conventional opinions about the "misticall sences" of "poeticall fictions," and carries out his principles in treating pagan divinities. A passage on Juno as Air, and the engendering of "creatures, trees and plants," is translated literally from Natalis Comes.[7] In his *Pleasant Dialogues and Dramma's* (1637), annotating Textor's *Dialogue of Earth and Age,* Heywood takes from Comes, whom he mentions, the notion that Eurydice represents the soul and Orpheus the body.[8]

The greatest repository of allegorized myth in English is the commentary which Sandys added to the 1632 edition of his translation of the *Metamorphoses.*[9] Sandys' list of authorities ranges from Plato to Bacon, and his interpretations, like those of earlier mythographers, are eclectic. Expositions may be theological, moral, euhemeristic, scientific. References in the text range from Fulgentius and Lactantius to Copernicus, Galileo, Tycho, and Kepler. Like Ralegh Sandys is critical, within the limits set by his fundamental assumptions. He

6. *Anatomy of Melancholy* (Bohn's Popular Library), III, 177. Cf. *ibid.,* I, 299, 499, etc., and index (for mythographers).

7. Heywood, pp. 6–7; Comes, p. 533.

8. Ed. W. Bang, *Materialien* (1903), p. 288; Comes, vii.14, p. 402.

9. Sandys issued five books in 1621, and the complete text in 1626. In view of the fact that the first work printed in English by Caxton was the *Recuyell,* it is noteworthy—as regards the prestige of our subject matter—that Sandys' *Ovid* seems to have been the first piece of literature achieved in the land of the pilgrims' pride. The University of Nebraska Press is issuing a paperback reprint of the 1632 edition.

For a critical account of Sandys as a translator see *Cambridge History of English Literature,* VII, 50 ff. It is there said, by the way, that Sandy's rendering of the tale of Actaeon gains strength from his finding appropriate equivalents for the names of Actaeon's hounds. It is hardly an accident that some eighteen of the names are the same as Golding's—not that it matters.

tries to disentangle fact from fiction, and to relate "history" to Biblical matter. The commentary, if one has a taste for that sort of thing, is never dull, and Keats did not find it so.[10] And perhaps Milton had read it, as footnotes in the following chapter may or may not suggest to the candid reader.

In the same year apparently was published the *Mythomystes* of Henry Reynolds. The essay is, as Spingarn said,

the chief example in English of the systematic application of Neoplatonism to the interpretation of poetry. Bacon had already indicated the road, but Reynolds follows it into a tropical forest of strange fancies: the Cabalists and Neoplatonists, Philo and Reuchlin, but especially Pico della Mirandola and Alessandro Farra, here find an English voice.[11]

But we cannot plunge into the tropical forest. Nor can we linger with Alexander Ross, to whom a casual couplet of Butler's gave an immortality doubtfully achieved in *Mel Heliconium* and *Mystagogus Poeticus*. Ross, said Addison, had dived deeper into Ovid's design than anyone else, "for he discovers in him the greatest mysteries of the Christian religion, and finds almost in every page some typical representations of the World, the Flesh, and the Devil." [12]

By this time the allegorical plant, though of sturdy ancestry, was drooping in the nipping air of reason. In 1674 Rymer declared in his downright way: "And it was the vice of those Times to affect superstitiously the Allegory; and nothing would then be currant without a mystical meaning. We must blame the Italians for debauching great Spencer's judgment . . ." [13] In the year following the very unmystical Hobbes surveyed Homer with unblinking eyes, and, mainly by negative implications, removed allegory from the field of discussion.[14] Yet the rising tide of rationalism represented by such names did not sweep away all vestiges of traditional opinion. The later history of allegory lies beyond our present limits, but we may remember

10. See E. de Selincourt's edition of Keats, for both parallels from the text of the translation and suggestions of symbolism probably derived from the commentary, which we know he read. In connection with *Hyperion* it may be noticed that Sandys (ed. 1632, p. 27) identifies the giants with ignorance, the gods with virtue.

11. *Critical Essays of the Seventeenth Century*, I, xxi. See the text, I, 141 ff., and my Appendix, under 1632.

12. *Miscellaneous Works, In Verse and Prose* (London, 1726), I, 236–37.

13. Spingarn, II, 168.

14. *Ibid.*, II, 67 ff. Cf. pp. 54 ff.

that Pope's preface to the *Iliad*, following Le Bossu, remarks on the breadth of knowledge embodied in Homer's allegories; [15] that in the essay contributed to the same work Parnell, though snorting at extreme allegorical vagaries, avowed that some rays of truth streamed through the darkness; [16] that Garth's preface to the translation of the *Metamorphoses* done by Dryden and others expounded Ovid's allegories and endorsed the work of Sandys. These are only a few examples. Such interpretations of myth lingered on in volumes like Tooke's *Pantheon*, which Keats read as a boy. The name of Keats reminds us that, so far as poetry is concerned, the distance between allegory and symbolism is not great. In general the best modern treatments of myth, unlike those of the common Renaissance type, have been poems in which more is meant than meets the eye.[17]

II

Although the allegorical theory of poetry had enabled Ovid and some Ovidian poems to take on a protective coloring, the best-known pieces, like Marlowe's and Shakespeare's, laid no claim to hidden moral truth. They were pagan, and it depended upon the reader's upbringing whether the paganism were glorious or wicked. In this section we must glance at representatives of the latter persuasion. The moral excesses and aesthetic deficiencies which are commonly associated with the puritan party (or rather parties) of the sixteenth and seventeenth centuries are found of course, with infinite variations of hue and degree, in all ages and countries; indeed one may well be chary of using a word that can be applied alike to Plato and to William Prynne. The so-called puritan reaction to imaginative literature, though always with us, is likely to be especially marked at any time when culture is rapidly broadening down from ignorance to ignorance, through layer after layer of the middle class. It was thus in our period.

In the sixteenth century, as in the fourteenth or the fourth, there

---

15. See A. F. B. Clark, *Boileau* (1925), p. 247; Austin Warren, *Alexander Pope* (1929), pp. 81, 100–01.

16. *The Iliad of Homer. Translated by Alexander Pope*, ed. G. Wakefield (London, 1796), I, clxii–clxiii, clxxxiii.

17. The list of references given above for allegorical doctrine might be expanded indefinitely. To go no further than this book, see in the Appendix: Fraunce, 1592; Brathwait, 1611, 1621; Digges, 1617; Brinsley, 1618; Hall, 1651, 1655; Jones, 1658. Since allegory was last discussed we have encountered such more or less sincere exponents as Basse, Chapman, Marmion.

were those who appreciated Ovid as a poet, those who compounded
for enjoying his tales by attaching a moral, and those who regarded
his pagan pantheon as the devil's chapel. Each group might contain
puritans. But as the third increased in numbers and shrillness it became more and more expressive of strict puritan sentiment. Ovid, like
Shaw's amiable dustman, found himself "up agen middle class
morality." Whereas a liberal puritan like Golding could enjoy a
moralized Ovid—and Golding's allegories were confined to his prefaces—the increasing majority of illiberal and dismal puritans would
have no such compromise. Some of these "painful" servants of God
we have listened to already.[18] We noticed also in an early chapter
the moralizing habit which, especially during the years 1560–70,
devitalized ballads and appended sermons to Ovidian tales; this was
one way of preventing the devil from having all the tunes.[19] It failed
to satisfy those who were resolved, as Sir Toby might have said, that
because they were virtuous there should be no more Cupids and
Venuses. Sylvester, though he made occasional use of mythology,
prayed

> O! furnish me with an un-vulgar stile,
> That I by this may wain our wanton Ile
> From Ovid's heires, and their un-hallowed spell
> Here charming senses, chaining soules in Hell.[20]

And the popularity of Sylvester's translation in the first half of the
seventeenth century is a most significant cultural phenomenon; it was
the epic of middle-class Protestantism, and it had some effect on
Milton, even the youthful Dryden.

When in the disreputable suburbs of London theaters rose and
flourished like evergreen trees of diabolical knowledge, puritan axes
began to be wielded with vigor. One might not have expected
mythology to come in for a share of the invective, but not the least
vigorous of Gosson's pages denounce the immoralities of the pagan
gods and the wickedness of the poets who write about them:

Whilest they make Cupide triumphe in heauen, and all the gods to
marche bounde like miserable captiues, before his charriot, they belie God,
and bewitch the reader with bawdie charmes . . .
Thus making gods of them that were brute beastes, in the likenes of men,

18. Chapter IV, note 10.
19. Page 60 above.
20. Ed. Grosart, I, 99.

diuine goddesses of common harlots; they robbe God of his honour, diminishe his authoritie, weaken his might, and turne his seate to a stewes.[21]

Gosson's work is a mere preface compared with the tremendous *Histriomastix* of 1632, and Prynne, by the way, quotes Gosson with approbation. In the general anathema against the stage mythology is included, and the tone is at once more medieval and more puritanical than Gosson's; Prynne's artillery is mostly charged from the early fathers. It is infamous for Christians even to read or hear the names of pagan gods, who were really devils or wicked men or mere fictions, and stories about them, sugared over with art and rhetoric, cool our love for the soul-saving word of God.[22]

Mythology, however, was coming into disfavor with more than puritans. The merely pagan impulses of the Renaissance were exhausted; they had not vitality enough to preserve them from putrefaction. They could still appeal to some genuine poets, but the metaphysical movement brought fresh life to another kind of writing. For an important group thoughts of God and judgment and eternity were replacing Olympus and Venus. Besides, puritanism, for good or ill, had leavened the lump; the slow and not always silent pressure of the middle class was, for a time, purifying literature and taste. Thus by the middle of the century we find a number of the literary men sharing the continental dislike for classical subjects. Whereas the ideal of the Renaissance had been an edifying but more or less secular heroic poem, the great aim now is the Christian epic.

In the preface to *Psyche,* the only part of that work that one can read, Joseph Beaumont declares his hope "That this Book may prompt better Wits to believe, that a Divine Theam is as capable and happy a Subject of Poetical Ornament, as any Pagan or Humane Device whatsoever." [23] Davenant, the unpuritanical loss of whost nose engendered so much delicate wit, made a well-known defense of a Christian subject in the preface to *Gondibert* (1650).[24] Still more sig-

---

21. *An Apologie of the Schoole of Abuse* (1579), ed. Arber, pp. 65–68.
22. Ed. 1633, pp. 28, 79–80.
23. *Psyche* (London, 1648).
24. Spingarn, II, 5, 9–10, and *passim.* The movement against paganism in poetry had begun quite early on the continent. One may recall again the case of Tasso (see H. M. Briggs, "Tasso's Theory of Epic Poetry," *MLR,* XXV, 457 ff.). Fairfax introduced into his translation mythological allusions which he did not find in the original (Courthope, *History of English Poetry,* III, 82 ff.). Further, as C. H. Herford says, "the fiends of the *Gerusalemme Liberata* are in essence medieval devils disguised under the names and characteristics of

nificant, as regards the soil out of which grew Milton's major poems, is Cowley's preface of 1656, especially when we remember that as a child he had been won to poetry by the benign and radiant Spenser, that his first production was an Ovidian tale, and that much of his best mature work was amorous and festive. The devil has reigned over the realm of poetry, says Cowley, and among poets' sins has been the handling of "confused antiquated Dreams of senseless Fables and Metamorphoses." These things "are all but the Cold-meats of the Antients," and nothing is left for modern writers. Anyhow Biblical stories are far better than "the obsolete threadbare tales of Thebes and Troy." "Can all the Transformations of the Gods give such copious hints to flourish and expatiate on as the true Miracles of Christ, or of his Prophets and Apostles?" [25] Cowley is far from desiring mere versified Scripture; he remains, whatever be thought of his own effort, an artist. It is partly as an artist too that he feels the exhaustion of the classic themes, though a greater poet might not have had the feeling. At the same time his Christian condemnation of mythology is quite as harsh as the outburst in *Paradise Regained,* and Cowley (who oddly enough was one of Milton's favorite English poets) is not branded a puritan.

the more monstrous figures of Greek myth" ("Dante and Milton," *The Post-War Mind of Germany,* p. 93). See, at the beginning of Tasso's fourth canto, the description of Pluto, with horns, fiery eyes, a mouth emitting blood, "sparks and smells."

25. Spingarn, II, 88–90. Cf. *Davideis* (*Poems,* ed. Waller, 1905, p. 243):

> Too long the Muses-Land have Heathen bin;
> Their Gods too long were Dev'ils, and Vertues Sin;
> But Thou, Eternal Word, hast call'd forth Me
> Th' Apostle, to convert that World to Thee;
> T'unbind the charms that in slight Fables lie,
> And teach that Truth is truest Poesie.

CHAPTER XIV

Milton

What besides God has resolved concerning me I know not, but this at least: He has instilled into me, if into anyone, a vehement love of the beautiful. Not with so much labour, as the fables have it, is Ceres said to have sought her daughter Proserpina as it is my habit day and night to seek for this idea of the beautiful, as for a certain image of supreme beauty, through all the forms and faces of things (for many are the shapes of things divine) and to follow it as it leads me on by some sure traces which I seem to recognize.

Letter to Diodati, 1637.[1]

Masson suggests that Shakespeare and Ben Jonson, as they went along Bread Street from the Mermaid Tavern, might have passed a small boy at play whose name was John Milton. It is probable that when Ben at least quitted his chair and his cup little John Milton had been some hours in bed, yet the pleasant fancy helps to emphasize the poet's close relation to the Elizabethans, to remind us that he was born nine years after the death of Spenser, when *The Tempest* was not yet staged, when England, if not merry—it never has been that—was still a land of music and song. Sixty years bring us to a worn champion of freedom, blind but cheerful, despite chalkstones and frustrated hopes, who publishes *Paradise Lost* when gentle George Etherege is rousing himself to produce *She Would If She Could;* and who, in the year of *The Rehearsal,* offers *Paradise Regained* and *Samson Agonistes* to the polite censure of the town.

We have, or think we have, a fairly definite notion of what we mean by "Elizabethan," and of what we mean by "neoclassical"; what lies between does not invite such easy labels. The modish one is "baroque," which means almost anything a critic wishes to make it mean. Among the various cross-currents in poetry the most important was the metaphysical. But from the first Milton moved in the main stream of Renaissance humanism, and he remained closer to

1. Masson, *Life*, I, 644–45.

Spenser than to any other single poet. Such a statement, concerning so potent an individuality as Milton's, is of course only comparative, and it is truer of his ethical thought than of his poetic expression. The latter is necessarily our chief interest. Yet Milton's treatment of classical myth does lead us sometimes to the center of his thought, and he is the last poet until the romantic period of whom that can be said.

Of the sources, ancient and modern, of Milton's mythology some account will have to be taken, but with a purpose rather different from that which governed similar discussions in earlier chapters. Spenser, Marlowe, Shakespeare, have highly individual styles, yet at times they reflect the tone of a particular source, such as Ovid. Milton knew Ovid better than any of these men, but almost from the beginning he wrote in such a consistently personal idiom that one can very rarely say "This is like Ovid," or "This is like Homer." Wherever Milton gets his material the result, except in a few early pieces, is simply John Milton.

Further, the mere extent of Milton's learning inclines one to accept the advice given to Adam and forbear inquiry. I may summarize the summary made in Mr. Osgood's standard work:

There are four poets from whom he certainly derived more help than from any others. These are Homer, Hesiod, Vergil, and Ovid . . . Next in importance to these four sources are Euripides, Pindar, Theocritus, and the *Homeric Hymns*. With these we may mention also the prose writers, Pausanias and Apollodorus. Milton has also drawn some of his mythology from Æschylus, Sophocles, Plato, the *Orphic Hymns*, and Apollonius of Rhodes; from Herodotus, Plutarch, Pliny, Diodorus, and Strabo; from Horace, Statius, Claudian, and the tragedies of Seneca. To these we may add, though the list will be by no means exhaustive, Cicero, Athenæus, Hyginus, Aratus, Macrobius, Lucretius, and most of the minor poets of the empire.[2]

In other words, and as everyone knows, Milton was steeped in ancient literature as no English poet before him had been, and in Greek no less than in Latin. He drank copiously from the sources which Spenser, with a few exceptions, only sipped, and from many sources

2. *The Classical Mythology of Milton's English Poems* (1900), pp. xlii–xliii. This chapter is everywhere indebted to Mr. Osgood's study of sources, and also to his general discussion, though I have tried as far as possible to avoid repetition of the latter. Starnes and Talbert (Bibliography, "General") show how much of Milton's mythology was in Renaissance dictionaries, though one may think that he assimilated it from more imaginative sources.

that Spenser did not know. Milton's Latin verse alone shows that as a young man he had Ovid and Virgil and other poets pretty well by heart. It shows too how critically he knew them, even to the minutiæ of style and versification. He was, in short, a classical scholar, in both an extensive and intensive sense that applies to no other poet we have met except Ben Jonson, and Milton's critical as well as his creative faculties were aesthetically more keen and delicate than Ben's. The significance of Milton's classical studies in his whole life and work is at once too large and too familiar a subject to be touched in such a sketch as this. It is enough to say that Latin and Greek literature colored everything he was and did, from his syntax to his love of liberty—and his equally strong love of self-discipline and obedience.

One would expect so learned a poet, with all ancient literature at his command, to deal with "authentic" classical mythology, and certainly Milton is not guilty of those innumerable "errors" which in Spenser reveal a much inferior familiarity with original sources, a larger infusion of medievalism, and in general a less scholarly attitude. Milton does now and then invent or adapt a non-classical story, but usually for obvious reasons, as in the genealogies of Melancholy and the Graces in *L'Allegro,* or the parentage of Comus. Commentators who seek to catch Milton in a mistake are generally caught soon or late themselves.

I

Nothing places Milton more clearly in the Renaissance tradition than his attachment to Ovid. Writing to Diodati in 1626 about his own exile from the university, he exclaims: "Would that no heavier blow had fallen on the lamentable bard who was exiled to the land of Tomis. In naught would he then have yielded to Ionian Homer, nor would the first praise be yours, O vanquished Maro." [3] When full allowance is made for boyish enthusiasm, and for the inflated style of Neo-Latin compliments, this is a large claim, larger, no doubt, than its author even then would have soberly supported. Milton knew Ovid through and through, and delighted to imitate him, but, for a young man preparing himself to be a Christian *vates,* other guides than "the smooth elegiac poets" were needed. Yet although in later

3. *El.* i.21–24 (W. MacKellar, *The Latin Poems of John Milton,* 1930, pp. 68–69).

years Milton's Heavenly Muse was not on speaking terms with the Roman lover of earth, many Ovidian offerings were still laid on the shrine. For Ovid was not with Milton a mere schoolboy passion—not that schoolboy passions are negligible. Dr. Johnson says: "The books in which his daughter, who used to read to him, represented him as most delighting, after Homer, which he could almost repeat, were Ovid's *Metamorphoses* and Euripides." [4]

Since Milton's enthusiasm for Ovid is so marked in his Latin verse, we may glance at it for a moment.[5] If we think of Milton's religious self-dedication to the office of poet-priest, of the *Nativity*, of his early pledge to live as ever in his great Task-master's eye, and then turn to gay and mundane pieces in Latin, we may experience a slight shock. Here we have the vagaries of Cupid in springtime, praise of wine as the fuel of poetry, a record of a fair face seen, loved, and never seen again, all in polished elegiacs, rich in mythological allusions and pagan sensuousness. The shock would be uncritical, of course, because Milton's Latin poems are thoroughly in the humanistic tradition of the Renaissance. Not merely Ovid and Virgil but George Buchanan and his kind are Milton's teachers, and in real charm as well as craftsmanship the young student excels most of his countrymen. When one wrote Latin one imitated the Latin poets, for even the religious humanist's fancy could move easily on pagan as well as Christian levels. So Milton, with no slackening of his high resolves, which indeed are proclaimed in a memorable passage of his Latin verse,[6] can quite naturally and whole-heartedly indulge in pagan manners as well as in pagan idiom. The obscurity of a learned language may even permit the revelation of more intimate personal feeling, whether grave or gay, than appears in English poems to be read by all and sundry. But paganism was never more innocent than here, for much of Ovid is left behind. In one poem, celebrating a happily concluded visit from Corinna, Ovid prays *proveniant medii sic mihi saepe dies*.[7] (It was this piece that contributed a good deal to Marlowe's picture

---

4. *Lives of the English Poets* (ed. G. B. Hill, Oxford, 1905), I, 154, 158, 199. Cf. Todd, *Life and Writings of Milton* (1809), p. 151; Masson, VI, 754.

5. No student of Milton needs to be reminded of two essays, E. K. Rand's vivacious "Milton in Rustication" (*SP*, XIX, 109 ff.), and Mr. Hanford's illuminating "Youth of Milton," *Studies in Shakespeare, Milton, and Donne* (1925). See also E. M. W. Tillyard, *Milton* (1930). Milton's Latin poems are cited from Mr. MacKellar's edition and translation.

6. *El.* vi.55 ff.

7. *Amores*, i.5.26.

of Hero naked before her lover.) Milton echoes the Ovidian phrase—in an elegy on the deceased bishop of Winchester.[8]

As we have noticed before, the mixing of pagan and Christian allusions, which we meet constantly in poetry of the Renaissance, began, like most Renaissance fashions, in the Middle Ages. And, as we also saw, the "naïve" medieval mixture persisted in the more decorative art of the Renaissance; though sometimes it became quite self-conscious, thanks to the paganizing habits of the Ciceronians and the virtual necessities of Neo-Latin verse-making. Milton of course observes the rules of the game. Satan is described in terms of Pluto:

> Cum ferus ignifluo regnans Acheronte tyrannus,
> Eumenidum pater, aethereo vagus exul Olympo.[9]

But the much-quoted conclusion of the *Epitaphium Damonis* is illustration enough. The soul of Milton's dearest friend is welcomed into heaven, "and the joyous revels rage under the thyrsus of Zion!"

Moreover, Milton's English poems, especially the later ones, are the great examples of the carrying over into English of the stylistic usages of Latin (and some Italian) verse, although the effects have commonly been exaggerated and the functional value has often been missed. But the alteration of normal word-order, some syntactical practices, some Latinate diction, allusive circumlocutions, a preference for unfamiliar proper names as more sonorous and suggestive than the familiar ones, these and other devices help to give Miltonic verse its special elevation.

However, these commonplaces have led us away from the particular question of Ovid and Milton. In his first enraptured study and imitation Milton had mastered the complete works, and, while a young Ovidian a generation earlier would have written a mythological tale in English, Milton, writing in Latin, responded to the amatory as well as the other poems.[10] He recoiled at all times from the vulgar amorists of his own day, but Ovid was long dead, and his form, lan-

8. *El.* iii.68. Rand (page 133) mentions another innocent application of a phrase from an Ovidian poem that modern translators commonly leave in Latin (*Am.* iii.7.68; Milton, *El.* v.8).

9. *In Quintum Novembris*, ll. 7–8. Cf. the reference to Tasso above, chapter XIII, note 24; Crashaw (ed. L. C. Martin), pp. 111–12; Giles Fletcher, *Christ's Victorie*, ii.22 (ed. Boas, I, 45). Fletcher's picture of hell in this stanza, by the way, obviously copies Spenser, *F.Q.*, I.v.32–33.

10. Milton's own account, in the *Apology for Smectymnuus*, of his early devotion to the Roman love-poets has been often quoted and will be below. See Hanford, "Youth of Milton," pp. 111 ff.

guage, workmanship, were elegance itself. Yet Ovid's love poems, however valuable in awakening senses and emotions, could never have satisfied more than a part of Milton's mind, and when this phase gave way to higher enthusiasms the *Metamorphoses* remained. The author of that book must have been, after a fashion, a prophet and priest of the wonder and bloom of the world, and, as such, a desirable supplement to Sylvester.[11]

Discussion of Milton's large debt to Ovid must be limited, here and elsewhere, to a few specimens, and specimens of Milton speak for themselves better than comment. On account of both his freedom of handling and his fusing of many sources one seldom, especially in the early poems, finds distinct echoes of Ovid. There is no happier example of that early manner than these lines from *L'Allegro:*

> That Orpheus' self may heave his head
> From golden slumber on a bed
> Of heaped Elysian flowers, and hear
> Such strains as would have won the ear
> Of Pluto to have quite set free
> His half-regained Eurydice.

This is not warmly voluptuous, softly flowing, elaborately pictorial, as when Spenser follows Ovid, but cool, plastic, economical, achieving a sensuous effect with hardly a sensuous word. It might be called Ovidian in its decorative objectivity, but the ideal beauty, the pure and not too glamorous magic (a good share of which lives in the melody), are beyond Ovid. Another instance of free and original re-creation of Ovidian motives, with a similar mixture of firm precision and suggestive generality, is the song of the Lady in *Comus:*

> Sweet Echo, sweetest nymph, that liv'st unseen
> Within thy airy shell
> By slow Meander's margent green,
> And in the violet-embroidered vale . . .

11. There is no need of discussing here the case elaborately argued in H. C. H. Candy's *Some Newly Discovered Stanzas Written by John Milton on Engraved Scenes Illustrating Ovid's Metamorphoses* (London, 1924). Candy dated the script *ca.* 1623. C. W. Brodribb showed that the author knew Golding and Sandys (probably the latter's edition of 1632 with the commentary as well as the first edition), and suggested that perhaps Sandys wrote the stanzas (*Notes and Queries*, CXLVII, 1924, 77–78). Candy's reply (*ibid.*, 122–24) was hardly convincing, as regards his main thesis at least. Metrical arguments are offered also (*ibid.*, CLIX, 1930, 165–67, 189–92).

It is a long way from such fanciful yet controlled delicacy to the style of the later heroic similes, or the lines on Orpheus in *Lycidas*.

II

That combination of qualities, imaginative, intellectual, ethical, stylistic, which we sum up in the rather intimidating word "Miltonic," is associated especially with *Paradise Lost*. But the essential elements, in somewhat different proportions, are manifest in the early poems, for Milton's total production, though covering forty-five years, is more of a unit than the work of Chaucer or Spenser or almost any great English poet. His course from the beginning, as both poet and publicist, was as straight as the career of any strong mind can be. The pseudo-Ovidian tone of a sheaf of Latin verse was artificial and transient, though the humanistic tradition left permanent marks upon his English style, and though Ovid's fables—not the love poems—remained attractive to the sense of beauty they had helped to nourish. *L'Allegro* and *Il Penseroso* are the expression of a mood too serene to endure or recur, and they are not typical in spirit of the early Milton, though even in them are revealed the lineaments of an uncommonly serious young man. But *Comus* is, as the event proved, central, and leads on naturally to *Paradise Lost, Paradise Regained*, and *Samson Agonistes*.[12]

Milton's conception of the disciplined life early became and remained his citadel, the fortress from which he sallied out to battle in the field of prose for the right to exercise self-government, the tower in which, under the guidance of Urania, he celebrated the struggles and victories of the resolved soul. While that tower stood apart from the world, new and untried as yet by severe assault, grass and flowers and trees flourished around it, pastoral music was in the air. When it was no longer on the outskirts of life but in the center, when years of warfare had battered its masonry and altered its contours, grass and flowers almost vanished, trees stood gaunt and leafless, there was no music but the trumpet's. This impromptu allegory embodies the history of Milton's poetic craftsmanship, and the changes are mirrored in his treatment of mythology. In this section we may run through a number of the poems with an eye to Milton's poetic evolution, the continuance in his early work of the Renaissance manner, and the emergence of a more classical style of his own. Of course the movement

12. Remarks on Milton's consistent development apply of course to central motives and principles, not to particular ideas, many of which were modified.

is not uniform, but the general tendency is clear enough, and familiar enough. Our special purpose, the attempt to view Milton's handling of mythology as the culmination of the Renaissance tradition, will perhaps—along with the relative bulk of the material—justify the disproportionate space given to the earlier poems.

Such an outline must consist of a selection of more or less obvious illustrations. There is hardly a late Elizabethan or Jacobean poet who has not been quoted in comments on the earlier, and often the later, work of Milton, with one notable exception already suggested. Both the profounder and the more external qualities of Donne were alien to Milton from the beginning, and even the conceits strewn about his early poems are in the fanciful rather than the metaphysical vein.[13]

To turn to the poems, the *Fair Infant* is, as Mr. Eliot might say, pustular with mythology, despite its sincerity and the occasional beauty of its Elizabethan sweetness or Elizabethan rhetoric. In the first mythological allusion [14] one line approaches the large accent of *Paradise Lost*—"By boisterous rape th' Athenian damsel got"—but more typical are these lines:

> For so Apollo, with unweeting hand,
> Whilom did slay his dearly-loved mate,
> Young Hyacinth, born on Eurotas' strand,
> Young Hyacinth, the pride of Spartan land;
> But then transformed him to a purple flower.

Their Elizabethan quality is sufficiently attested by a bit of Spenser:

> And all about grew euery sort of flowre,
> To which sad louers were transformd of yore;
> Fresh Hyacinthus, Phœbus paramoure,
> And dearest loue,
> Foolish Narcisse, that likes the watry shore,
> Sad Amaranthus, made a flowre but late,
> Sad Amaranthus, in whose purple gore . . .[15]

13. Sir H. J. C. Grierson, *Cross Currents in English Literature of the 17th Century* (1929), p. 241; G. R. Potter, *PQ*, VI, 396–400.

14. One might notice the veiled reference at the end of the first stanza to Winter's thinking to kiss and killing instead. See above, p. 138, for the conceit about the boar and Adonis, and also *The Purple Island*, c. 5, st. 61.

15. *F.Q.*, III.vi.45. Cf. *Astrophel* (ll. 7–8):
> Young Astrophel the pride of shepheards praise,
> Young Astrophel the rusticke lasses loue . . .

In the *Vacation Exercise* (1628) the poet aspires to a theme

> Such as may make thee search thy coffers round,
> Before thou clothe my fancy in fit sound:
> Such where the deep transported mind may soar
> Above the wheeling poles, and at Heav'n's door
> Look in, and see each blissful deity
> How he before the thunderous throne doth lie,
> Listening to what unshorn Apollo sings
> To th' touch of golden wires, while Hebe brings
> Immortal nectar to her kingly sire.

Milton is adapting the picture given at the end of the first book of the *Iliad*, and the lines have the Miltonic dignity, the Miltonic sense of space, which are lacking in the plaintive bit about Hyacinth. The effect can best be measured by means of another quotation from Spenser:

> There thou them placest in a Paradize
> Of all delight, and ioyous happie rest,
> Where they doe feede on Nectar heauenly wize,
> With Hercules and Hebe, and the rest
> Of Venus dearlings, through her bountie blest,
> And lie like Gods in yuorie beds arayd,
> With rose and lillies ouer them displayd.[16]

It is needless to emphasize the spacious and exalted gravity, economy, and coolness of Milton's lines.

On the Morning of Christ's Nativity (1629) marks in more than one way the young poet's coming of age. It contains in embryo the mixed elements, classical, medieval, modern, which were to receive full expression in *Paradise Lost*. Not only is Christ Pan—we are used to that—but he is also an infant Hercules who, paradoxically, controls "the damned crew" of pagan divinities. Of the twenty lines beginning "For, if such holy song . . . ," Mr. Osgood remarks, and the summary is true in spirit of other parts of Milton: "Various sources of details in this passage from the Psalms, the *Iliad*, the Fourth Eclogue of Virgil, and Horace, have been noted by the editors. But the thought as a whole is that in the Fifth Book of the *Divine Institutes* of Lactantius."[17] The stanza on the cessation of oracles—

---

16. *Hymne in Honour of Love*, ll. 280 ff. Cf. *Odyssey*, xi.601 ff.
17. *American Journal of Philology*, XLI, 76 ff.

which Keats turned to other uses—seems to be compounded out of
authors ranging from Plutarch and Prudentius to Giles Fletcher.[18]
From medieval allegory, perhaps by way of Fletcher, we have the four
daughters of God, who are destined to reappear in Milton; one of
them, Peace, comes down to earth in the manner of Iris or the Virgilian Mercury, or some figure in a masque.[19] Finally, Milton utilizes
the patristic and medieval doctrine that the pagan gods were demons,
a doctrine important in *Paradise Lost*. He is not untouched—as the
warmth of the fifth *Elegy* showed—by the attractions of pagan
polytheism, and delight in handling exotic names and attributes is
blended with militant exultation in the overthrow of idolatry by "The
dreaded Infant's hand." But, for all its concreteness of reference, the
poem is concerned with the meaning of the Incarnation, not with the
Gospel story of the Nativity. In its unified structure, purity of texture,
rapidity of movement, and volume of sound it is far beyond the
reach of the Fletchers, in spite of some conceits which they might have
owned.

In *L'Allegro* and *Il Penseroso* Milton comes under the sway of
more secular and more lyrical masters. For sources and analogues,
general or specific, commentators have cited most Elizabethan and
Jacobean poets, and, though such lines as the following are in the
best sense original, the names of Jonson and Shakespeare help to
explain their dew-washed purity, the airy delicacy and precision of
their mythological invention:

> Or whether (as some sager sing)
> The frolic wind that breathes the spring,
> Zephyr, with Aurora playing,
> As he met her once a-Maying,
> There on beds of violets blue,
> And fresh-blown roses washed in dew,

18. A. S. Cook, "Notes on Milton's Ode on the Morning of Christ's Nativity," *Transactions of the Connecticut Academy of Arts and Sciences*, XV
(1909), 349–51. E. K. had told the story "Great Pan is dead" in his gloss
on Spenser's eclogue for May. It is also in Sandys' *Relation* (ed. 1627, p. 11).
See Osgood, *Classical Mythology*, p. xlvii. One might compare Ralegh's account of the overthrow of paganism, *History*, i.6.8 (1829, II, 185). Tasso's
Canzone sopra la Cappella del Presepio has been cited as a general parallel to
Milton's poem.

19. Cook, pp. 322–24. See Ben Jonson's *Masques* (ed. H. Morley), p. 390;
Ben Jonson, VII, 97; R. L. Ramsay, "Morality Themes in Milton's Poetry,"
SP, XV, 133–36; Enid Welsford, *The Court Masque*, pp. 310–11.

> Filled here with thee, a daughter fair,
> So buxom, blithe, and debonair.[20]

Milton's next few lines, with the help of Burton and others, present an Elizabethan or Jacobean Hebe:

> Nods and Becks, and wreathed Smiles,
> Such as hang on Hebe's cheek,
> And love to live in dimple sleek.

The Olympian cupbearer is by way of becoming a pastoral nymph. A quality barely hinted in these lines, and quite agreeably, is more marked in a passage of *Il Penseroso:*

> Thus, Night, oft see me in thy pale career,
> Till civil-suited Morn appear,
> Not tricked and frounced, as she was wont
> With the Attic boy to hunt,
> But kerchieft in a comely cloud . . .

"Civil-suited"—apparently derived from Juliet's

> Come, civil night,
> Thou sober-suited matron, all in black—

and the other epithets make Aurora a sort of damsel at a *fête champêtre.*[21] When Milton writes

20. See the lyric in Jonson's *Penates* sung by Aurora, Zephyrus, and Flora (*Masques*, ed. Morley, p. 420; *Ben Jonson*, VII, 139), and the lyrical allusions to the same characters (Morley, pp. 221, 421). Cf. Campion's *Maske . . . in honour of the Lord Hayes* (*Works*, ed. P. Vivian, Oxford, 1909, p. 64).

Petruchio declares that when Katherine frowns he will say she looks as clear "As morning roses newly wash'd with dew." The opening chorus of *Pericles* tells of a female heir "so buxom, blithe, and full of face." Commentators have cited Randolph's "blithe, buxom, and debonair" (*Aristippus*, in *Works*, ed. Hazlitt, London, 1875, I, 21); see G. C. M. Smith in *TLS*, January 19, 1922, p. 44.

Foster Damon called attention to the resemblance between the first thirty lines of *L'Allegro* and the first part of the last satire in Marston's *Scourge of Villanie* (*PMLA*, XLII, 1927, 873–74; Marston, ed. Bullen, III, 371). The not improbable relation, which was observed by Warton, illustrates Milton's ability to extract gold from ore.

21. Mr. Rylands discusses the "urban" quality of a number of Milton's epithets in *Words and Poetry*, page 113.

> While Cynthia checks her dragon yoke
> Gently o'er th' accustomed oak,

he is not, like the more primitive Marlowe, soaring skyward with a
cosmic divinity; he is a bookish young poet who watches the moon
glide above a familiar tree near his home and recalls Elizabethan
rather than classical allusions to Cynthia.[22] Of course the tone of
all these references is quite in keeping with Milton's themes and
moods. And nowhere in these serene and lovely poems is there a hint
that the classical deities which adorn them are of the tribe of Satan;
"yet there was no fear of Jove." Troy is "divine." Country games
and dances, the well-trod stage, and the Anglican church service, all
are good, and none are unworthy of a young man who aspires to be
himself a true poem.

The mythology of *L'Allegro* and *Il Penseroso* shows that the waywardness and conceits of the Spenserians have given place to the purer,
more classical influence of Jonson. It was especially Jonson who
helped Milton to find his own lyric style, to achieve crisp diction and
definiteness of line and form without altogether losing Elizabethan
opulence. The mythological allusions are often Jonsonian also in their
civilized, courtly, masque-like quality. Milton's study of Jonson's
masques and lyrics is very apparent in the plot, details, and tone of
Arcades, for instance:

> This, this is she alone,
> Sitting like a goddess bright
> In the center of her light.

The first line echoes "This is she, this is she" of Jonson's *A Satyr,*[23]
and the second line (which originally read "Seated") recalls "Queen
and huntress, chaste and fair." Milton's "glassy, cool, translucent"
mythology is much more Jonsonian than Elizabethan.

22. Marlowe's lines are quoted above, near the end of chapter VI.

23. Morley, p. 411; *Ben Jonson,* VII, 124. Cf. Marston, ed. Bullen, III,
391. With the third stanza of Jonson's *Satyr* compare the last lines of Milton's
third song. As for the "plot," the discourse of the Genius of the Wood is somewhat in Jonson's vein and might have been prompted by the business of the
Genius and the Fates in Jonson's entertainment given at Theobalds (Morley,
pp. 428 ff.; *Ben Jonson,* VII, 154 ff.).

L'Allegro and *Il Penseroso* have in the past been assigned to the beginning
of the "Horton period," 1632 ff.; modern opinion has inclined to Milton's last
long vacation in 1631. The date of *Arcades* is presumably 1630–32; some
scholars favor 1632.

III

When one begins "Before the starry threshold of Jove's court. . . . ," one shrinks from soiling the pure ambrosial weeds of *Comus* with the rank vapors of annotation, but something must be done. Though the two aspects of the masque can hardly be separated, we may postpone the moral and religious theme and consider first the aesthetic quality of the texture.

We have seen the young poet, with the classics in his head, and Jonson as a further corrective to Elizabethan fluency, richness, and eccentricity, emerging on a *via media* of his own. It is that starry path (*via lactea*, one might say, though not in Phineas Fletcher's sense) which Milton follows with such triumphant originality in *Comus*. Yet there are occasional deviations, for the style now and then recalls the past or anticipates the future. Passages of modified Elizabethan sensuousness may be followed by lines of expository bareness approaching the manner of *Paradise Regained;* we have some Elizabethan or Jacobean conceits,[24] a few traces of turgid Jacobean rhetoric,[25] and some lines of smooth eighteenth-century classicism.[26] The

24. Cf. ll. 139 ff., and *Venus and Anchises* (ed. Seaton, p. 4):
    The thick-lac'd boughs shutt out the Telltale Sunne.
    For Venus hated his all-blabbing light.
A conceit involving Scylla and Charybdis (ll. 257–59) was apparently suggested by Silius Italicus, xiv.471–74 (quoted in Osgood, page 76). Milton might perhaps have reached the fourteenth book of such a poet, but he might have remembered the lines from Sandys' *Relation* (ed. 1627, p. 237). Both in the *Relation* (p. 248) and the *Metamorphosis* (ed. 1632, p. 476), Sandys, in translating an epigram, has "fell Charybdis." Todd cites the same phrase in Sylvester.
    While speaking of Sandys I may add another item, in connection with *Comus*, ll. 675 ff., where Milton describes the "nepenthes" given to Helen as "to life so friendly." He is recalling the *Odyssey*, iv.219–30, where the words are φάρμακα μητιόεντα, ἐσθλά. We expect Milton's phrases to be freely original, but, in view of his knowledge of the *Relation*, it may be more than coincidence that Sandys, who quoted part of the Homeric passage, in Latin as usual, rendered *pharmaca utilia bona* by "a friend to life" (page 126).
    25. E.g., ll. 597–99, 603 ff. These last lines are not quite Virgilian (cf. *Aen.* vi.287 ff.). The "sooty flag" of Acheron comes from Phineas Fletcher's *Apollyonists* (ed. Boas, I, 151, st. 39), and with the two following lines compare Fairfax's *Jerusalem Delivered* (bk. xv, st. 51, ed. H. Morley, 1901, p. 312).
    26. Ll. 984–87. Gray of course registers the fact by his borrowing of "the rosy-bosom'd Hours," for his spring is also "spruce and jocund." Yet Milton's

mythology woven into the texture naturally partakes of both the dominant and the occasional qualities.

Very seldom, even in Milton's earliest poems, is there writing that approaches the sensuous warmth, the soft fluidity, of Spenser. Remembering the stanza in which Spenser united a radiant Phoebus with the sun of the psalmist—and remembering also the conceits about the sun in the *Nativity*—we can measure the cool restraint of Milton when he handles the same combination:

> And the slope sun his upward beam
> Shoots against the dusky pole,
> Pacing toward the other goal
> Of his chamber in the east.[27]

That is Milton's more characteristic tone, and even these lines in *L'Allegro* seem luxuriant:

> Right against the eastern gate,
> Where the great sun begins his state,
> Robed in flames and amber light,
> The clouds in thousand liveries dight.[28]

Although a learned scholar, Milton borrows mythological allusions from his immediate predecessors, and, further, he often gives them a didactic application. When he writes that she who is chaste "may pass on with unblenched majesty," that Diana "set at naught The frivolous bolt of Cupid," he has been thinking of Plato, and of Belphoebe and Britomart, but he has not forgotten "the imperial votaress" who

> passed on,
> In maiden meditation, fancy-free.

When, at the conclusion of the same speech, the Second Brother exclaims that divine philosophy is "musical as is Apollo's lute," he is

---

lines follow the magical phrase that sang in Tennyson's head to such romantic effect.

27. Ll. 98 ff. Cf. *F.Q.*, I.v.2 (quoted above, page 106).

28. Cf. *Midsummer Night's Dream*, III.ii.391: "Even till the eastern gate, all fiery-red . . . ," and Milton's Elizabethan and Jonsonian *Song on May Morning*. See Osgood, page xxxii.

quoting the un-Platonic Berowne's praise, not of chastity, but of love.[29] And when the Lady declares

> Were it a draught for Juno when she banquets,
> I would not taste thy treasonous offer,

is she not echoing, with some unconscious irony, Jonson's most famous lyric? We do not have the devil citing Scripture, but we do have Comus quoting Sylvester, and combining him with Homer—"Love-darting eyes, or tresses like the morn." Shakespeare's Ariel was content to be Ariel; the Spirit of Milton, after celebrating the mystic marriage of Cupid and Psyche, echoes Ariel, and ends with praise of Virtue.

The actual space that Milton gives to the story of Circe is small, and some details seem to follow Ovid more than Homer.[30] Homer and Ovid, however conscious of didactic implications, were disinterested story-tellers, Milton is not, and though the myth itself contains the essence of romance much of that is inevitably strained out in the Miltonic version. *Comus* is more romantic than Milton's other work, but its beauty is a clear, finite beauty, without much strangeness added to it, except—and it is a large exception—in the author's ever-present vision of celestial purity. While the poem is not romantic in spirit, it is full of romantic details. It could hardly be otherwise when to such a myth were added, from Spenser, Shakespeare, Fletcher, and the rest, all manner of pastoral decoration, magic spells, fairy lore, British legend. As Warburton said, "Though Milton builds his fable on classick mythology, yet his materials of magick have more the air of enchantments in the Gothick romances." [31] But Milton could not, like Spenser, wander delightedly through a world of enchantment; his classical instincts, the weighty discourses on virtue, and the formal

---

29. *Love's Labour's Lost*, IV.iii.342.

30. See Warton's notes on ll. 252, 637, 651, 815, 880, 981 (and Osgood, page 24). Warton remarked upon the fact that in his sixth Elegy Milton chose to illustrate Homer's poetical character by the *Odyssey* and not by the *Iliad*, and Keightley added "which was quite natural in one who was so fond of Ovid" (MacKellar, p. 232).

Considerations of allegory and dramatic presentation would account for some changes in the classical story, such as the figure of Comus himself, his parentage, the incomplete metamorphosis of the victims of enchantment, and their unconsciousness of degradation. The last two items are found in the *Orlando Furioso*, vi.60–66 (E. G. Ainsworth, *MLN*, XLVI, 91–92). We need not repeat the facts and opinions about the influence of Jonson and others.

31. Quoted in Todd (1809), VI, 245.

requirements of the masque, all were a check upon extravagance. Yet the thread of mythology is more or less colored, like classical tales in *The Faerie Queene,* by the partly "Gothick" texture into which it is woven. Thus we hear of Circe surrounded by "the Sirens three" and "flowery-kirtled Naiades." [32] We have water-nymphs with pearled wrists, Sabrina under the waves and in her chariot, and we owe something to Jonson, Drayton, and others for such pleasant apparitions. There is the song to Sabrina which, if not—like "Full fathom five"—of the water watery, at any rate contrives by means of more or less classical allusions to divinities of the sea to create an atmosphere and a picture. One says "more or less classical" because of

> fair Ligea's golden comb,
> Wherewith she sits on diamond rocks
> Sleeking her soft alluring locks.[33]

We have noticed before some hints of "urban" mythology in Milton, and even romantic bits of *Comus* may be touched with that quality. "The pert fairies and the dapper elves," whatever is allowed for a change of meaning in the words, are not quite a wood-note wild. There is a clue to this somewhat spruce vein of writing in these lines:

> . . . and such court guise
> As Mercury did first devise
> With the mincing Dryades
> On the lawns and on the leas.

Milton is thinking of masques, and "mincing" is more suited to dryads of the court than to those of the woods.[34]

32. Homer and Ovid do not give Circe sirens as attendants, but Browne does, and sirens were welcome in *Comus* as traditional symbols of fleshly delights. Mr. Osgood has dwelt upon the distilled charm of "flowery-kirtled Naiades," a Botticellian picture at once definite and vaguely suggestive (pp. lxvi, 58).

33. Ovid's Salmacis and Galatea comb their hair, and cf. *Georg.* iv.336–37:
> Drymoque Xanthoque Ligeaque Phyllodoceque,
> caesariem effusae nitidam per candida colla.

The gold comb and diamond rocks, as Warton observed, are new allurements for the unwary.

In the episode of Sabrina, J. Arthos (*Anglia,* 79, 1962, pp. 204–13) finds echoes of Virgil's tale of Aristaeus and Cyrene (*Georg.* iv.315 ff.).

34. Mr. Osgood (pp. 42, 65) finds only rather vague classical authority for Mercury's dancing with the dryads, and it is not our common conception of

Finally, there are sixteen lines which not every reader of Milton knows. There is no better proof of Milton's sense of form than that, after writing such a passage, he could strike it out, perhaps because the sensuous luxuries of traditional earthly paradises blurred the contrast between the purity of heaven and the sinful earth. I can quote only part of it, beginning with four lines which preceded it and which still remain:

> Before the starry threshold of Jove's court
> My mansion is, where those immortal shapes
> Of bright aerial spirits live insphered
> In regions mild of calm and serene air
>
> Amidst the Hesperian gardens, on whose banks
> Bedewed with nectar and celestial songs
> Eternal roses grow and hyacinth
> And fruits of golden rind, on whose fair tree
> The scaly-harnessed dragon ever keeps
> His unenchanted eye . . .[35]

Here, says J. W. Mackail, classical and romantic elements are for a moment in perfect fusion, and he quotes two other passages in *Comus* which deal with the Hesperides. One is the magical phrase already referred to,

> Of Hesperus, and his daughters three
> That sing about the golden tree.

The other is this:

> But Beauty, like the fair Hesperian tree
> Laden with blooming gold, had need the guard
> Of dragon watch with unenchanted eye
> To save her blossoms, and defend her fruit,
> From the rash hand of bold Incontinence.

---

him. Cf. Jonson's *Pan's Anniversary* (Morley, p. 336; *Ben Jonson*, VII, 535):
> Of Pan we sing, the best of leaders, Pan,
>   That leads the Naiads and the Dryads forth;
>   And to their dances more than Hermes can.
One is reminded of masques by such lines as *Paradise Lost*, iv.266 ff.

35. The whole passage is quoted by Mackail (*Spring of Helicon*, p. 155), with admirable comments. It is on page 10 in the *Facsimile of the Manuscript of Milton's Minor Poems*, ed. W. A. Wright (Cambridge University Press, 1899), and in the facsimile edition of the *Complete Poetical Works*, ed. H. F. Fletcher, I (University of Illinois Press, 1943), 398.

The central line "gives the concentrated essence of the suppressed passage," fuses classical and romantic; "the rest is hardening into classicism."

Before we leave the opening lines of *Comus*, in their printed form, we may observe that they are an excellent specimen of Milton's combining of pagan and Christian materials in harmonious unity. The speech is a sort of Euripidean prologue, spoken by a Platonic daemon who is also a guardian angel, about angels and the souls of the good, who live in Hesperian gardens that stand for the Christian heaven. The description of the gardens seems to unite traditional accounts of happy isles with the Olympus of the *Odyssey*. "Above the smoke and stir" is a clear echo of Horace's *fumum et opes strepitumque Romae*. And with "sainted seats" we come to the white-robed elders seated round the throne in Revelation (iv.4). But all things have the purity of tone that goes with Milton's vision of the contrast between heaven and earth.

Comus is the chief example of Milton's use of allegorized mythology and we may look briefly at its background.[36] The traditional interpretation of the myth of Circe commended itself to Milton as inevitably as it had to Ariosto, Tasso, Spenser, and others for the presentation of virtue's conflict with sensuality. No myth left a deeper or more permanent impress upon him. At the end of his first Elegy, in which he had glorified the beauty of English girls, he had taken the magical herb moly as a symbol of the classical and Christian teaching that governed his conduct; and when in his last work Samson achieves victory over the temptation that had ruined him, Dalila is another embodiment of Circe:

> Thy fair enchanted cup and warbling charms
> No more on me have power.

Milton's choice of such a subject for a masque was natural, although of course he freshened the fable by making Comus the son of Circe.

36. There is the concrete fact that Milton owned a copy of *Heraclidis Pontici Allegoriae in Homeri Fabulas*, but he would, like other poets, encounter traditional interpretations in Renaissance handbooks and elsewhere. Allegorized myths appear in his academic prolusions, but they are rather like pulpit anecdotes and need not imply serious conviction.

See the chapter on *Comus* in W. G. Madsen's "The Idea of Nature in Milton's Poetry," in *Three Studies in the Renaissance: Sidney, Jonson, Milton*, by Richard B. Young, W. T. Furniss, and Madsen (Yale University Press, 1958).

That personification of revelry had already appeared in the Neo-Latin fantasy *Comus* (1608) by the Dutch Erycius Puteanus [37] and, as a crude belly-god, in Jonson's *Pleasure Reconciled to Virtue* (acted in 1618). As a writer of masques Jonson had led the way in combining classical myth and personified abstractions to produce a more or less edifying spectacle, but Milton went far beyond him in didactic seriousness; *Comus* could in no wise be entitled *Pleasure Reconciled to Virtue*.

One main element in Milton's thought and feeling, now and in later years, was Plato, whom he knew or came to know well at first hand, [38] unlike his poetic predecessors and still more unlike contemporary authors of the "Platonics" relished at the Caroline court. How much he knew of the Platonic tradition remains conjectural. At any rate the best introduction to *Comus* is that personal passage in the *Apology for Smectymnuus* (1642) in which—replying to opponents' charges of immorality—Milton looked back on the reading that especially nourished his ideal of chastity and love. The climactic teachers were Plato and the Bible:

> Thus, from the laureate fraternity of poets, riper years and the ceaseless round of study and reading led me to the shady spaces of philosophy, but chiefly to the divine volumes of Plato and his equal [i.e., contemporary], Xenophon: where, if I should tell ye what I learnt of chastity and love, I mean that which is truly so, whose charming cup is only virtue, which she bears in her hand to those who are worthy (the rest are cheated with a thick intoxicating potion which a certain sorceress, the abuser of love's name, carries about), and how the first and chiefest office of love begins and ends in the soul, producing those happy twins of her divine generation, knowledge and virtue. . . .
>
> Last of all, not in time, but as perfection is last, that care was ever had of me, with my earliest capacity, not to be negligently trained in the precepts of Christian religion: this that I have hitherto related hath been to show that, though Christianity had been but slightly taught me, yet a certain reservedness of natural disposition, and moral discipline learnt out of the noblest philosophy, was enough to keep me in disdain of far less incontinences than this of the bordello. But having had the doctrine of Holy Scripture, unfolding those chaste and high mysteries, with timeliest care infused, that "the body is for the Lord, and the Lord for the body," thus also I argued to myself: that if unchastity in a woman, whom St. Paul terms

37. See R. H. Singleton, "Milton's *Comus* and the *Comus* of Erycius Puteanus," *PMLA*, LVIII (1943), 949–57.

38. Irene Samuel, *Plato and Milton* (Cornell University Press, 1947).

the glory of man, be such a scandal and dishonor, then certainly in a man, who is both the image and glory of God, it must, though commonly not so thought, be much more deflowering and dishonorable . . . Nor did I slumber over that place [Rev. xiv.1–5] expressing such high rewards of ever accompanying the Lamb with those celestial songs to others inapprehensible, but not to those who were not defiled with women, which doubtless means fornication; for marriage must not be called a defilement.[39]

It is the more general and positive parts of what is said here that are embodied in *Comus*. The masque is not concerned with mere abstinence; chastity is an all-embracing vision of perfection, the Platonic and Christian love of the good. The Lady is not tempted, to be sure, and there is no inward and little outward drama; but a masque was by definition undramatic, and *Comus* might be called an extended—and fervently idealistic—"emblem."

Another general influence was Spenser, whom Milton, after dallying with the Spenserians, had come to know as a poet who treated ethical and religious ideas with imaginative artistry. Spenser's partly Platonic handling of temperance and temptation made a strong impression upon a nature strongly predisposed to feel it, as the familiar eulogy in *Areopagitica* sufficiently indicates. Spenser had wholly rejected the kind of license that was urged by Marlowe's Leander and by Donne in some early poems, and there were later exponents of the conventional libertinism that is put into the mouth of Comus.[40] In the second half of her reply to Comus (lines 780–99, one of the passages not in the acting version), the Lady rises above Spenser to a religious intensity which is thoroughly Miltonic.

Finally—for we cannot touch innumerable "sources"—we may note parts of George Sandys' traditional and markedly Platonic interpretation of the myth of Circe, in the *Ovid* (1632) that Milton may have known:

39. *Works*, III, i, 305–06 (modernized).
40. At times Comus' speeches may echo Marlowe; see L. C. Martin's edition of Marlowe's poems, and below, note 68. Part of Comus' central speech (ll. 710–42) has been related particularly to the passage in Thomas Randolph's *Muses' Looking-Glass* that begins "Nature has been bountiful" (*Works*, ed. W. C. Hazlitt, ii.3, I, 208–09). The play was not printed until 1638, but was probably acted at Cambridge while Milton was there. For references to these ideas in Elizabethan poetry, see above, chapter VI, note 26. Although they soon became commonplaces, Randolph seems now and then to echo Marlowe; see his *Epithalamium to Mr. F. H., A Pastorall Courtship*, and *Upon Love fondly refus'd for Conscience sake.*

That the upper part of her [Scylla's] body, is feigned to retaine a humane figure, and the lower to be bestiall; intimates how man, a divine creature, endued with wisdome and intelligence, in whose superiour parts, as in a high tower, that immortall spirit resideth, who only of all that hath life erects his lookes unto heaven, can never so degenerate into a beast, as when he giueth himselfe over to the lowe delights of those baser parts of the body, Dogs and Wolues, the blind & saluage fury of concupiscence . . .

Yet Ulysses could not loose his shape with the rest, who being fortifyed by an immortall power, was not subiect to mutation. For the diuine & cœlestiall soule, subsisting through the bounty of the Creator, can by no assault of nature be violated, nor can that bee conuerted into a beast, which so highly participates of reason . . . [Circe's sensual charms] are not to bee resisted, but by the diuine assistance, Moly, the guift of Mercury, which signifies temperance . . .

Sandys proceeds to explain

their head strong appetites, which reuolt from the soueraignty of reason (by which wee are onely like unto God, and armed against our depraued affections) nor euer returne into their Country (from whence the soule deriueth her cœlestiall originall) unlesse disinchanted, and cleansed from their former impurity. For as Circes rod, waued ouer their heads from the right side to the left: presents those false and sinister perswasions of pleasure, which so much deformes them: so the reuersion thereof, by discipline, and a view of their owne deformity, restores them to their former beauties.[41]

In addition to making explicit—and religious—the moral import of the whole fable, Milton has the Attendant Spirit affirm the general doctrine of divine truth concealed in poetic story; this, however traditional and orthodox, is a dramatic speech in the only work of Milton's grounded on classical myth, so that something may be allowed for a special apologia. And the terms of the reference, from "sage" and "the heavenly Muse" to the "rifted rocks," suggest that

41. *Ovid's Metamorphosis* (1632), pp. 475, 480–81. In Sandys' *Relation* (ed. 1627, p. 308) moly is also said to signify temperance.

The reversing of Comus' rod and spells has been emphasized as the clearest parallel, in plot, between *Comus* and the rescue of Amoret (*Comus*, 816 ff.; *F.Q.*, III.xii.36; Hanford, "Youth of Milton," p. 141; *A Milton Handbook*, ed. 1946, pp. 162–63). Without discounting Spenserian influence we may observe the last sentence quoted from Sandys, which is his comment on *Metam.* xiv.300–01, thus rendered in his translation (p. 462):

Sprinkled with better juyce, her wand reuerst
Aboue our crownes, and charmes with charmes disperst.

For Milton's use of Ovid rather than Homer, see note 30 above.

Milton had Spenser especially in mind.[42] But in other places ancient myth is allegorized in a more or less traditional way. The Elder Brother, the exponent of rational temperance, in a speech akin to Milton's academic prolusions, invokes "the old schools of Greece" on the theme of invincible chastity, and sees that virtue symbolized in the bow of Diana and the Gorgon-shield of Minerva.[43] More complex and important is the latter half of the epilogue. With the parenthetical warning, "List, mortals, if your ears be true," it sums up the meaning of the masque in allusive symbols. The love of Venus ("th' Assyrian queen") and Adonis seems to carry the idea Spenser had given it in the "Gardens of Adonis," the perpetual generation of physical life. Then, on a higher level, the union of Cupid and Psyche will give birth to "Youth and Joy." We might have expected the Platonic twins of the *Apology for Smectymnuus*, "knowledge and virtue"; but these the whole masque has celebrated, and the "Youth and Joy" that Comus has falsely claimed for himself are identified with love of the good.[44]

IV

Lycidas, written in November, 1637, came more than three years after *Comus* and, what is much more significant, after Milton had spent more than five years in arduous, private, and outwardly unrewarding study in preparation for his unknown future. The serenely

42. *Comus*, 513 ff. See Osgood, pp. xlix, 23. We recall "the sage and solemn tunes" of chivalric romance, in whose enchantments "more is meant than meets the ear" (*Il Penseroso*, 116–20); the presumable inclusion of Spenser among "those lofty fables and romances which recount in solemn cantos the deeds of knighthood," one of the kinds of writing that nourished Milton's youthful love of chastity (*Apology for Smectymnuus*, *Works*, III, i, 304); "the sage And serious doctrine of Virginity" (*Comus*, 786–87); and the "sage and serious poet Spenser" of *Areopagitica* (*Works*, IV, 311).

"Enchanted isles" include Spenser's as well as Homer's and Tasso's, and the rifted rocks, while perhaps partly Virgilian (Osgood, p. 23), suggest the cave of Mammon (*F.Q.*, II.vii.28), to which, along with the Bower of Bliss, Milton alluded in *Areopagitica*.

43. Ll. 438 ff. The linking of the two goddesses here, as proof against Cupid, might occur to anyone who knew mythology, but Milton might remember Lucian's *Venus and Cupid* (trans. Fowler, I, 77; see Todd, VI, 316). Jonson, in *The Haddington Masque* (Morley, pp. 91–93; *Ben Jonson*, VII, 252–55), quotes Lucian; cf. *Cynthia's Revels*, I.i. Sandys also quotes Lucian concerning Cupid and Diana (*Ovid*, p. 70).

44. See A. S. P. Woodhouse, "The Argument of Milton's *Comus*," *University of Toronto Quarterly*, XI (1941–42).

joyous idealism of the masque has given place to deep disturbance. As all modern readers recognize, this poem, which begins and ends with allusions to Milton's own career, is not so much a lament for the drowned Edward King as it is an impassioned meditation on the extinction of any promising young life; though it is almost wholly impersonal, its intensity comes from the clash between its author's high hopes and the doubts and fears this event has stirred in his mind. *Lycidas* is in a sense one of those lofty inventories that Milton took at successive stages in his life, but it gains universal dimensions and resonance in facing the apparent wrongness of things in a divinely ordered world. *Lycidas* has of course been long admired, but, in the past, in a rather external way; it is only in criticism of this past generation that the poem has really come into its own as a masterpiece of controlled passion, depth, and complexity.[45] In that complexity, that *concordia discors*, the opposition and fusion of pagan and Christian make a conspicuous strain.

The pastoral convention and the form of the canzone together gave Milton the mixture of discipline and freedom to which his genius responded. Within that frame the mixing of pagan and Christian elements operates in more than one way. The conventional appeal to the Muses leads into the only overt identification of the living poet's possible fate with that of the dead man. The dancing satyrs and fauns belong to the natural world of youth, unclouded by any thought of death. The conventional appeal to the nymphs comes to a climax with the hideous end of Orpheus, the archetype of the poet, whom even his mother the Muse could not save. The next paragraph, the argument on fame, is an oblique exposure of Milton's own questioning; and, if we remember that for a devoutly Christian poet King's death was not a distressing accident but the result of God's will, we feel the shock of

> Comes the blind Fury with th' abhorred shears,
> And slits the thin-spun life.

Atropos, the third Fate, is not enough; God's providence seems to act with more malign irresponsibility. But there follows at once a pagan allusion which reflects Christian truth: Phoebus' definition of true fame is an abstract statement of what is to be the ultimate reassurance.[46] Then come the first individual mourners, the herald of the

45. Much modern criticism is assembled in Milton's *Lycidas: the Tradition and the Poem*, ed. C. A. Patrides (New York, 1961).

46. For the same idea, in purely Christian terms, cf. *Paradise Regained*, iii.60–64.

sea and Hippotades, and through their testimonies the poet gropes in the natural world for some natural, immediate cause of the shipwreck. In the end, when the vision of Lycidas welcomed into heaven banishes all doubts and fears, the spirit of the dead man becomes a protective "Genius of the shore." In the earlier line 164, "And, O ye dolphins, waft the hapless youth," Milton was probably thinking of Palaemon, whose drowned body dolphins carried to shore, and whom the Romans identified with Portunus or Portumnus, the god of harbors.[47] Thus a Christian spirit from heaven becomes, as a pagan divinity, a symbol of divine love and care for man, "the dear might of him that walked the waves." But such a blending is only the initial item in the poet's return to pastoral order and serenity, in the total reconciliation which comprehends nature, God's providential wisdom, and man's acceptance of the conditions of life.

V

Paradise Lost, with its divine, angelic, and two superhuman beings (Adam and Eve sink to the human level only when they sin), presented much greater difficulties than Homer or Virgil had had to face. In following, as he was bound to do, the concrete pattern of the classical epic, Milton could use—and re-create—the established narrative conventions, but he still had the problem of putting flesh on the Biblical skeleton. There were of course many traditional accretions, theological and imaginative, not to mention the whole Bible, and there was also the whole body of classical literature and mythology, which Milton could handle with the ease of lifelong familiarity. His sacred theme did not forbid embellishments from pagan sources. These served quite diverse functions; they might illustrate the idyllic beauty of the unfallen world or the evil of hell and the fallen world. Sometimes Milton appropriates and adapts such material silently, expecting it to be recognized by some readers at least; sometimes a reference is open and express, whether a mere name or phrase or a full-blown epic simile.

Thus—to put in a conscious way what was instinctive with Milton —how would the revolt of the angels be conceived? There were the wars of gods and giants and Titans. What would be the character of Satan? To the established image of the Evil One and of Mephistopheles might be added the heroic qualities of ancient epic heroes

47. T. O. Mabbott, *The Explicator,* V (1947), 26.

and such a rebel as Prometheus. How would the fallen angels, reassembled, parade before their leader? As Plutarch, in his life of Lycurgus, described the marching of Spartan soldiers. How would Satan and Gabriel confront each other? Like Turnus and Aeneas in their last combat.[48] What would Eve do when she was first created? She might give a quite innocent hint of future self-centeredness by falling in love with her face in a pool, like Narcissus. What would Adam do at the first sight of Eve? He might give a quite innocent hint of potential excess of devotion by pursuing her as Apollo pursued Daphne. How would they behave after they had eaten of the tree of knowledge? Like the wanton Paris and Helen and like Zeus and Hera when the goddess had put on the girdle of Aphrodite.[49] How were the animals created? They broke out of the ground, like the warriors in the tales of Cadmus and Medea.[50] What was the nature of the flood? Ovid was more detailed than Genesis. But such silent adaptations did not bring in the world of paganism and raised no question of religious or literary decorum. Open references to myth were another matter.

When at last Milton came to write *Paradise Lost*, age and experience had deepened still further his early conviction that his end was not

to be obtained by the invocation of Dame Memory and her siren daughters; but by devout prayer to that eternal Spirit who can enrich with all utterance and knowledge, and sends out his Seraphim, with the hallowed fire of his altar, to touch and purify the lips of whom he pleases.[51]

It is wholly natural, then, that at intervals he should declare that his purpose and his theme—as artist he is humble enough—elevate his work above its ancient models. He intends to soar above the Aonian mount, to sing with other notes than to the Orphean lyre. Compared

48. A. S. Ferguson (*MLR*, XV, 168–70) showed that the last forty lines of *P.L.* iv are a highly original manipulation of the last three hundred lines of the *Aeneid*. The significance of the parallel—and of many others—is interpreted by D. P. Harding, *The Club of Hercules* (1962).

49. *P.L.*, ix.1029 ff.; *Iliad* iii.442 ff., xiv.315 ff.

50. *P.L.*, vii.463–74. J. D. Bruce (*Englische Studien*, XLI, 166 ff.) pointed out a parallel in Apollonius Rhodius (iii.1354 ff.), whom Milton knew well, and a closer one in the less familiar *Dionysiaca* of Nonnus (iv.427–40). Ovid (*Metam.* iii.104 ff., vii.121 ff.) is not so close to Milton.

51. *Works*, III, i, 241. Cf. Isaiah, vi.6–7.

with Orpheus' mother, the Muse Calliope, the Christianized Urania
is "heav'nly, she an empty dream." [52] Milton's argument is

> Not less but more heroic than the wrath
> Of stern Achilles on his foe pursued
> Thrice fugitive about Troy wall; or rage
> Of Turnus for Lavinia disespoused;
> Or Neptune's ire or Juno's, that so long
> Perplexed the Greek and Cytherea's son.

When a great poet embarks, with the prayerful consciousness of divine guidance, upon the most sacred theme, for which his whole life
has been a preparation, it is hardly matter for surprise or regret that
he rarely hints at hidden truth in classical myth but often labels it
pagan untruth. Yet that does not prevent his making abundant,
splendid, and functional use of it; he is still a poet of the Renaissance.
When Milton was beginning or about to begin *Paradise Lost,* the
not very profoundly religious Abraham Cowley, as we observed at
the end of the last chapter, harshly condemned mythologizing and
urged Biblical themes (of which his own *Davideis* was an uninspiring
example); and in one of his best poems, *On the Death of Mr.
Crashaw,* he could write thus:

> Still the old heathen gods in numbers dwell,
> The heav'nliest thing on earth still keeps up hell;
> Nor have we yet quite purged the Christian land;
> Still idols here, like calves at Bethel, stand,
> And though Pan's death long since all oracles broke,
> Yet still in rhyme the fiend Apollo spoke.[53]

52. For a parallel of a sort there is Sylvester's account of the tree of life in
Eden. After naming various famous juices and herbs, such as nectar, am-
brosia, nepenthe, moly, he proceeds (ed. Grosart, I, 101, lines 256 ff.):
> No, none of these: these are but forgeries,
> But toyes, but tales, but dreams, deceits, and lies.
> But Thou art true, although our shallow sense
> May honour more, then sound thine Excellence.

53. In 1679 appeared an imitation of *Paradise Lost* called *Order and Dis-
order;* the author's first object "was to remove from the Mosaic legend all
accretions from heathen fable and philosophy" (C. A. Moore, *MP,* XXIV,
1926–27, pp. 321–22). Blackmore's denunciation of pagan mythology is
notorious; see A. F. B. Clark, *Boileau,* pp. 308 ff. Some readers found *Paradise
Lost* dangerously pagan; witness Addison's censure, *Spectator* 297.

We might notice some expressions of Christian scruple that belong to Milton's epic subject and his later years.[54] The word "scruple" is hardly adequate for the identification of the fallen angels with the heathen gods of the fallen world. The venerable tradition was very convenient for Milton's epic scheme and acceptance of it had no puritan implications; it was endorsed by Hooker and Sandys as well as by Stephen Gosson and William Prynne.[55]

While Milton often alludes to myths without any skeptical comment, he does also often remind us that such tales are fiction. Satan sees Eve among her flowers in a

> Spot more delicious than those gardens feigned
> Or of revived Adonis, or renowned
> Alcinous, host of old Laertes' son,
> Or that, not mystic, where the sapient king
> Held dalliance with his fair Egyptian spouse.[56]

Here "mystic" seems to mean "mythical" and contrasts pagan fancy with scriptural truth. The most arresting example is the account of Mulciber:

> and how he fell
> From heav'n, they fabled, thrown by angry Jove

54. E.g., *P.L.*, i.197, ii.627–28, iv.250–51, 706, x.578–84, xi.10–14. Some of these items are quoted below.
A first and isolated scruple had appeared in the youthful *On the Death of a Fair Infant* when he mentioned Elysian fields, "if such there were." But the thought of the Christian heaven causes only a momentary qualm, for in the next stanza heaven is enveloped in mythology. In the earlier Latin poems on the death of bishops and academic officers such allusions are thick.

55. Hooker, *Eccles. Pol.*, i.4.3; Sandys, *Ovid*, p. 392 and elsewhere. Cf. Burton, *Anatomy* (Bohn's Popular Library), I, 214 ff.
The roll-call of pagan gods in *P.L.*, i.376 ff. may remind us of the passage in *Areopagitica* (*Works*, IV, 338) in which the dismembered body of "the good Osiris" is likened to the scattered fragments of the virgin Truth. Miss Seaton (*MLR*, XVII, 168–70) suggested that Milton might have seen and remembered the pictorial representation of the myth of Osiris in the Vatican. He might also have remembered that Clement of Alexandria compared Truth to the body of Pentheus, torn asunder by fanatics (Sandys, *History of Classical Scholarship*, I, 324). The story of Osiris is told, for example, in Plutarch's treatise and in Diodorus Siculus, i.21; see Ralegh, *History*, ii.2.5.; Selden, *De Diis Syris*, Syntagma i.4.

56. *P.L.*, ix.439–43. See Osgood, p. xlix; Greenlaw, *SP*, XIV, 209. Sandys (*Ovid*, p. 452) speaks of the "Iland famous for the Hortyards of Alcinoë, and wonderfull pregnancy of the soyle (a fable deriued from the terrestriall Paradice)." Cf. Ralegh, i.3.3; i.4.1.

Sheer o'er the crystal battlements: from morn
To noon he fell, from noon to dewy eve,
A summer's day; and with the setting sun
Dropped from the zenith like a falling star,
On Lemnos th' Aegean isle. Thus they relate,
Erring. . . .[57]

This allusion is a sort of postscript to the catalogue of false gods and
is prefaced and concluded with expressions of hostile disbelief, while
the myth itself is told with quite unnecessary richness of detail and is
notable even in Milton for beauty of phrase and sound; there seems
to be a momentary divorce between the Christian and the imaginative
artist in this transmutation of Homeric comedy into romantic vision.
Another example of the contrast between fiction and truth is more
implicit than explicit, though the tone is set by "amorous ditties" and
"supposed"; but much of the contrast is in the rhythm:

Thammuz came next behind,
Whose annual wound in Lebanon allured
The Syrian damsels to lament his fate
In amorous ditties all a summer's day,
While smooth Adonis from his native rock
Ran purple to the sea, supposed with blood
Of Thammuz yearly wounded: the love-tale
Infected Sion's daughters with like heat,
Whose wanton passions in the sacred porch
Ezekiel saw, when by the vision led
His eye surveyed the dark idolatries
Of alienated Judah.[58]

On the other hand, as we noticed in the preceding chapter, tradition permitted, indeed encouraged, the habit of seeing classical myth
and Biblical history as a single body of material, the former a distorted
version of the latter; it was an early and uncritical impulse toward

57. *P.L.*, i.740–47. Sandys, as I remarked before, tries both to link Biblical
and classical stories and to separate truth from fiction. In the *Relation* (ed.
1627, p. 23) he refers to "Lemnos; famous for the fabulous fall of Vulcan."
After quoting and translating Homer's lines, he adds: "The Grecians there now
inhabiting, do relate
—(What dares not lying Greece
In histories insert?)—
that he brake his thigh with a fall from a horse. . . ."
58. *P.L.*, i.446–57.

modern anthropology and comparative religion.[59] It is a question if
Milton was thinking in those terms when he borrowed for his sacred
epic all sorts of pagan material; but now and then he writes in that
tradition. Thus after the fall Adam and Eve, offering contrite prayers,
are likened to

> th' ancient pair
> In fables old, less ancient yet than these,
> Deucalion and chaste Pyrrha. . . .[60]

If that is a noncommittal comparison, Milton makes an explicit connection in these lines:

> The rest were long to tell, though far renowned,
> Th' Ionian gods, of Javan's issue held
> Gods, yet confessed later than Heav'n and Earth,
> Their boasted parents; Titan, Heav'n's first-born. . . .[61]

59. One compendious extract from Ralegh's *History* illustrates the method
used by him, by Sandys, Henry Reynolds, and others:
"And as Adam was the ancient and first Saturn, Cain the eldest Jupiter,
Eva, Rhea, and Noema, or Naamah, the first Venus; so did the fable of the
dividing of the world between the three brethren, the sons of Saturn, arise from
the true story of the dividing of the earth between the three brethren the sons
of Noah: so also was the fiction of those golden apples kept by a dragon taken
from the serpent which tempted Evah: so was paradise itself transported out
of Asia into Africa, and made the garden of the Hesperides: the prophecies,
that Christ should break the serpent's head, and conquer the power of hell,
occasioned the fables of Hercules killing the serpent of Hesperides, and de-
scending into hell, and captivating Cerberus. . . ." *History*, i.6.4 (II, 167).
Cf. *ibid.*, II, 130–31, 163.
60. *P.L.*, xi.10–12. Sandys discusses the problem of chronology (*Ovid*,
p. 31; cf. p. 218). Cf. Ralegh, i.7.3, ii.6.5.
61. *P.L.*, i.507–10. Miss Hartwell (*Lactantius and Milton*, p. 54) remarks
that "this idea of the priority of heaven and earth over the earliest gods is part
of the argument against the Greek deities in the first book of Lactantius." Cf.
Hesiod, *Theog.* 45, and Ralegh, i.8.5: "True it is that the Greeks had their
Janus, but this was not Noah; so had they Ion the son of Xuthus, the son of
Deucalion, from whom they draw the Iones, who were indeed the children of
Javan, the fourth son of Japhet"; and *ibid.*, i.8.7.
Miss Hartwell observes (pp. 47 ff., 147, 181–82) that Keightley, Verity,
and others have been wrong in charging Milton with an error in alluding to
a single Titan, and she records the story of Titan and Saturn, as Milton uses
it, in Lactantius, Boccaccio's *De Genealogia Deorum*, and Caxton's *Recuyell*.
As these names imply, it was quite common. Cf. Warner, *Albion's England*,
i.1–3; Natalis Comes, ii.1–2 (Padua, 1616, pp. 40, 56–57); Ralegh, i.6.5.
Mr. Osgood had pointed out the commentators' errors, and Milton's choice of
a patristic version, in *MLN*, XVI, 282–85.

He again makes a connection when he speculates about stories of Satan:

> However, some tradition they dispersed
> Among the heathen of their purchase got,
> And fabled how the Serpent, whom they called
> Ophion, with Eurynome, the wide-
> Encroaching Eve perhaps, had first the rule
> Of high Olympus, thence by Saturn driv'n
> And Ops, ere yet Dictaean Jove was born.[62]

For a last example, Eden is said to be fairer than

> that Nyseian isle,
> Girt with the river Triton, where old Cham,
> Whom Gentiles Ammon call and Libyan Jove,
> Hid Amalthea and her florid son
> Young Bacchus from his stepdame Rhea's eye.[63]

In the tradition Cham is Ham, Noah's son, and also Jupiter Ammon.

Of overt mythological allegory there seems to be only one clear case in *Paradise Lost*, the birth of Sin from the head of Satan when in heaven he first conceived of rebellion against God (ii.748 ff.). The whole account of Sin and Death, the one thread of allegory in the poem, starts of course from James i.15: "Then when lust hath conceived, it bringeth forth sin; and sin, when it is finished, bringeth forth death." Along with the grisly parody of God and the Son

---

62. *P.L.*, x.578–84. Osgood (p. 34) shows that the mythological source is Apollonius Rhodius, *Arg.* i.503 ff. The story is also told by Natalis Comes (ii.2, p. 61). Sandys' discussion adds some things that Milton would not find in classical authorities: "Pherecides the Syrian writes how the Divels were throwne out of heauen by Iupiter (this fall of the Gyants perhaps an allusion to that of the Angells) the chiefe called Ophioneus, which signifies Serpentine: hauing after made use of that creature to poyson Eue with a false ambition" (*Ovid*, p. 27).

63. *P.L.*, iv.275–79. The story of Amalthea is told by Diodorus Siculus, iii.67–70, and repeated from Diodorus by Ralegh, i.6.5 (II, 175); see Verity (II, 685), who does not notice Ralegh, and Starnes and Talbert, *Classical Myth and Legend*, pp. 236–38. A few pages further on Ralegh says: "But the Egyptians, even after the flood, began (somewhat before this Chaldean Jupiter) to entitle Cham, the parent of their own Mizraim, Jupiter Chammon, or Hammon" (i.6.6). And a few pages earlier (i.6.4) Ralegh speaks of "Mizraim, the son of Cham, who had learnt the same of Cham, and Cham of his father Noah." Cf. Sandys, *Ovid*, pp. 111, 191–92; and Osgood, p. 7.

there is the initial ironic contrast between Sin and Satan and Athene, the goddess of wisdom, and Zeus. It is not clear how far the golden chain by which the created world hangs from heaven is related to the age-old and especially Neo-Platonic interpretation of Homer's chain as a symbol of unity and concord in the universe. Milton had taken that view of the chain in his second Cambridge prolusion, on the music of the spheres, and its presence in the poem is further suggested by his linking the chain with a stairway like that of Jacob's vision—a contrast, by anticipation, with the bridge from hell to the world built by Sin and Death after Satan's triumph.[64]

In general, Milton's mythological allusions are the continuation and the culmination of Renaissance art; as in Marlowe, Spenser, Shakespeare, and the rest, such allusions operate as a language of richly imaginative intensification that goes beyond the capacity of merely abstract terms. They suggest degrees of magnitude, power, horror, beauty, above human and natural limits, and, in serving such purposes, they carry not only a symbolic tinge but, especially in Milton, a judgment of value. This last and usually latent factor is far from a poetic blemish; it is embedded in the nature of the allusion itself and dominates our response. Large portions of *Paradise Lost* obviously forbid mythological references and, as we should expect, the chief clusters have to do with hell and Eden and their inhabitants.

The first simile in the poem (i.197–201) links the huge Satan with the "Titanian or Earth-born, that warred on Jove"—and also with the Biblical Leviathan. The review of the diabolic troops inspires a resounding list of famous armies of myth and romance, beginning with "all the giant brood Of Phlegra" and "th' heroic race . . . That fought at Thebes and Ilium" (i.576 ff.). The pastimes of the fallen angels include contests like the Olympic and Pythian games.

> Others with vast Typhoean rage more fell
> Rend up both rocks and hills, and ride the air
> In whirlwind; Hell scarce holds the wild uproar;

64. Homer, *Iliad*, viii. 18 ff.; *P.L.*, ii.1005, 1051, iii.501 ff. For two out of countless references there are Sir John Davies, *Nosce Teipsum* (ed. Grosart, 1876, I, 53–54), and Jonson's *Hymenaei* (Morley, pp. 69–70; *Ben Jonson*, VII, 221). Jonson cites the original interpretation in Plato's *Theaetetus* (153C) but names Macrobius as his chief authority. As we noted in earlier pages, Spenser and Chapman, following Natalis Comes, took the chain as a symbol of misguided ambition. See the studies by Emil Wolff and L. Edelstein (Bibliography, "General").

> As when Alcides from Oechalia crowned
> With conquest, felt th' envenomed robe, and tore
> Through pain up by the roots Thessalian pines,
> And Lichas from the top of Oeta threw
> Into th' Euboic sea.

This, like the revolt against God, is an explosion of blind, destructive, futile energy. Those who explore hell find a mixture of classical and medieval horrors which, like martial activities, reflect their mental state of anarchy and despair: the four rivers of Hades associated with hate, sorrow, lamentation, and fiery rage; harpy-footed Furies; Lethe, the river of forgetfulness, of which they cannot drink because

> Medusa with Gorgonian terror guards
> The ford.

Hell is a universe of death, filled with prodigies worse

> Then fables yet have feigned, or fear conceived,
> Gorgons and Hydras, and Chimeras dire.

The figure of Sin is girt with hell-hounds of "wide Cerberean mouths," like Scylla. Her son Death is black as Night, "Fierce as ten Furies."

In contrast, the idyllic beauties of the garden surpass all those of traditional earthly paradises. Even the serpent that Satan enters has had no rival in tradition (and Milton's serpent lore, like some other allusions, makes him in a sense familiar and credible as well as uniquely beautiful); there has been none

> Lovelier; not those that in Illyria changed
> Hermione and Cadmus, or the god
> In Epidaurus; nor to which transformed
> Ammonian Jove, or Capitoline was seen,
> He with Olympias, this with her who bore
> Scipio, the highth of Rome.[65]

65. *P.L.*, ix.505–10. The preceding physical description is adapted from Virgil, *Aen.* v.84–90. Milton would know of these various serpents from various sources, but one might refer to Sandys. The story of Aesculapius is in *Metam.* xv.622 ff. (Sandys, *Ovid*, pp. 504–07). In his comment Sandys quotes Lactantius for the view that this serpent was "the great Divell; called a Serpent in the sacred Scriptures" (p. 526). The other two that Milton names Sandys links together (p. 319):

The unearthly perfections of such a garden only mythological allusion can suggest—although, because of Satan's presence and purpose, its short-lived beauties are seen in the light of compassionate
irony. "Universal Pan"—the epithet brings in the allegorical "All"—

> Knit with the Graces and the Hours in dance,
> Led on th' eternal spring. Not that fair field
> Of Enna, where Proserpine gathering flowers,
> Herself a fairer flower, by gloomy Dis
> Was gathered, which cost Ceres all that pain
> To seek her through the world. . . .[66]

This, perhaps the most famous simile in English poetry, compresses
a whole Ovidian tale into a four-line "conceit" (if the term may be
used here); every word and syllable counts in the verbal and rhythmical pattern, and the emotional effect is far beyond anything Ovidian.
Beside these lines we might set one of Spenser's more casual stanzas,
from one of his most luxuriant cantos:

> More sweet and holesome, then the plesaunt hill
> Of Rhodope, on which the Nimphe, that bore
> A gyaunt babe, her selfe for griefe did kill;
> Or the Thessalian Tempe, where of yore
> Fair Daphne Phoebus hart with loue did gore;
> Or Ida, where the Gods lou'd to repaire,
> When euer they their heauenly bowres forlore;
> Or sweet Parnasse, the haunt of Muses faire;
> Or Eden selfe, if ought with Eden mote compaire.[67]

Spenser's crowded, glancing allusions, his particularizing details, are
not salient; his epithets—and sacred Eden—slip by unnoticed, while

---

"A Serpent was said to haue beene found about Olympia's bed, that night
wherein she conceaued with Alexander; which gaue a colour to the claime of
his descent from Iupiter. The like the Romans divulged of Scipio Africanus,
both reports no doubt but proceeding from the Serpents amorous inclination."

Mr. Osgood showed that Milton had good precedent, in editions of Horace
and elsewhere, for using "Hermione" instead of "Harmonia" (*American
Journal of Philology*, XLI, 76 ff.). It may be added that "Hermione" is
Sandys' regular form, in text and commentary.

66. *P.L.*, iv.266–72. For examples of this favorite Miltonic formula,
"Not . . . ," cf. Dante, *Paradiso*, ix.97 ff. (and *passim*); Spenser, *F.Q.*,
I.xi.27 (quoted above, page 95); Giles Fletcher, *Christ's Victorie*, I, 50,
stanza 40.

67. *F.Q.*, II.xii.52.

economy and arrangement make Milton's significant (contrast the
use of "fair" in the two extracts). Nor have the lines any weight of
emotion, though Spenser could hardly write anything without reveal-
ing his love of beauty. Milton's simile suggests the wonder and the
fragility of beauty, the actuality of loss and pain, and along with such
general feelings there is the special feeling stirred by the tacit anticipation of the fate of Eve. (In the ninth book the same pattern is
beautifully varied, without mythological reference, in the picture of
Eve among her flowers when Satan, now a serpent, sees her.) The
ominous—and sympathetic—note is audibly sounded when Adam
and Eve come to their nuptial bower (iv.705 ff.), a lovelier retreat
than any known to Pan or Silvanus or Faunus, and Eve is likened to
Pandora. But normally there is no hint of trouble to come, or no more
than an overtone. When Eve welcomes the angel Raphael she is

> Undecked save with herself, more lovely fair
> Than wood-nymph, or the fairest goddess feigned
> Of three that in Mount Ida naked strove. . . .[68]

Later when she has got her way and left Adam to work alone, she
goes off (ix.386 ff.)

>   like a wood-nymph light,
> Oread or Dryad, or of Delia's train. . . .

But the word "light" is ambiguous, and, if Eve surpasses Delia in
gait and "goddess-like deport" and resembles Pales or Pomona or
Ceres, we think not merely of her beauty but of her ambition and
weakness that Satan is soon to play upon with his arguments that she
should be "A goddess among gods."

VI

Samson Agonistes has three brief allusions, two to Atlas and
Tantalus (146–50, 499–501), both, in accordance with Hebraic decorum, referred to as "Gentile" fables; and a third, a veiled allusion
to Circe, Milton's last (934–35). While *Paradise Regained* does not
allow of many references, what there are range from argumentative

68. *P.L.*, v.380–82. Is Milton recalling *Hero and Leander*—"Where Venus
in her naked glory strove"? For other possible echoes of the poem in Milton
see above, note 40, and, in L. C. Martin's edition of Marlowe's poems, the
notes on *Hero and Leander*, i.31, 197, 241, 249, 251, 262, 265, 301, 325, 393.

or astringent bareness to opulence. Of the former kind is Satan's list of nymphs waylaid by amorous gods, in his reply to Belial's suggestion that Christ be tempted through women; Milton may be only recollecting Ovid, but a number of the names and the flavor of the passage perhaps derive from a less tolerant source, Clement of Alexandria.[69] In the same speech Satan refers to what "fables tell" of the "effect on Jove" of "the zone of Venus." Although a woody scene in which Satan reappears to Christ is akin to Eve's bower or one of Il Penseroso's retreats, the description (ii.294–97) is less sympathetic. But the luxurious banquet, the first stage of the second temptation, demands a purple patch, and—even though the lavish display reveals Satan's inability to comprehend Christ's nature—all Milton's old love of romance as well as myth is poured into the lines:

> Tall stripling youths rich clad, of fairer hue
> Than Ganymede or Hylas; distant more
> Under the trees now tripped, now solemn stood
> Nymphs of Diana's train, and Naiades
> With fruits and flowers from Amalthea's horn,
> And ladies of th' Hesperides, that seemed
> Fairer than feigned of old, or fabled since
> Of fairy damsels met in forest wide
> By knights of Logres, or of Lyonnesse,
> Lancelot or Pelleas, or Pellenore.[70]

Three other bits are noteworthy in more special ways. In his long and vehement rejection of Greek culture (a speech that has needlessly disturbed many readers), Christ himself makes metaphorical use of the myth of Ixion (iv.318–21):

> Who therefore seeks in these
> True wisdom, finds her not, or by delusion
> Far worse, her false resemblance only meets,
> An empty cloud.

Since the reference is veiled, it cannot be called a breach of decorum, and we cannot think of the smallest detail in Milton as happening by chance or oversight; yet, in such a context, the item is odd, and it is quite a different matter from Christ's Miltonic—though hostile —knowledge of Greek literature.

69. *P.R.*, ii.185–91; Osgood, p. 10.
70. *P.R.*, ii.352–61.

More arresting and important is the single mythological simile, in the vein of *Paradise Lost,* which Milton uses at the swift and ironic climax when the temptation of the pinnacle reveals Christ's divinity to both himself and Satan:

> To whom thus Jesus: "Also it is written,
> 'Tempt not the Lord thy God.'" He said, and stood.
> But Satan smitten with amazement fell,
> As when Earth's son Antaeus (to compare
> Small things with greatest) in Irassa strove
> With Jove's Alcides, and oft foiled still rose,
> Receiving from his mother Earth new strength,
> Fresh from his fall, and fiercer grapple joined,
> Throttled at length in the air, expired and fell;
> So after many a foil the Tempter proud,
> Renewing fresh assaults, amidst his pride
> Fell whence he stood to see his victor fall.

This may be an ordinary heroic simile (and it is followed, in Homeric fashion, by another one, about the Theban sphinx), but we may recall Milton's association of Christ with Hercules in the early *Passion* (lines 13–14), and we may ask if he remembered the traditional interpretation: that Hercules is the soul (or prudence, reason) which must raise Antaeus, the sensual body, above the contagion of earthly things.[71]

The quiet conclusion begins:

> So Satan fell; and straight a fiery globe
> Of angels on full sail of wing flew nigh,
> Who on their plumy vans received him soft
> From his uneasy station, and upbore
> As on a floating couch through the blithe air;
> Then in a flow'ry valley set him down
> On a green bank, and set before him spread
> A table of celestial food, divine, ...

While Luke has Satan quote to Christ the assurance of angelic aid, there is no such thing in his narrative, and Milton seems to be fol-

71. Fulgentius, ii.7; Sandys, *Ovid,* p. 322. In *F.Q.,* II.xi.42–46, Spenser had made veiled use of the myth when Arthur (Grace) found a way of overcoming Maleger (Original Sin, in Arthur Woodhouse's cogent interpretation). Cf. Ralegh's parallels between Christ and Hercules in note 59 above.

lowing Giles Fletcher; but he is surely thinking also of Psyche's airy voyage to her lover's mansion in the "myth" of Apuleius.[72]

Looking back over the arduous road Milton had traveled since his first poems in Latin and English, one cannot miss the artistic growth and independence that kept pace with his deepening experience and deepening poetic purposes. Almost from the start he had his own voice, and although the timbre altered, its individual quality became more and more distinct, complex, and powerful. Perhaps the most suggestive summary of his artistic and spiritual evolution is given in his allusions to Orpheus. The passage in *L'Allegro* partook of the unclouded lyricism of the whole (and that, to be sure, represented only one side of the serious young poet). Then, half a dozen years later, came the disenchanted questioning of the harsh lines in *Lycidas* on the death of the archetypal poet. Some thirty years later we have a partly similar antithesis between two allusions in the invocations of *Paradise Lost*. In the invocation to Light, when Milton is moving his scene from hell to heaven, he turns into metaphor the underworld journeys of Orpheus and Aeneas:

> Thee I revisit now with bolder wing,
> Escaped the Stygian pool, though long detained
> In that obscure sojourn, while in my flight
> Through utter and through middle darkness borne
> With other notes than to th' Orphean lyre
> I sung of Chaos and eternal Night,
> Taught by the Heav'nly Muse to venture down
> The dark descent, and up to reascend,
> Though hard and rare.[73]

Here the poet is relatively confident and serene, in spite of his blindness, as the rest of the grand passage makes amply clear. But, half way through the poem, when the story shifts from the war in heaven to the creation of the world, Milton prays to his Heavenly Muse to

72. *P.R.*, iv.583 ff.; Luke iv.10–11; Fletcher, ii.38, 61 (Boas, I, 49, 56); Apuleius, *The Golden Ass*, the end of book iv.

73. *P.L.*, iii.13–21. With the last lines cf. Virgil, *Aen*. vi.125–31; Ovid, *Metam*. x.53–55. Ovid's lines are translated by Sandys (p. 338) with a free turn of phrase which might almost seem to prepare them for Milton's use— not that one needs to invoke Sandys:

> A steepe ascent, dark, thick with fogges, they clime
> Through euerlasting Silence. By this time
> Approach the confines of illustrious Light.

The last phrase renders *telluris margine summae*.

guide him down to earth (lest he fall like Bellerophon on Pegasus),
and his mood recalls that of *Lycidas,* though the cause is different:

> Standing on earth, not rapt above the pole,
> More safe I sing with mortal voice, unchanged
> To hoarse or mute, though fall'n on evil days,
> On evil days though fall'n, and evil tongues;
> In darkness, and with dangers compassed round,
> And solitude; yet not alone, while thou
> Visit'st my slumbers nightly, or when morn
> Purples the east. Still govern thou my song,
> Urania, and fit audience find, though few.
> But drive far off the barbarous dissonance
> Of Bacchus and his revelers, the race
> Of that wild rout that tore the Thracian bard
> In Rhodope, where woods and rocks had ears
> To rapture, till the savage clamor drowned
> Both harp and voice; nor could the Muse defend
> Her son. So fail not thou who thee implores;
> For thou art heav'nly, she an empty dream.

CHAPTER XV

Travesties of Classical Themes and Poems

A chronological sketch of changing tastes in classical matters compels us to employ the art of sinking and descend from Milton to the travesties that litter the second half of the seventeenth century. They may be roughly classified as dull and obscene, and merely dull. Wit is not always absent, but it is likely to be drowned in a flood of boisterous high spirits. Yet the mere bulk of such pieces forces upon our attention a distinct if unattractive phase of our subject, so that this book may, like the phoenix, in aromatic odors end.

Travesty is a free, humorous reworking of a serious narrative which retains the characters and at least a recognizable amount of the subject matter of the original, but reduces everything to the level of bourgeois comedy or farce. The impulse toward travesty is almost as old as literature, but it was not an accident that in Italy, France, Spain, England, a wave of burlesque followed in the wake of the classical revival. Extreme and often wrong-headed veneration for the classics, the hardening of neoclassical dogmas of imitation, the extravagances of mythological poems, produced the logical reaction. The bolder spirits very early began to ask if nature had expended all its energy in the creation of the ancients, if moderns might not hope for an equal gift of genius, and there was born the quarrel of ancients and moderns which was to last for generations. A few at least of the men who wrote travesties may be regarded as the light cavalry in the army of the moderns. The influence of Scarron established the travesty as a popular form, and dozens of lesser men, without Scarron's talent and taste, set about debasing traditional idols and ideals with all the zest of Stracheyan biographers.

So far as England is concerned the critical significance of the movement should not be exaggerated. The most important representative, Charles Cotton, was as a writer of travesty far inferior to Scarron. The Elizabethan age, with its ethical reading of the ancients, its general moral seriousness and glowing idealism, gave way to the easy immorality, sophistication, and sometimes blunt common sense, of the Restoration. Travesties of the classics could hardly have flourished in the time of Spenser, and to remember that they did flourish in the time of Milton is to remember that Milton's soul dwelt apart. The majority of English burlesques, lacking the wit and critical seasoning which make a number of French pieces documents, if nothing more, in the history of taste, seem merely to have gratified a desire in writers and readers to abandon tragic passions and high imaginings and indulge, as Boileau said, in "le langage des halles." Travesties at their best were not exactly refined, and in England the reaction against puritanism contributed to a rather self-conscious coarseness.

In 1644 Scarron published his *Typhon,* which was not strictly a travesty, since it did not caricature any particular poem, but as a humorous treatment of a serious mythological subject it led the way for the *Virgile travesti.* The first books of that famous work appeared in 1648, and many imitations quickly followed. Scarron had seized upon the poet whose qualities lent most piquancy to burlesque, and Virgil was at first the chief victim. But there was plenty of other material available, and Ovid was soon undergoing a variety of metamorphoses, as in Richer's *Ovide bouffon* and the *Ovide en belle humeur* of D'Assoucy.[1]

While Scarron exerted some influence upon a few of the later English travesties, there were in English traces of at least a jocose or satirical handling of classical stories long before Scarron wrote. Pettie's prose adaptations of Ovidian and other tales were not very serious, and added abundant courtly and bourgeois elements. Whetstone's *Rocke of Regard,* also of 1576, tells the story of Venus, Mars, and Vulcan in a half-realistic manner—Vulcan being "a Croydon chuffe" —in order to illustrate "the discommodities of forst marriages." [2] We have noticed that Warner used mythological figures as a stalkinghorse for homely satire. Marston's assertion regarding his tale of Pygmalion at least shows that he could entertain the notion of a mythological burlesque, though not of the bourgeois kind.

1. See Victor Fournel's introduction to his edition of *Le Virgile travesti* (1858); S. E. Leavitt, "Paul Scarron and English Travesty," *SP,* XVI, 108; Albert H. West, *L'influence française dans la poésie burlesque en Angleterre entre 1660 et 1700* (Paris, 1931).

2. Ed. Collier, page 131. Peend's poem of 1565 (see the Appendix) contained a brief version of the story in much the same vein. Indeed there is a similar "explication" in the *Ovide moralisé* (ed. De Boer, iv.1538).

We should not pass by the highly unromantic prose version of the story of Hero and Leander in Nashe's *Prayse of the Red Herring* (1599).[3] Though Nashe has only respect for Marlowe he turns his back on passion and splendor.[4] His alert common sense observes a difficulty in the traditional tale: why did Leander have to swim instead of taking a boat? The parents, he says, were unfriendly, and the towns were "at wrig wrag." Short work is made of courtship and of Hero's scruples. Nashe's slangy mockery is sometimes vivid and amusing, sometimes merely crude. When Hero found her lover on the beach, "sodden to haddocks meate" ("drowndead," as a later inhabitant of Yarmouth expressed it), and was about to kiss his "blew iellied sturgeon lips," the waves carried the body out again. "At that she became a franticke Bacchanal outright, & made no more bones but sprang after him, and so resignd up her Priesthood, and left worke for Musæus and Kit Marlowe." The gods' interest in the lovers is burlesqued, like everything else. Instead of Chapman's metamorphoses, Leander becomes the fish called "ling," Hero a "Cadwallader Herring," while the old nurse, "a shrewish snappish bawd," is turned into mustard seed. Thus it is that "the red Herring and Ling, neuer come to the boord without mustard, their waiting maid." [5]

3. *Works*, ed. McKerrow, III, 195 ff. In addition to Marlowe and Chapman Nashe evidently made use of Ovid. One may recall Ben Jonson's burlesque puppet play on Hero and Leander in *Bartholomew Fair* (Act V), which belongs to the same tradition as Shakespeare's Pyramus and Thisbe.

4. There is at least one touch not unworthy of Marlowe: "Yet towards cocke-crowing she caught a little slumber, and then shee dreamed that Leander and shee were playing at checkestone with pearles in the bottome of the sea."

5. In earlier chapters we have noticed that the injection of humor or satire into mythological poems was one of the marks of the transition from the Elizabethan to the Jacobean manner. In addition to examples just cited in the text there were such later pieces as the *Salmacis and Hermaphroditus* of 1602, Drayton's *Man in the Moone*, and Basse's *Urania*. See also, in the Appendix, *The Metamorphosis of Tabacco*, 1602; Brathwait's *Birth of Tobacco*, 1617; Henry Hutton's *Follie's Anatomie*, 1619. One might notice the fanciful or burlesque use of mythology in Dekker's *A Knights Coniuring* (1607), in particular the burlesque story of Orpheus and Eurydice (ed. Rimbault, Percy Society, 1842, pp. 24–25).

I can only mention the use of mythology as a framework in satire of a more literary kind, the critical survey of poets. The form was made popular by Boccalini, and the best-known English example is Suckling's *Sessions of the Poets*; see Spingarn, *Cambridge History of English Literature*, VII, 273–74, and *Critical Essays of the Seventeenth Century*, I, xxiii. Such writing is of course remote from the travesties we are considering, but the satirical adaptation of the old roll-call of poets springs from the same irreverent impulse.

The first real travesty appears to have been *The Innovation of Penelope and Ulysses,* by James Smith. It was included in the doggish *Wit Restor'd* of 1658, but evidently written in or before 1640. Thus, although it is in the farcical bourgeois vein of the imitations of Scarron, it seems to have preceded both the *Typhon* and the *Virgile travesti.*[6] The poem's chief merit is the light-heartedness characteristic of its reverend author's unclerical muse. Penelope and Ulysses and the Trojan war are brought down to the level suggested by this greeting to the absent husband:

> My pretty Duck, my Pigsnie, my Ulysses,
> Thy poor Penelope sends a thousand Kisses . . .

Stricken with love-longing, Ulysses washes his hands and hastens homeward, while Penelope

> had her shoes rub'd over with Lamp blacking,
> Her new rebato, and a falling band,
> And Rings with severall poesies on her hand.

At the feast a song in praise of blacksmiths is sung, "collected out of Homer, Virgill and Ovid"; it has the lusty classical refrain "Which Nobody can deny." The narrative is furnished with burlesque footnotes.[7] The only respect in which the *Innovation* fails to conform to the later convention is that it does not burlesque one particular poem, although it has obvious and avowed connections with Ovid's epistle. Some of the commendatory lines, including the author's own, show

6. For the text of the *Innovation* see *Musarum Deliciæ* (Hotten, London, 1874), I, 255 ff. A commendatory piece has the signature of Philip Massinger, who died in March, 1640.

For the influence on Mennes and Smith of satirical and facetious French verse, see, for example, Spingarn, *Critical Essays of the Seventeenth Century,* III, 310–11.

7. A *Carmen Heroicum* in *Wit Restor'd* (page 153) has still more remarkable footnotes. One may be quoted to indicate how far we have moved from *Endimion and Phœbe:*

"Endimion was a handsome young Welshman, whom one Luce Moone lov'd for his sweet breath; and would never hang off his lips: but he not caring for her, eat a bundance of toasted cheese, purposely to make his breath unsavory; upon which, she left him presently, and ever since 'tis proverbially spoken (as inconstant as Luce Moone.) The Vatican coppy of Hesiod, reades her name, Mohun, but contractedly it is Moone. *Hesiod. lib. 4. tom. 3.*"

This last sentence marks the arrival of sophisticated scholarship.

that the novelty was appreciated. Massinger, more friendly than critical, declares that the *Culex* showed more art than the *Aeneid*, and as
for the *Innovation*,

> Methinks I do behold in this rare birth
> A temple built up to facetious mirth.

Smith's verse-letters and other pieces are written in a vein of col-
loquial jocoseness, with occasional burlesque references to mythology,
and here, whether or not the idea was original, he applied his normal
style to a traditionally lofty theme.

There is hardly any better proof of the strong stomachs possessed
by some of our ancestors than *The Loves of Hero and Leander*,
which perhaps first appeared in 1651.[8] In addition to the almost inevitable allusion to *Venus and Adonis* (the amorous horse this time),
there is some burlesque of *Hero and Leander*, of the crudest kind.[9]
Some lines may refer to the popular literary firm of Mennes and
Smith, and seem to recognize the pair as models of the new style.[10]

Richard Flecknoe at any rate paid open tribute to Dr. Smith,
"whose muse so bonny is and blithe," and to Mennes, in his *Diarium*
(1656). In the same work Flecknoe mentions Scarron and imitates
a passage in the *Virgile travesti*.[11] He appears to be one of the earliest
links between the native tradition and the foreign. From this time on-

8. It was reprinted in 1653, and, bound up with Heywood's translation of
the *Ars Amatoria*, in 1662 and later years. See above, p. 187, n. 25, for references to articles by A. M. Clark, which straighten out bibliographical puzzles.
The title of the 1662 edition is: *Ovid De Arte Amandi and the Remedy of
Love Englished As also the Lovs of Hero & Leander, A mock-Poem. Together
with Choice Poems, and rare pieces of Drollery.*

9. The motives burlesqued are Leander's swim (including the fish playing
round him and the dalliance of Neptune), and the metamorphosis of the lovers
into a crab and a flounder, inspired doubtless by Chapman or Nashe. Leander's
telling of the story of Cophetua to Hero might have been suggested by Chapman's tale of Teras, though there is no actual similarity.

10. The dubious lines are these:

> Know all, I value this rich Gem,
> With any piece by C. J. M.
> Nay more then so, I'le go no less,
> Then any script of Friends, J. S.

The *Innovation* had contained allusions to the story of Hero and Leander
(pp. 269, 277). In *Wits Recreations* of 1640 (reprint of Hotten, II, 106) an
epigram *On a Coy Woman* recasts a distich of Marlowe's:

> She seems not won, yet won she is at length;
> In loves war, women use but halfe their strength.

11. Leavitt, p. 110. For the mention of Smith, see *Musarum Deliciæ*, I, 7.

ward travesties sometimes reveal the direct or indirect influence of Scarron, but, unless they name their model or clearly imitate him, influence is hard to prove. The formula was easy to apply, after a fashion, and the English writer of travesty had no more need to know Scarron than the composer of a limerick to have read Lear.

In 1664 appeared Charles Cotton's *Scarronides*, a travesty of the first book of the *Aeneid*; a version of the fourth book was added later. The work was extremely popular and stirred up a host of imitators. The title acknowledges a debt to Scarron, and Cotton follows him in choice of subject, in meter, in the constant use of comic anachronisms; there is also some direct borrowing. But there is little in the piece that might not have been as it is if Scarron had never written. Cotton in general is closer to the earthy buffoonery of Smith than to the barbed satirical wit which strikes through the genial irreverence of Scarron. This is Scarron's invocation of the muse, in part:

> Petite muse au nez camard,
> Qui m'as fait auteur goguenard,
> Et qui, quoique mon mal empire,
> Me fais pourtant quelquefois rire,
> Dis-moi bien comment, et pourquoi,
> Junon, sans honneur et sans foi,
> Persécuta ce galant homme,
> Sans lequel nous n'aurions pas Rome,
> Ni tous ces illustres Romains
> A qui nous baisons tous les mains.
> Elle fit bien la furieuse
> Contre personne si pieuse:
> Ils se fâchent donc comme nous!
> Je ne les croyois pas si fous,
> Et les croyois être sans bile,
> Ces beaux dieux d'Homère et Virgile!

Scarron is not invariably delicate, but here we have a scholar and a gentleman permitting himself a holiday from orthodox respect for antiquity, employing both sophisticated and affectedly naïve irony to reduce mythological beings to the humdrum level of prose. Cotton was a scholar and gentleman also, but he produces a daub of coarse liveliness:

> But oh, my Muse! put me in mind,
> To which o' th' Gods was he unkind:
> Or, what the Plague did Juno mean,

(That cross-grain'd, peevish, scolding Quean,
That scratching, cater-wawling Puss)
To use an honest Fellow thus?
(To curry him like Pelts at Tanners)
Have Goddesses no better Manners? [12]

If one reads more than a few pages one may wonder how even a fond editor of Cotton can describe the work as "exceedingly witty." [13] Cotton's travesty of Lucian, *The Scoffer Scofft* (1675), is equally dull and coarse.

In 1664 the first book of the *Iliad* was travestied by J. Scudamore, as *Homer à la Mode*. In the following year Scarron's *Typhon* was translated as *The Gyants War with the Gods*,[14] and the second book of the *Aeneid* was burlesqued by R. Mounsey under the now conventional title of *Scarronides*. Passing over some other minor pieces we may notice a burlesque *Hero and Leander* of 1669 which has been attributed to Wycherley. The work does not seem to reveal any debt to Scarron's *Léandre et Héro* (1656), but it does apparently hark back to Marlowe's elaborate descriptions of Leander and the temple, and perhaps Marlowe's dialogue as well.[15]

In 1672–73 John Phillips translated the fifth and sixth books of *Le Virgile travesti* as *The Maronides, or Virgil Travesty*. As a rule he followed Scarron closely, though he substituted English for French allusions. But from this time onward Ovid was the most popular victim. In 1673 appeared *Ovidius Exulans*, a travesty of five epistles from the *Heroides*. The author calls himself "Naso Scarronnominus," and mentions Scarron in his preface, but his work, which applies the common formula, gives no evidence of any special debt. He declares that he has not written in order to get credit, or pay a bookseller, or flatter a patron, but out of spite, because he sees daily such elaborate

12. *Poetical Works of Charles Cotton* (London, 1765), p. 6. It is pleasant to read that Denham, having burlesqued as well as translated Virgil, burned the travesty, "sayeing that 'twas not fitt that the best poet should be so abused" (Aubrey's *Brief Lives*, ed. Clark, I, 218; *Works of Sir John Denham*, ed. T. H. Banks, p. 42, note 181).

13. John Beresford, *Poems of Charles Cotton* (1923), p. 8.

14. This translation is attributed to John Phillips by the *D.N.B.* and the *Cambridge History of English Literature* (IX, 268), but Leavitt thinks it unworthy of Phillips' linguistic knowledge and experience as a translator (page 113).

15. *Works of Wycherley*, ed. M. Summers, IV, 76, 84 ff. M. Charles Perromat does not accept the notion of Wycherley's authorship (*William Wycherley*, Paris, 1921).

pieces of nonsense creeping out under patronage, and wonders "whether this would pass among them that dote on such Rubbish Learning." The work has no more subtlety than its fellows. Leander would go to Hero on the Bankside if the Thames were not so plaguy rough. Laodamia grieves in this fashion:

> Before that I could fetch my Scarf,
> Your nimble feet had reach'd the Wharf.
> Nay you were got quite out of hear-
> Ing, e're the Cat could lick her ear . . .

If *Ovidius Exulans* is dull, *The Wits Paraphras'd* (1680) falls into the category of the dull and obscene.[16] It burlesques the translation of the *Heroides* (1680) done by Dryden, Flatman, and others. Not many shreds of Ovid are left. In the same year Alexander Radcliffe published an *Ovid Travestie*. His preface ridicules *The Wits Paraphras'd* and its author, "an unlucky Pretender to Poetry." Radcliffe burlesqued some epistles from the *Heroides;* the number was increased in later editions. The popularity of the work was doubtless owing to the fact that Radcliffe was one of the most obscene of his tribe.

There is no need of prolonging a catalogue of such drolleries, since their general character is much the same. It is clear that while a few paid lip service to Scarron, and while Scarron must have encouraged the growth of travesty in England, no English writer had the talent, or perhaps the desire, to emulate his real cleverness. Besides, the simple tricks which the English writers relied upon—anachronism, coarseness, general vulgarizing of theme and characters—were, as we have seen, being practiced before Scarron wrote. Even the continental travesties need not be taken too seriously as a reaction against idolatry of the ancients, since it is only in an age of faith that a feast of fools can be enjoyed, and the English pieces were mostly the hasty scribbling of pot-poets. In the whole mass of tawdry stuff one can find hardly anything that approaches the satirical neatness of Butler's famous lines:

> The Sun had long since in the Lap
> Of Thetis, taken out his Nap,
> And like a Lobster boyl'd, the Morn
> From black to red began to turn.

16. There is a dedication signed "M. T." The Bodleian Catalogue gives the piece to Matthew Stevenson.

Conclusion

Whatever conclusions have emerged from this study may have been repeated so often, since they were first announced in the introduction (and admitted as obvious), that perhaps nothing should be added here to delay the reader's arrival at the Appendix. Yet a few main threads may be picked up.

In the first place, the rise, flourishing, and decline of classical myth in English poetry from Chaucer to the Augustan age is roughly parallel to the pattern we find, over a longer stretch of time, in antiquity: Homer's relatively "primitive" simplicity and piety (which permits comedy); the high philosophized piety and grand art of Pindar, Aeschylus, Sophocles, and Virgil; and the skeptical view and treatment of myth which, beginning in Euripides, ends with the mockery of Lucian. Such phases—matter-of-fact acceptance, philosophic reinterpretation, and skeptical reaction—constitute a logical and predictable process in both the ancient and the modern world; in both, a venerable religious and imaginative tradition of myth and poetry is eventually dissolved by more or less scientific and critical rationalism.

A number of chapters in this book have been concerned with narratives representing Elizabethan Ovidianism (along with the opposed, less popular, and potentially more fruitful kinds represented by Chapman and Drayton). Some of these poems have intrinsic value, and the earlier and better ones had a share in transforming medieval drabness of style into Italianate gold or gilt. They also contributed, if this was a virtue, to emancipation from what may be called Elizabethan Victorianism; there was a whole tribe of young Swinburnes.

But, when we scan the broad horizon, the most significant representatives of myth and poetry are of course the three major nondramatic poets, Chaucer, Spenser, and Milton. For one thing, they represent successive stages of the Renaissance. Chaucer, like most poets of his time, has little scholarly and historical knowledge of the ancient world; as a matter of course he uses an undifferentiated mixture of classical and medieval themes and gives them a more or less medieval costume. His religious faith is assured and sincere, if not intense, and when he is troubled, as he is at the end of *Troilus,* the pagan gods are one cause or symptom of the passions and vanities that turn "yonge, fresshe folkes" away from God and eternal things.

Two centuries later, Spenser has the cultivated Renaissance man's degree of classical knowledge, of the elements of ancient and especially Platonic ethical thought (however indirect), and the Christian humanist's confidence in the bonds of mutual support between pagan reason and Christian faith; and he has the Renaissance humanist's didactic, semi-allegorical view of the heroic poem, ancient and modern. He has too his own special devotion to medieval forms, themes, and language, while his imagination and art have assimilated much from the modern re-creators of heroic romance, Ariosto and Tasso. Thus Spenser's treatment of myth, notably in the Bower of Bliss, combines didactic seriousness of purpose with a sensuous lavishness and lusciousness that outdoes Ovid and the Italians in suggestive subtlety of texture. There is no real antinomy between his sensuous and richly imaginative romanticism and his sober ethical and religious aims. While his employment of myth is mainly ethical (and always decorative as well), he can also make it the vehicle for a metaphysical view of world-order, in the "Gardens of Adonis" and the *Cantos of Mutability.* At the end of the latter, like Chaucer at the end of *Troilus,* Spenser can have a revulsion, though it is not of the same kind: Spenser's conflict is within himself, between his Christian belief in God's providential sway and his instinctive and overwhelming sense of a world of meaningless chance and change.

We may suppose that Spenser and Chaucer—both capable public officials, by the way—would have got on well together, but one difference is relevant here. Spenser's didactic view of the heroic poets, from Homer down, naturally took in the allegorical conception of myth. That conception had been widespread in and long before Chaucer's age, but he, though able to write some unconscionably didactic tales, was unusual in not being attracted to anything allegorical. The tradition has an importance far wider than the limits of this book. Cultural history shows that the vitality of myth is partly imaginative, in man's response to a story that crystallizes and universalizes experience or vision, and partly in the extension of story to ethical *exemplum* or explicit allegorization. This second impulse, whatever its occasional vagaries, was not a late and spurious one. It was active in Greece before Plato, it was increasingly reinforced and enriched by medieval and Renaissance exegesis, and in some form or other it is alive as long as poetry lives by symbols. What has been said already of the rise and decline of myth in English poetry includes the rise and decline of the allegorical or symbolic conception, as some sections of this book have indicated.

Milton made his nearest approach to the allegorical tradition in *Comus,* which links itself with Spenser's book of temperance. The body of Milton's poetry is of course less many-sided and more completely religious than Spenser's. Even more ardently and devoutly than Spenser, Milton held the Renaissance belief in the didactic function of poetry, especially the heroic poem. As Spenser repudiated the doctrine of courtly love, Milton repudiated the traditional epic ideal of martial heroism. Spenser was Milton's great English exemplar in the imaginative handling of moral and religious ideas; we remember Milton's high praise of the sage and serious teacher, and his saying— according to Dryden—that Spenser was his "original," a word that may take in both teaching and technique. Milton was born only nine years after Spenser died, but his deep and sophisticated classical learning went further beyond Spenser's than Spenser's went beyond Chaucer's. As artist, he learned far more from the classics, though he learned much also from Italian theory and practice; but whereas Spenser had assimilated Italian fluidity and sensuous expansiveness, Milton assimilated the devices that made for muscularity and elevation. While Spenser had his full portion of the Elizabethan Protestant's anti-Catholic feeling, he had something too of the Catholic instinct that the senses may share in the glory of God. Milton's sensuous faculties were intense, but both as a disciplined classicist and a puritan he seldom gave them free rein. When he does so, as in the picture of Eden, the supreme earthly paradise and symbol of perfection, his mythological allusions are the *ne plus ultra* of Renaissance art, idealistic and idyllic, concentrated, arresting, rich in overtones, and, from the nature of his fable, poignantly ironic. At the opposite pole, mythological allusions heighten the horrors of hell, of minds cut off from God. Spenser had freely blended the pagan and Christian without misgiving, in the normal sixteenth-century way. Milton, in *Comus, Lycidas,* and *Paradise Lost,* blended these elements with a more conscious, discriminating, and functional sense of both harmony and disharmony. In the sacred epic he may, even in creating a beautiful mythological image, feel at times the need of calling it pagan fiction. Only now and then does he seem to subscribe to the traditional view that pagan myth has a degree of validity in being a partial perversion of Biblical truth. But whatever minor difficulties Milton's

all-embracing religious commitment put in his way, they did not injure the poetic result; indeed they raised and intensified its significance
and power.

Chaucer, Spenser, and Milton, with all their individual differences,
had a large view of poetry, a view which comprehended the realistic,
the romantic, the visionary, the religious, and, along with such diversity, all kinds of "unclassical" incongruity, even in Milton. While
he was by far the greatest of neoclassicists, he was not bound by
neoclassical theory, which during his lifetime was narrowly constrict-
ing the poetic world. He was the last poet who had the vatic stature
and outlook, the mastery of knowledge which justified him, like
Dante, in the claim to be a teacher of mankind. While the humanistic
and aesthetic values of the classical tradition were united with the religious and ethical force of the Catholic and Protestant tradition,
Milton was still possible. But the new philosophies, beginning with
Bacon and especially Descartes, had been undermining the ground
on which Milton stood, had been killing the essence of the classical
tradition, of religion, of myth, of poetry. Besides, while for Milton
poetry and knowledge were still one, as they had been for Dante,
science had set out on its own independent path, which was to lead
beyond the horizon of any one man, any one poet. Through the
division of labor the unacknowledged legislators of the world had
lost their leadership. Milton is a poet; Dryden is a man of letters.

When Milton's major poems appeared, crude travesties of the
classics were (within our limited area) all the rage; the allegorical
tradition had been pretty well dissolved by skeptical rationalism; the
intensities of Reformation religion were subsiding into cool Anglican-
ism and cooler Deism; and the newly established aim of poetry was
the realistic and satirical depiction of men and manners, in substance
and style freed from all that was visionary, mythic, and irrational.
Thus, in the serious use of classical myth, our great classical age is
the age of sterility. (The virtues of the age do not concern us here.)

But the mythological barrenness of full-blown neoclassicism was,
in the long perspective of poetry, only a temporary hiatus. The romantic movement, a slowly rising revolt against the constrictions of
rationalism, brought back a large conception of poetic vision. The
great stream of classical myth and the allegorical or symbolic tradition
emerged from underground and resumed its fertilizing course. It
was, to be sure, flowing through a new world. Whereas during the
centuries of the Renaissance the use of myth had been as natural as
breathing, the romantic revival was attended, in the age of the in-

dustrial revolution, by a more conscious nostalgia. But the ideal function and value of myth were still there:

> The intelligible forms of ancient poets,
> The fair humanities of old religion,
> The Power, the Beauty, and the Majesty,
> That had their haunts in dale, or piny mountain,
> Or forest by slow stream, or pebbly spring,
> Or chasms and wat'ry depths; all these have vanished.
> They live no longer in the faith of reason!
> But still the heart doth need a language, still
> Doth the old instinct bring back the old names.[1]

1. Coleridge, *Wallenstein*, Part I, II.iv.123 ff.

Appendix

This appendix has two main objects, first, to provide a chronological conspectus of mythological poems (and a few related works in verse and prose) up to 1680; and, secondly, to include brief accounts of a number of minor works not discussed in the text. The list aims, of course in vain, at something like completeness, within necessarily arbitrary limits, since hardly any book of the period is free from mythology. In its original manuscript state this appendix had swollen into another volume, and it has been reduced to more tolerable size by the exclusion of nearly all ballads, lyrics, and brief pieces generally, and of almost all formal translations from classical poems except some few mentioned in the text. Up to 1600 all translations of Ovid's *Metamorphoses* and *Heroides* are included. A few other items not covered by these general exceptions appear on account of some special significance.

For the sake of uniformity titles are almost always given as they appear in the *Short-Title Catalogues* of Pollard and Redgrave and Wing. Exceptions to this rule comprise titles of books not published or not extant and a few cases in which a title is abridged or given in full.

No attempt has been made to supply full references and bibliographical information. "Text" means a reference to the earlier pages of this book. For the titles of Hazlitt, Palmer, Scott, see Bibliography, "General." "Collier," unless a title is given, means *A Bibliographical and Critical Account*, etc., 4 vols., New York, 1866.

1475? William Caxton, The recuyell of the historyes of Troye. Text, II.ii.

ca. William Caxton, Thhistories of Jason.
1477.

1480. William Caxton, Ovyde hys booke of Methamorphose. Text, II.ii.

1490. William Caxton, Eneydos.
Text, II.ii.

1508? Robert Henryson, The traitie of Orpheus.

1518? This boke treath of the lyfe of Virgilius.
> The legendary life of Virgil the wizard. See under 1562, and Palmer, p. 117.

1520–
1540? A lire of love etc.
> A poem of 273 lines, printed by Padelford along with many others from MS. Rawlinson C. 813 (*Anglia*, XXXI, 1908, 385 ff.). The date of the MS is placed between 1520 and 1540; some of the poems are much older. The first 35 lines of our piece describe the judgment of Paris. The author proceeds, in exuberantly aureate language, to praise love and women and especially his own "redolent flowre." The medieval flavor is strong. The poet borrows from an odd pair, Tibullus and Hawes. See W. Bolle, *Anglia*, XXXIV, 275, 290, 299–300, 306; and Padelford, *Anglia*, XXXV, 185.

1521. Brian Anslay, The boke of the Cyte of Ladyes.
> The book contains many stories of goddesses, etc. A translation of Christine de Pisan's *Livre de la Cité des Dames*, which itself is modeled on, and borrows largely from, Boccaccio's *De Claris Mulieribus*. See text, II.ii.

1526. The letter of Dydo to Eneas.
> Printed in Pynson's edition of Chaucer, 1526. Apparently a free and abridged paraphrase of the epistle in the *Heroides*, whether direct or not. See E. Hammond, *Chaucer*, p. 436.

Before
1531. La conusaunce damours.
> A poem containing thirty pages of rhyme royal, printed by Pynson. To gain inspiration for a poem in honor of "dames and pusels" the writer calls on a young woman and her friends. The hostess tells in thirty stanzas of not unpleasing verse the story of Pyramus and Thisbe. It is a close paraphrase, direct or indirect, of Ovid; the chief departure, a medieval one, is the expansion of *audacem faciebat amor* into a couple of stanzas on the power of love. At the end of the story comes a discussion of love, with contributions from "Reason" and "Thought-and-hevynesse." There is an allusion to the *Troilus* of "our ornate Chaucer." The poem was said by Collier (IV, 161) to be from the French—as the title might suggest—but I do not know any original.

1534–
1547. Henry Parker, Lord Morley (1476–1556) translated but did not publish 46 lives from Boccaccio's *De Claris Mulieribus*. They were edited by H. G. Wright, E.E.T.S., 1943.

1536–
1545. The C. hystoryes of Troye.
> A translation of Christine de Pisan's *L'Epistre d'Othea*, probably done by the printer, Robert Wyer.

1553. The faythfull and true storye of the destruction of Troye, compyled by Dares Phrigius, which was a souldier while the siege lasted, Translated into Englyshe by Thomas Paynell. (Palmer, p. 40).

1557. Giovanni Battista Gelli, Circes. *Tr.* out of Italyon H. Iden. Text, II.ii.

1557. Songes and sonettes, written by Henry Haward late Earle of Surrey, and other.

Tottel's *Miscellany* contains many amatory poems employing myths; for some of these see text, III.iii. Other pieces of classical interest are a translation of the opening lines of Penelope's epistle to Ulysses (*Heroides*); Wyatt's *Song of Iopas;* and Grimald's *Ciceroes Death* (from Beza's Latin), one of Grimald's two experiments in blank verse. See also text, II.i.

1560. The fable of Ovid treting of Narcissus.
Text, III.i.

1561. The nine ladies worthy.

A piece on famous heroines, printed in Stow's edition of Chaucer, 1561. See Skeat, *Chaucerian and Other Pieces,* p. xii; Hammond, p. 441.

How Mercurie with Pallas, Venus and Minarua, appered to Paris.

Also in Stow. See Skeat, p. xiii; and *Romaunt of the Rose: Minor Poems,* p. 33; Hammond, p. 427.

1562– A boke intituled Perymus and Thesbye.
1563. Entered to W. Griffith, *Stat. Reg.,* I, 215. Warton mentions a quarto on the same theme, licensed in 1562 to T. Hacket (*History of English Poetry,* 1871, IV, 297). See *Gorgeous Gallery,* ed. Rollins, pp. 198, 203; Chambers, *William Shakespeare,* I, 363.

1562? Virgilius. This boke treateth of the lyfe of Virgil.
An account of the wizard. See under 1518.

1563. A myrroure for magistrates.
This edition contained Sackville's *Induction.* Text, III.v.

Before Sir Thomas Chaloner (d. 1565) wrote, but apparently did not
1565. publish, a rendering of the epistle of Helen to Paris (*Heroides*). Printed in *Nugae Antiquae* (1804), II, 372–89.

1565. The fyrst fower bookes of P. Ouidius Nasos worke, intitled Metamorphosis. *Tr.* into Englishe meter by A. Golding.

1565. The pleasant fable of Hermaphroditus and Salmacis [*tr.*] by T. Peend.

Ovid is treated rather freely in 166 lines of jog-trot verse. The rest of the 340 lines expound the allegory. Hermaphroditus represents youthful purity, Caria the world, Salmacis all the allurements of vice. A similar interpretation is given in the *Ovide moralisé* (ed. De Boer), iv.2284 ff. There are also euhemeristic explanations of Actaeon and other figures which go back at least as far as Fulgentius and Servius. Apparently with the help of the *Ars Amatoria* (i. 269 ff.) Peend rebukes the "folysh fyts" of passionate women, citing such examples as Venus, Hero, Juliet.

Peend says that he gave up a projected version of the *Metamorphoses* on being "prevented" by another—evidently Golding. One is not left inconsolable. Brydges prints extracts in *Brit. Bibl.*, II, 344; I used the Bodleian copy of Peend. See L. Rick, *Ovids Metamorphosen in der englischen Renaissance*, pp. 32–35, and Hallett Smith, *Elizabethan Poetry*, pp. 68–69.

1565– Very pleasaunte sonettes and storyes in myter.
1566.   First edition of *Handful of Pleasant Delights* (1584). See *Handful*, ed. Rollins, introduction. On particular ballads, text above, III.iv.

1566.   William Painter, The palace of pleasure [vol. I].
Text, II.iii.

1566.   John Partridge, The notable hystorie of two famous princes Astianax and Polixena.
A piece of about 220 long lines, written ostensibly to show the horrors of war. Though said by the author to be a translation, it seems to be based on those parts of Seneca's *Troades* (in Heywood's translation) which deal with Astyanax and Polyxena. Use is made of the speech of Achilles added by Heywood to the original. Some details, especially about Polyxena, are possibly from *Metam*. xiii. 449 ff., or Lydgate, *Troy Book*, iv. 6635 ff., 6684 ff. Brief extracts are given in Collier, III, 147.

1566.   Thomas Underdowne, The excellent historye of Theseus and Ariadne.
I have not seen the whole poem. It is described, with excerpts, in Brydges, *Brit. Bibl.*, II, 534, and Collier, IV, 183. The myth receives a strongly didactic and misogynistic coloring.

1567.   The XV. bookes of P. Ouidius Naso, entytuled Metamorphosis. *Tr.* into English meeter by A. Golding.
Text, IV.i, and see index.

1567.   William Painter, The palace of pleasure [vol. II].
Text, II.iii.

1567.   James Sanford, The amorous and tragicall tales of Plutarch.
A prose version of Plutarch's five tales of love. See *Moralia*, ed. Bernardakis, IV, 463 ff.; *Morals*, ed. Goodwin (Boston, 1878), IV, 312–22. The translator's epistle censures "the fruites which spring of

hote Loue and fleshly lust." The volume contains also a version of parts of Heliodorus, beginning with bk. iv.

1567. George Turberville, The heroycall epistles of Pub. Ouidius Naso, in Englishe verse . . . With A. Sabinus aunsweres.

The *Stat. Reg.* for 1566–67 (I, 328, 329, 335) has three entries to Denham for epistles of Ovid. These were doubtless a precautionary announcement of Turberville's work, though one or two may have appeared separately. See H. E. Rollins, *MP*, XV (1918), 519. The book was reprinted by F. S. Boas (Cresset Press, 1928).

1567. George Turberville, Epitaphes, epigrams, songs and sonets. Text, III.ii.

1568. William Fulwood, The enimie of idlenesse. Teaching how to indite epistles.

This manual gives a model poem, of ten stanzas, the "story of Pigmalions ill," in which the myth is applied to the case of an unhappy lover; the hard-hearted statue does not come to life. For a piece on Troilus and Cressida see Rollins, *PMLA*, XXXII, 391.

1568. Thomas Howell, The arbor of amitie or pleasant poems.

——————, Pleasant sonnets and prettie pamphlets.

Text, III.ii.

1569. W. Hubbard, The tragicall and lamentable historie of Ceyx, kynge of Thrachine, and Alcione his wife.

Reprinted in Collier, *Illustrations of Old English Literature*, III (and see *Bibl. Acct.*, II, 143). Hubbard treats Ovid (*Metam.* xi. 346 ff.) freely, abridging the description of the storm, and omitting mythological machinery in the account of Alcyone's dream. Lines and phrases are frequently borrowed from Golding.

1570. B. G., Helen's epistle to Paris.

Hazlitt, p. 429. Warton (IV, 301) records the piece, calling it a "ballet." The title of course suggests translation or adaptation of Ovid.

1573. James Sanford, The garden of pleasure.

Re-issued in 1576 as *Houres of recreation* (Scott, p. 27). The book includes short tales and anecdotes, ancient and modern, such as those concerning the wife of Candaules; Mercury and Battus; Atalanta; the three Graces.

1574. Richard Robinson, The rewarde of wickednesse.

Described in Collier, III, 330; Brydges, *Censura Lit.*, IV, 36; *Mirror for Magistrates*, ed. Haslewood, pp. xxiii ff. I used the British Museum copy. The piece is strongly didactic and anti-Romanist. The author visits Hades and hears the confessions of sundry notable sinners, Helen, Pope Alexander VI, Tarquin, Medea, Tantalus, Midas, etc. One is reminded of the *Mirror*, and also of the dialogue of

Ravisius Textor, *Earth and Age,* which Thomas Heywood translated in his *Pleasant Dialogues and Dramma's.*

1574– George Turberville, Tragical tales.
1575.   Text, III.ii.

1575.   W. Painter, The palace of pleasure beautified; Corrected and augmented.

1576.   The paradyse of dainty deuises.
        This popular miscellany included four poems, by Edwards, illustrating the cardinal virtues. They deal with the story of Damocles; a young man of Egypt and Valerian; Zaleuch and his son; and Spurina. See Rollins' ed., pp. 55 ff., and notes. Text, II.ii.

1576.   George Gascoigne, The steele glas. A satyre, togither with the Complainte of Phylomene.
        Text, III.iii.

1576.   George Pettie, A petite pallace of Pettie his pleasure.
        Text, II.iii.

1576.   George Whetstone, The rocke of regard.
        The book includes three moralistic poems, on Cressida, Medea, Venus and Vulcan (Collier's reprint, pp. 36, 108, 131). On the last, see text, XV.

1577.   Stephen Batman, The golden booke of the leaden goddes.
        Text, II.ii. Available in M.L.A. rotograph series, No. 76.

1577?   " 'The historie of Leander and Hero, written by Musæus, and Englished by me a dozen years ago, and in print.' So mentioned by Abraham Fleming in his Virgil's Georgics, 1589. Not otherwise known." (Palmer, p. 74.) See Hazlitt, p. 410; Collier, II, 27.

1577.   John Grange, The golden Aphroditis.
        A.O., the heroine of this piece of prose fiction, is the daughter of Diana and Endymion and there is much decorative mythology. Like Pettie's shorter tales, this is full of love-making and letter-writing. See Hyder Rollins' edition (Scholars' Facsimiles & Reprints, 1939).

1578.   A gorgious gallery of gallant inuentions.
        Text, III.i–ii.

1579.   H. C., The forrest of fancy.
        A miscellany of prose and verse, described in Brydges, *Restituta,* III, 456; Collier, II, 30; Koeppel, *Quellen und Forschungen,* LXX (1892), 44–46; Scott, pp. 36–38. A few short tales about such characters as Eteocles and Polynices (this inspired perhaps by the Senecan translations); King Antigonus; Meleager.

1579.   A poor Knight, his pallace of priuate pleasures. Written by a student in Cābridge. And published by J. C. Gent.

Reprinted by Sir H. Ellis, *Three Collections of English Poetry of the Latter Part of the Sixteenth Century* (Roxburghe Club, 1845). A piece of thirty pages uses the dream-allegory to describe, somewhat in the manner of Lydgate or Googe's *Cupido Conquered*, a battle between the forces of Diana and Cupid and a trial before the gods. There is also a poem of nearly two hundred lines, which combines broadside style with historical detail, *The lyfe and death of Maister, T. Cicero.* Cf. Lydgate, *Fall of Princes*, ed. Bergen, vi. 2948–3276.

1579. **Thomas Salter, A mirrhor mete for all mothers, matrones, maidens, intituled the mirrhor of modestie.**

Reprinted in Collier, *Illustrations of Old English Literature*, I. The author is indignant that women able to read Prudentius and other Christian poets should prefer "Lascivious bookes of Ovide, Catullus, Propercius, Tibullus, and in Virgill of Eneas, and Dido; and amonge the Greeke poettes of the filthic love (if I maie terme it love) of the Goddes themselves, and of their wicked adulteries and abhominable fornications, as in Homer and suche like" (p. 17). There are classical anecdotes of a moral turn, and a quite unclassical dialogue between Mercury and Virtue.

1579. **Edmund Spenser, The shepheardes calender.**
See index.

1580. **Humfrey Gifford, A posie of gilloflowers.**

Contains *A straunge historie*, which tells of Camma, Sinatus, and Sinorix (pp. 60–62 in original ed. of *Posie;* pp. 122 ff. in Grosart's reprint). Gifford's names in his book are Camna, Sinatus, Sinoris. The piece had been issued as a broadside ten years earlier. H. E. Rollins took this ballad to be the same as another issued in the same year (1569–70), *The Revenge yat a Woman of Grece toke of hym that slewe hyr husbounde* (see his *Analytical Index*, 2284 and 2452). But Baskervill suggested that "the publication of 2452 by Jones may have called forth another ballad on the same theme from the press of Arnold" (*MP*, XXIII, 1925–26, 123). This seems probable, for Gifford's ballad (if, as one may assume, it was *Sinorex, Cania et Sinatus*) is based on *The Courtier* (Tudor Translations, pp. 236–37), while the title of the other, as Rollins points out, is summarized from the title in North's translation of Guevara, bk. ii, c.5.

1581. **William Goodyear, The voyage of the wandering knight.**

Translated from the French of Jean de Cartigny. One of the illustrations of Folly's dominion over man is the Trojan war, which is outlined, in two and a half pages, from the judgment of Paris to the lonely old age and death of Helen. Apparently the ultimate source is Dictys. Extracts from other parts of the book are given in the *Retrospective Review*, I (1820), 250–58. The work was discussed by D. F. Atkinson, *Huntington Library Quarterly*, VII (1943–44), 109–34, and edited by her, now D. A. Evans (University of Washington Press, 1951).

1581.   Thomas Howell, Howell his deuises for his owne exercise, and his friends pleasure.
Text, III.ii.

1582.   *Cal. St. Pap. Dom. Add.*, XII, 77, Oct. 14, 1582.
"John de Critz to Sec. Walsingham: 'Pardon my slackness in not sending oftener . . . Meantime I send two pieces, the one of St. John, the other a poetical story taken out of Ovid, where Neptune took Coenis by the seaside, and having ravished her, for some amends changed her into the form of a man. Take this little present in good part. I trust to send something better next time.' "
This irrelevant reference to pictorial art is included here for the sake of its atmosphere. See *D.N.B.* on De Critz.

1584.   A handefull of pleasant delites by C. Robinson and diuers others.
See under 1565–1566, and text, III.iv.

1585.   Robert Greene, Planetomachia.

1585?   Thomas Procter, The triumph of trueth.
Reprinted in Collier, *Illustrations of Old English Literature*, II. There are classical tales of the didactic sort. Caesar's glory was "blemisht with desire of Lucre." "The Gretians Conquest" tells the story of the Trojan war in five pages. The account of the capture of Troy seems to follow Virgil; other parts suggest the *Heroides* or Dictys, though the matter was common property.

1585.   Thomas Watson, *Amyntas.*
See W. F. Staton (Bibliography, IV).

1586.   John Shepery, Hyppolitus Ouidianæ Phædræ respondens.

1586.   William Warner, Albions England.
The first edition, comprising four books and the prose tale of Aeneas.
Text, III.v.

1586.   Helenæ raptus, Latinus, paraphraste T. Watsono.
Watson's Latin translation of the poem of Colluthus.

1586.   Geffrey Whitney, A choice of emblemes and other deuises.
Emblems mostly taken from Alciati, and others. Dozens of myths are briefly recounted and often allegorized. Reprinted by Henry Green, London, 1866. See M.A. Scott, p. 470, and my index.

1587.   Robert Greene, Euphues his censure to Philautus.
————————, Penelopes web.
Text, II.iii.

1587.   Mathew Grove, The most famous and tragicall historie of Pelops and Hippodamia.
Ed. Grosart, 1878. See also Collier, II, 95, and *Catalogue . . . of*

Early English Literature at Bridgewater House (1837), p. 134. The poem occupies 44 pages in Grosart. The story, taken perhaps from Diodorus Siculus (iv.73), is amplified with speeches, moralizing, descriptions, in the feeble, jog-trot style of Ovidian poems of twenty years earlier. The author plagiarized somewhat from Tottel's *Miscellany* (ed. Rollins, II, 112).

1587.   The mirror for magistrates.
         The edition containing lives of Roman emperors. Text, III.v.

1587?   Christopher Marlowe, The rape of Helen.
         "Marlowe is credited with a translation of Coluthus which no longer exists" (Palmer, p. 39). See *Marlowe's Poems*, ed. L. C. Martin, p. 22.

1587.   Antonius Thylesius, Cassius of Parma his Orpheus. *Tr.* Roger Rawlyns.
         Thirty-five lines tell the story of Orpheus (without Eurydice) to show that the musician must work in order to reach the top of the tree.
         The same translator produced a similar inspirational piece called *Nestor his Antilochus.*

1587.   George Turberville, Tragical tales.
         See under 1574–1575.

1588.   In William Byrd's *Psalms, sonets and songs* appeared a piece of eight lines, a translation of the opening portion of Ovid's epistle from Penelope to Ulysses. The author is unknown. Reprinted in Bullen, *Some Shorter Elizabethan Poems* (1903), p. 14; Arber, *English Garner*, II, 84.

1588.   Sixe idillia.
         Text, III.ii.

1589.   Thomas Lodge, Scillaes metamorphosis.
         Re-issued in 1610 as *A most pleasant historie of Glaucus and Scilla.* Text, IV.iii.

1589.   George Peele, A farewell. Entituled to the famous generalls of our English forces: Sir J. Norris & Syr F. Drake. Whereunto is annexed: a Tale of Troy [in verse].
         Text, III.i.

1589.   W. Warner, The first and second parts of Albions England, reuised and corrected.
         Second edition, containing bks. i–vi. Text, III.v.

1590.   Thomas Fenne, Fennes frutes.
         An extraordinary hodge-podge, mainly in prose, heavily didactic, with scores of classical anecdotes from the usual sources, Plutarch, Justin, etc., some taken verbatim from Fleming's translation of Aelian. Somewhat in the manner of Valerius Maximus, tales are

marshaled to illustrate temperance, modesty, etc. There is a detailed account of the Trojan war, citing Dares and Dictys. Fenne protests against the derivation of Britons from "such an unfaithfull stock" as the Trojans.

Forty pages of verse on "Hecubaes mishaps" also recount the Trojan story; the matter seems to be taken from Dares, Dictys, Lydgate, Ovid, Homer, Virgil.

1590. Edmund Spenser, The Faerie Queene [Bks. i–iii]. Text, V.

1590. Edmund Spenser, Muiopotmos.

The title-page of this poem in *Complaints* (1591) is dated 1590.

1590. William Vallans, A tale of two swannes.

Reprinted in Hearne's edition of Leland's *Itinerary* (vol. V). A topographical poem about Hertfordshire, with a slight mythological framework involving Venus and Mercury. Venus sits by a river side "Tuning her Lute unto the waters fall." See Carpenter, *Reference Guide to Spenser* (1923); Robert A. Aubin, *Topographical Poetry in XVIII-Century England* (1936).

1591. Thomas Bradshaw, The shepherds starre.

A much amplified "paraphrase upon the third of the Canticles of Theocritus, Dialogue wise." Inset is a piece of verse, *A Dialogue betwixt Hercules and the two Ladies, Voluptuous, and Vertuous,* with a reference to "Xenophon. li. 2. Memorabilium"; see Xenophon, ii.1.21 ff. Cf. Whitney, *Choice of Emblemes,* p. 40.

1591. John Clapham, Narcissus, siue amoris iuuenilis descriptio.

An elaborate didactic, allegorical version of the story, in Latin verse.

1591. Jo. M., Philippes Venus. Wherein is pleasantly discoursed sundrye fine and wittie arguments in a senode of the gods and goddesses assembled for the expelling of wanton Venus from among their sacred societie.

Esdaile, *English Tales and Prose Romances,* p. 96; Hazlitt, p. 365; Collier, III, 195.

1592. Abraham Fraunce, The third part of the Countesse of Pembrokes Yuychurch: entituled, *Amintas Dale.* Wherein are the most conceited tales of the pagan gods in English hexameters: together with their auncient descriptions and philosophicall explications.

The book has been made available in the M.L.A. rotograph series, No. 75. Inset in a pastoral framework are sixteen narratives in verse, the subjects roughly covering the fifteen books of the *Metamorphoses.* An extract from one tale is given above, VII, note 18. Most of the stories are fairly close paraphrases of Ovid, with more or less Italianate ornament and an occasional interpolation.

The prose sections constitute a dictionary of allegorized mythology. Innumerable and varied authorities are cited, many demonstrably at second hand; such references as those to Spenser, Boscán, Belleau, Tasso, seem to be Fraunce's own. His allegorical matter seems to be compiled chiefly from Vincenzo Cartari, Natalis Comes, an annotated edition of Ovid (Cambridge, 1584), and Leo Hebraeus.

1592.   William Warner, Albions England. The third time corrected. Books i–ix.

1593.   Gervase Markham "revised for the press 'Thyrsis and Daphne,' a poem not known to be extant (cf. *Stationers' Reg.* 23 April 1593)" (*D. N. B.*). The piece may have been pastoral or mythological or both.

1593.   Christopher Marlowe, Hero and Leander. Entered to J. Wolf, September 28, 1593, but no edition is known previous to that of 1598. Text, VI.

1593.   William Shakespeare, Venus and Adonis. Text, VII.i.

1594.   Richard Barnfield, The affectionate shepheard. The volume includes *Hellens Rape. Or a light Lanthorne for light Ladies* (*Poems*, ed. Arber, p. 38). The poem's 75 creaking hexameters suggest that the imitative Barnfield's idol of the moment was Abraham Fraunce. The Trojan saga receives some apparently original additions, such as Paris' "Aunt Amaryllis" and a variegated Elizabethan banquet. H. Morris has a full account of the book in *Tulane Studies in English*, X (1960).

1594.   George Chapman, Σκιὰ νυκτός. The shadow of night: containing two poeticall hymnes. Text, X.

1594.   T. H., Oenone and Paris. Text, IX.v.

1594.   I. O., The lamentation of Troy, for the death of Hector. About 200 sixain stanzas, presenting a series of Trojan characters, Priam, Andromache, and others, lamenting in speeches of varying length. The initial idea perhaps came from Seneca's *Troades* or *Iliad* xxii, xxiv; the author praises Homer. Details and some verbal parallels suggest that the main source was Lydgate's *Troy Book*. The framework—the ghost of Troy appearing in a dream—and the gloomy subject recall the *Mirror for Magistrates*. There is a reference to *Astrophel and Stella*. Spenser is hailed as "the only Homer liuing." The influence of the new mellifluous style, especially Spenser's, is quite marked in elaborate similes; rhythm and style in general often suggest the sixains of Lodge and Shakespeare. The poem has been edited by E. C. Wilson (Institute of Elizabethan Studies, Chicago, 1959), who suggests Spenser's *Ruines of Time* as its immediate inspiration and finds the most likely author in a young soldier, Sir John Ogle (1569–1640).

1594. William Shakespeare, Lucrece.
Text, VII.ii.

1595. R. B., Orpheus his iourney to hell and his music to the ghosts.
A poem of 24 pages in sixains. In general it follows the orthodox story, with rather more action and less decoration than the new mode prescribed. Orpheus sings some lyrics about love. See the note on Colse, under 1596.

1595. Richard Barnfield, Cynthia, with certaine Sonnets and the legend of Cassandra.
The author claims *Cynthia* as the first imitation of the verse of *The Faerie Queene*. Using the device of the dream-vision and a variation on the judgment of Paris, Barnfield achieves the inevitable compliment to Elizabeth.
Cassandra is a more ambitious piece, in 78 sixain stanzas. The poet tells of Cassandra's relations with Apollo, then with Agamemnon. After the murder of the king she laments, in prison, on such topics as fortune, ambition, chastity. Finally, with a knife "her purest soule was eased." There is an obvious debt to Shakespeare, especially *Lucrece*. (For Barnfield's imitation of Shakespeare and Marlowe, see Pooler's edition of *Venus and Adonis*, pp. ix–xii; Charles Crawford, *Collectanea*, First Series, and *Notes and Queries*, Ninth Series, VIII, 217, 277.)
Much of the Trojan matter seems to be taken from the *Recuyell* (ed. Sommer, pp. 509, 526 ff., 658 ff., 667, 673). For the death of Agamemnon external probability, and some parallels in detail, favor the *Agamemnon* of Seneca.

1595. George Chapman, Ouids banquet of sence.
Text, X.

1595. Michael Drayton, Endimion and Phœbe. Ideas Latmus.
Text, VIII.i.

1595. Thomas Edwards, Cephalus and Procris: Narcissus.
Edited, with a very full apparatus criticus, by W. E. Buckley (Roxburghe Club, 1882). On the identity of Edwards see Mrs. Stopes, *MLR*, XVI, 209. *Cephalus and Procris* was entered October 22, 1593 (*Stat. Reg.*, II, 639).
The Ovidian fables are almost lost sight of on account of Edwards' endless elaboration and fanciful additions. Aurora's wooing of Cephalus follows *Venus and Adonis*. A few details suggest a knowledge of Pettie's romantic prose version. There are also such un-Ovidian episodes as a meeting between Procris and Lamia, and an uncivil swain's somewhat violent expression of admiration when he finds Procris asleep. The story of Narcissus is padded with a long account of

women's efforts to captivate him, and with discussions of love and beauty. At times both poems achieve some mild charm and grace.

Edwards' debt to his models is obvious. He salutes Spenser, Daniel, Watson, Marlowe, Shakespeare. Marlowe is his chief creditor, for luxuriant description, arguments against chastity, myth-making, and many incidental phrases. There are over forty clear echoes or imitations of Marlowe's poem, not to mention other possible ones.

1595. John Trussell, Raptus I Helenæ. The first rape of faire Hellen.

> The *Stat. Reg.* (II, 296) gives *Raptus Helenæ* [,] *Helens Rape by the Athenian Duke Theseus*. The poem was edited by M. A. Shaaber, *Shakespeare Quarterly*, VIII (1957), 407–48.

1596. Sir John Davies, Orchestra, or a poeme of dauncing. Text, IX.iv.

1596. Peter Colse, Penelopes complaint.

> For the Shakespearian puzzles connected with this poem see G. B. Harrison's edition of *Willobie his Avisa* (1926) and reviews of the book; F. S. Boas, *Marlowe and His Circle*, pp. 88–89; Chambers, *William Shakespeare*, I, 570.
>
> As verse *Penelopes complaint* is sad stuff. The plan of the numerous sections, and the moralizing, are indebted to *Willobie*; the significant subtitle is "A Mirrour for wanton Minions." The Homeric story is followed, at a distance, so far as it concerns Penelope, Telemachus. the wooers, and the return of Ulysses; Penelope and the wooers are much more articulate than they are in Homer (cf. the very different *Orchestra* of Davies). The letter of Penelope in the *Heroides* is used, and one section seems to be based on the epistle from Ulysses to Penelope which Sabinus added to Ovid (Colse, ed. Grosart, pp. 177–78).

1596. The auncient historie of the destruction of Troy, newly corrected by W. Fiston.

> An edition of Caxton's *Recuyell*.

1596. Dunstan Gale, Pyramus and Thisbe.

> The dedication is dated 1596; no edition is known earlier than that of 1617. The poem is in couplets, divided into forty twelve-line stanzas. A fanciful elaboration of Ovid, describing the childhood of the lovers, the agency of Venus and Cupid, etc. I do not find any certain evidence of a relation to earlier pieces on the same theme. *Venus and Adonis* is alluded to, and Gale's lion, like the boar, only wanted a kiss. There are many echoes and imitations of Marlowe, in the description of Thisbe, in conceits, gnomic lines, etc. The poem is a feeble effort in the conventional Italianate style.

1596. Edmund Spenser, The Faerie Queene [Bks. i–vi]. Text, V. See under 1590.

1597. G. B., Ludus Scacchiæ: Chesse-play. [Anon.] Containing also a poem [a translation of the Ludus Scacchiæ of H. Vida] Written by G. B.

> Vida's poem has a mythological framework. See R. W. Bond, *Poetical Works of William Basse*, pp. xxxix–xl; Brydges, *Brit. Bibl.*, I, 382.

1597. [   ] of Loues complaint; with the legend of Orpheus and Euridice.

> Lownes, the printer, has an epistle to Anthony Gibson (see under 1599). Collier's excerpts from the piece (II, 281–84) suggest the conventional manner. Some satire on women is put in the mouth of Orpheus.

1597. Robert Parry, Sinetes passions uppon his fortunes.

> Related to the story of Sinatus, Sinorix, and Camma? See Hazlitt, p. 697. On pp. xiii ff., in his edition of Robert Chester (see under 1601), Grosart gives extracts from Parry's work.

1598. Samuel Brandon, The tragicomœdi of the vertuous Octauia [and epistles].

> Both drama and epistles (exchanged between Antony and Octavia) are among the manifestations of interest in Garnier's *Marc Antoine* displayed by the Countess of Pembroke's circle. Daniel's *Cleopatra* had appeared in 1594.
>
> The epistles derive of course from Ovid, and more directly from Drayton. Brandon lacks dignity of feeling and style; his Octavia seldom rises above tedious moralizing and shrill nagging.

1598. Christopher Marlowe, Hero and Leander.

> The earliest known edition of Marlowe's fragment. See under 1593.

1598. George Chapman, Hero and Leander.

> An edition of Marlowe's fragment, with Chapman's continuation. Text, X.

1598. John Marston, The metamorphosis of Pigmalions image; and certaine satyres.
Text, IX.i.

1598. Henry Petowe, The second part of Hero and Leander.

> A curious continuation of Marlowe. Petowe states, whether on good authority or not, that Marlowe's work was interrupted by his sudden death. A good part of the poem as well as the preface is taken up with mingled self-depreciation and praise of Marlowe. Petowe professes, doubtless with the license allowed romancers, to have been "inriched by a Gentleman a friend of mine, with the true Italian discourse, of those Louers further Fortunes." The story is a mosaic of well-worn motives of chivalric romance; after a lifetime of felicity the pair undergo an Ovidian metamorphosis. There is an abundance of romantic rhetoric, drawn largely from Tottel's *Miscellany* (see

Rollins' edition of Tottel, II, 112 ff.). There are echoes of Marlowe, a few of *Venus and Adonis;* the idea of Venus' anger at Hero may have come from the tale of Cupid and Psyche, to which Petowe elsewhere alludes. The poem is reprinted in L. Chabalier, *Héro et Léandre* (1911). Extracts are given in Rollins, in Dyce's edition of Marlowe (1858, pp. 398–401); I used the Bodleian copy of Petowe. For a sketch of chapbooks in a similar vein see A. T. Crathern, *MLN*, XLVI (1931), 382.

1598. Thomas Powell, Loues leprosie.

Reprinted by Rimbault, *Ancient Poetical Tracts* (Percy Society, 1842). About 320 ll. in couplets, on the love of Achilles for Polyxena and his death at the hands of Paris. Based probably on Caxton or Lydgate; the style is suggestive of Lydgate on stilts. Along with aureate diction we have (p. 73) at least one distinct echo of *Hero and Leander* (ii.9, etc.).

1599. Samuel Daniel, A letter from Octauia to Marcus Antonius.

Much superior to Brandon's epistles, which may have given Daniel some hints. There is not lacking the note of sober moral earnestness so characteristic of Daniel. On the possible Shakespearian interest of the letter see H. Norgaard, *Notes & Queries*, II (1955), 56–57.

1599. Anthony Gibson, A womans woorth, defended against all the men in the world.

The large claims of the title-page are perhaps slightly weakened by addresses to various Maids of Honor, including Mistress Fitton. The book is translated from the French of the Chevalier de l'Escale (A.M. Clark, *Thomas Heywood*, p. 97). Some seventy authorities are named, from Orpheus to Bandello. The thesis is proved with many brief anecdotes or sayings about Penthesilea, Dido, etc. The section on beauty has a speech by Leander to Hero. Gibson praises Spenser and Daniel.

1599. R. Linche, The fountaine of ancient fiction.
Text, II.ii, and Scott, p. 76.

1599. Thomas Moffett (Moufat, etc.), The silkewormes, and their flies.

A long didactic poem on silkworms, clothes, etc., dedicated to the Countess of Pembroke by a well-known physician attached to her circle. An inset story, in twenty-three stanzas, tells of Pyramus and Thisbe; it seems to be a paraphrase, sometimes close, sometimes free, of Ovid. A marginal note on the metamorphosis refers to Natalis Comes. The latest argument for Shakespeare's use of the poem in *A Midsummer Night's Dream* is by K. Muir, *Shakespeare Quarterly*, V (1954). See also M. Doran (Bibliography, "General") and her further references.

1599. Thomas Nashe, Nashes Lenten stuffe.
Text, XV.

1600. Englands Helicon.

This golden treasury of Elizabethan pastoral verse has been edited by H. Macdonald (London, 1925) and, with full scholarly apparatus, by Hyder E. Rollins (2 vols., Harvard University Press, 1935).

1600. Henry Chettle, The sheepheards song of Venus and Adonis.

This lyrical poem, which used to be ascribed to Henry Constable (see *England's Helicon*, ed. Rollins, II, 133, 180–81), has a special interest because of the verbal parallels between it and Shakespeare's narrative. Most scholars have taken Chettle's presumably later piece to be the debtor.

1600. F. L., Ovidius Naso his remedie of love.

Described by Collier, III, 95. In addition to a freely expanded version of Ovid's poem, there is a translation of the Ovidian epistle of Dido to Aeneas and an answer to it. The answer is said to be the work of "the thrice renowned Sapho of our times," a phrase which suggests the Countess of Pembroke. But it is subscribed "Tout Seule," and the Countess did not become a widow until 1601.

1600. Thomas Middleton, The ghost of Lucrece.

A continuation of Shakespeare's poem, in the same stanza, which came to light in 1920. It was edited by J. Q. Adams (New York and London, 1937).

1600. Samuel Nicholson, Acolastus his after-witte.

Described by Collier (III, 58) as a pastoral poem with flagrant plagiarisms from *Venus and Adonis*, *Lucrece*, some of Shakespeare's plays, and from other authors. See Carpenter, *Reference Guide to Spenser*, p. 247; H. C. Bartlett, *Mr. William Shakespeare* (1922), p. 158.

1600. Cyril Tourneur, The transformed metamorphosis.

This harsh and obscure satire, listed here because of its use of mythology, is discussed by Allardyce Nicoll in his edition of *The Works of Cyril Tourneur* (1930).

1600. John Weever, Faunus and Melliflora; or, the original of our English saytres.

This pastoral-mythological-satirical tale belongs in part to the Ovidian convention and echoes Sidney's *Arcadia*, *Hero and Leander*, *Venus and Adonis*, Spenser, etc. It was edited by A. Davenport (Liverpool University Press, 1948), who had a note, "Weever, Ovid and Shakespeare," in *Notes & Queries*, CXCIV (1949), 524–25, and is discussed by Hallett Smith (Bibliography, "General").

1600. E. W[ilkinson] his Thameseidos.

A pastoral-mythological-topographical poem which "may have imitated Spenser and influenced Drayton" (H. Taylor, *Topographical Poetry in England during the Renaissance, University of Chicago Abstracts of Theses, Humanistic Series*, V, 1926–27, 493–97). It tells

of Neptune's unsuccessful pursuit of the chaste "Thamesis," and the
ravishing of her nymph Medway by a satyr, etc.

1601. **Robert Chester, Loues Martyr; or, Rosalins complaint.**

Ed. Grosart, 1878. The piece opens with a half-medieval assembly
of the gods. A very Italianate anatomical catalogue is put in the mouth
of Dame Nature, who prays to Jove. Chester's work has naturally
been buried under discussion of *The Phoenix and the Turtle.* See
Shakespeare: The Poems, ed. H. E. Rollins (1938).

1602. **Francis Beaumont (?), Salmacis and Hermaphroditus.**
Text, IX.ii.

1602. **The metamorphosis of tabacco.**

Reprinted in Collier, *Illustrations of Early English Popular Literature,* and *Poems of Sir John Beaumont,* ed. Grosart (1869), pp. 275–
321. The poem is apparently accepted as Sir John Beaumont's by
R. J. Kane, *Tobacco in English Literature to 1700* (*Harvard University Summaries of Theses, 1929,* p. 163). A framework of pseudo-
Ovidian myth is used for a light-hearted eulogy of tobacco. Cf. Brathwait, under 1617.

1603. **Hugh Holland, Pancharis.**

A piece in *terza rima,* reprinted in Collier, *Illustrations of Old English Literature,* II. Katharine, widow of Henry V, was so good that
Diana came down to Windsor to see her. Venus also paid a visit, but
was refused admittance. The rest of the poem tells how Venus and
Cupid contrived to make the queen fall in love with Owen Tudor,
and it ends with an Ovidian account of the elements reduced to order
by Love. Chaucer and Lydgate are referred to (p. 34). A tree-list
(pp. 20–21) perhaps alludes to Spenser's February eclogue. (For
some lines by Holland in praise of Spenser, see H. E. Sandison, *MLN,*
XLIV, 161.) A debate on the relative happiness of maid, wife, and
widow (pp. 38 ff.) was doubtless imitated from the playlet by Sir
John Davies which was produced in 1602 and included in the 1608
edition of the *Poetical Rhapsody* (ed. Rollins, 1931, I, 247).

1606? **Michael Drayton, Poemes lyrick and pastorall: odes, eglogs,
the man in the moone.**
Text, VIII.i.

1607. **William Barksted, Mirrha the mother of Adonis, with certain
eclogs by L. M[achin].**
Text, IX.iii.

1607. **W. N., Barley-breake, or a warning for wantons.**

Ed. Grosart, 1877. A pastoral of native and old-fashioned flavor.
The girl Euphema plays at barley-break with her friends. Old Elpin,
disliking the freedoms of young Streton, calls her away, and later,
as a warning, tells her the story of Jupiter and Callisto, in about 230
lines. The author follows Ovid in the main, though he had read

Warner's version (see text, III.v), to which he alludes. Euphema is deaf to the cautionary tale and is betrayed by Streton. When she returns in the same condition as Callisto, Elpin dies, and she stabs herself. Streton, pursued by wild beasts, finds his victim, while birds and beasts crowd around. One bird cries "A rope!" another "Goe hang thee in thy garters!" This last suggestion is followed, and Streton is finished by the birds and flies.

1607.   Richard Niccols, The cuckow.

Fifty-one pages, in couplets, describe the birth of Flora; a gathering of birds to welcome Lady Ver; a contest between the "cuckow," which has sung unchaste songs, and Philomel or Casta, whose themes have been innocent. The contest takes place in a "bower of blisse" thronged by nymphs, ladies, knights, the chief member of the last group being "Vanitie," who is the favorite of the mistress of the bower. In this belated treatment of medieval motives, Philomel tells, in over forty lines, the story of her ravishment. The book has an allusion to Spenser's squire who had such a long search for a chaste woman; and there are other Spenserian echoes. See Carpenter, *Reference Guide*, p. 246; Brydges, *Restituta*, II, 1 ff.; Collier, *Catalogue of Bridgewater House*, p. 220.

1608.   W. Bettie, The historie of Titana and Theseus.

A partly mythological, euphuistic romance, with a plot based largely on Greene's *Pandosto* (J. S. Weld, *PQ*, XXVI, 1947, pp. 36–44).

1609.   F. Baconi De sapientia veterum liber.
Text, XIII.i.

1609.   Thomas Heywood, Troia Britanica, or Great Britaines Troy.
Text, IX.v.

1609.   Edmund Spenser, Two cantos of mutabilitie.
Text, V, and see index.

1610.   Giles Fletcher, Christs victorie, and triumph.
Text, VIII.ii.

1611.   Richard Brathwait, The golden fleece.

A sermon in verse, of about thirty-six pages, "shadowing under this title of Golden Fleece, the reward of a sincere and prouident pilgrim, who with Iason endureth patiently the surging Sea of persecution . . ." Appended elegies on Narcissus and Aeson are cautionary tales based on Ovid.

1611.   George Chapman, The Iliads of Homer.
First complete edition.

1611.   Sir David Murray, The tragicall death of Sophonisba.

Reprinted by the Bannatyne Club, Edinburgh, 1823. Murray evidently took his subject matter from Painter's *Palace of Pleasure*, since the version of Bandello in Painter contains moralizing and rhetorical elements which are absent from Livy's brief account (Livy, bk. xxx, cc. 13–15; Painter, ii.7, vol. II, pp. 236 ff., in Jacobs' ed.). (Bandello, by the way, had followed Livy and the fifth book of Petrarch's *Africa;* see *MLN*, XXXII, 374–75, *MLR*, XX, 191, and XXI, 195.) Murray's twelve hundred lines have a minimum of action and maximum of rhetoric. As befitted both a "Scoto-Brittaine" and a tutor of royalty, Murray was one of the wiser sort who preferred Shakespeare's *Lucrece* to *Venus and Adonis,* and he faithfully follows his model.

1611.   Sands Penven, Ambitions scourge, described in the morall fiction of Ixyon.
  Hazlitt, p. 453. I have not seen this work, but the title is equally suggestive and satisfying.

1606–   William Basse, Urania.
1612.   Text, IX.vi.

1612–   Michael Drayton, Polyolbion.
1622.

1612.   "A booke to be prynted when it is translated and further Alowed. Called. *Les Metamorphoses, D' Ovide De nouueau traduytes en Ffrancois avec. xv. Discours. Contenans L'explication Morales Des fables."*
  Stat. Reg. III, 489. I do not know any record of the book's being published.

1612.   The passionate pilgrime.
  See index.

1613.   H. A. (editor?), The scourge of Venus.
  Ed. Grosart, 1876. Another version of the story of Myrrha. For a clearing-up of the uncritical legend which made "H. A." the Austin whom Heywood denounced for stealing his translations of the *Ars Amatoria* and *De Remedio Amoris,* see A. M. Clark, "Thomas Heywood's 'Art of Love,' " *Library,* Fourth Series, III (1923), 210 ff.
  The 161 six-line stanzas are abundantly padded with dialogue, soliloquy, and psychological analysis of prolix simplicity. The author is not averse to lingering over erotic details, but amply atones by referring to "God's holy Bible" and by expressing horror. The opening lines reveal a debt to *Venus and Adonis,* and the whole poem, wherever it sticks to Ovid, is full of phrases from Golding. It is said to have first appeared in 1613, though the edition of 1614 is the earliest extant; it was, unaccountably, reprinted in 1620.

1613.   William Browne, Britannia's pastorals [bk. i].
  Text, VIII.iii.

1613–   Thomas Milles, The treasurie of auncient and moderne times.
1619.   An immense prose miscellany compiled from Mexia and similar sources. There are classical stories without end. Chapter 33, in the fourth book, rejects the view that the Trojan matter is fabulous, and

appeals to the eyewitnesses Dares and Dictys, as well as to Homer, Herodotus, Euclid. Skeptics are advised to visit the ruins of Troy.

1613. S[amuel] P[age], The love of Amos and Laura.

This non-classical poem (of which the second edition, 1619, was dedicated to Izaak Walton) is included here because of its wholesale plagiarism from *Hero and Leander*. The chief matter of the piece is based on Leander's pleading; there are the usual decorative imitations and dozens of lines echo Marlowe. *Venus and Adonis* also receives some attention.

1614. George Chapman, Andromeda liberata. Or the nuptials of Perseus and Andromeda.

Text, X.

1614. The life and death of Hector.

A modernization, in thirty thousand lines, of Lydgate's *Troy Book*. The attribution to Thomas Heywood has been thoroughly disposed of (J. S. P. Tatlock, *PMLA*, XXX, 691 ff.; A. M. Clark, *TLS*, October 2, 1924, p. 612; *Thomas Heywood*, pp. 340–41; C. A. Rouse, *PMLA*, XLIII, 1928, 779 ff.). To mention only one detail which will illustrate the degree of the writer's literacy, he refers to Petrarch as "Patricke Franke." Now Heywood was the first Englishman to quote the Italian text of Dante (*SP*, XX, 176), and he mentions Petrarch several times (*SP*, *loc. cit.*, and *Exemplary Lives*, p. 99, "the famous Italian Poet, Francis Petrarch"). The *Life and Death* is cheap hack work, but its appearance tells something about popular taste.

1614– J. M., The newe metamorphosis.
1615?

A huge unpublished MS, described, with extracts, by J. H. H. Lyon, *A Study of The Newe Metamorphosis* (Columbia University Press, 1919). It was begun in 1600 and apparently completed about 1614–15. Lyon is inclined to assign the work to Gervase Markham.

It is an extraordinary jumble which "mingles classical figures and motifs with medieval legends, with metrical romances, with the ribald jests of the *fabliau*, with the witchcraft theme, and with the erotic and intricate intrigue of the *novelle*" (Lyon, p. 34). The author's first intention, a pseudo-Ovidian framework, gave way to other devices as he proceeded. A number of poets, such as Sidney and Spenser, are laid under contribution, and *Venus and Adonis* is paralleled "with some closeness."

1615. Richard Brathwait, Loves labyrinth, or the true lovers knot.

In *A Strappado for the Diuell*, ed. Ebsworth (1878), pp. 252 ff. This very long poem deals with "the disastrous fals of two star-crost Louers Pyramus & Thysbe." "Varietie of inuention," if not "proprietie of passion," fills about twenty-three hundred lines. Among un-Ovidian episodes is a meeting between Thisbe and Silvanus, who is a sort of Comus; on her refusing his offers, he asks how a vestal comes to be roaming in the gloaming, and later sends a lion after her. The chief embellishment is rhetoric. "Thysbe address'd to die, yet long in dying," addresses everything in sight, and when her breath has happily departed ten more pages are devoted to lamentations from wood-nymphs and parents.

Erotic pieces in the same volume (*The Ciuill Deuill, Frankes Anatomie, The Wooer*) contain clear echoes of *Hero and Leander*, but Brathwait's talent was too pedestrian and slipshod to learn much from Marlowe. In *Loves labyrinth* he could catch the note of Leander's argument, could strew mythological conceits and gnomic lines everywhere, but these things had become commonplaces. (Hero is mentioned on p. 303; and see pp. 88–89.) Some faint echoes of *Venus and Adonis* appear in the first two of the erotic pieces mentioned, and perhaps in the long poem. In *The English Gentlewoman* (ed. 1641, p. 349), among his precepts for female conduct, Brathwait includes an injunction against reading about Venus and Adonis.

The *Strappado* contains also *The Epistle of Hyppolitus unto Phedra*, in the semi-Ovidian fashion revived by Drayton. Ovid had neglected to write a *suasoria* in favor of chastity, and Brathwait's hero seems to owe something to Seneca's play. His notes in the volume refer twice to Senecan drama, though not to the *Hippolytus*. Cf., in this Appendix, John Shepery's Latin piece of 1586.

1615? George Chapman, Homers Odysses.
       First complete edition.

1615. T[homas] E[vans], Œdipus: Three cantoes. Wherein is contained: 1. His unfortunate infancy. 2. His execrable actions. 3. His lamentable end.
       Palmer, p. 100; Collier, I, 321, and *Catalogue of Bridgewater House*, p. 115.

1616. George Chapman, The divine poem of Musaeus.
       Text, X.

1617. That which seems best is worst. Juvenals tenth satyre: with Virginias death. By W. B[arksted?].
       Text, IX.iii.

1617. R. Brathwait, The smoaking age.
       The section called "The Birth of Tobacco" uses mythology in the manner of the work which doubtless inspired his own, the *Metamorphosis of Tabacco* of 1602. "Tobacco" is an illegitimate son of Bacchus and Proserpine, who is changed by Jove into a plant and by Pluto banished from Hades to earth, where he receives his bad name, derived from that of his father. Brathwait's sentiments are in harmony with his royal master's, and contrary to those of the *Metamorphosis*. See Matthew W. Black, *Richard Brathwait* (Philadelphia, 1928), p. 70.

1617. Leonard Digges, The rape of Proserpine. Translated out of Claudian in Latine, into English verse.

The poem has been edited by H. H. Huxley (Liverpool, 1959). In dedicating the poem to his sister, Digges remarks that it was intended for her "as a Patterne for a piece of Needle-work," for which no poet would be more suggestive than Claudian. The translation sometimes becomes free elaboration, especially in picture-making. Thus two lines (i.257–58) are explained into nearly twenty, and into the embroidery are woven the story of Narcissus and "the thorne-prick't goddesse loue to Adon." The Elizabethan luxuriance is not unattractive.

The three prose prefaces set forth a threefold allegory, historical, natural, allegorical, in the manner of the *Ovide moralisé*, etc. They are taken, with hardly any alteration, and without acknowledgment, from the Italian (*Il Ratto di Proserpina di Claudiano da Giovan Domenico Bevilacqua in ottaua rima tradotto . . . Con gli argomenti, & Allegorie di Antonino Cingale. Palermo, MDLXXXVI*).

1617.   Dunstan Gale, Pyramus and Thisbe.
See under 1596.

1618.   J. Brinsley, Ouids Metamorphosis *tr.* grammatically, etc.
A school version, mentioned here because of its didactic and allegorical notes. See G. W. McClelland, *Schelling Anniversary Papers* (1923), pp. 189 ff., 207.

1618.   James Shirley, Ecc[h]o and Narcissus.
Stat. Reg., III, 618. Text, IX.viii.

1619.   The wisedome of the ancients. *Tr.* Sir A. Gorges.
Translation of Bacon's work of 1609.

1619.   Henry Hutton, Follie's anatomie: or satyres and satyricall epigrams.
Reprinted by Percy Society, 1842. The volume contains "a compendious History of Ixion's Wheele" which is of some slight interest as regards the beginnings of mythological travesties. The piece is in much the same style as the satires, so that, though not strictly a burlesque, it often reads like one:
Hermes did trudge, a iolly foote-mans pase,
T'inuite the Rectors of the Spheres sublime.
The whole poem is gritty with legal jargon. The end is didactic. There is a conventional Shakespearian allusion—"chast Adonis blush"—and a possible echo of Marlowe in the lines "The modest queen . . ." (p. 51).

1620.   The destruction of Troy. *Tr.* out of the second booke of the Aeneads by Sir T. Wrothe.
Quite free and un-Virgilian, according to Collier, IV, 290.

1621.   R. Brathwait, Natures embassie.
Ed. Ebsworth (1877). The book contains a series of didactic satires, or partly satirical sermons, attached to mythological figures, and

modeled perhaps on Bacon's *De Sapientia Veterum*. Through the "deuine Morals" embodied in fable "the very heathen Poets" taught virtue and reproved vice (p. 31).

There followed three "funerall Elegies, concerning sundry exquisite Mirrours of true loue," namely, Hero and Leander, Pyramus and Thisbe, and Dido. The first reveals a trace of Marlowe, and echoes a couplet from Chapman's continuation (Sest. iii, ll. 231–32). The account of Dido uses Virgil and Ovid. Moral lessons are summarized at the end.

Another series of mythological satires follows the same plan as the first. The array of authorities is as heterogeneous as ever, including Gergory's commentary on *Job*, Boethius, Alanus de Insulis. All the pieces are old-fashioned.

1621. George Sandys, The first five bookes of Ovids Metamorphosis.

This supposedly lost book, discovered in 1947, was described by J. G. McManaway, *Papers of the Bibliographical Society* (University of Virginia), I (1948–49), and R. B. Davis (*ibid.*, VIII, 1956).

1622. Patrick Hannay, The nightingale. Sheretine and Mariana, etc.

Reprinted in *Minor Caroline Poets*, I. Preceding the 1,680 lines of *Philomela* is the calm statement that it "is to be sung (by those that please) to the tune set down before in the frontispiece." There is abundant padding, though actual departures from Ovid's story are slight. The opening recalls Gascoigne's tale. Nearly a hundred lines describe the mythological pictures in Philomela's gown. The general style suggests Turberville, and the structure of the stanza is an invitation to bathos which the poet commonly accepts. But, in this poem and *Sheretine*, there are echoes of Marlowe: e.g., p. 626, ll. 361–62; p. 627, l. 432; p. 663, l. 169; p. 665, ll. 269–70. Cf. Marlowe, i.184, ii. 8–9, i.428, i.167–68. For a probable allusion to *Venus and Adonis*, see p. 633, ll. 929 ff.

ca. 1623? On a manuscript, which H. C. H. Candy ascribed to Milton, containing stanzas about Ovidian engravings, see text, XIV, note 11.

1624. Thomas Heywood, Γυναικεῖον.
Text, IX.v, XIII.

1626? (pub. 1651). William Bosworth, The chast and lost lovers . . . Arcadius and Sepha.
Text, IX.vii.

1626. James Gresham, The picture of incest.

Ed. Grosart, 1876. Over seven hundred lines, in couplets, on the story of Myrrha. A number of phrases establish one more debt to Golding. The poem follows Ovid more closely than its predecessors of 1607 and 1613, though speeches are expanded and decorative details added. Gnomic lines are frequent enough to satisfy the moral sense. The most obvious characteristic of Gresham's style is the use of compound epithets, which are of varying success—"her azure-veyned necke"; "sence-delighting-rare-delitiousnesse"; "tree-chang'd-mothers-barke."

1626. George Sandys, Ovid's Metamorphosis.

1628. The true history of the tragicke loves of Hipolito and Isabella, Neapolitans. Englished.

> Taken from *Histoire des tragiques Amours d'Hipolite et d'Isabelle,* 1597 (A. H. Upham, *French Influence,* p. 369). The work, which I have not seen, included "the tale of Narcissus out of Ovid's third booke of his Metamorphosis."

1628. Phineas Fletcher, Venus and Anchises (Brittain's Ida). Text, VIII.ii.

1628. Henry Reynolds, T. Tassos Aminta. Englisht. To this is added Ariadne's complaint in imitation of Anguillara.

> Reynolds, the friend of Drayton, supplies a close link with the Italianate Ovid. *Ariadne's Complaint* is a paraphrase of one of the interpolated passages in Anguillara's "translation" of the *Metamorphoses* (bk. viii, pp. 136 ff., in edition published at Venice, 1575). Anguillara apparently developed his story from the epistle in the *Heroides,* and the episode of Bacchus in the *Fasti* (iii.459–516), perhaps drawing also upon the *Ars Amatoria* (i.527 ff.) and the tale of Olimpia in Ariosto. For details see *MLN,* XLI (1926), 510. Cf. *Narcissus,* below, under 1632.

1632. Martin Parker, The nightingale warbling forth her owne disaster, or, the rape of Philomela.

> The man destined to be a popular laureate here essays a literary flight, and commendatory verses, more candid than tactful, express surprise at the erudition displayed. But, though a detail or two may have come from Ovid, the piece is almost wholly a versification of Pettie's prose tale. For details see *MLN,* XL, 486–88. The bird's singing to the poet in a grove recalls the poems of Gascoigne and Hannay on the same theme. Daniel Price, author of one of the commendatory pieces, died in 1631; see *D.N.B.*

1632. Henry Reynolds, Mythomystes . . . The tale of Narcissus.

> *Mythomystes* was entered and presumably printed in 1632. Reynolds says the poem on Narcissus was "diuerse yeares since, put into English," and that he has paraphrased Ovid "after my owne way," but this piece also is a more or less free paraphrase of Anguillara. Reynolds is at least quite successful in reproducing in English the liquid movement of the Italian. Ovid's 170 lines (*Metam.* iii.341–510) become 504 in Italian, 448 in English. *Narcissus* was reprinted in *Englische Studien,* XXXV (1905), 260 ff., and in the Orinda Booklets (J. R. Tutin, Hull, 1906).
>
> The poem is appended to *Mythomystes* as an illustration of Reyn-

olds' mystical and allegorical theory of poetry. He expounds the geographical, physical, moral, and divine senses of the allegory in the medieval manner of a seventeenth-century Platonist and Cabbalist. See text, XIII.

1632. George Sandys, Ovid's Metamorphosis Englished, mythologiz'd, and represented in figures. An essay to the translation of Virgil's Æneis.
See index.

1633. Abraham Cowley, Poetical blossomes.
Text, IX.ix.

1637. Thomas Heywood, Pleasant dialogues and dramma's.
Text, IX.v, XIII.i.

1637. Shakerley Marmion, A morall poem, intituled the legend of Cupid and Psyche.
Text, XII.i.

1637. John Milton, A maske [Comus] presented at Ludlow Castle, 1634.
Text, XIV.iii.

1638. John Milton, Lycidas.
Text, XIV.iv.

1639. Jean Ogier de Gombauld, Endimion. An excellent fancy, interpreted by R. Hurst.
The plot of this once popular *roman à clef* makes Keats's poem seem meager. Incidentally, we have here an aërial voyage, and Endymion, though devoted to Diana, stirred by the appearance of a mortal maiden whom he had seen before. Rossetti had a copy, and supposed that "Keats had probably never seen it. If he had, he might really have taken a hint or two for his scheme, which is hardly so clear even as Gombauld's, though its endless digressions teem with beauty" (A letter quoted in Hall Caine, *Recollections of D. G. Rossetti*, London, 1882, p. 181). See the poem of Henry Vaughan, *Works*, ed. L. C. Martin, I, 48 (2nd ed., 1957, p. 48).

1639. George Rivers, The heroinæ: or the lives of Arria, Paulina, Lucrecia, Dido, etc.
A prose work dedicated to Lady Dorothy Sidney. The story of Lucrece employs Augustine's famous argument. That of Dido is quite un-Virgilian, and Rivers vindicates her honor by showing that Virgil's matter was fabulous. Each tale is followed by arguments pro and con regarding the problem involved (cf. G. Pettie, in 1576). Verbal quotations show a debt to Heywood's *Gunaikeion* (pp. 128–30) for the story of Aretaphila; Heywood also (p. 152) had given references for the un-Virgilian account of Dido, etc.

1640   James Smith, The innovation of Penelope and Ulysses.
or ear-   Burlesque. Pub. 1658. Text, XV.
lier?

1640.   Thomas Heywood, The exemplary lives and memorable acts
of nine the most worthy women of the world.
Text, IX, v.

Before   Sidney Godolphin, [A translation of part or all of *Aen.* iv].
1642.   Text, XII.ii.

1642.   Sir Francis Kynaston, Leoline and Sydanis.
Minor Caroline Poets, II, 70 ff. This non-classical poem is men-
tioned on account of its abundant mythology and its echoes of Mar-
lowe. E.g., cf. p. 72, ll. 92 ff. (the enamorment), with Marlowe, i.
91–96, 157 ff.; p. 113, l. 1720, with Marlowe, i.338; etc. Finsler
(*Homer in der Neuzeit*, p. 282) remarks: "Für die Trojasage verweist
Kynaston ausdrücklich auf Dares." There is an occasional echo of
Spenser.

1642.   Alexander Ross, Mel Heliconium.
Text, XIII.

1646.   John Milton, Poems, both English and Latin.

1646.   J. Shirley, Narcissus.
See under 1618.

1647.   Alexander Ross, Mystagogus Poeticus.
Text, XIII.

1647.   Thomas Stanley, Poems and translations.
The volume contained translations from Theocritus, Ausonius, etc.,
reprinted, with many omissions and additions, in 1651.

1647.   Sir Robert Stapylton, Musaeus on the loves of Hero and Leander.
This formal translation may be mentioned because, while the author does not seem to have known Marlowe—at any rate does not
mention or echo him—he frequently echoes Chapman's translation of
1616. Natalis Comes is quoted in the notes. The volume also contained
versions of the two epistles of Ovid on Hero and Leander.

1648.   Sir Richard Fanshawe, Il Pastor Fido . . . with an addition
of divers other poems.
The volume contained a translation of *Aen.* iv. Text, XII.ii.

1649.   Robert Baron, An apologie for Paris.
Ninety-six pages of prose tell of the judgment of Paris in the vein
of pastoral romance. There is a long prose version of the story in a
French Ovid of 1539 (above, III, note 7), pp. 9–24; though Baron
does not seem to owe anything specific to it he may have used it or some

similar elaboration. His particular figures for the forces of Greeks and Trojans testify to the spirit of Dictys and Dares (the figures differ in many books; cf. Burton, *Anatomy*, Bohn's Popular Library, I, 59). Apart from quotations the tale has obvious echoes of Warner, *Venus and Adonis, Henry IV*, Pt. I, etc.

Baron's notorious piece of plagiarism, *The Cyprian Academy* (1647), had contained abundant mythology, including pictures of Daphne and Apollo, Venus and Adonis, Hero and Leander.

1651. William Bosworth, Arcadius and Sepha.
       See under 1626.

1651. Thomas Hall, Wisdoms conquest, or, an explanation of the thirteenth book of Ovids Metamorphoses, containing that curious and rhetoricall contest between Ajax and Ulysses, for Achilles armour: where is set forth to the life the power of valour, and the prevalence of eloquence.
       An edifying work by a schoolmaster, citing such authorities as Sabinus, Golding, Sandys. "The scope and drift of this Fable and fiction is, to shew the folly of those, who preferre Strength before Policy, Warriours before Scholars, and Weapons before Wisdome," etc. See under 1655.

1651. The lovs of Hero and Leander.
       Travesty. Text, XV.

1651. Sir Edward Sherburne, Salmacis . . . the rape of Helen, etc.
       Text, XII.iii.

1651. Thomas Stanley, Anacreon. Bion. Moschus, etc.
       Text, XII.iii, and see under 1647.

1652. The gallery of heroick women. Written in French by Peter Le Moyne, of the Society of Jesus. *Tr.* into English by the Marquesse of Winchester.
       A collection of tales, with moral reflections, from *La Gallerie des Femmes Fortes*, Paris, 1647. Among the classical heroines are Panthea, Camma, Artemisia, Zenobia, Lucrece, etc.

1655. Thomas Hall, Phaetons folly, or, the downfal of pride: being a translation of the second book of Ovids Metamorphosis . . . where is lively set forth the danger of pride and rashness, with the safety of moderation . . .
       A schoolbook, with moral lessons. Natalis Comes is referred to.

1655. The rape of Lucrece, committed by Tarquin the sixt; and the remarkable judgments that befel him for it. By . . . Will. Shakespeare gent. Whereunto is annexed, the banishment of Tarquin: or, the reward of lust. By J. Quarles.

For data and a reprint of the text see Shakespeare's *Poems*, ed. Rollins, pp. 411–13, 439–46.

1658. N. Billingsley, ΚΟΣΜΟΒΡΕΦΙΑ, or the infancy of the world . . . with a taste of poetical fictions.

The latter section is an ample taste in the form of a series of poems on Jupiter, Apollo, and other mythological figures, apparently based on Cartari or some such book. One religious poem, *Genethliacon*, seems to be an imitation of Milton's *Nativity*.

1658. The passion of Dido for Æneas, translated by Edmund Waller and Sidney Godolphin.
Text, XII.ii.

1658. John Jones, Ovid's invective or curse against Ibis . . . translated . . . and the histories therein contained . . . briefly explained . . . with natural, moral, poetical, political, mathematical, and some few theological applications.

A number of interpretations are taken from Natalis Comes. Sandys is sometimes cited, and his explanation of the tale of Tereus and Progne is used (see text, III, note 34). It was presumably the same Jones who translated *Hero and Leander* (*Notes and Queries*, Third Series, VII, 435).

1658. James Smith, The innovation of Penelope and Ulysses.
Burlesque. See under 1640.

1660. Philander, The history of Tarquin and Lucretia.
Hazlitt, p. 456.

1664. Charles Cotton, Scarronides; or Virgile travestie.
Text, XV.

1664. James Scudamore, Homer à la mode.
Travesty. Text, XV.

1665. Charles Cotton, Scarronides.
Including travesty of *Aen.* iv. Text, XV.

1665. Lanii triumphantes, or the butchers prize. Being a description of the famous battel, between Achilles, a butcher of Greece, and Hector, a weaver of Troy, occasion'd by the rape of a daughty damosell y-clep'd Hellen the bright.

Obviously a travesty. The title is quoted from Catalogue No. 265, Pt. x, of Pickering & Chatto (item 8497).

1665. R. Mounsey, Scarronides: or, Virgil travestie.
Text, XV. Hazlitt, p. 403.

1665. Typhon, or the gyants war with the gods.
Travesty. Text, XV.

1667.   John Milton, Paradise lost.
Text, XIV.v.

1669.   W. Wycherley (?), Hero and Leander.
Travesty. Text, XV.

1671.   John Milton, Paradise regain'd: Samson Agonistes.
Text, XIV.vi.

1672.   Cataplus, or Aeneas his descent into hell.
Travesty.

1672.   Chaucer's ghoast: or, a piece of antiquity. Containing twelve
pleasant fables of Ovid penn'd after the ancient manner of
writing in England. Which makes them prove mock-poems
to the present poetry . . . By a lover of antiquity.
     The tales are those of Pygmalion; Actaeon; Jupiter, Juno, and
Tiresias; Apollo and Coronis, etc. This precious lover of antiquity
should have been haunted by the ghosts of both Chaucer and Gower,
for the tales are lifted from the *Confessio Amantis* "with few and
slight modernizations, but enough to render them easily intelligible"
(Lounsbury, *Studies in Chaucer*, III, 118–19). See Caroline Spurgeon,
Five Hundred Years of Chaucer Criticism and Allusion, I, 248.

1672.   John Phillips, The Maronides, or Virgil travesty.
     A translation of the fifth book of Scarron; followed in 1673 by a
translation of the sixth. Text, XV.

1673.   Ovidius exulans.
Travesty. Text, XV.

1675.   Charles Cotton, The scoffer scofft.
Travesty. Text, XV.

1680.   The wits paraphras'd.
Travesty. Text, XV.

1680.   Alexander Radcliffe, Ovid travestie.
Text, XV.

Bibliography

Although this book owes much to general scholarship and criticism, this bibliography is necessarily limited, with a few exceptions, to items directly concerned with the uses of mythology and to a selection from them. Since the book was first published in 1932 much of the older material has been gathered up in such works as the Variorum Edition of Spenser, Hyder E. Rollins' edition of Shakespeare's poems, and the like, and much will be assembled in the forthcoming variorum commentary on Milton. In the present skeleton list references pertaining to more than one chapter are mostly put in the first general section.

Abbreviations used in the notes, appendix, and bibliography are: *E.E.T.S.*, Early English Text Society; *ELH, English Literary History; JEGP, Journal of English and Germanic Philology; MLN, Modern Language Notes; MLR, Modern Language Review; MP, Modern Philology; PMLA, Publications of the Modern Language Association of America; PQ, Philological Quarterly; RES, Review of English Studies; SP, Studies in Philology; STC, Short-Title Catalogue . . . 1475–1640*, ed. A. W. Pollard and G. R. Redgrave (London, 1926); *TLS, London Times Literary Supplement.*

One may refer to the annual bibliographies in *SP, PMLA*, and *PQ*, and to that published by the Modern Humanities Research Association.

GENERAL

Amos, Flora R., *Early Theories of Translation.* Columbia University Press, 1920.

Baldensperger, F., and W. P. Friederich, *Bibliography of Comparative Literature.* University of North Carolina Press, 1950.

Baldwin, Thomas W., *William Shakspere's Small Latine & Lesse Greeke.* 2 vols. University of Illinois Press, 1944.

Boccaccio, Giovanni, *De Genealogia Deorum* (ed. Venice, 1511); *Genealogie Deorum Gentilium Libri*, ed. V. Romano. 2 vols. Bari, 1951.

Bolgar, R. R., *The Classical Heritage and Its Beneficiaries*. Cambridge University Press, 1954.

Bradbrook, M. C., *Shakespeare and Elizabethan Poetry*. London, 1951.

Brewer, Wilmon, *Ovid's Metamorphoses in European Culture*. 3 vols. Boston and Francestown, N.H., 1933–57.

Brown, Huntington, "The Classical Tradition in English Literature: A Bibliography." *Harvard Studies and Notes in Philology and Literature,* XVIII (1935), 7–46.

Brydges, Sir Egerton, *The British Bibliographer*. 4 vols. London, 1810–14.

————, *Censura Literaria*. 10 vols. London, 1805–09.

————, *Restituta*. 4 vols. London, 1814–16.

Bush, Douglas, *Classical Influences in Renaissance Literature*. Harvard University Press, 1952.

————, *English Literature in the Earlier Seventeenth Century 1600–1660* (with general and individual bibliographies). Revised edition. Clarendon Press, 1962.

Cambridge Bibliography of English Literature, ed. F. W. Bateson. 4 vols. Cambridge University Press, 1940. *Supplement,* ed. G. Watson, 1957.

Cartari, V., *Vincentii Chartarii Rhegiensis Imagines Deorum*. Moguntiae [Mainz], 1687.

Caxton, William, *Eneydos*, ed. W. T. Culley and F. J. Furnivall. E.E.T.S., 1890.

————, *Recuyell of the Historyes of Troye*, ed. O. Sommer. 2 vols. London, 1894.

Collier, John Payne, *A Bibliographical and Critical Account of the Rarest Books in the English Language*. 4 vols. New York, 1866.

————, *Illustrations of Old English Literature*. 3 vols. London, 1866.

Comes, Natalis [Natale Conti], *Mythologiae*. Patavii [Padua], 1616.

Doran, Madeleine, "Pyramus and Thisbe Once More." *Essays on Shakespeare and Elizabethan Drama in Honor of Hardin Craig*. University of Missouri Press, 1962, pp. 149–61.

Edelstein, L., "The Golden Chain of Homer." *Studies in Intellectual History* (Johns Hopkins Press, 1953), pp. 48–66.

Finsler, Georg, *Homer in der Neuzeit von Dante bis Goethe*. Leipzig and Berlin, 1912.

Foster, Finley M. K., *English Translations from the Greek*. Columbia University Press, 1918.

Friederich, W. P., et al., *Yearbook of Comparative and General Literature*. University of North Carolina Press, 1952 ff.

Fulgentius, Fabius Planciades, *Mythologiae* and *Liber de Expositione Virgilianae Continentiae*, in *Mythographi Latini*, ed. T. Muncker, Amsterdam, 1681.

Galinsky, Hans, *Der Lucretia-Stoff in der Weltliteratur*. Breslau, 1932.

Genouy, Hector, *L'élément pastoral dans la poésie narrative et le drame en Angleterre, de 1570 à 1640*. Paris, 1928.

Gordon, George S., ed., *English Literature and the Classics*. Clarendon Press, 1912.

————, "Virgil in English Poetry." *Proceedings of the British Academy*, XVII (1931); *The Discipline of Letters*. Clarendon Press, 1946.

Greg, Sir Walter W., *Pastoral Poetry and Pastoral Drama*. London, 1906.

Gruppe, Otto, *Geschichte der klassischen Mythologie und Religionsgeschichte während des Mittelalters im Abendland und während der Neuzeit.* Leipzig, 1921.

Hazlitt, William C., *Hand-Book to the Popular, Poetical, and Dramatic Literature of Great Britain.* London, 1867.

Highet, Gilbert, *The Classical Tradition: Greek and Roman Influences on Western Literature.* Oxford University Press, 1949.

Hoffmann, Adolf, *Das Psyche-Märchen des Apuleius in der englischen Literatur.* Strassburg, 1908.

Hutton, James, "The First Idyl of Moschus in Imitations to the Year 1800." *American Journal of Philology,* XLIX (1928), 105–36; supplemented by J. G. Fucilla, *Classical Philology,* XXVI (1931), 135–52.

Jacobsen, Eric, *Translation: A Traditional Craft.* Copenhagen, 1958.

Jellinek, Max H., *Die Sage von Hero und Leander in der Dichtung.* Berlin, 1890.

Jiriczek, Otto L., ed., *Specimens of Tudor Translations from the Classics.* Heidelberg, 1923.

Lascelles, Mary, "The Rider on the Winged Horse." *Elizabethan and Jacobean Studies Presented to Frank Percy Wilson* (Clarendon Press, 1959), pp. 173–98.

Lathrop, Henry B., *Translations from the Classics into English from Caxton to Chapman 1477–1620.* University of Wisconsin Press, 1933.

Lewis, C. S., *The Allegory of Love: A Study in Medieval Tradition.* Clarendon Press, 1936; corrected reprint, 1938.

———, *English Literature in the Sixteenth Century, excluding Drama* (with general and individual bibliographies). Clarendon Press, 1954.

Lydgate's Troy Book, ed. H. Bergen. 4 vols. E.E.T.S., 1906–35.

Mackail, John W., *The Springs of Helicon.* New York, 1909.

McPeek, James A. S., *Catullus in Strange and Distant Britain.* Harvard University Press, 1939.

Miller, P. W., "The Elizabethan Minor Epic." *SP,* LV (1958), 31–35.

Nitchie, Elizabeth, *Vergil and the English Poets.* Columbia University Press, 1919.

Le Metamorfosi di Ovidio, Ridotte da Giouanni Andrea dell' Anguillara, in ottaua rima, impressione quinta. Venice, 1575.

Ovid's Metamorphosis Englished, Mythologiz'd, and Represented in Figures, by George Sandys. Oxford, 1632.

Palmer, Henrietta R., *List of English Editions and Translations of Greek and Latin Classics Printed before 1641.* London, 1911.

Panofsky, Dora and Erwin, *Pandora's Box: The Changing Aspects of a Mythological Symbol.* New York, 1956; rev. ed., 1962.

Panofsky, Erwin, *Studies in Iconology: Humanistic Themes in the Art of the Renaissance.* Oxford University Press, 1939.

Papajewski, H., "Die literarische Wertung Ovids am Ausgang des 17. und zu Beginn des 18. Jahrhunderts." *Anglia,* 78 (1960), 422–48.

Rand, Edward K., *Ovid and His Influence.* Boston, 1925; New York, 1928.

Rick, Leo, *Ovids Metamorphosen in der englischen Renaissance.* Münster i. W., 1915.

Sandys, Sir John E., *A History of Classical Scholarship.* 3 vols. Cambridge University Press, 1903–08.

Schirmer, Walter F., *Antike, Renaissance und Puritanismus.* Munich, 1924; rev. ed., 1933.

Scott, Mary A., *Elizabethan Translations from the Italian.* Boston, 1916.

Seznec, Jean, *La survivance des dieux antiques: essai sur la rôle de la tradition mythologique dans l'humanisme et dans l'art de la renaissance.* London, 1940. Trans. as *The Survival of the Pagan Gods.* New York, 1953; reprint 1961.

Smith, Hallett, *Elizabethan Poetry: A Study in Conventions, Meaning, and Expression.* Harvard University Press, 1952.

Soellner, Rolf, "The Madness of Hercules and the Elizabethans." *Comparative Literature,* X (1958), 309–24.

Starnes, DeWitt T., and E. W. Talbert, *Classical Myth and Legend in Renaissance Dictionaries.* University of North Carolina Press, 1955.

Stanford, W. B., *The Ulysses Theme: A Study in the Adaptability of a Traditional Hero.* Oxford and New York, 1954.

Steadman, J. M., " 'Perseus upon Pegasus' and *Ovid Moralized.*" *RES,* IX (1958), 407–10.

Stevens, L. C., "A Re-evaluation of Hellenism in the French Renaissance," *SP,* LVIII (1961), 115–29.

Tatlock, J. S. P., "The Siege of Troy in Elizabethan Literature." *PMLA,* XXX (1915), 673–770.

> Thomson, J. A. K., *The Classical Background of English Literature.* London, 1948.

———, *Classical Influences on English Poetry.* London, 1951.

Warton, Thomas, *History of English Poetry,* ed. W. C. Hazlitt. 4 vols. London, 1871.

Wilkinson, L. P., *Ovid Recalled.* Cambridge University Press, 1955.

Williams, Arnold, *The Common Expositor* (University of North Carolina Press, 1948), chap. xii, "The Classics."

Wind, Edgar, *Pagan Mysteries in the Renaissance.* Yale University Press, 1958.

Wirl, Julius, *Orpheus in der englischen Literatur. Wiener Beiträge,* XL (1913).

Wittkower, Rudolf, "Transformations of Minerva in Renaissance Imagery." *Journal of the Warburg Institute,* II (1938–39), 194–205.

Wolff, Emil, *Die goldene Kette. Die aurea catena Homeri in der englischen Literatur.* Hamburg, 1947.

Wright, C. T., "The Amazons in Elizabethan Literature." *SP,* XXXVII (1940), 433–56.

Zocca, Louis R., *Elizabethan Narrative Poetry.* Rutgers University Press, 1950.

CHAPTER I

Benoit de Sainte-Maure, *Le Roman de Troie,* ed. L. Constans. 5 vols. Paris, 1904–12.

> Born, L. K., "Ovid and Allegory." *Speculum,* IX (1934), 362–79.

Bourne, Ella, "Classical Elements in the *Gesta Romanorum.*" *Vassar Mediæval Studies.* Yale University Press, 1923.

———, "The Mediæval Wanderings of a Greek Myth." *JEGP,* XXIV (1925), 184–94.

Callan, Norman, "Thyn Owne Book: A Note on Chaucer, Gower and Ovid." *RES,* XXII (1946), 269–81.

Chaucer, *Complete Works of Geoffrey*, ed. F. N. Robinson. 2nd ed. Boston, 1957.

Chaucer, Geoffrey, *The Book of Troilus and Criseyde*, ed. R. K. Root. Princeton University Press, 1926.

Comparetti, Domenico, *Vergil in the Middle Ages*, trans. E. F. M. Benecke. London and New York, 1895.

Constans, L., "L'épopée antique." *Histoire de la langue et de la littérature française*, ed. Petit de Julleville, I (Paris, 1896), 171–253.

Cooke, J. D., "Euhemerism: A Mediaeval Interpretation of Classical Paganism." *Speculum*, II (1927), 396–410.

Coulter, C. C., "Boccaccio's Acquaintance with Homer." *PQ*, V (1926), 44–53.

Crosland, J., " 'Eneas' and the 'Aeneid.' " *MLR*, XXIX (1934), 282–90.

———, "Ovid's Contribution to the Conception of Love Known as 'L'Amour Courtois.' " *MLR*, XLII (1947), 199–206.

Curry, Walter C., "Astrologising the Gods." *Anglia*, XLVII (1923), 213–43.

———, "The Judgment of Paris." *MLN*, XXXI (1916), 114–16.

> Curtius, Ernst R., *European Literature and the Latin Middle Ages*, trans. W. R. Trask. New York, 1953.

Dares Phrygius, *De Excidio Troiae Historia*, ed. F. Meister. Leipzig, 1873.

Davies, C., "Notes on the Sources of 'Sir Orfeo.' " *MLR*, XXXI (1936), 354–57.

Dictys Cretensis, *Ephemeris de Historia Belli Troiani*, ed. F. Meister. Leipzig, 1872.

Donovan, M. J., "The Image of Pluto and Proserpine in The Merchant's Tale." *PQ*, XXXVI (1957), 49–60.

Eneas: roman du XIIe siècle, ed. J.-J. S. de Grave. 2 vols. Paris, 1925–29.

Faral, Edmond, *Les arts poétiques du XIIe et du XIIIe siècle*. Paris, 1924.

———, *Recherches sur les sources latines des contes et romans courtois du moyen age*. Paris, 1913.

Ghisalberti, F., "L' «Ovidius Moralizatus» di Pierre Bersuire." *Studi Romanzi*, XXIII (1933), 5–136.

Green, R. H., "Classical Fable and English Poetry in the Fourteenth Century." *Critical Approaches to Medieval Literature*, ed. D. Bethurum (Columbia University Press, 1960), pp. 110–33.

Griffin, Nathaniel E., *Dares and Dictys*. Baltimore, 1907.

———, "Un-Homeric Elements in the Medieval Story of Troy." *JEGP*, VII (1907–08), 32–52.

Griffin, N. E., and A. E. Beckwith, eds., *The Filostrato of Giovanni Boccaccio*. University of Pennsylvania Press, 1929.

Haskins, Charles H., *The Renaissance of the Twelfth Century*. Harvard University Press, 1928; reprint, New York, 1957.

Haynes, French, *Shakespeare and the Troy Story. Howard College Bulletin*, LXXX, No. 3 (1922), 67–131.

Hill, A. A., "The Traditional Development of a Character" [Diomede]. *Essays and Studies in English and Comparative Literature by Members of the English Department of the University of Michigan* (University of Michigan Press, 1932), pp. 1–25.

Knowlton, Edgar C., "Notes on Early Allegory." *JEGP*, XXIX (1930), 159–81.

Krey, A. C., "John of Salisbury's Knowledge of the Classics." *Transactions of the Wisconsin Academy of Sciences, Arts and Letters,* XVI, Part 2 (1910), 948–87.

Manitius, M., "Beiträge zur Geschichte des Ovidius und andrer römischer Schriftsteller im Mittelalter." *Philologus,* Supplementband VII (1899), 723–68.

Meech, S. B., "Chaucer and an Italian Translation of the *Heroides*." *PMLA,* XLV (1930), 110–28.

——, "Chaucer and the *Ovide Moralisé*—a Further Study." *PMLA,* XLVI (1931), 182–204.

Miller, F. J., "Ovid's *Aeneid* and Vergil's." *Classical Journal,* XXIII (1927–28), 33–43.

Munari, Franco, *Ovid im Mittelalter (Lebendige Antike).* Zurich and Stuttgart, 1960.

Osgood, Charles G., *Boccaccio on Poetry.* Princeton University Press, 1930.

Ovide Moralisé, ed. C. de Boer. *Verhandelingen der Koninklijke Akademie van Wetenschappen te Amsterdam.* Afdeeling Letterkunde, Nieuwe Reeks, Deel XV, 1916 ff.

Philomena, ed. C. de Boer. Paris, 1909.

Piramus et Tisbé, ed. C. de Boer. Paris, 1921.

Rand, E. K., "The Classics in the Thirteenth Century." *Speculum,* IV (1929), 249–69.

Root, R. K., "Chaucer's Dares." *MP,* XV (1917–18), 1–22.

Schirmer, Walter F., *John Lydgate: A Study in the Culture of the XVth Century,* trans. A. E. Keep. London, 1961.

Sedgwick, W. B., "The *Bellum Troianum* of Joseph of Exeter." *Speculum,* V (1930), 49–76.

The Seege or Batayle of Troye, ed. M. E. Barnicle. E.E.T.S., 1927.

Shannon, Edgar F., *Chaucer and the Roman Poets.* Harvard University Press, 1929.

Sir Orfeo, ed. A. J. Bliss. Oxford University Press, 1954.

Spargo, John W., *Virgil the Necromancer: Studies in Virgilian Legends.* Harvard University Press, 1934.

Wilkins, E. H., "Descriptions of Pagan Divinities from Petrarch to Chaucer." *Speculum,* XXXII (1957), 511–22.

CHAPTER II

Bush, Douglas, "The Classical Tales in Painter's *Palace of Pleasure*." *JEGP,* XXIII (1924), 331–41.

——, *The Renaissance and English Humanism.* University of Toronto Press, 1939; slightly rev., 1956.

Campbell, P. G. C., "Christine de Pisan en Angleterre." *Revue de littérature comparée,* V (1925), 659–70.

Caxton, William, *Ovyde Hys Booke of Methamorphose,* ed. S. Gaselee and H. F. B. Brett-Smith. Oxford, 1924.

Christine de Pisan, *The Epistle of Othea to Hector,* trans. S. Scrope, ed. G. F. Warner, Roxburghe Club, 1904; another translation, ed. J. D. Gordon, Philadelphia, 1942.

Clark, A. C., "The Reappearance of the Texts of the Classics." *Library,* Fourth Series, II (1922), 13–42.

Conley, Carey H., *The First English Translators of the Classics*. Yale University Press, 1927.
Coulter, C. C., "The Genealogy of the Gods." *Vassar Mediæval Studies*. Yale University Press, 1923.
Dearing, Bruce, "Gavin Douglas's *Eneados:* A Reinterpretation." *PMLA*, LXVII (1952), 845–62.
Gilmore, Myron P., *The World of Humanism 1453–1517*. New York, 1952.
Gordon, George S., "The Trojans in Britain." *Essays and Studies by Members of the English Association*, IX (1924), 9–30; *The Discipline of Letters*. Clarendon Press, 1946.
Greenlaw, Edwin, "The Battle of the Books." *Studies in Spenser's Historical Allegory*. Johns Hopkins Press, 1932.
Hall, Louis B., "An Aspect of the Renaissance in Gavin Douglas' *Eneados*." *Studies in the Renaissance*, VII (1960), 184–92.
Hunter, G. K., *John Lyly: The Humanist as Courtier*. London, 1960.
Kendrick, Sir Thomas D., *British Antiquity*. London, 1950.
Kristeller, Paul O., *Renaissance Thought: The Classic, Scholastic, and Humanist Strains*. New York, 1961.
Laigle, Mathilde, *Le livre des trois vertus de Christine de Pisan*. Paris, 1912.
Parsons, A. E., "The Trojan Legend in England." *MLR*, XXIV (1929), 253–64, 394–408.
Pinet, M. J., *Christine de Pisan*. Paris, 1927.
Schirmer, Walter F., *Der englische Frühhumanismus*. Leipzig, 1931.
Shackford, Martha H., *Plutarch in Renaissance England*. Wellesley College, 1929.
Stephens, George R., *The Knowledge of Greek in England in the Middle Ages*. Philadelphia, 1933.
Tilley, Arthur, "Greek Studies in England in the Early Sixteenth Century." *English Historical Review*, LIII (1938), 221–39, 438–56.
Tilley, M. P., "*Euphues* and Ovid's *Heroical Epistles*." *MLN*, XLV (1930), 301–08.
Weiss, R., *Humanism in England During the Fifteenth Century*. Oxford, 1941.
———, "The Study of Greek in England during the Fourteenth Century." *Rinascimento*, II (1951), 209–39.
Wolff, Samuel L., *The Greek Romances in Elizabethan Prose Fiction*. Columbia University Press, 1912; reprint, New York, 1961.

CHAPTER III

Baker, Herschel C., "Classical Material in Broadside Ballads, 1550–1625." *PMLA*, LIV (1939), 981–89.
Bush, Douglas, "Classical Lives in *The Mirror for Magistrates*." *SP*, XXII (1925), 256–66.
Dowling, H. M., "Miscellaneous Notes on Peele." *Notes and Queries*, CLXV (1933), 272–74.
Ekeblad, I.-S., "On the Background of Peele's 'Araygnement of Paris.'" *Notes and Queries*, III (1956), 246–49.
Hart, Georg, *Ursprung und Verbreitung des Pyramus-und-Thisbe-Sage*. Passau, 1889.
———, *Die Pyramus-&-Thisbe-Sage in Holland, England, Italien, & Spanien*. Passau, 1891.

Huf, Hans, *William Warner, Albion's England. Quellenuntersuchungen zu den ersten Büchern.* Munich, 1912.

Peele, *The Life and Minor Works of George*, ed. David H. Horne. Yale University Press, 1952.

Reeves, J. D., "The Judgment of Paris as a Device of Tudor Flattery." *Notes and Queries*, I (1954), 7–11.

——, "The Cause of the Trojan War, according to Peele." *Notes and Queries*, II (1955), 333.

Rodger, Gillian, "Hero and Leander in Scottish Balladry." *Comparative Literature*, IX (1957), 1–16.

Rollins, Hyder E., "An Analytical Index to the Ballad-Entries in the Registers of the Company of Stationers of London." *SP*, XXI (1924), 1–324.

——, "The Troilus-Cressida Story from Chaucer to Shakespeare." *PMLA*, XXXII (1917), 383–429.

CHAPTER IV

Belloni, Antonio, *Il poema epico e mitologico*. Milan, 1912.

Cooper, Clyde B., *Some Elizabethan Opinions of the Poetry and Character of Ovid*. Menasha, 1914.

Flamini, Francesco, *Studi di storia letteraria italiana e straniera*. Livorno, 1895.

Rick, Leo (see "General").

Schevill, Rudolph, *Ovid and the Renascence in Spain*. University of California Press, 1913.

Staton, Walter F., "The Influence of Thomas Watson on Elizabethan Love Poetry." *Studies in the Renaissance*, VI (1959), 243–50.

Witz, E., *Die englischen Ovidübersetzungen des 16. Jahrhunderts*. Leipzig, 1915.

CHAPTER V

Cumming, W. P., "The Influence of Ovid's *Metamorphoses* on Spenser's 'Mutabilitie' Cantos." *SP*, XXVIII (1931), 241–56.

Durling, Robert M., "The Bower of Bliss and Armida's Palace." *Comparative Literature*, VI (1954), 335–47.

Evans, Maurice, "Platonic Allegory in *The Faerie Queene*." *RES*, XII (1961), 132–43.

Hamilton, A. C., *The Structure of Allegory in The Faerie Queene*. Clarendon Press, 1961.

Hughes, Merritt Y., "Spenser and the Greek Pastoral Triad." *SP*, XX (1923), 184–215.

——, *Virgil and Spenser*. University of California Press, 1929.

——, "Virgilian Allegory and *The Faerie Queene*." *PMLA*, XLIV (1929), 696–705.

——, "Spenser's Acrasia and the Circe of the Renaissance." *Journal of the History of Ideas*, IV (1943), 381–99.

Lemmi, C. W., "The Symbolism of the Classical Episodes in *The Faerie Queene*." *PQ*, VIII (1929), 270–87.

Lewis, C. S. (see "General").

Lotspeich, Henry G., *Classical Mythology in the Poetry of Edmund Spenser*. Princeton University Press, 1932.

MacLure, Millar, "Nature and Art in *The Faerie Queene.*" *ELH*, XXVIII (1961), 1–20.
The Works of Edmund Spenser: A Variorum Edition, ed. E. Greenlaw, C. G. Osgood, F. M. Padelford, et al. 10 vols. John Hopkins Press, 1932–57.
Starnes, D. T., and E. W. Talbert (see "General").
Steadman, J. M., "Spenser's *Errour* and the Renaissance Allegorical Tradition." *Neuphilologische Mitteilungen*, LXII (1961), 22–38.
Williams, K., "Venus and Diana: Some Uses of Myth in *The Faerie Queene.*" *ELH*, XXVIII (1961), 101–20.
Woodhouse, A. S. P., "Nature and Grace in *The Faerie Queene.*" *ELH*, XVI (1949), 194–228.

CHAPTER VI

Bakeless, J. M., *The Tragicall History of Christopher Marlowe*. 2 vols. Harvard University Press, 1942.
Baldwin, T. W., "Marlowe's Musaeus." *JEGP*, LIV (1955), 478–85.
Chabalier, L., *Héro et Léandre*. Paris, 1911.
Fraser, R. A., "The Art of *Hero and Leander.*" *JEGP*, LVII (1958), 743–54.
Jacobsen, Eric (see "General").
Jellinek, M. H. (see "General").
Lazarus, Gertrud, *Technik und Stil von Hero und Leander*. Bonn, 1915.
Levin, Harry, *The Overreacher: A Study of Christopher Marlowe*. Harvard University Press, 1952.
Marlowe's Poems, ed. L. C. Martin. London and New York, 1931.
Miller, P. W., "A Function of Myth in Marlowe's 'Hero and Leander.' " *SP*, L (1953), 158–67.
Poirier, Michel, *Christopher Marlowe*. London, 1951.
Smith, Hallett (see "General").

CHAPTER VII

Allen, Don C., "On *Venus and Adonis.*" *Elizabethan and Jacobean Studies Presented to Frank Percy Wilson* (Clarendon Press, 1959), pp. 100–11.
————, "Some Observations on *The Rape of Lucrece.*" *Shakespeare Survey*, XV (1962), 89–98.
Baldwin, Thomas W., *On the Literary Genetics of Shakspere's Poems & Sonnets*. University of Illinois Press, 1950.
Bullough, Geoffrey, ed., *Narrative and Dramatic Sources of Shakespeare*, I. London and Columbia University Press, 1957.
Bush, Douglas, "Classical Myth in Shakespeare's Plays." In *Studies*, cited under Allen, pp. 65–85.
Dickey, F. M., *Not Wisely But Too Well: Shakespeare's Love Tragedies* (Huntington Library, 1957), chap. V.
Hamilton, A. C., "Venus and Adonis." *Studies in English Literature*, I.i (1961), 1–15.
Hatto, A. T., " 'Venus and Adonis'—and the Boar." *MLR*, XLI (1946), 353–61.
Jackson, R. S., "Narrative and Imagery in Shakespeare's *Venus and Adonis.*" *Papers of the Michigan Academy of Science, Arts and Letters*, XLIII (1958), 315–20.
Miller, R. P., "Venus, Adonis, and the Horses." *ELH*, XIX (1952), 249–64.

———, "The Myth of Mars' Hot Minion in *Venus and Adonis*." *ELH*, XXVI (1959), 470–81.

Palmatier, M. A., "A Suggested New Source in Ovid's *Metamorphoses* for Shakespeare's *Venus and Adonis*." *Huntington Library Quarterly*, XXIV (1960–61), 163–69.

Presson, Robert K., *Shakespeare's Troilus and Cressida & the Legends of Troy*. University of Wisconsin Press, 1953.

Price, H. T., "Function of Imagery in *Venus and Adonis*." *Papers of the Michigan Academy of Science, Arts, and Letters*, XXXI (1945), 275–97.

Putney, R., "*Venus and Adonis*: Amour with Humour." *PQ*, XX (1941), 533–48.

———, "*Venus Agonistes*." *University of Colorado Studies*, Series in Language and Literature, No. 4 (1953), 52–66.

Rick, Leo, "Shakespeare und Ovid." *Jahrbuch der deutschen Shakespeare-Gesellschaft*, LV (1919), 35–53.

Root, Robert K., *Classical Mythology in Shakespeare*. New York, 1903.

Shakespeare, *Poems*, ed. C. K. Pooler (Arden ed., London, 1911); ed. Hyder E. Rollins (New Variorum ed., Philadelphia, 1938); ed. F. T. Prince (Arden Shakespeare, London and Harvard University Press, 1960).

Shakespeare: The Sonnets. A New Variorum Edition, ed. H. E. Rollins. 2 vols. Philadelphia, 1944.

Smith, Hallett (see "General").

Thomson, J. A. K., *Shakespeare and the Classics*. London, 1952.

Whitaker, Virgil K., *Shakespeare's Use of Learning: An Inquiry into the Growth of His Mind & Art*. Huntington Library, 1953.

Wilson, J. Dover, "Shakespeare's 'Small Latin'—How Much?" *Shakespeare Survey*, X (1957), 12–26.

CHAPTER VIII

Cory, H. E., "The Golden Age of the Spenserian Pastoral." *PMLA*, XXV (1910), 241–67.

———, "Spenser, the School of the Fletchers, and Milton." *University of California Publications in Modern Philology*, II (1912), 311–73.

Drayton, Michael, *Endimion and Phoebe*, ed. J. W. Hebel. Oxford and Boston, 1925.

Drayton, Complete Works of Michael, ed. J. W. Hebel, K. Tillotson, and B. H. Newdigate. 5 vols. Oxford, 1931–41.

Fletcher, Phineas, *Venus and Anchises (Brittain's Ida) and Other Poems*, ed. Ethel Seaton. Oxford University Press, 1926.

Genouy, H. (see "General").

Greg, Sir W. W. (see "General").

Grundy, Joan, "William Browne and the Italian Pastoral." *RES*, IV (1953), 305–16.

CHAPTER IX

Bush, Douglas, "The Influence of Marlowe's *Hero and Leander* on Early Mythological Poems." *MLN*, XLII (1927), 211–17.

Caputi, Anthony, *John Marston, Satirist*. Cornell University Press, 1961.

Clark, Arthur M., "A Bibliography of Thomas Heywood." *Oxford Bibliographical Society Proceedings and Papers*, I, Part 2 (1925).

Clark, Arthur M., "Thomas Heywood's *Art of Love* Lost and Found." *Library*, Fourth Series, III (1923), 210–22.
———, *Thomas Heywood*. Oxford, 1931.
Cross, G., "Marston's 'Metamorphosis of Pigmalion's Image': A Mock-Epyllion." *Etudes Anglaises*, XIII (1960), 331–36.
Davies, Sir John, *Orchestra*, ed. E. M. W. Tillyard. London, 1945.
Heywood, Thomas [?], *Oenone and Paris by T.H.*, ed. J. Q. Adams. Folger Shakespeare Library, 1943.
Marston, Poems of John, ed. A. Davenport. Liverpool University Press, 1961.
Tillyard, E. M. W., "Sir John Davies: *Orchestra 1594*." *Five Poems 1470–1870*. London, 1948.

CHAPTER X

Chapman, The Poems of George, ed. Phyllis B. Bartlett. New York, 1941.
Chapman's Homer, ed. A. Nicoll. 2 vols. New York, 1956.
Bartlett, P. B., "Chapman's Revisions in his *Iliads*." *ELH*, II (1935), 92–119.
———, "The Heroes of Chapman's Homer." *RES*, XVII (1941), 257–80.
———, "Stylistic Devices in Chapman's *Iliads*." *PMLA*, LVII (1942), 661–75.
Fay, H. C., "Chapman's Materials for His Translation of Homer." *RES*, II (1951), 121–28.
———, "Poetry, Pedantry, and Life in Chapman's *Iliads*." *RES*, IV (1953), 13–25.
Gordon, D. J., "Chapman's Use of Cartari in the Fifth Sestiad of 'Hero and Leander.'" *MLR*, XXXIX (1944), 280–85.
———, "Chapman's 'Hero and Leander.'" *English Miscellany*, ed. M. Praz, V (1954), 41–94.
Lewis, C. S., "Hero and Leander." *Proceedings of the British Academy*, XXXVIII (1952), 23–37.
Lord, G. de F., *Homeric Renaissance: The Odyssey of George Chapman*. Yale University Press, 1956.
Rees, Ennis, *The Tragedies of George Chapman: Renaissance Ethics in Action*. Harvard University Press, 1954.
Schoell, Franck L., *Études sur l'humanisme continental en Angleterre*. Paris, 1926.
Schrickx, W., "Chapman's Borrowings from Natali Conti." *English Studies*, XXXII (1951), 107–12.
Smalley, D., "The Ethical Bias of Chapman's *Homer*." *SP*, XXXVI (1939), 169–91.
Sühnel, R., *Homer und die englische Humanität: Chapmans und Popes Übersetzungskunst im Rahmen der humanistischen Tradition*. Tübingen, 1958.

CHAPTER XI

Carew, The Poems of Thomas, ed. R. Dunlap. Clarendon Press, 1949.
Emperor, John B., *The Catullian Influence in English Lyric Poetry circa 1600–1650*. University of Missouri Studies, 1928.
Gilbert, Allan H., *The Symbolic Persons in the Masques of Ben Jonson*. Duke University Press, 1948.

Herrick, *The Poetical Works of Robert,* ed. L. C. Martin. Clarendon Press, 1956.

Jonson, Ben, ed. C. H. Herford and P. and E. M. Simpson. 11 vols. Clarendon Press, 1925–52.

McEuen, Kathryn E., *Classical Influence upon the Tribe of Ben.* Cedar Rapids, 1939.

Wheeler, C. F., *Classical Mythology in the Plays, Masques, and Poems of Ben Jonson.* Princeton University Press, 1938.

CHAPTER XII

Amos, F. R. (see "General").

Conington, John, "The English Translators of Virgil." *Quarterly Review,* CX (1861), 38–60; *Miscellaneous Writings,* ed. J. A. Symonds (London, 1872), I, 137 ff.

Frost, William, *Dryden and the Art of Translation.* Yale University Press, 1955.

Marmion, Shakerley, *Cupid and Psyche,* ed. Alice J. Nearing. Philadelphia, 1944.

Praz, Mario, "Stanley, Sherburne and Ayres as Translators and Imitators of Italian, Spanish and French Poets." *MLR,* XX (1925), 280–94, 419–31.

Proudfoot, L., *Dryden's Aeneid and Its Seventeenth Century Predecessors.* Manchester University Press, 1960.

Sherburne, Sir Edward, *The Poems and Translations . . . excluding Seneca and Manilius,* ed. F. J. Van Beeck. Assen, 1961.

Stanley, *The Poems and Translations of Thomas,* ed. G. M. Crump. Clarendon Press, 1962.

Thomas, Sir Henry, "Three Translators of Góngora." *Revue Hispanique,* XLVIII (1920), 180–256, 311–16.

CHAPTER XIII

Lemmi, C. W., *The Classic Deities in Bacon: A Study in Mythological Symbolism.* Johns Hopkins Press, 1933.

Rossi, Paolo, *L'interpretazione baconiana delle favole antiche.* Milan, 1953 (incorporated in Rossi's *Francesco Bacone: dalla magia alla scienza,* Bari, 1957).

Schirmer, W. F. (see "General").

Sewell, Elizabeth, *The Orphic Voice: Poetry and Natural History.* London, 1960.

CHAPTER XIV

Stevens, David H., *Reference Guide to Milton from 1800 to the Present Day.* University of Chicago Press, 1930.

Huckabay, Calvin, *John Milton: A Bibliographical Supplement 1929–1957.* Duquesne University Press, 1960.

Allen, Don C., "Milton and the Descent to Light." *JEGP,* LX (1961), 614–30.

Arthos, John, "Milton's Sabrina, Virgil and Porphyry." *Anglia,* 79 (1962), 204–13.

Buff, Friedrich, *Miltons Paradise Lost in seinem Verhältnisse zur Aeneide, Ilias, und Odyssee.* Hof a. S., 1904.

Bowra, Sir Maurice, *From Virgil to Milton.* London, 1945.

Bush, Douglas, "Virgil and Milton." *Classical Journal*, XLVII (1951–52), 178–82, 203–04.

Connely, W., "Imprints of the *Aeneid* on *Paradise Lost.*" *Classical Journal*, XVIII (1922–23), 466–76.

Hammond, Mason, "*Concilia Deorum* from Homer through Milton." *SP*, XXX (1933), 1–16.

Hanford, J. H., "The Pastoral Elegy and Milton's *Lycidas.*" *PMLA*, XXV (1910), 403–47.

———, "The Youth of Milton." *Studies in Shakespeare, Milton and Donne by Members of the English Department of the University of Michigan.* New York, 1925.

Harding, Davis P., *Milton and the Renaissance Ovid.* University of Illinois Press, 1946.

———, *The Club of Hercules: Studies in the Classical Background of Paradise Lost.* University of Illinois Press, 1962.

Hughes, Merritt Y., "The Christ of *Paradise Regained* and the Renaissance Heroic Tradition." *SP*, XXXV (1938), 254–77.

———, "Milton's Celestial Battle and the Theogonies." *Studies in Honor of T. W. Baldwin* (University of Illinois Press, 1958), pp. 237–53.

Le Comte, Edward S., *A Milton Dictionary.* New York, 1961.

MacCaffrey, Isabel G., *Paradise Lost as "Myth."* Harvard University Press, 1959.

Mackail, J. W. (see "General").

Madsen, William G., "The Idea of Nature in Milton's Poetry." *Three Studies in the Renaissance: Sidney, Jonson, Milton,* by Richard B. Young, W. T. Furniss, and W. G. Madsen. Yale University Press, 1958.

Milton: Complete Poems and Major Prose, John, ed. M. Y. Hughes. New York, 1957.

Milton: Paradise Lost, John, ed. M. Y. Hughes. New York, 1962.

Milton, A Variorum Commentary on the Poems of, ed. M. Y. Hughes et al. 3 vols. (forthcoming, London and Columbia University Press).

Milton, *Paradise Lost,* ed. A. W. Verity, vol. II. Cambridge University Press, 1929.

Milton, The Latin Poems of John, ed. Walter MacKellar. Yale University Press, 1930.

Moore, O. H., "The Infernal Council." *MP*, XVI (1918–19), 169–93; XIX (1921–22), 47–64.

Nicolson, Marjorie, "Milton's Hell and the Phlegraean Fields." *University of Toronto Quarterly,* VII (1937–38), 500–13.

Nitchie, Elizabeth (see "General").

Osgood, Charles G., *The Classical Mythology of Milton's English Poems.* New York, 1900.

———, "Milton's Classical Mythology." *MLN*, XVI (1901), 282–84.

Patrides, C. A., ed., *Milton's Lycidas: The Tradition and the Poem.* New York, 1961.

Rand, E. K., "Milton in Rustication." *SP*, XIX (1922), 109–35.

Riley, E. H., "Milton's Tribute to Virgil." *SP*, XXVI (1929), 155–65.

Samuel, Irene, *Plato and Milton.* Cornell University Press, 1947.

Tillyard, E. M. W., "Milton and the Classics." *Essays by Divers Hands: . . . Transactions of the Royal Society of Literature,* XXVI (1953), 59–72.

Woodhouse, A. S. P., "The Argument of Milton's *Comus.*" *University of Toronto Quarterly,* XI (1941–42), 46–71; XIX (1949–50), 218–23.

CHAPTER XV

Kitchin, George, *A Survey of Burlesque and Parody in English.* Edinburgh and London, 1931.

Leavitt, S. E., "Paul Scarron and English Travesty." *SP,* XVI (1919), 108–20.

Scarron, Paul, *Le Virgile travesti,* ed. V. Fournel. Paris, 1858.

West, Albert H., *L'influence française dans la poésie burlesque en Angleterre entre 1660 et 1700.* Paris, 1931.

INDEX